Princess Resurrection

5

Yasunori Mitsunaga

Translated by
Satsuki Yamashita

Adapted by
Joshua Hale Fialkov

Lettered by
North Market Street Graphics

Ballantine Books · New York

A Del Rey Manga/Kodansha Trade Paperback Original

Princess Resurrection volume 5 copyright © 2007 by Yasunori Mitsunaga
English translation copyright © 2009 by Yasunori Mitsunaga

Published in the United States by Del Rey, an imprint of The Random House Publishing Group, a division of Random House, Inc., New York.

DEL REY is a registered trademark and the Del Rey colophon is a trademark of Random House, Inc.

Publication rights arranged through Kodansha Ltd.

First published in Japan in 2007 by Kodansha Ltd., Tokyo.

ISBN 978-0-345-50668-9

Printed in the United States of America

www.delreymanga.com

9 8 7 6 5 4 3 2

Translator: Satsuki Yamashita
Adapter: Joshua Hale Fialkov
Lettering: North Market Street Graphics

Contents

That is not dead
which can eternal lie,
and with strange eons
even death may die.

Honorifics Explained

Throughout the Del Rey Manga books, you will find Japanese honorifics left intact in the translations. For those not familiar with how the Japanese use honorifics and, more important, how they differ from American honorifics, we present this brief overview.

Politeness has always been a critical facet of Japanese culture. Ever since the feudal era, when Japan was a highly stratified society, use of honorifics—which can be defined as polite speech that indicates relationship or status—has played an essential role in the Japanese language. When addressing someone in Japanese, an honorific usually takes the form of a suffix attached to one's name (example: "Asuna-san"), is used as a title at the end of one's name, or appears in place of the name itself (example: "Negi-sensei," or simply "Sensei!").

Honorifics can be expressions of respect or endearment. In the context of manga and anime, honorifics give insight into the nature of the relationship between characters. Many English translations leave out these important honorifics and therefore distort the feel of the original Japanese. Because Japanese honorifics contain nuances that English honorifics lack, it is our policy at Del Rey not to translate them. Here, instead, is a guide to some of the honorifics you may encounter in Del Rey Manga.

-*san:*   This is the most common honorific and is equivalent to Mr., Miss, Ms., or Mrs. It is the all-purpose honorific and can be used in any situation where politeness is required.

-*sama:* This is one level higher than "-san" and is used to confer great respect.

-*dono:* This comes from the word "tono," which means "lord." It is an even higher level than "-sama" and confers utmost respect.

-*kun:*   This suffix is used at the end of boys' names to express familiarity or endearment. It is also sometimes used by men among friends, or when addressing someone younger or of a lower station.

-chan: This is used to express endearment, mostly toward girls. It is also used for little boys, pets, and even among lovers. It gives a sense of childish cuteness.

Bozu: This is an informal way to refer to a boy, similar to the English terms "kid" and "squirt."

Sempai/
Senpai: This title suggests that the addressee is one's senior in a group or organization. It is most often used in a school setting, where underclassmen refer to their upperclassmen as "sempai." It can also be used in the workplace, such as when a newer employee addresses an employee who has seniority in the company.

Kohai: This is the opposite of "sempai" and is used toward underclassmen in school or newcomers in the workplace. It connotes that the addressee is of a lower station.

Sensei: Literally meaning "one who has come before," this title is used for teachers, doctors, or masters of any profession or art.

[blank]: This is usually forgotten in these lists, but it is perhaps the most significant difference between Japanese and English. The lack of honorific means that the speaker has permission to address the person in a very intimate way. Usually, only family, spouses, or very close friends have this kind of permission. Known as *yobisute,* it can be gratifying when someone who has earned the intimacy starts to call one by one's name without an honorific. But when that intimacy hasn't been earned, it can be very insulting.

Princess Resurrection

5

Yasunori Mitsunaga

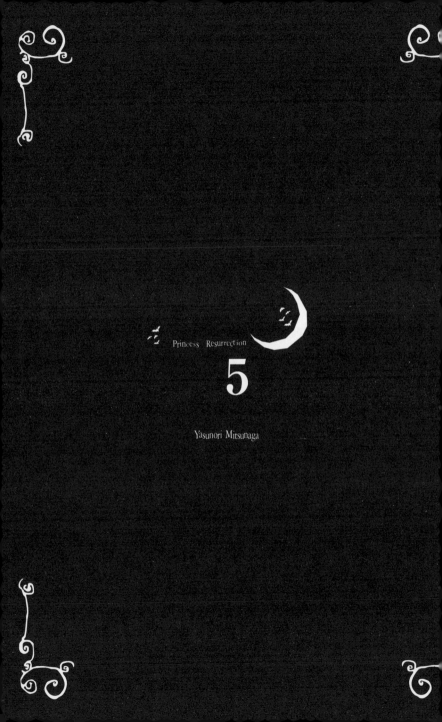

5
Contents

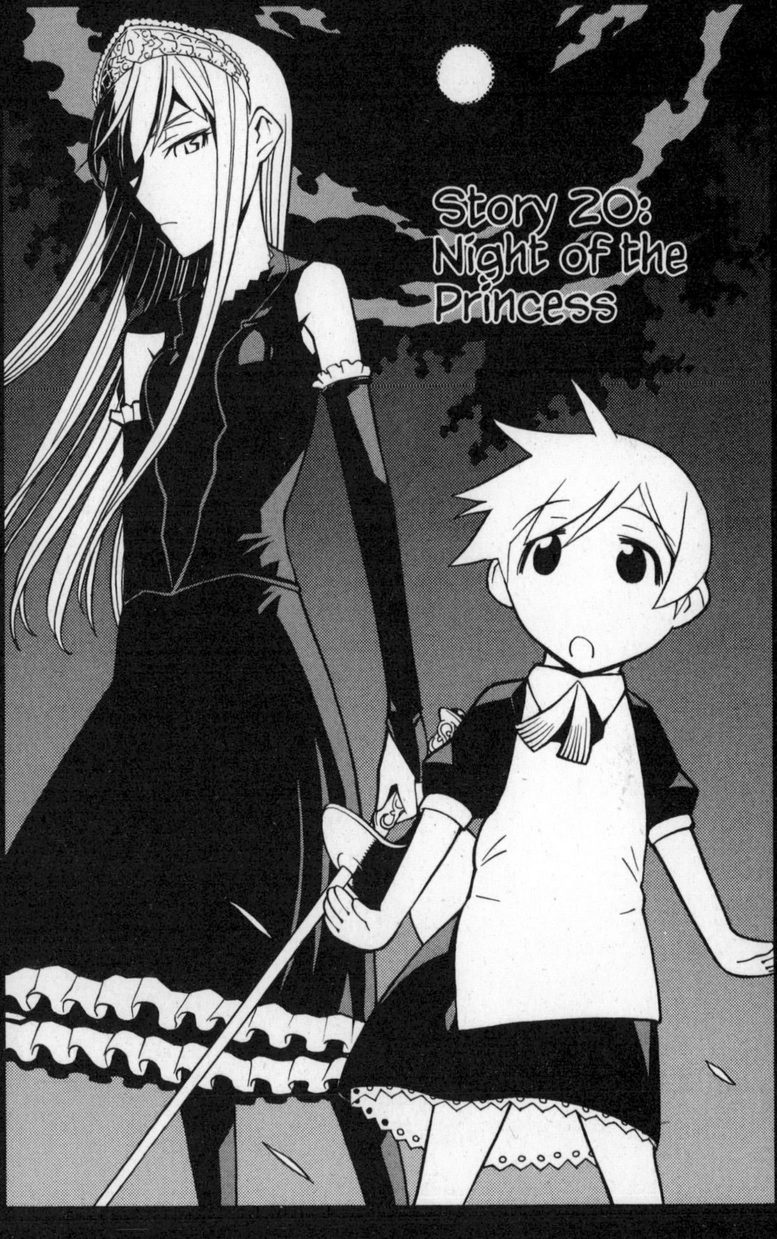
Story 20:
Night of the Princess

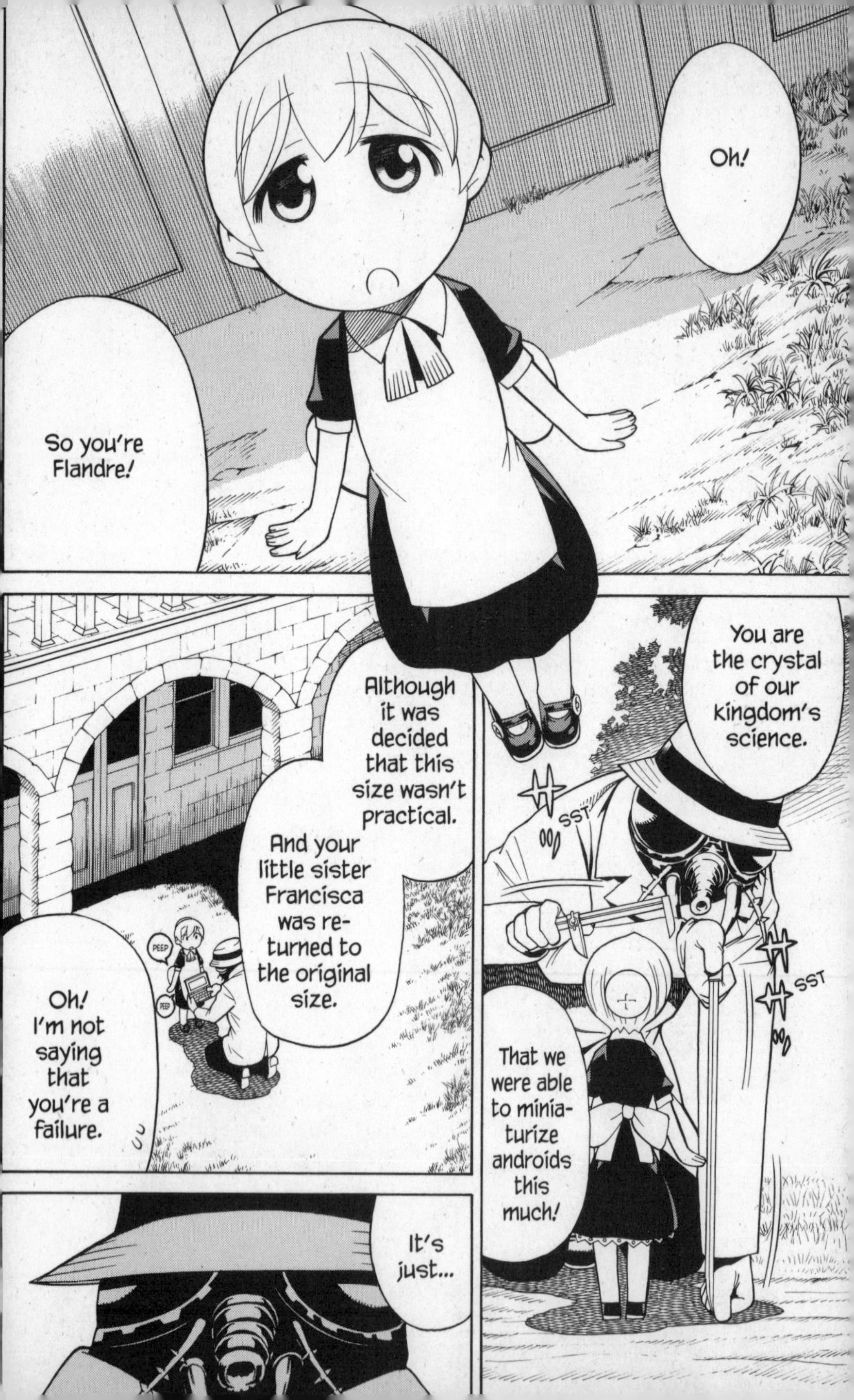
Oh!
So you're Flandre!
You are the crystal of our kingdom's science.
SST
SST
That we were able to miniaturize androids this much!
Although it was decided that this size wasn't practical.
And your little sister Francisca was returned to the original size.
PEEP
PEEP
Oh! I'm not saying that you're a failure.
It's just...

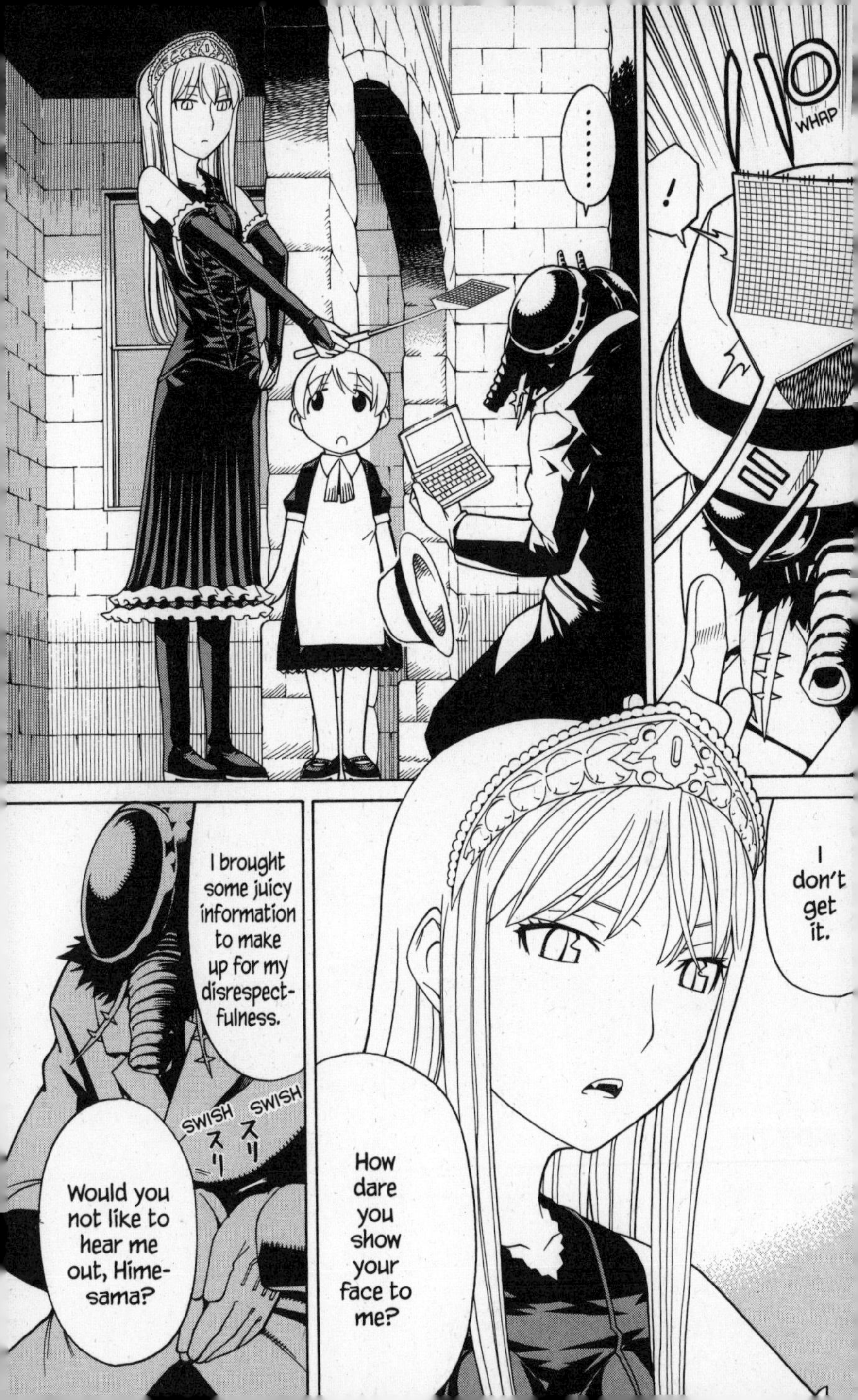
WHAP
!
......
I don't get it.
How dare you show your face to me?
I brought some juicy information to make up for my disrespect-fulness.
SWISH SWISH
スリ スリ
Would you not like to hear me out, Hime-sama?

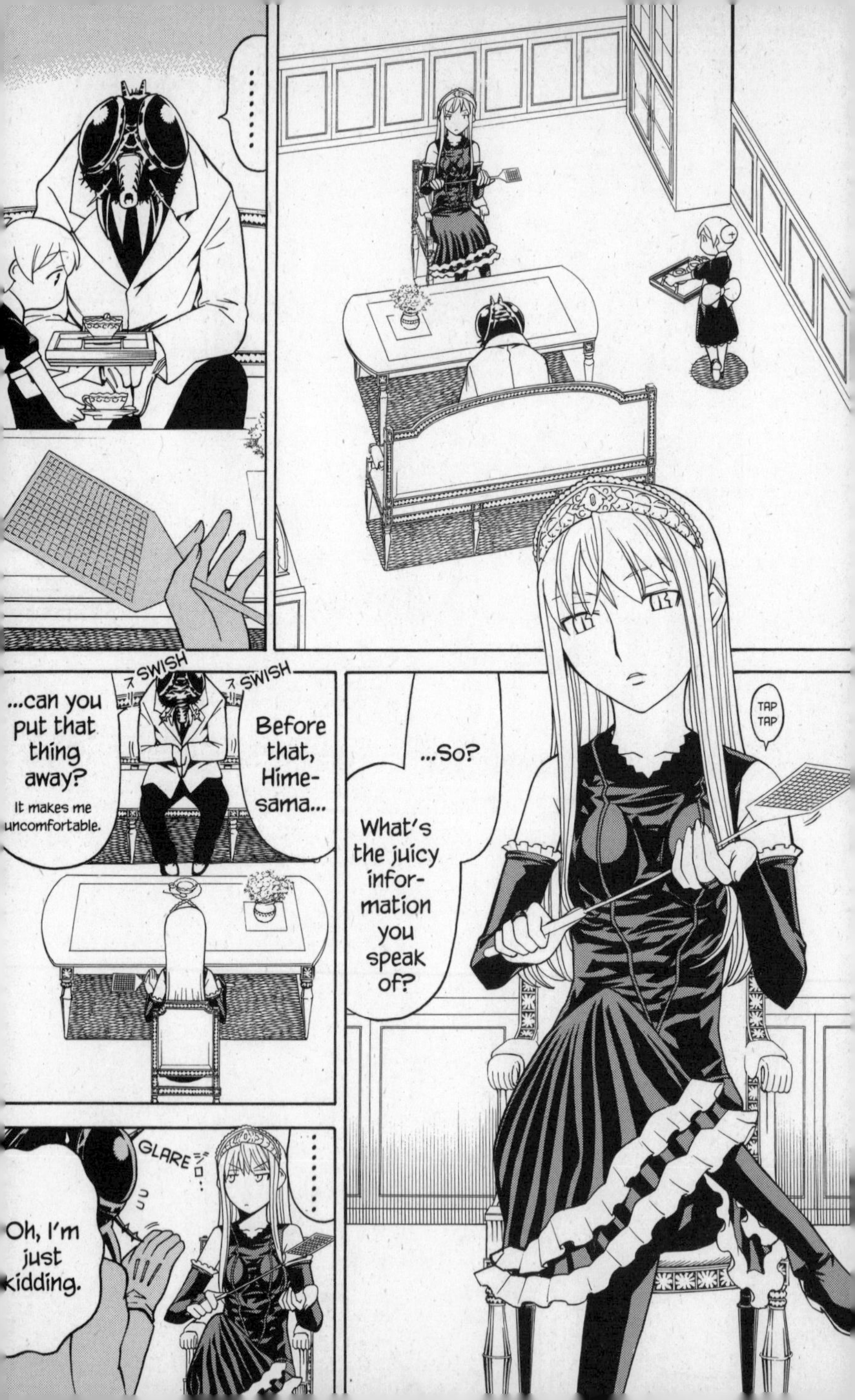
......
TAP TAP
...So?
What's the juicy information you speak of?
SWISH SWISH
Before that, Hime-sama...
...can you put that thing away? It makes me uncomfortable.
GLARE
......
Oh, I'm just kidding.

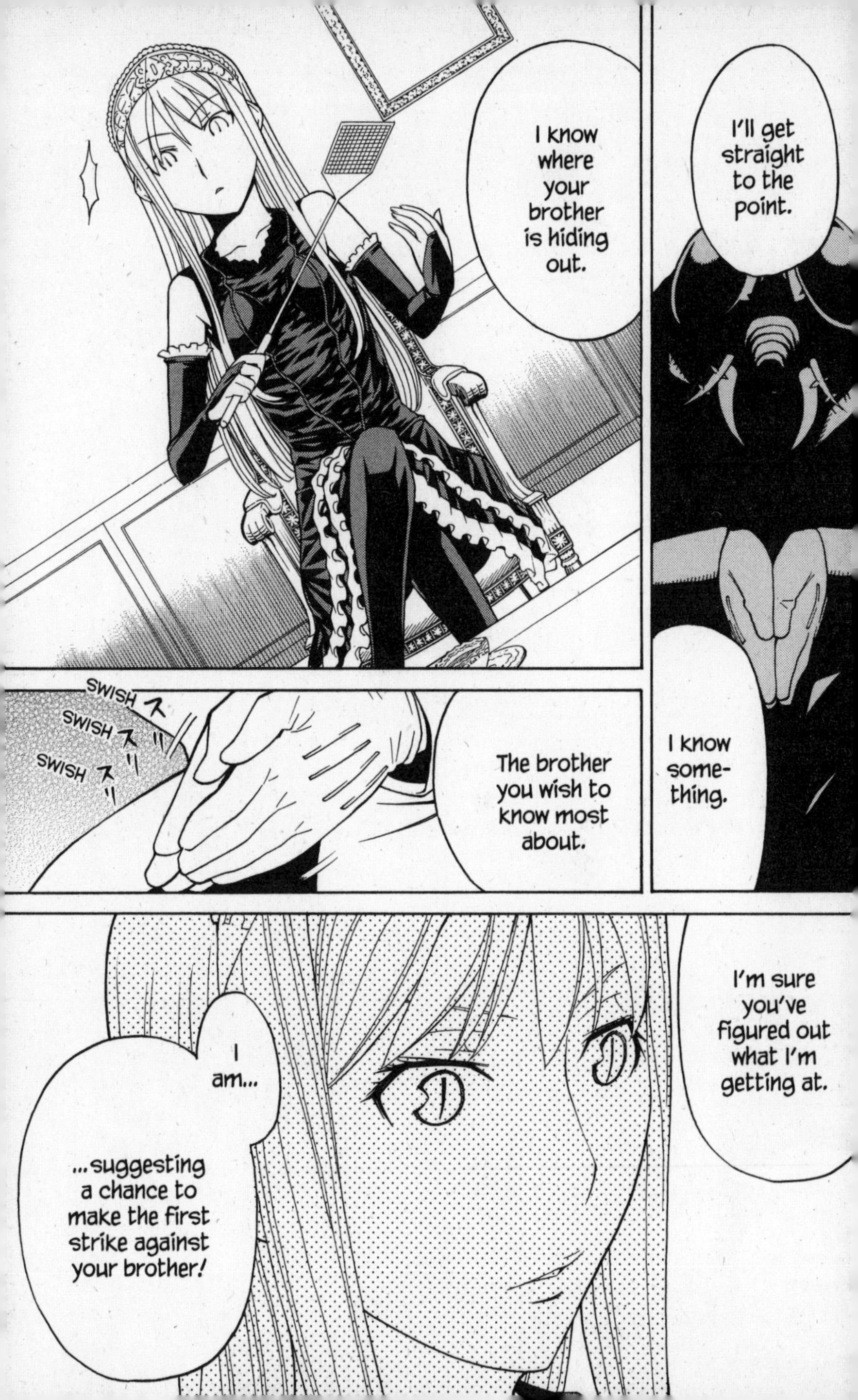
I'll get straight to the point.
I know something.
I know where your brother is hiding out.
The brother you wish to know most about.
SWISH
SWISH
SWISH
I'm sure you've figured out what I'm getting at.
I am...
...suggesting a chance to make the first strike against your brother!

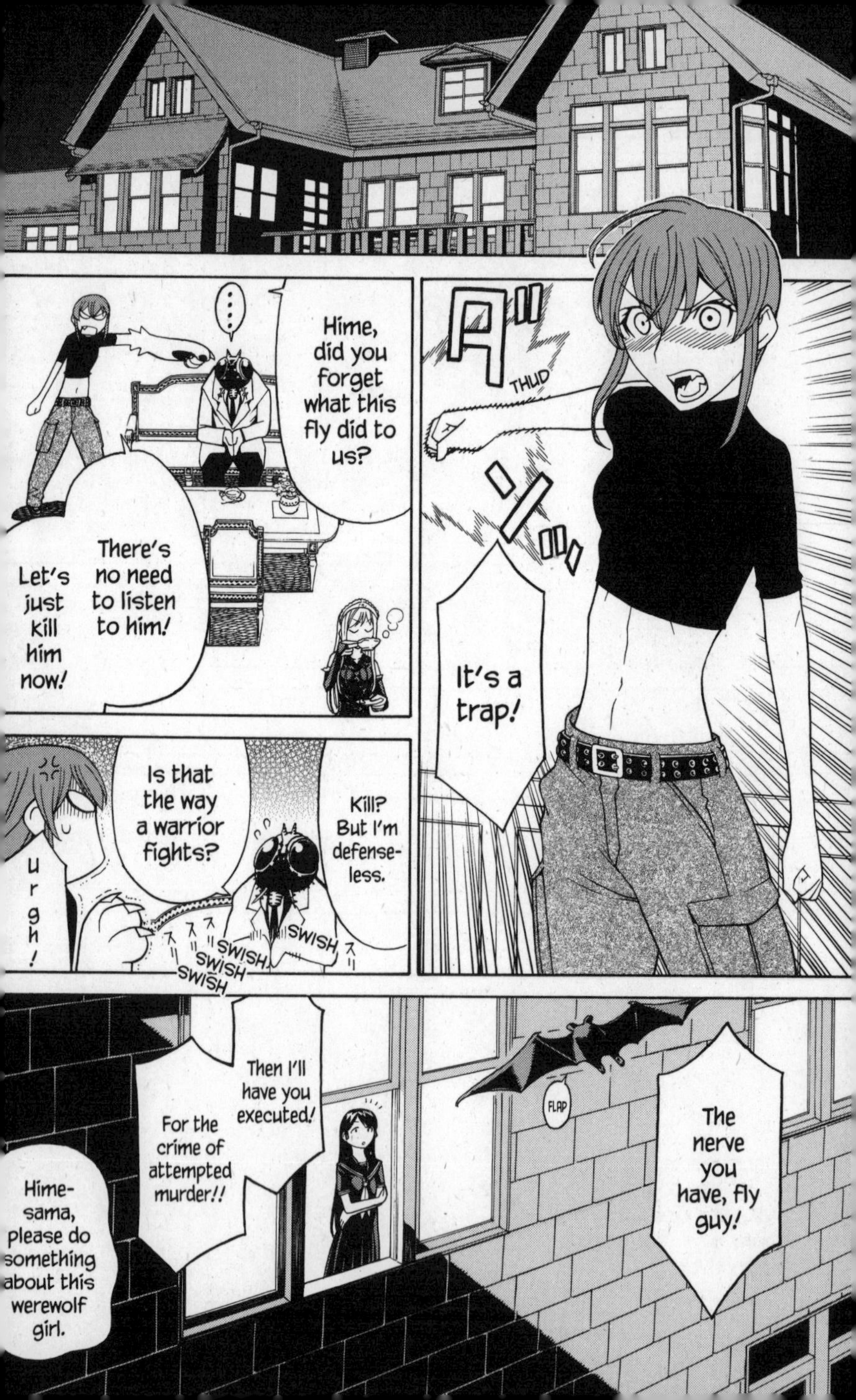
THUD
It's a trap!
…
Hime, did you forget what this fly did to us?
There's no need to listen to him!
Let's just kill him now!
Kill? But I'm defenseless.
Is that the way a warrior fights?
urgh!
SWISH
SWISH
SWISH
SWISH
The nerve you have, fly guy!
FLAP
Then I'll have you executed!
For the crime of attempted murder!!
Hime-sama, please do something about this werewolf girl.

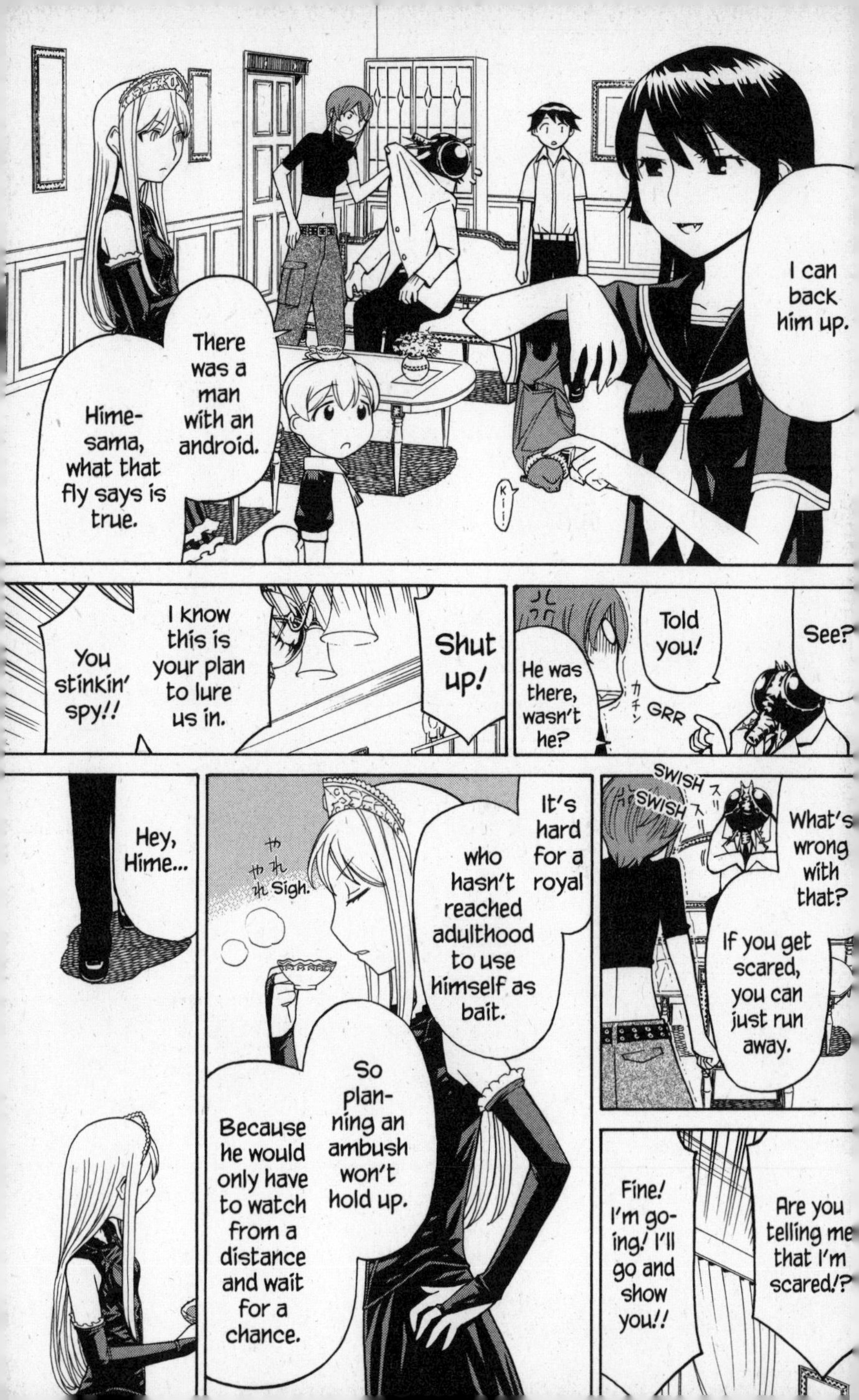
I can back him up.
KI!
There was a man with an android.
Hime-sama, what that fly says is true.
See?
Told you!
He was there, wasn't he?
カチン
GRR
Shut up!
I know this is your plan to lure us in.
You stinkin' spy!!
SWISH
SWISH
What's wrong with that?
If you get scared, you can just run away.
Are you telling me that I'm scared!?
Fine! I'm go-ing! I'll go and show you!!
It's hard for a royal who hasn't reached adulthood to use himself as bait.
やれやれ Sigh.
So plan-ning an ambush won't hold up.
Because he would only have to watch from a distance and wait for a chance.
Hey, Hime...

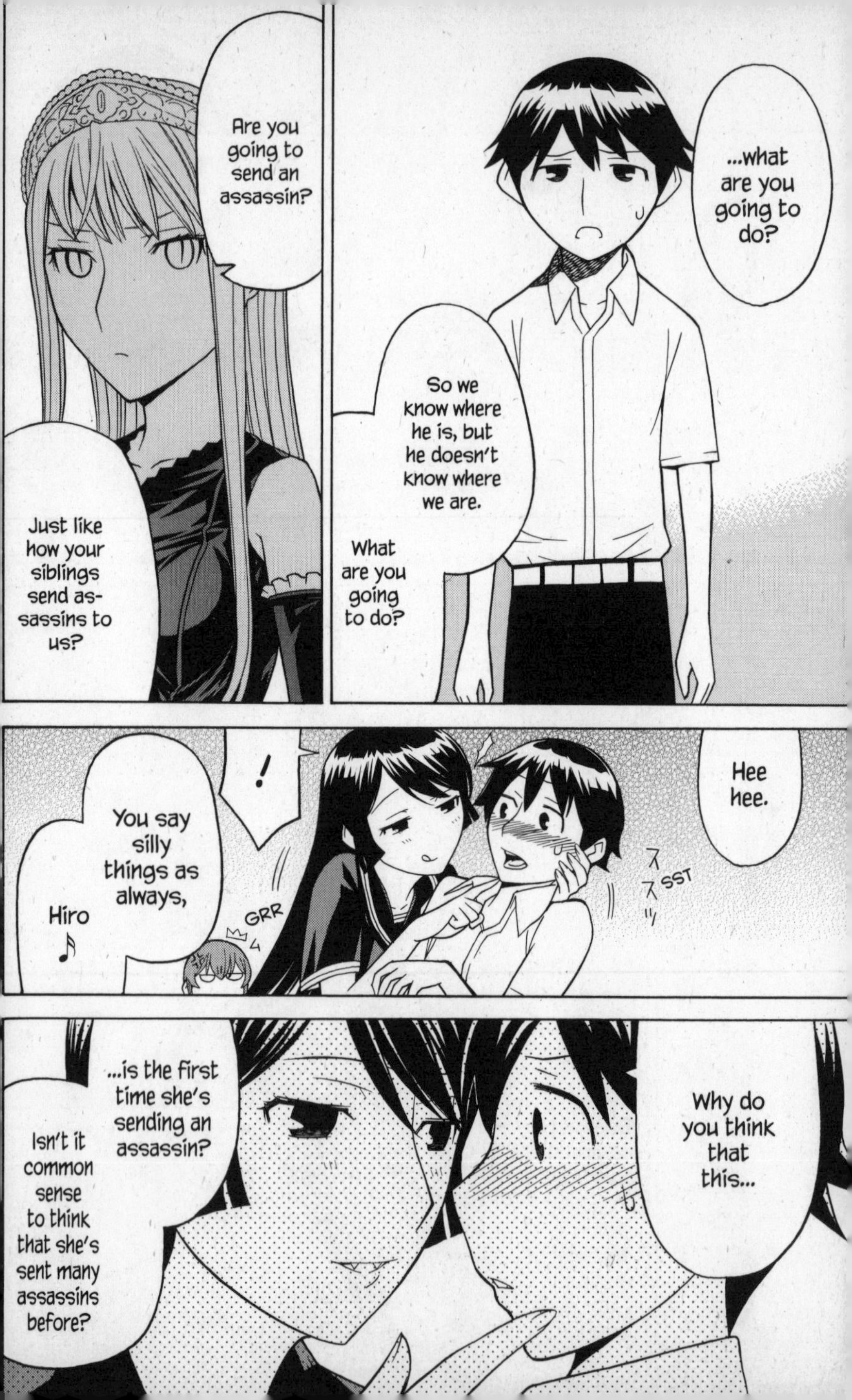

...what are you going to do?
So we know where he is, but he doesn't know where we are.
What are you going to do?
Are you going to send an assassin?
Just like how your siblings send assassins to us?
Hee hee.
ススッ SST
!
You say silly things as always,
Hiro ♪
GRR
Why do you think that this...
...is the first time she's sending an assassin?
Isn't it common sense to think that she's sent many assassins before?

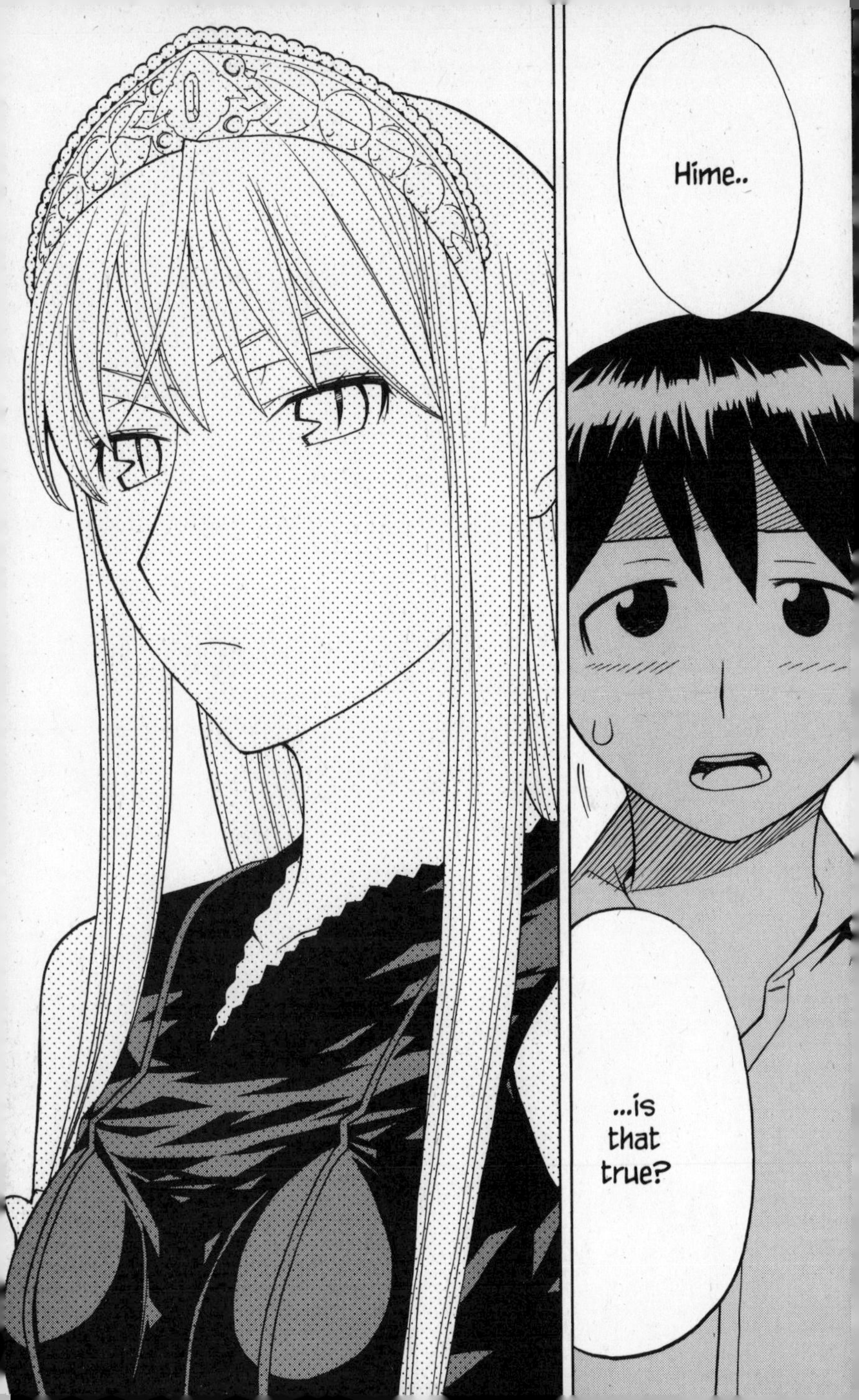
Hime..
...is that true?

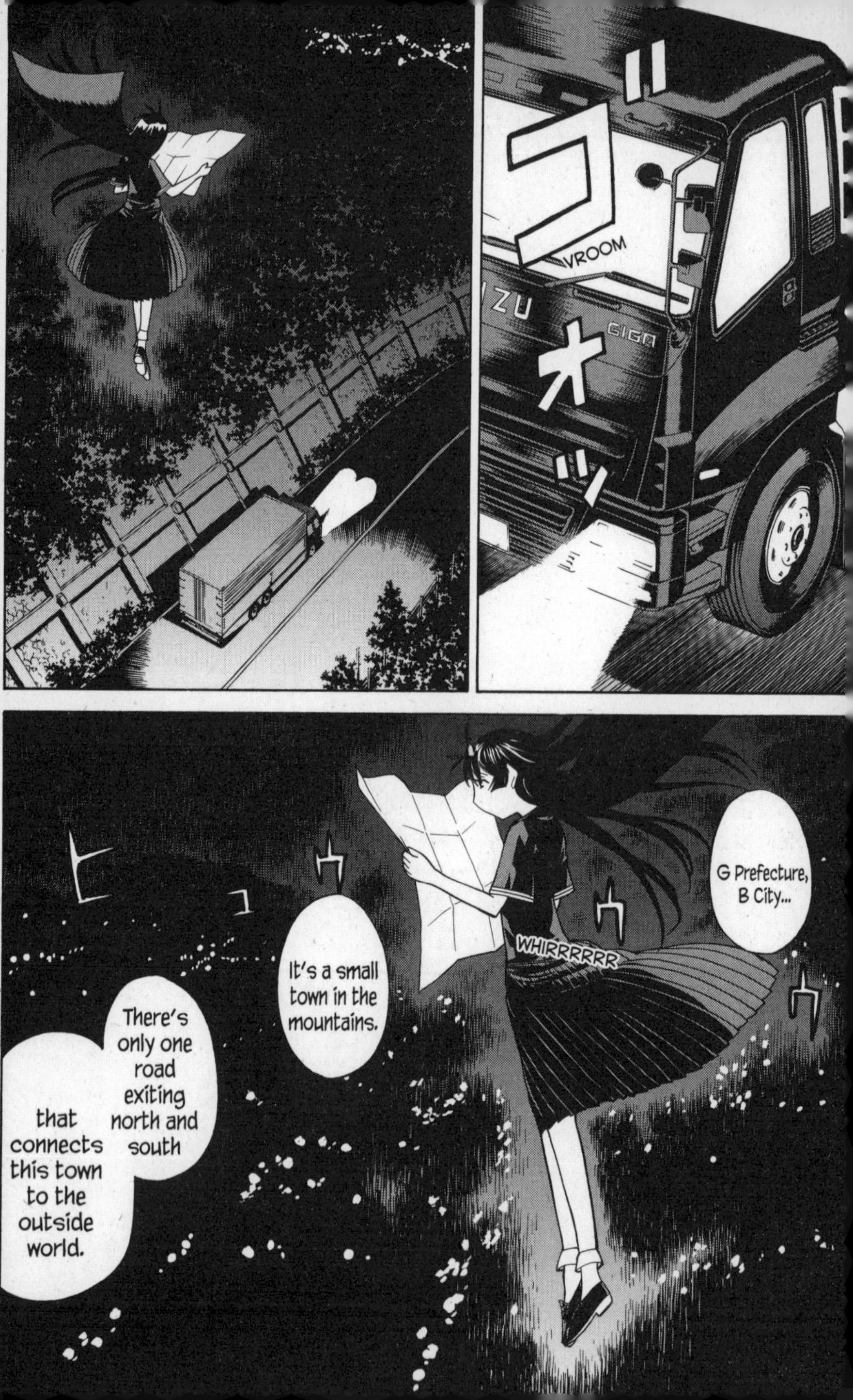
VROOM
G Prefecture, B City...
WHIRRRRRRR
It's a small town in the mountains.
There's only one road exiting north and south
that connects this town to the outside world.

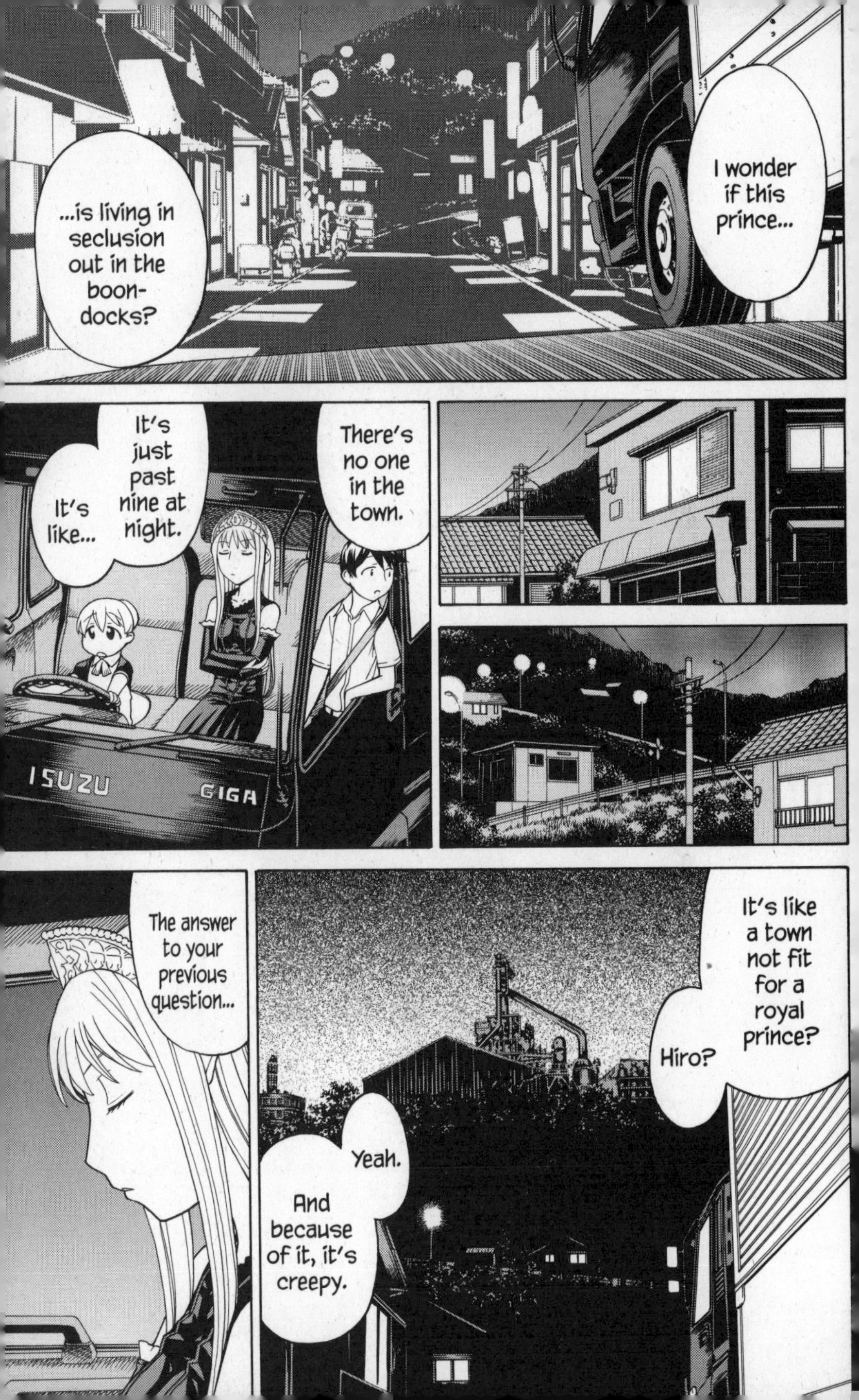
I wonder if this prince...
...is living in seclusion out in the boon-docks?
There's no one in the town.
It's just past nine at night.
It's like...
ISUZU GIGA
It's like a town not fit for a royal prince?
Hiro?
Yeah.
And because of it, it's creepy.
The answer to your previous question...

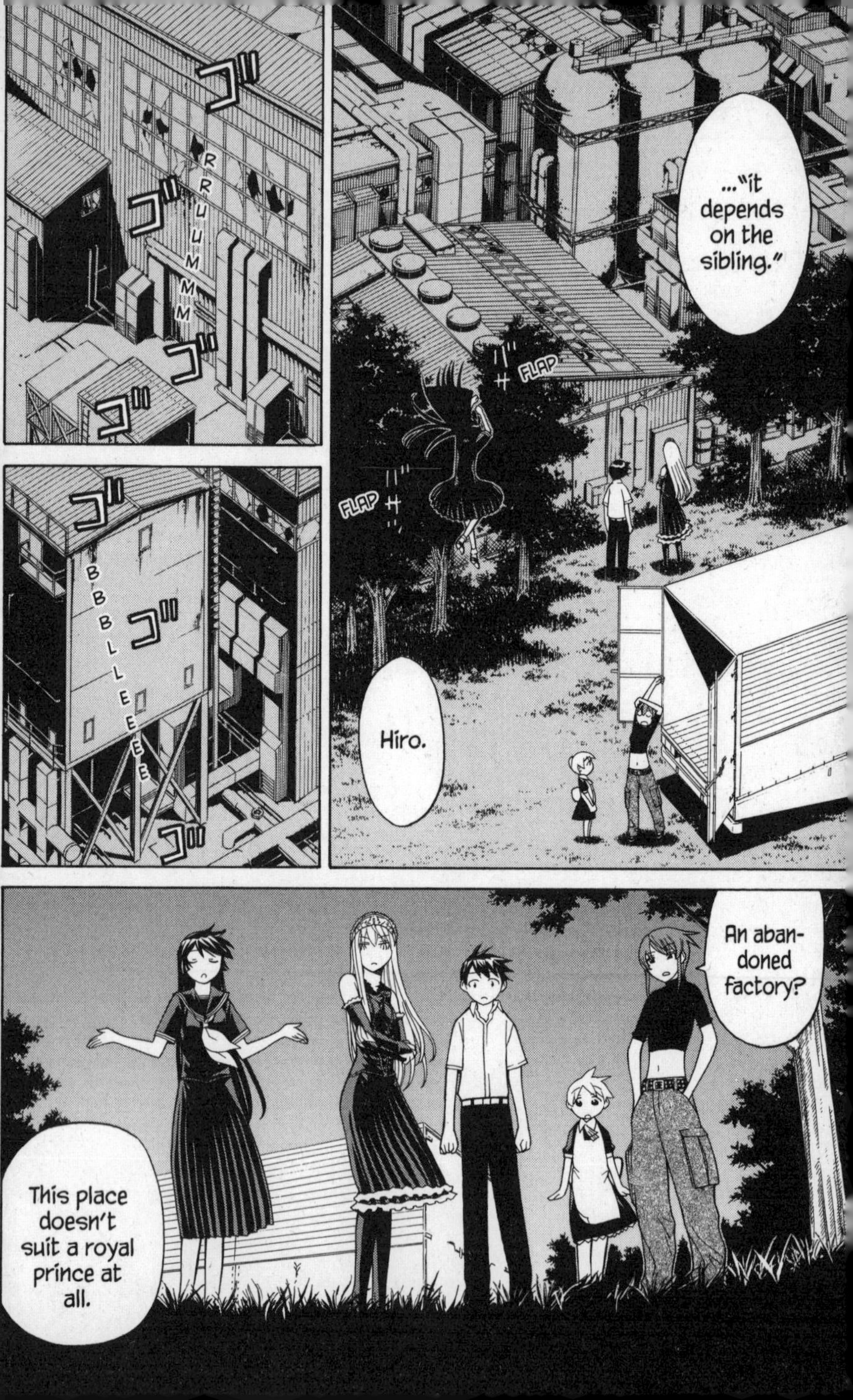
..."it depends on the sibling."
FLAP
FLAP
Hiro.
ゴ
RRUUMMMM
ゴ
ゴ
ゴ
ゴ
BBBLLEEEEE
ゴ
ゴ
An aban-doned factory?
This place doesn't suit a royal prince at all.

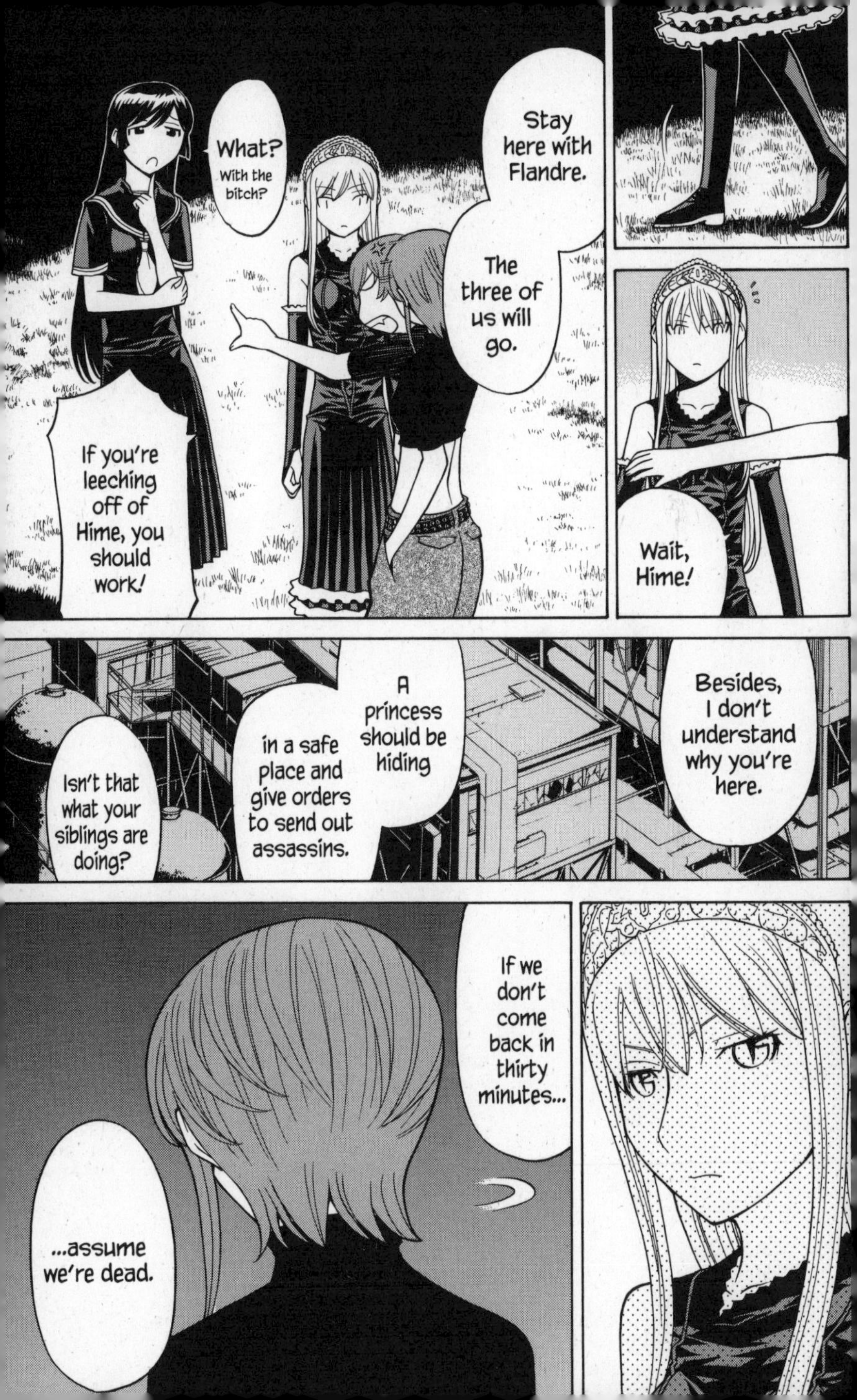
Wait, Hime!
Stay here with Flandre.
The three of us will go.
What? With the bitch?
If you're leeching off of Hime, you should work!
Besides, I don't understand why you're here.
A princess should be hiding
in a safe place and give orders to send out assassins.
Isn't that what your siblings are doing?
If we don't come back in thirty minutes...
...assume we're dead.

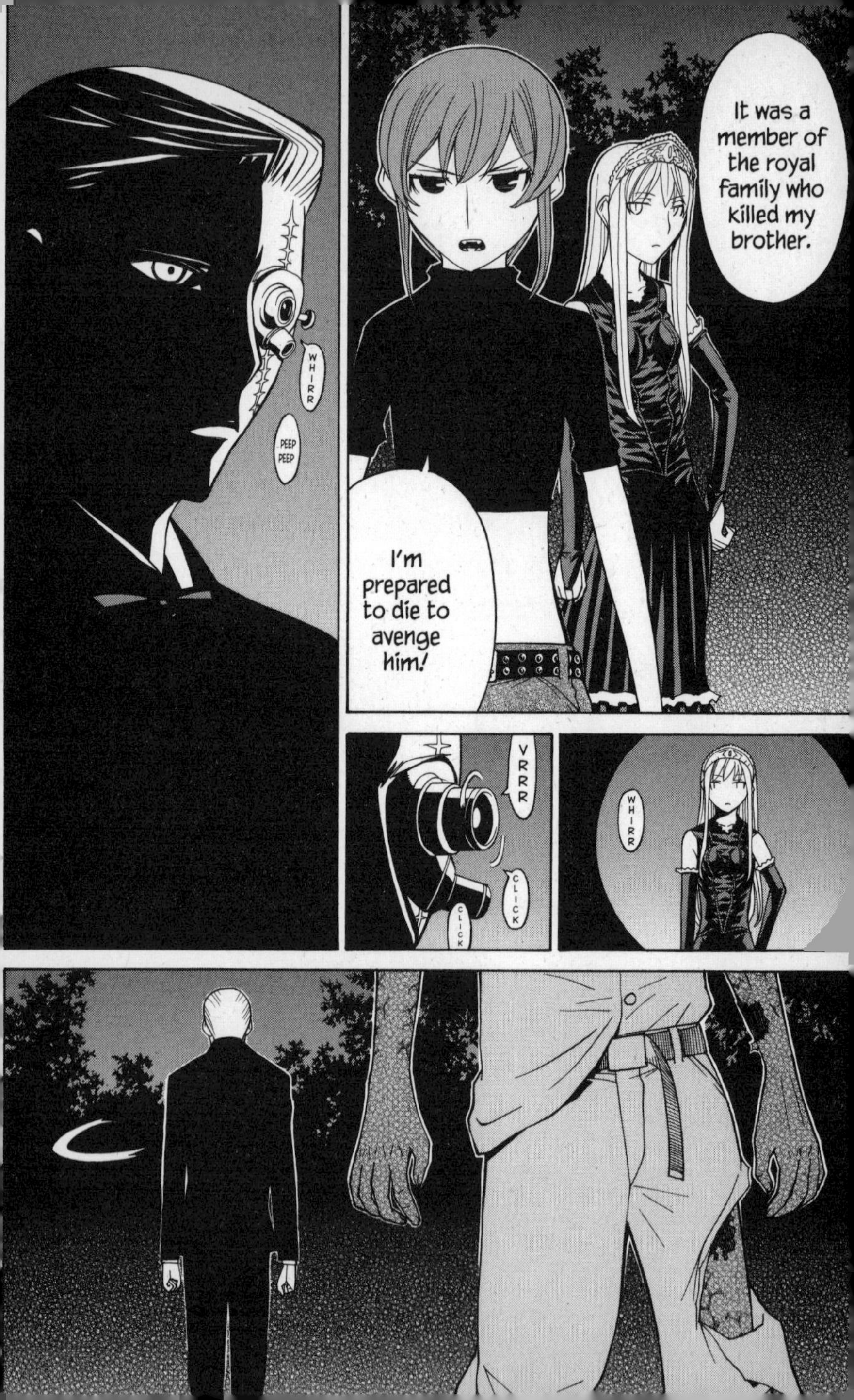
It was a member of the royal family who killed my brother.
I'm prepared to die to avenge him!
WHIRR
VRRR
CLICK
CLICK
WHIRR
PEEP PEEP

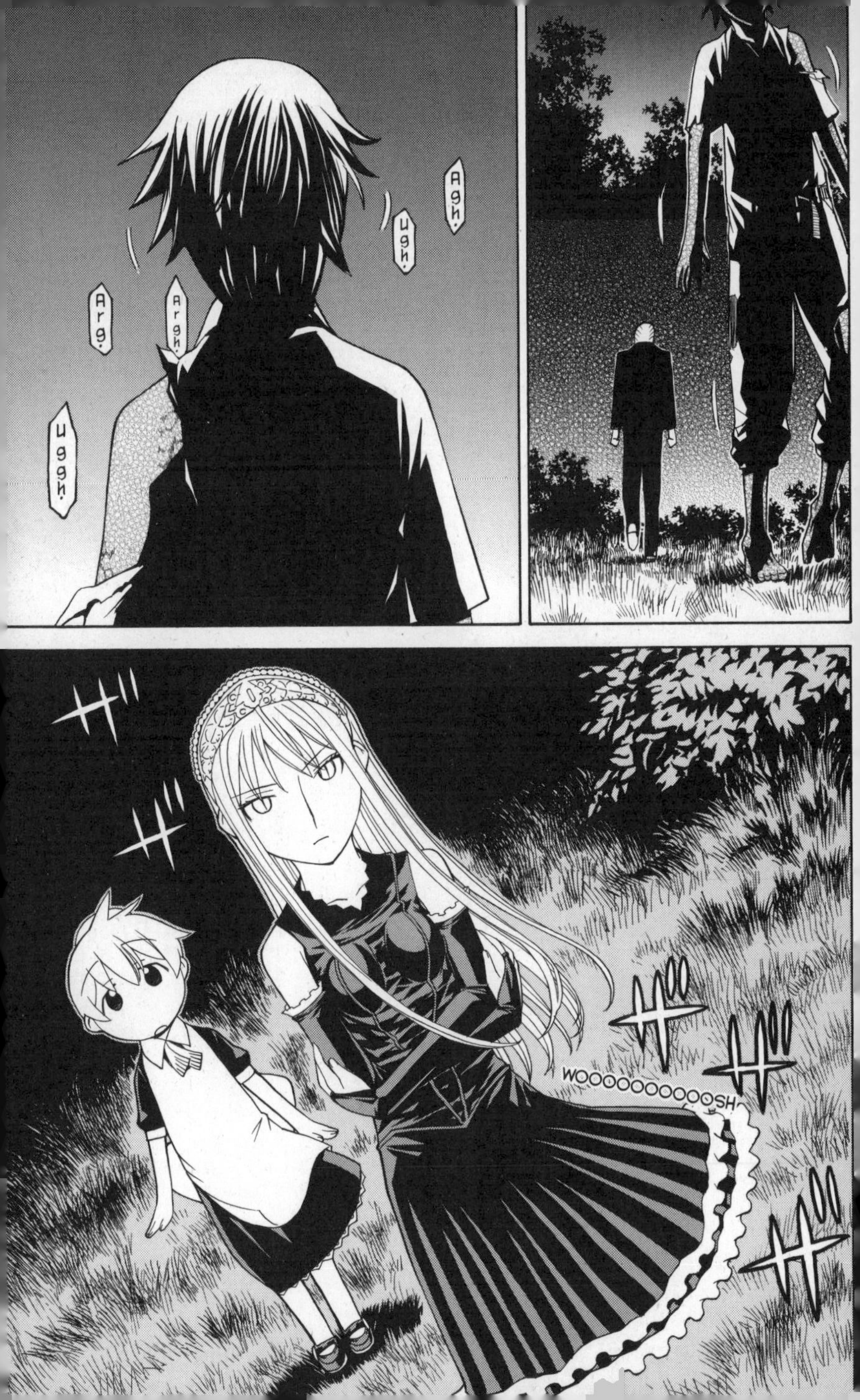

Agh.
Ugh.
Argh.
Arg.
Uggh.
WOOOOOOOOOOSH

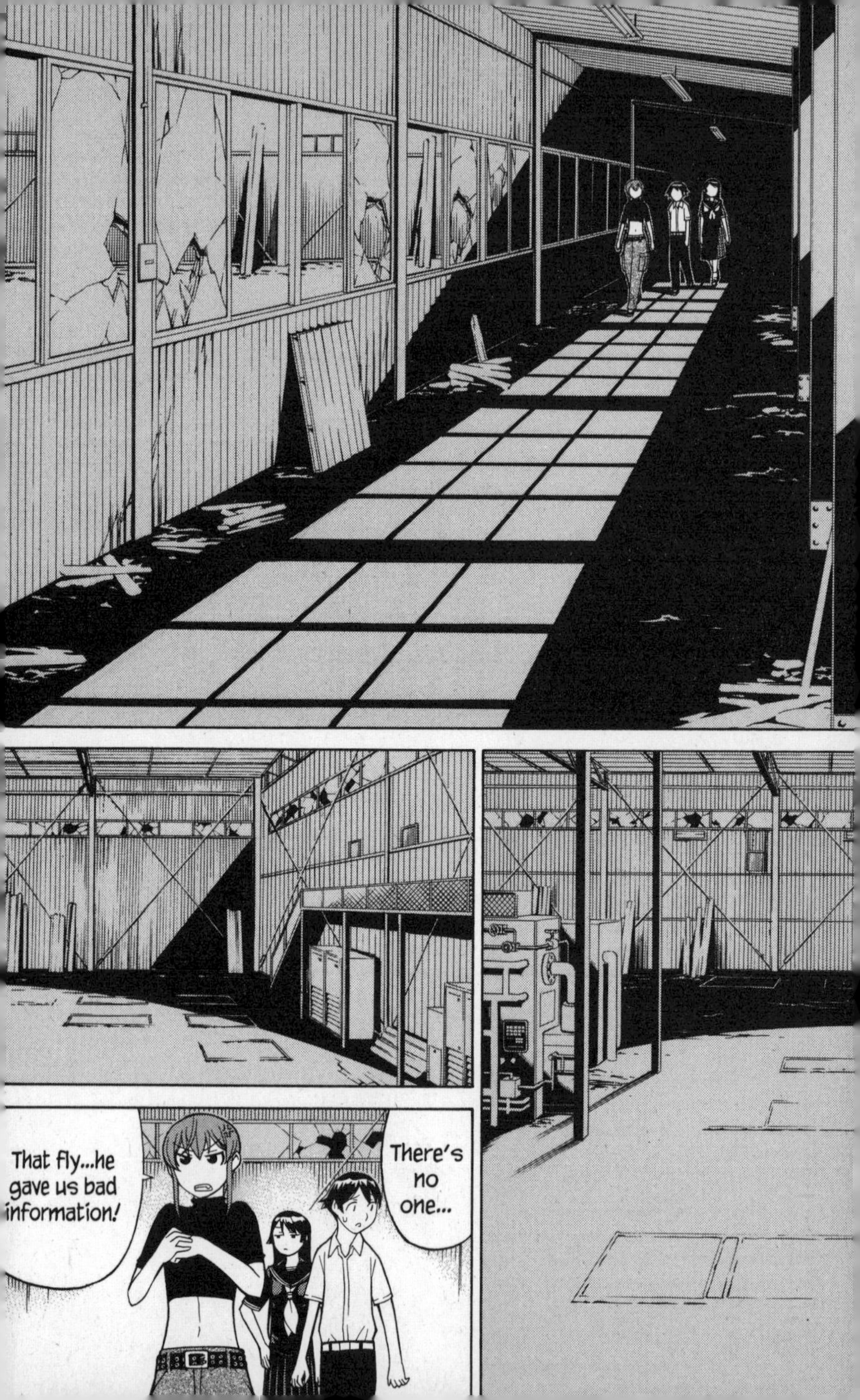
There's no one...
That fly...he gave us bad information!

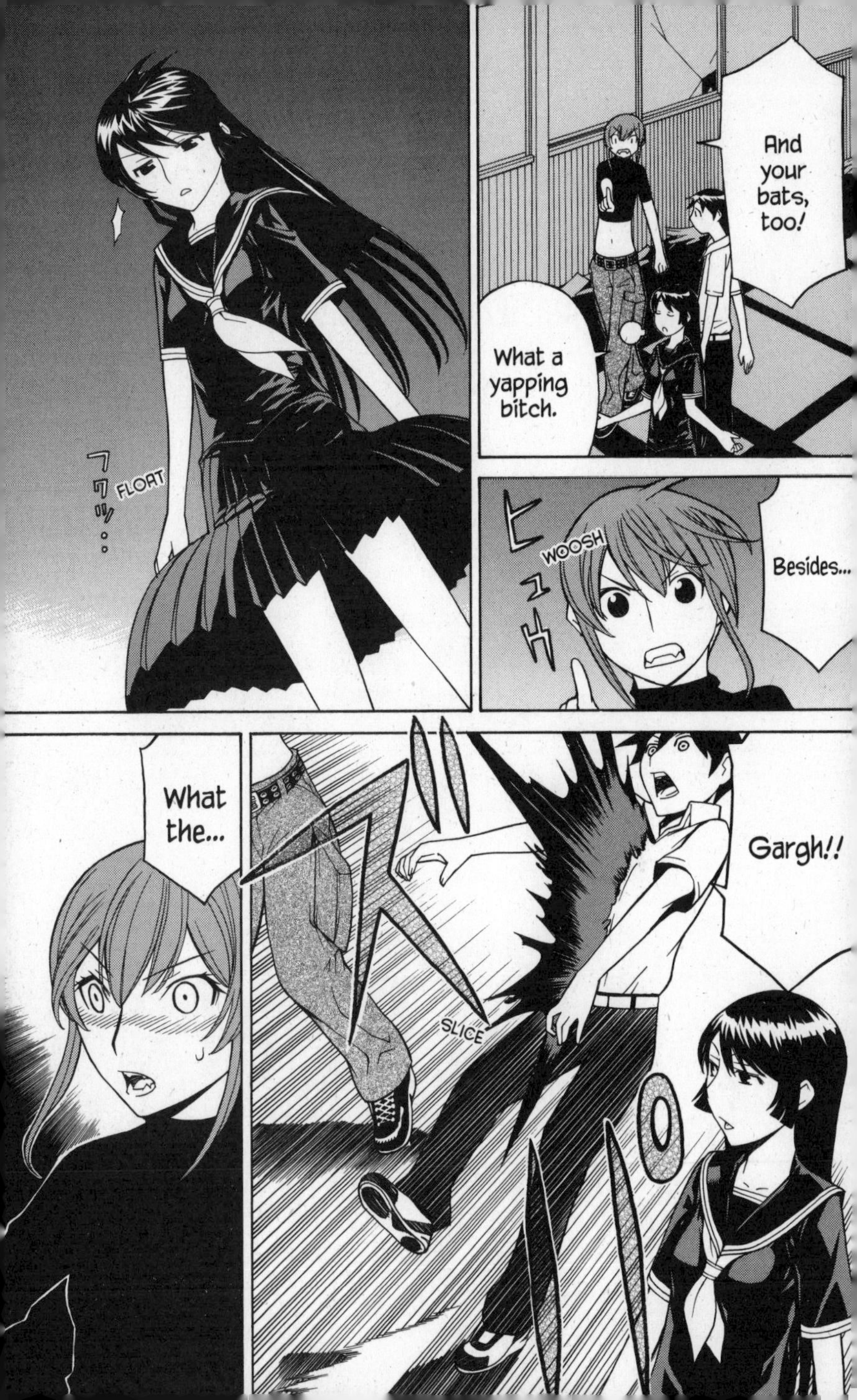
And your bats, too!
What a yapping bitch.
Besides...
ヒュッ
WOOSH
フワッ..
FLOAT
Gargh!!
SLICE
What the...

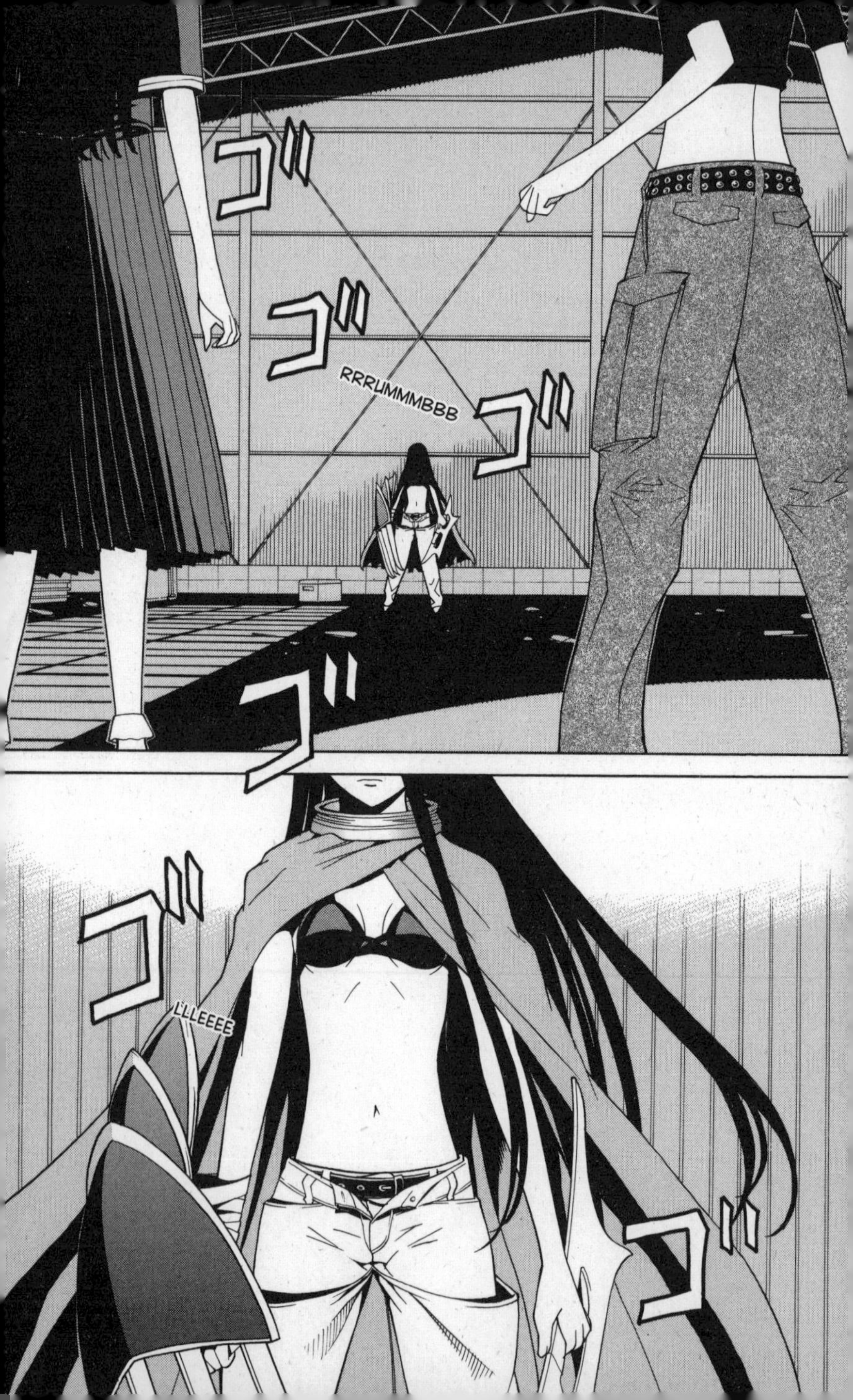
ゴ
ゴ
ゴ
RRRUMMMBBB
ゴ
ゴ
ゴ
LLLEEEE
ゴ

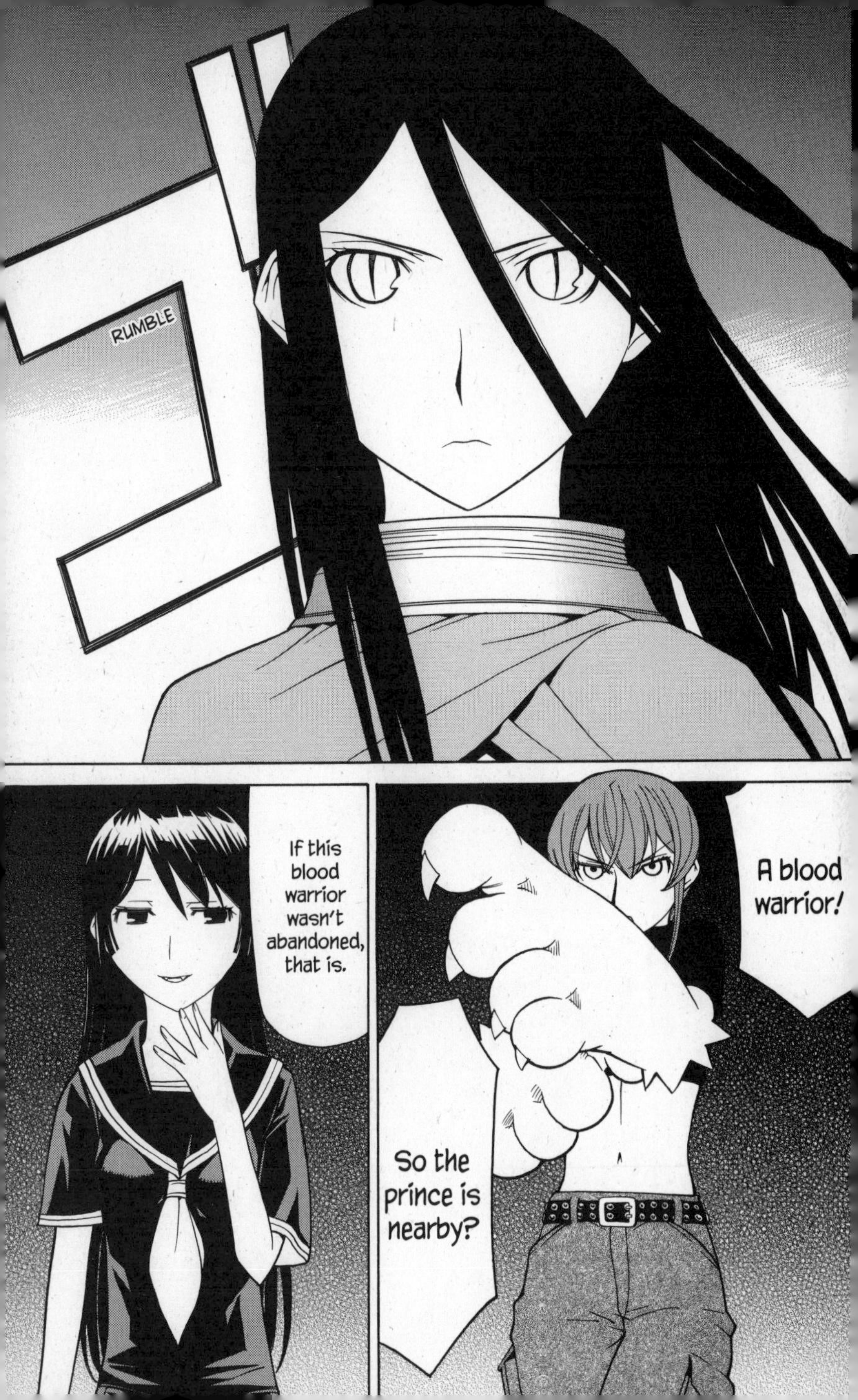
RUMBLE
A blood warrior!
So the prince is nearby?
If this blood warrior wasn't abandoned, that is.

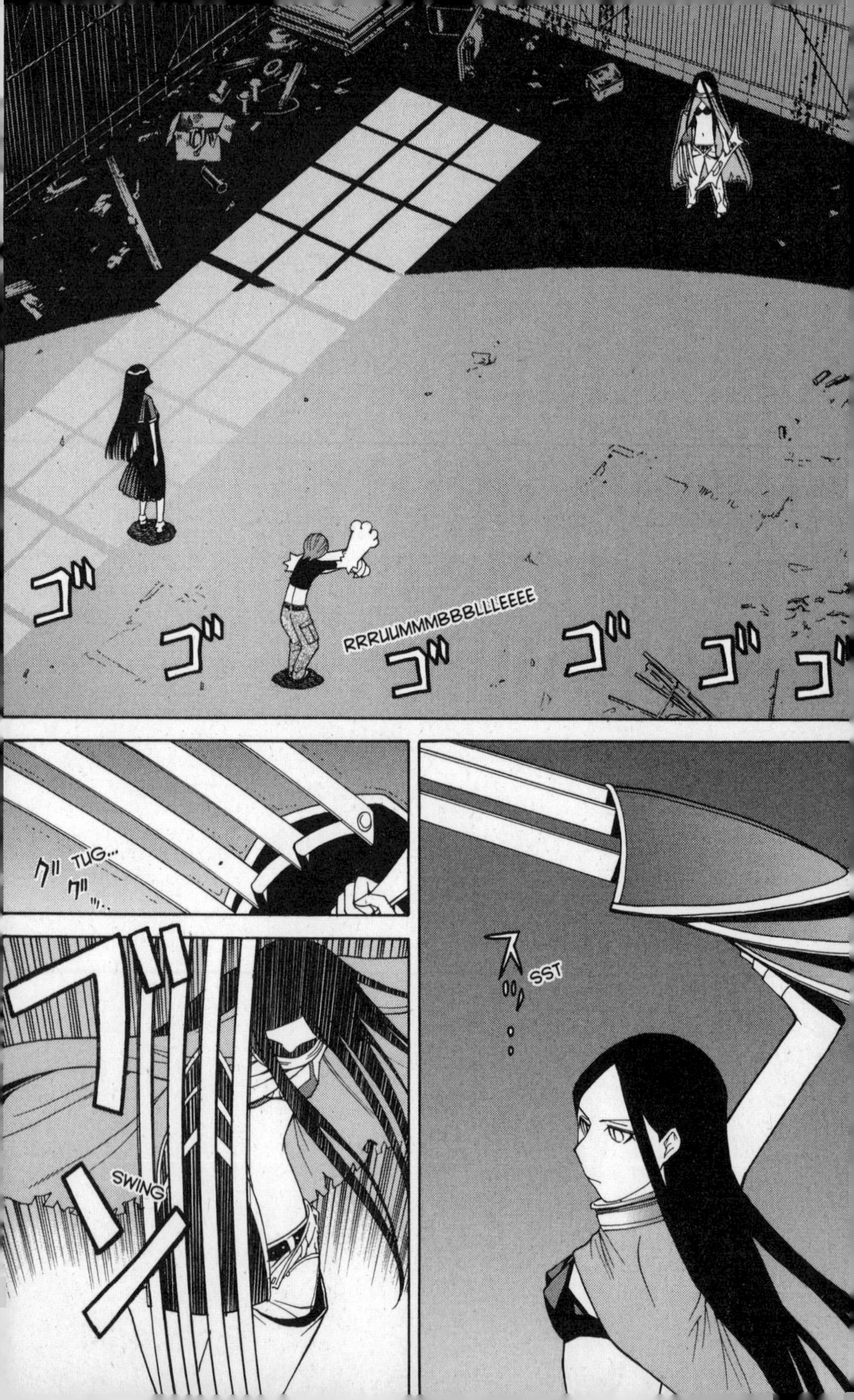
ゴ ゴ ゴ ゴ ゴ ゴ
RRRUUMMMBBBLLLEEEE
ス…
SST
グ グ…
TUG...
SWING

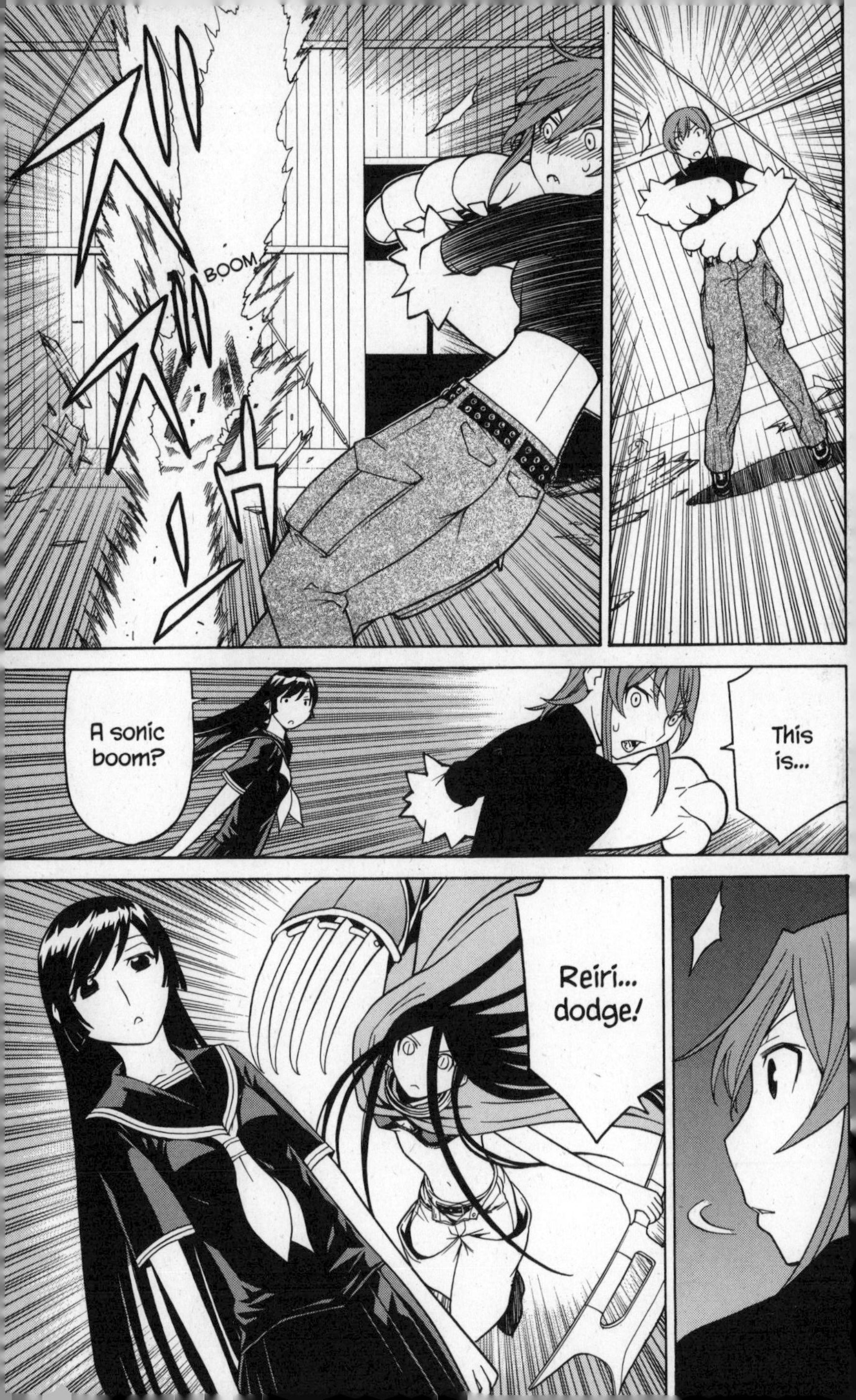
BOOM
This is...
A sonic boom?
Reiri... dodge!

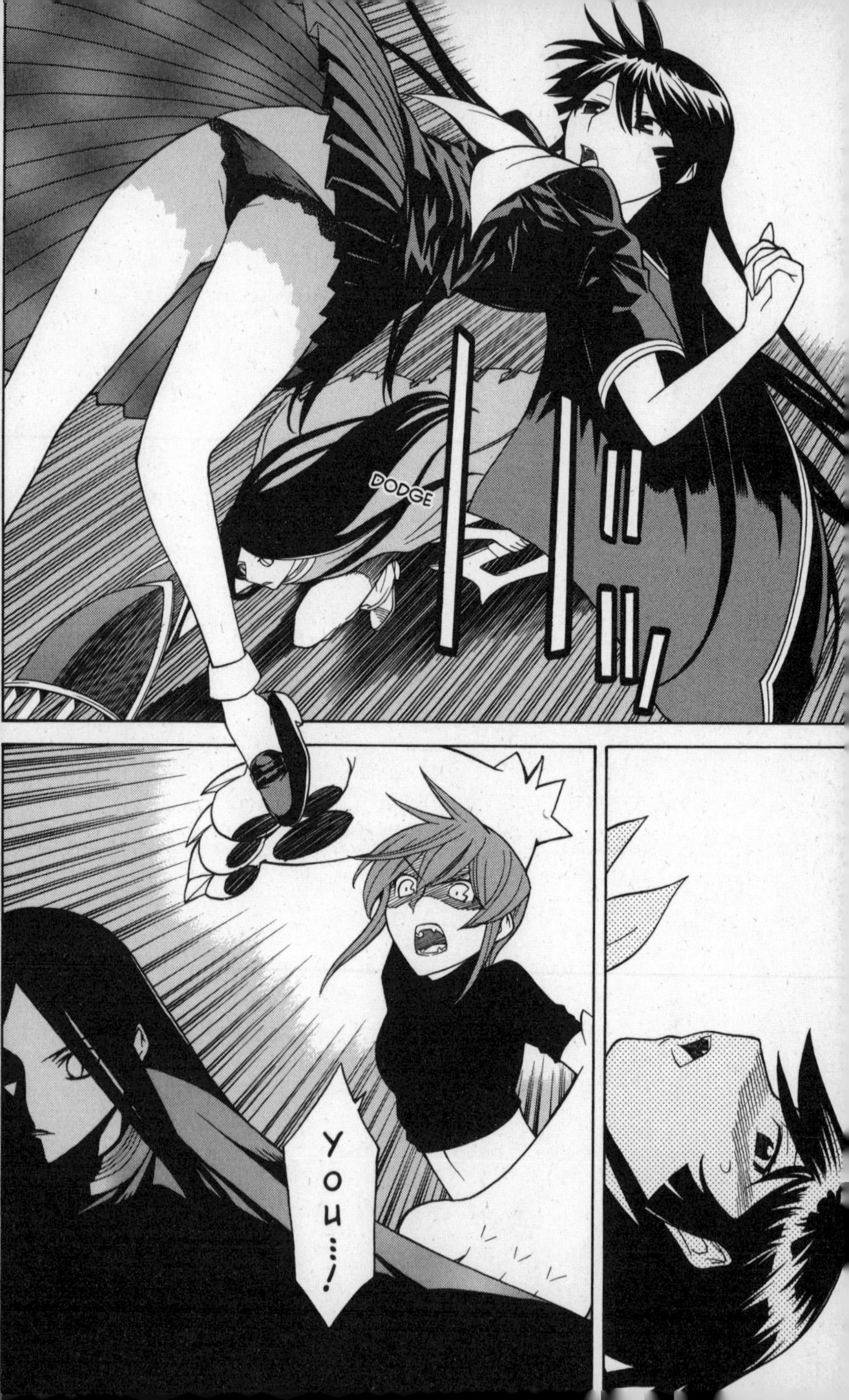
DODGE
YOU...!

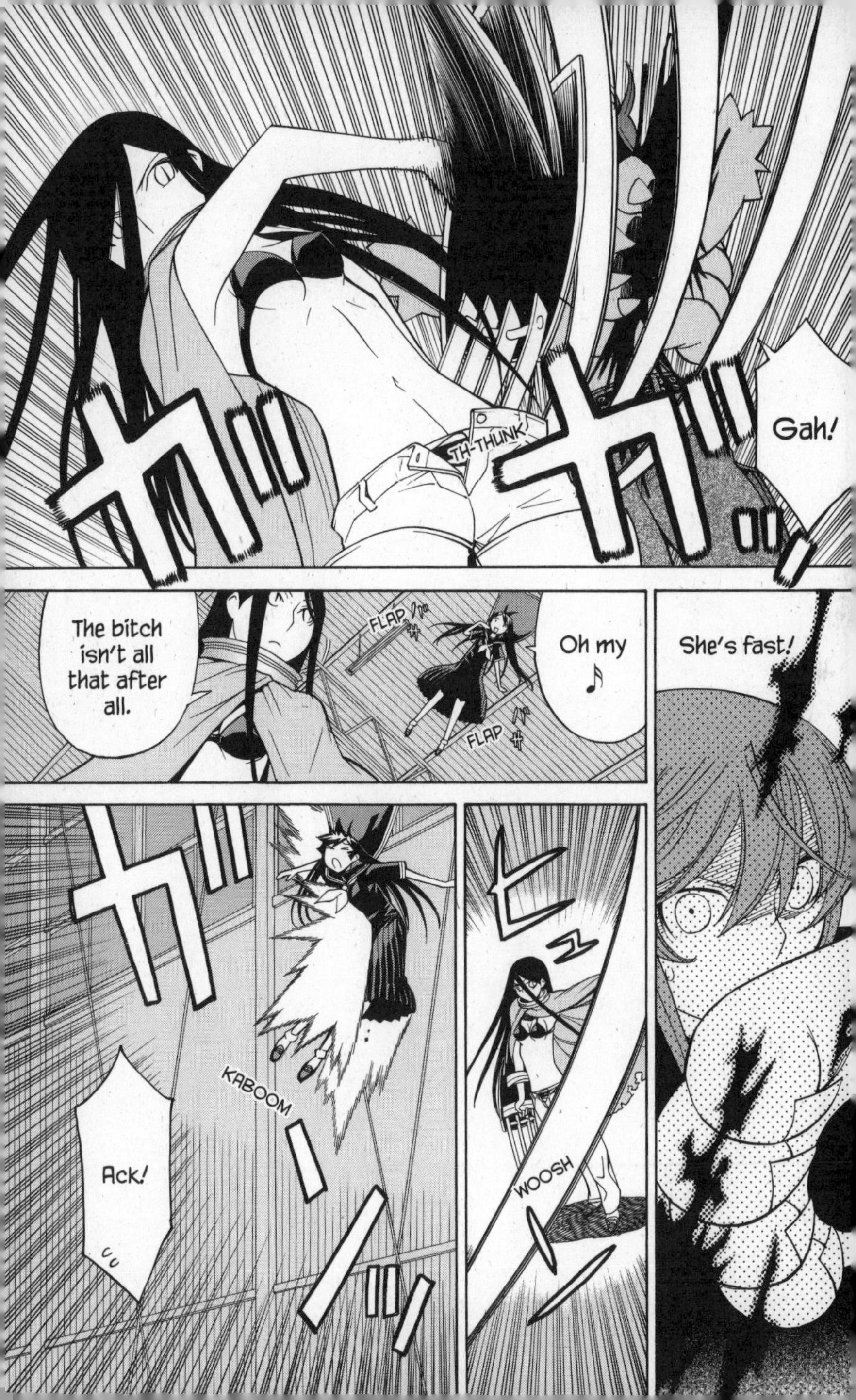
Gah!
TH-THUNK
She's fast!
Oh my ♪
FLAP
FLAP
The bitch isn't all that after all.
WOOSH
KABOOM
Ack!

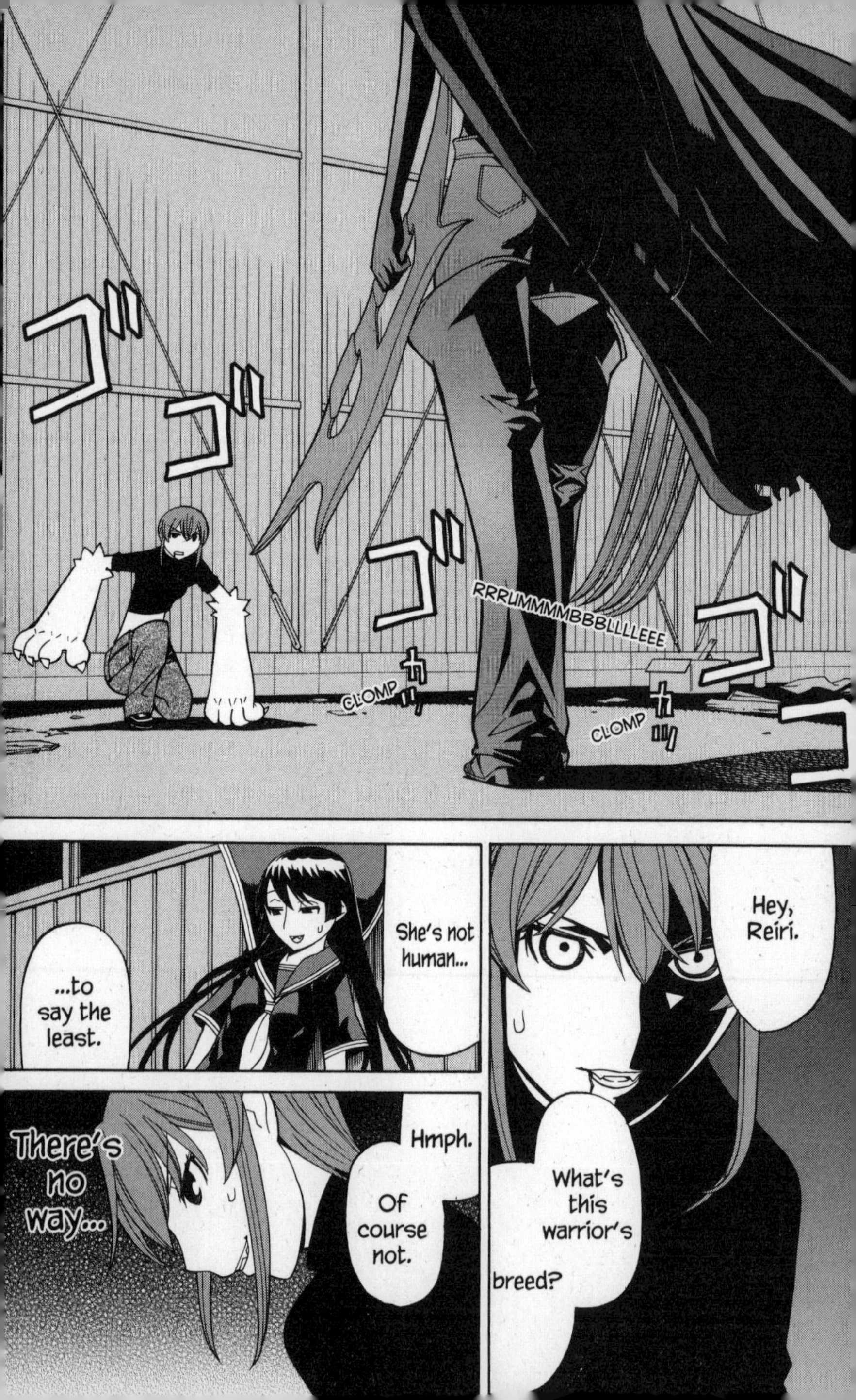
RRRUMMMMBBBLLLLEEE
CLOMP
CLOMP
Hey, Reiri.
What's this warrior's breed?
She's not human...
...to say the least.
Hmph.
Of course not.
There's no way...

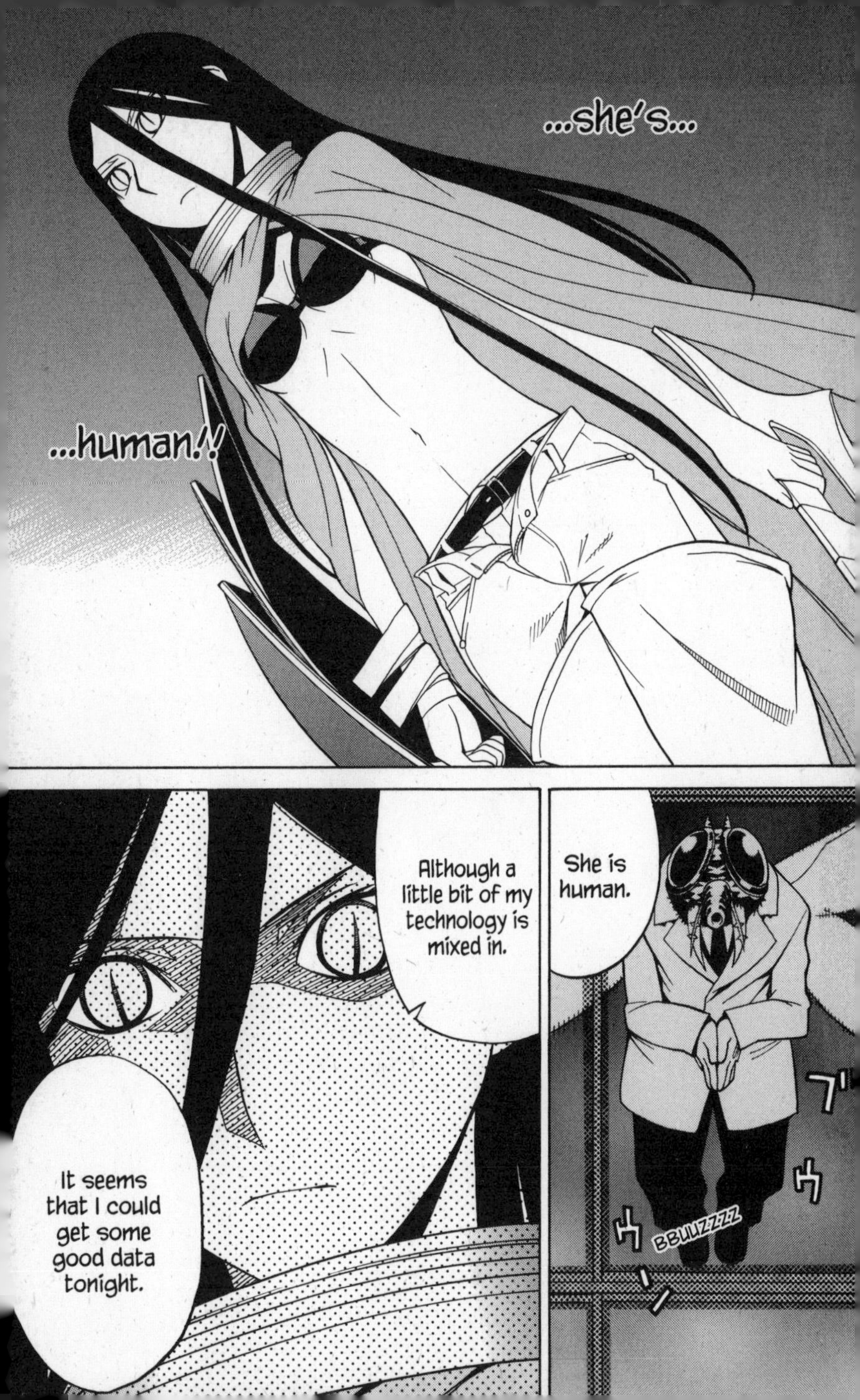
...she's...
...human!!
She is human.
BBUUZZZZ
Although a little bit of my technology is mixed in.
It seems that I could get some good data tonight.

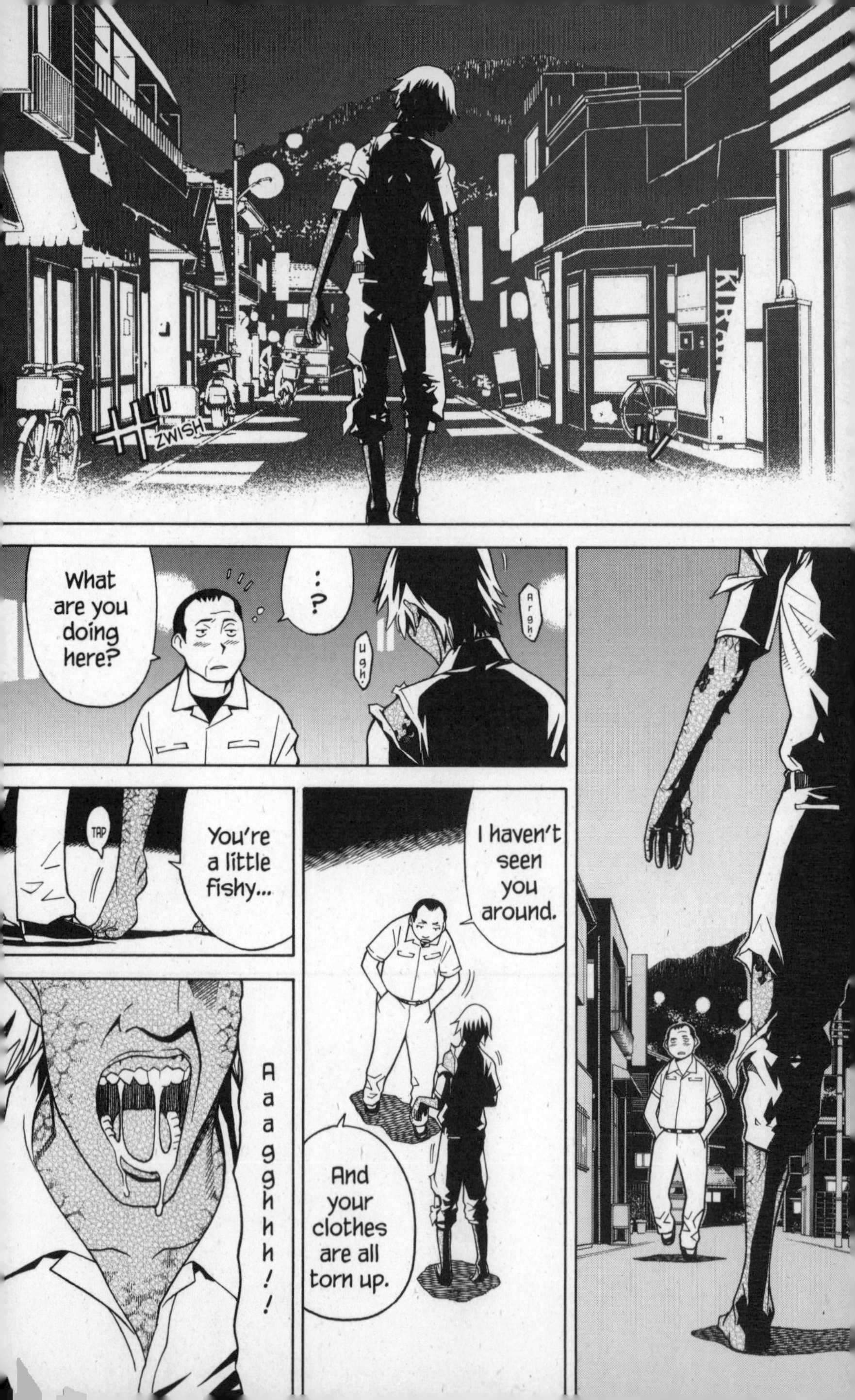
ZWISH
Argh
Ugh
?
What are you doing here?
I haven't seen you around.
And your clothes are all torn up.
TAP
You're a little fishy...
Aaagghhh!!

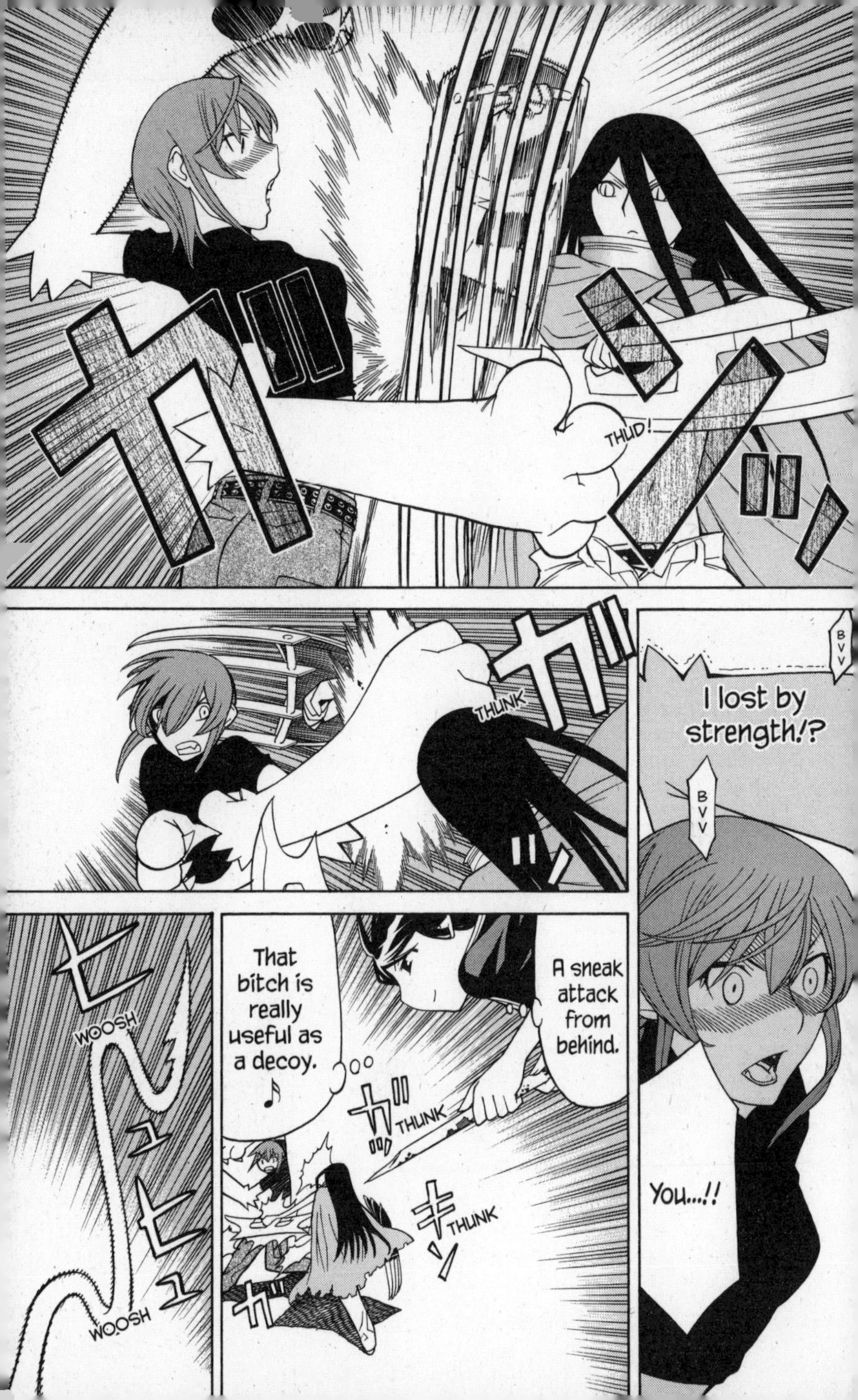
THUD!
BVV
I lost by strength!?
BVV
You...!!
THUNK
A sneak attack from behind.
That bitch is really useful as a decoy. ♪
THUNK
THUNK
WOOSH
WOOSH

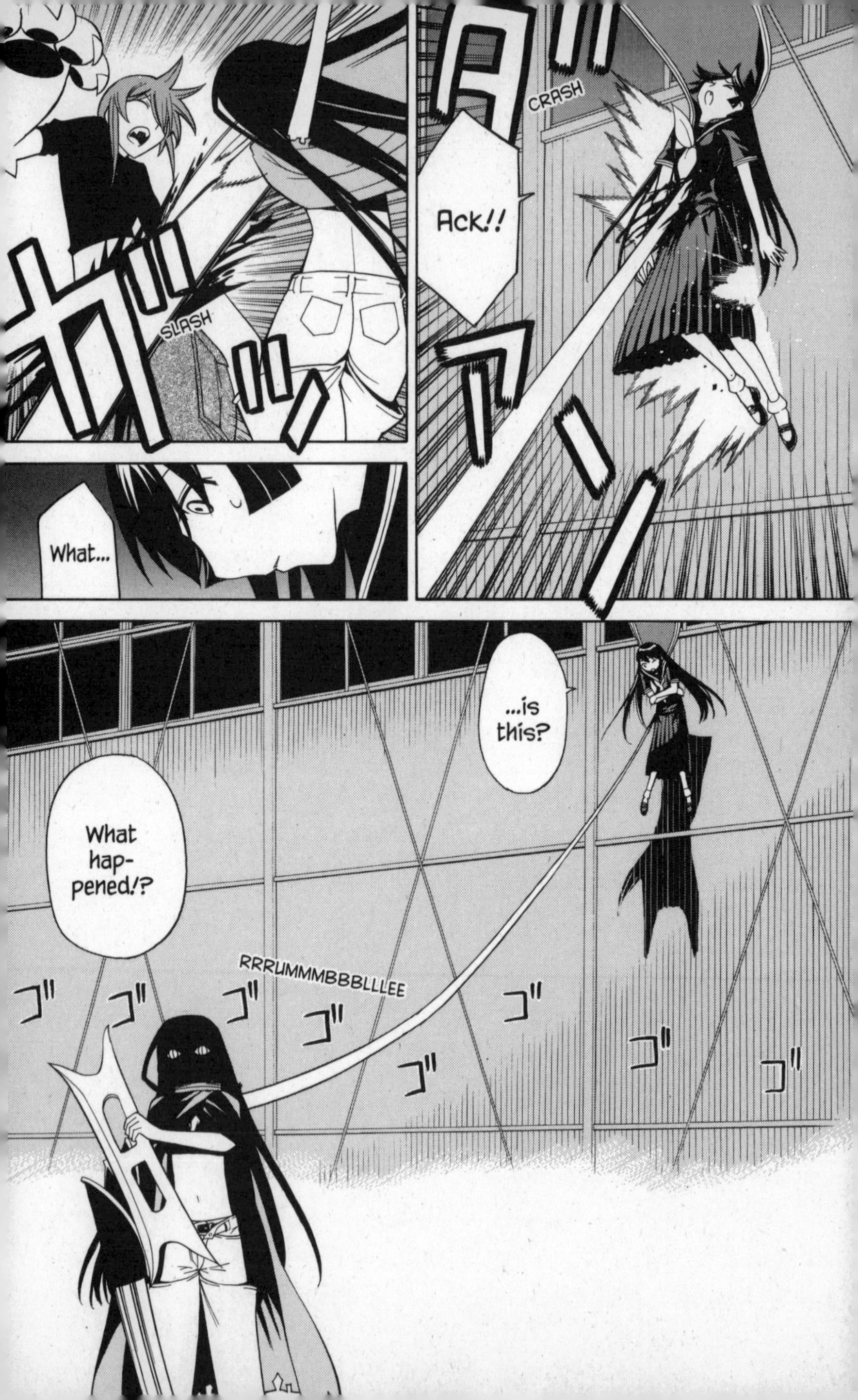
CRASH
Ack!!
SLASH
What...
...is this?
What hap-
pened!?
RRRUMMMBBBLLLEE

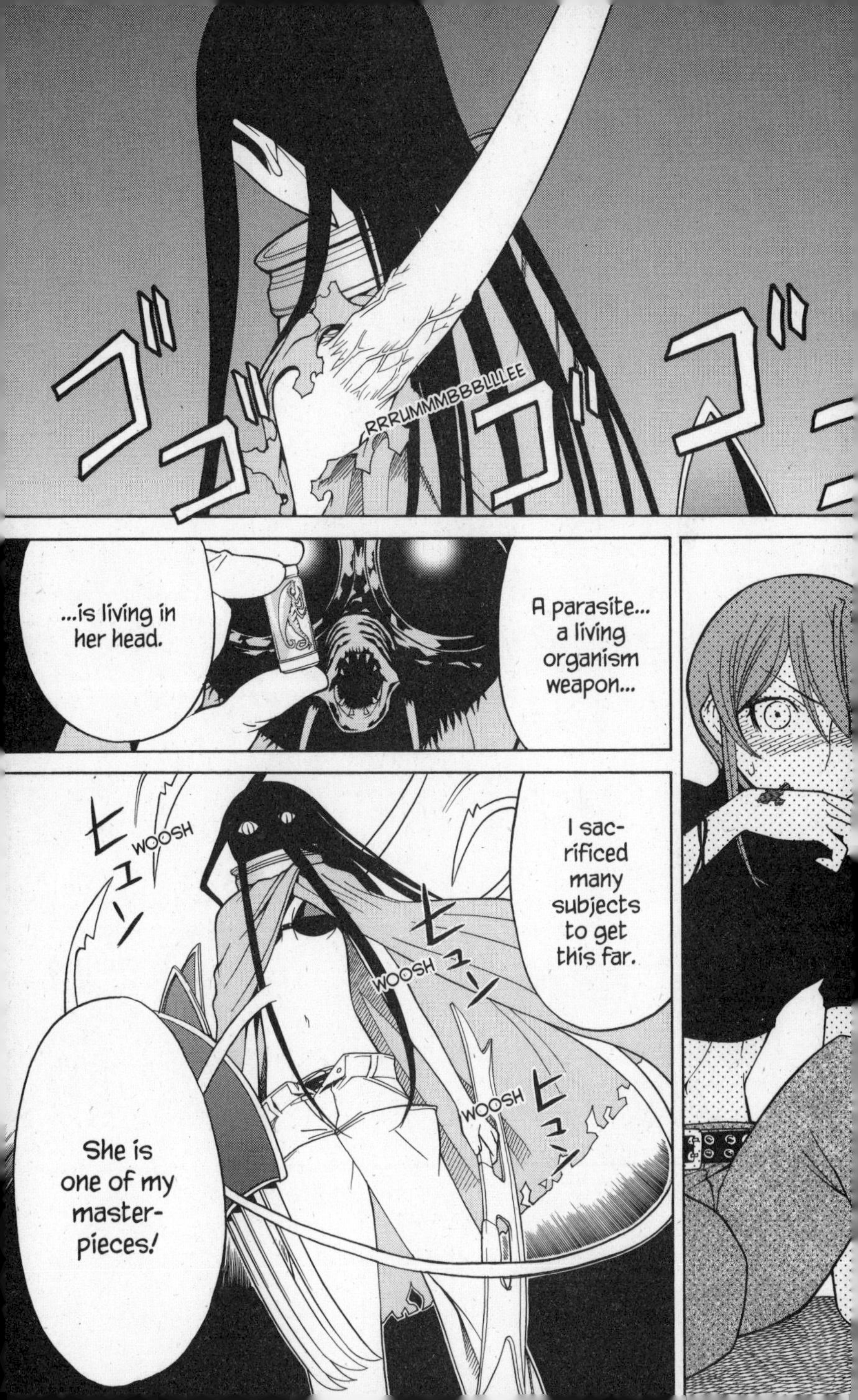

ゴゴゴゴ
RRRUMMMBBBLLLEE
A parasite... a living organism weapon...
...is living in her head.
I sacrificed many subjects to get this far.
ヒューン
WOOSH
ヒューン
WOOSH
ヒューン
WOOSH
She is one of my masterpieces!

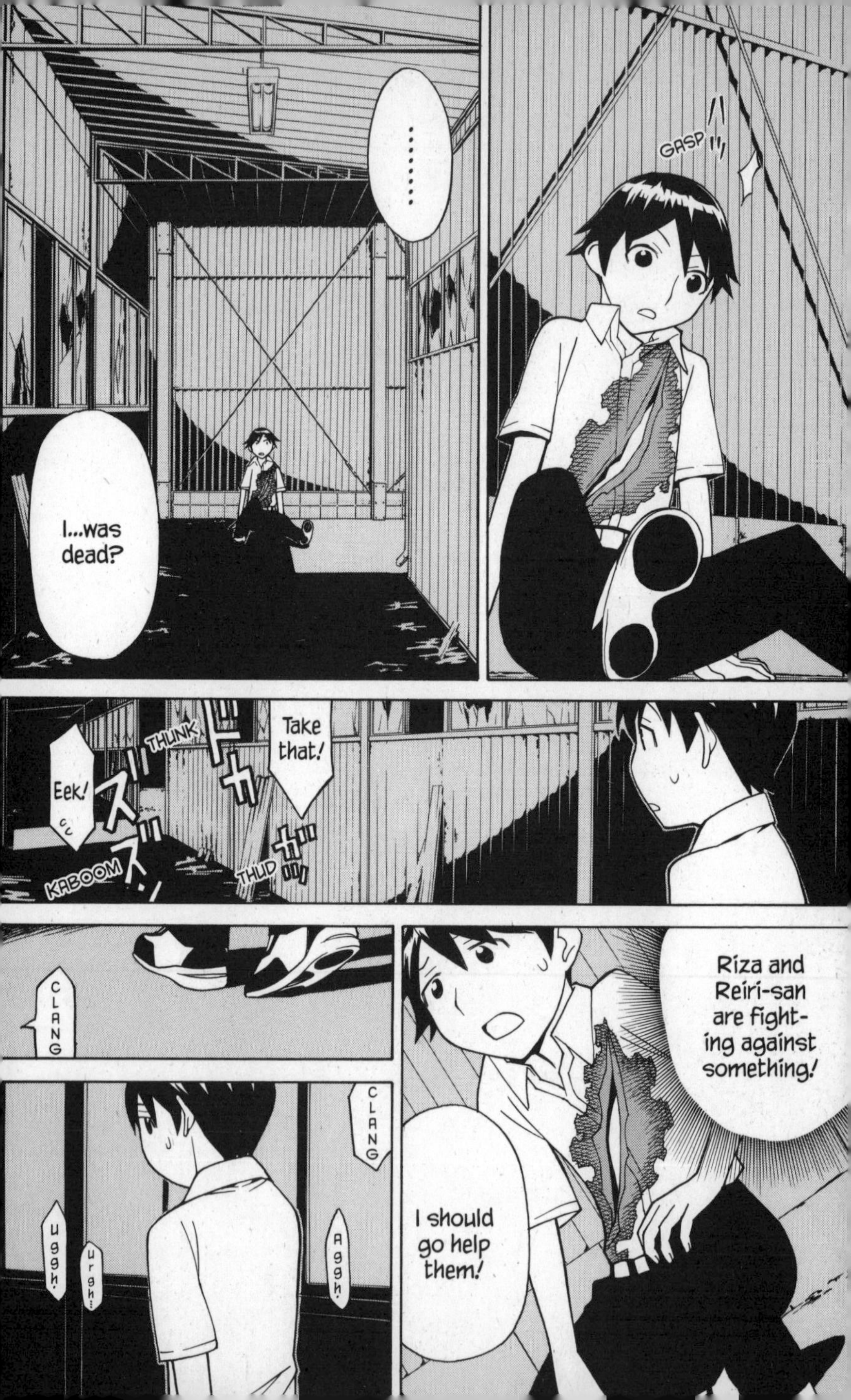
GASP
......
I...was dead?
Take that!
THUNK
Eek!
THUD
KABOOM
Riza and Reiri-san are fight-ing against something!
I should go help them!
CLANG
CLANG
Aggh.
urgh...
Uggh.

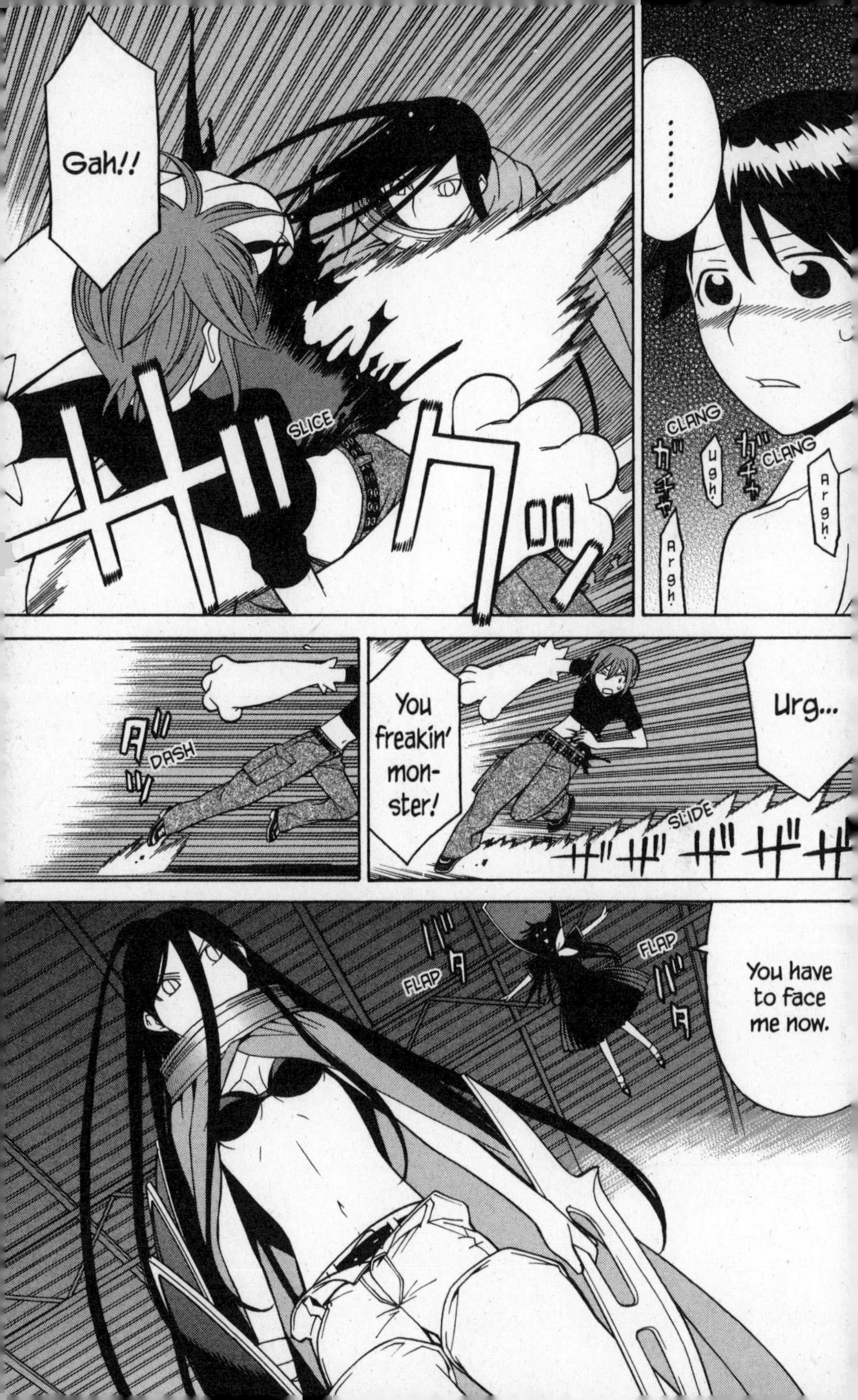

……
CLANG
Argh.
CLANG
Ugh.
Argh.
Gah!!
SLICE
Urg...
You freakin' monster!
SLIDE
DASH
You have to face me now.
FLAP
FLAP

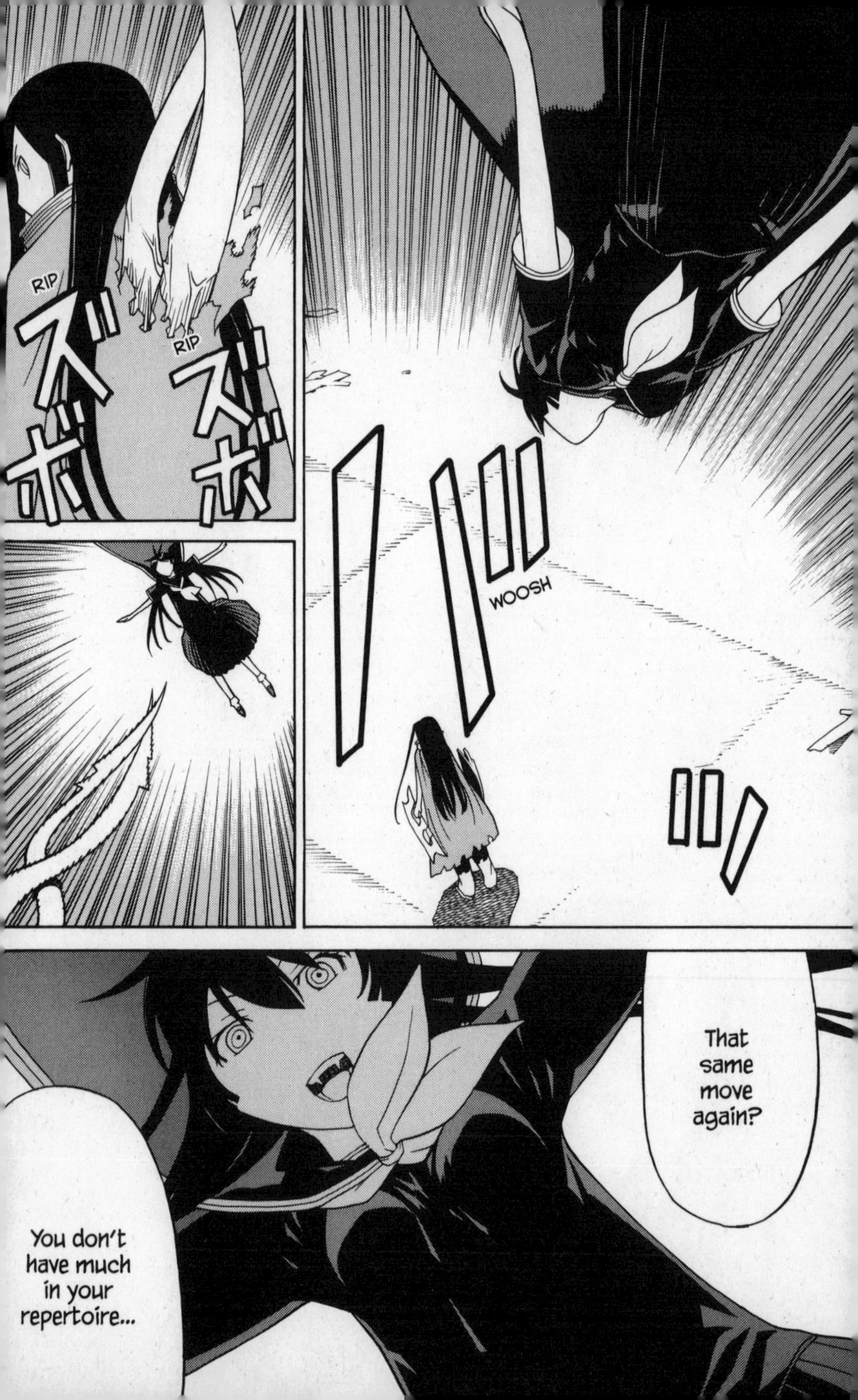

WOOSH
RIP
ズボ
RIP
ズボ
That same move again?
You don't have much in your repertoire...

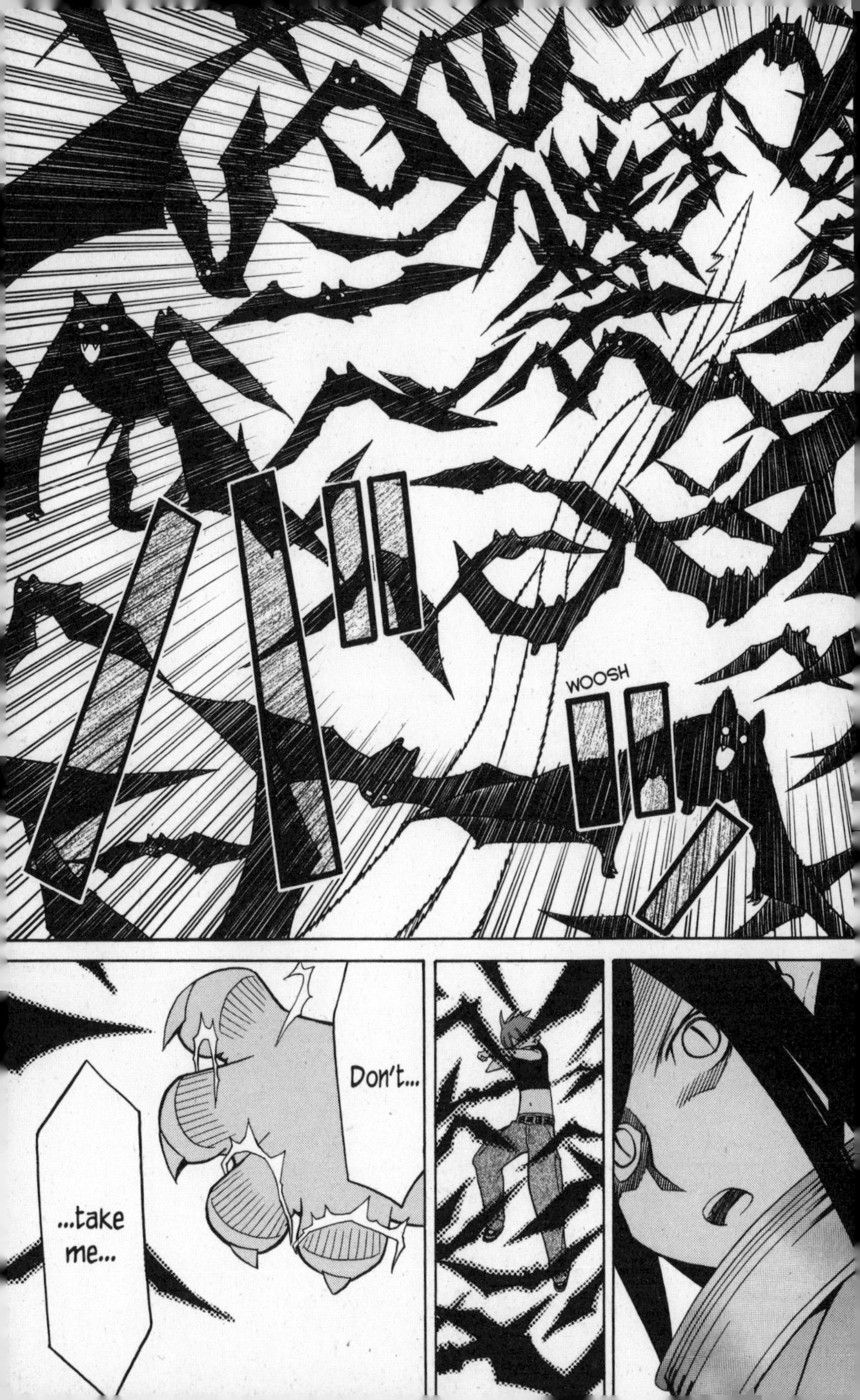
WOOSH
Don't...
...take me...

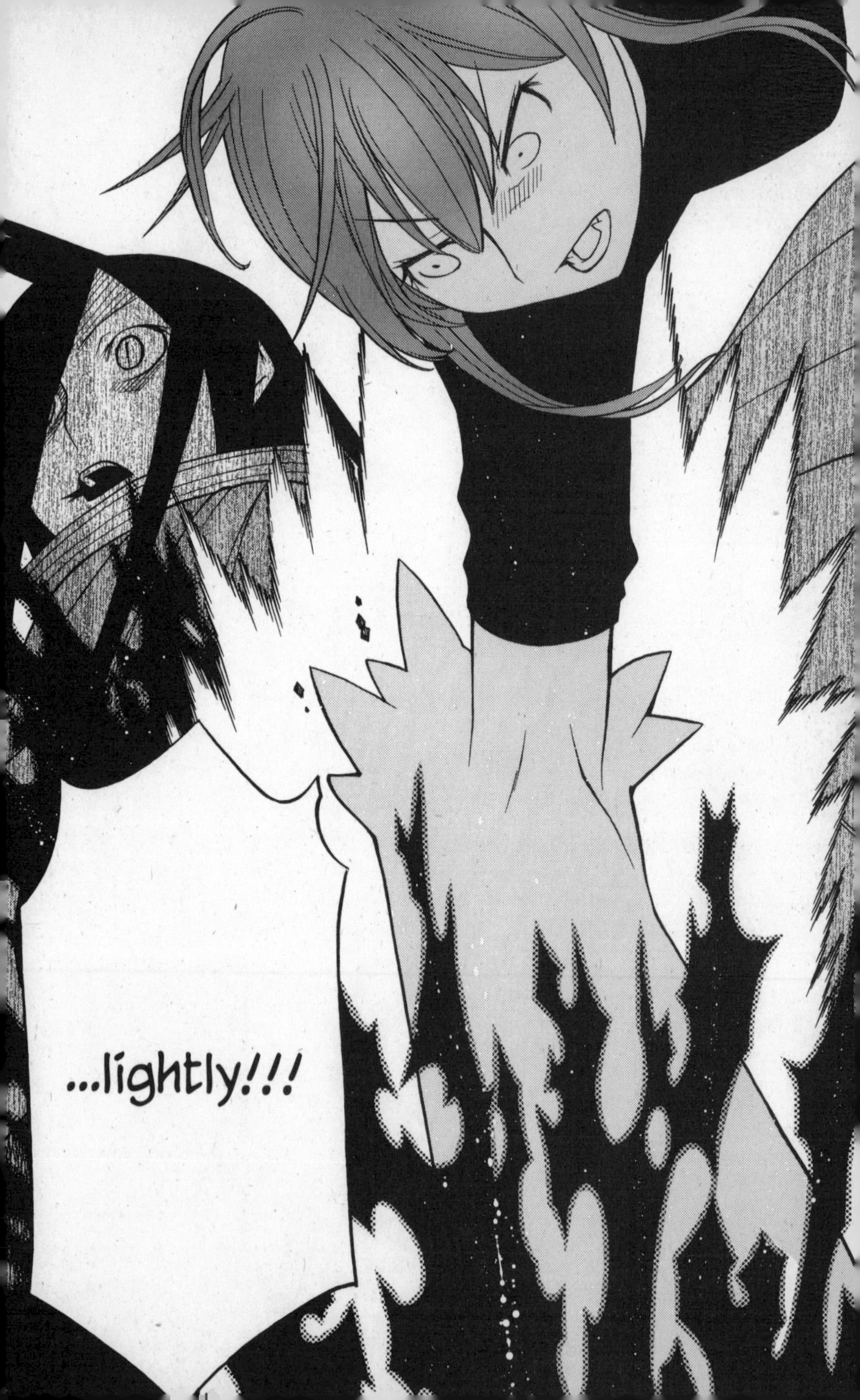
...lightly!!!

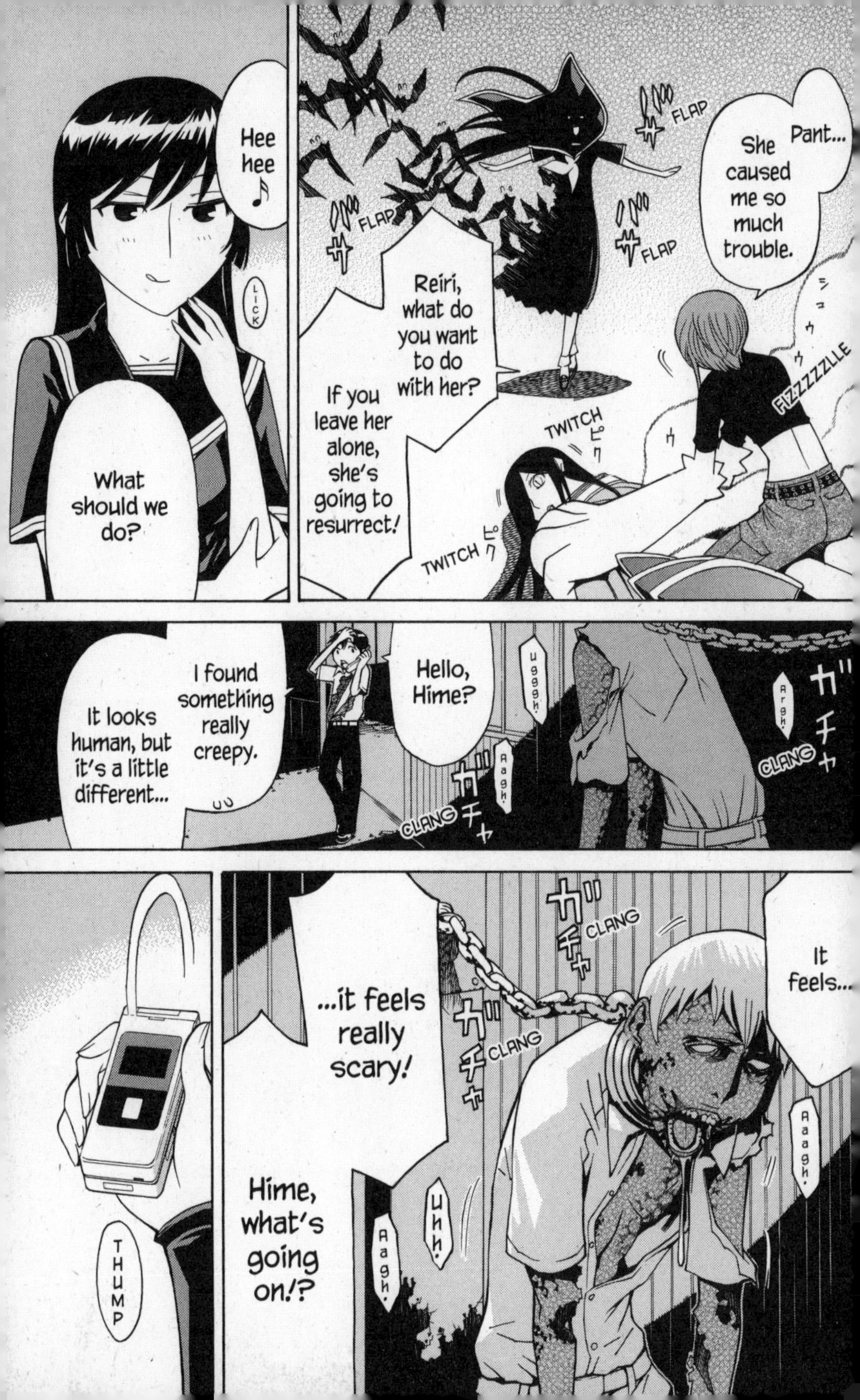
FLAP
FLAP
FLAP
Pant...
She caused me so much trouble.
FIZZZZZLLE
Reiri, what do you want to do with her?
If you leave her alone, she's going to resurrect!
TWITCH
TWITCH
Hee hee ♪
LICK
What should we do?
CLANG
Argh.
Hello, Hime?
Uggh.
Aagh.
CLANG
I found something really creepy.
It looks human, but it's a little different...
It feels...
CLANG
CLANG
...it feels really scary!
Aaagh.
Uhh.
Aagh.
Hime, what's going on!?
THUMP

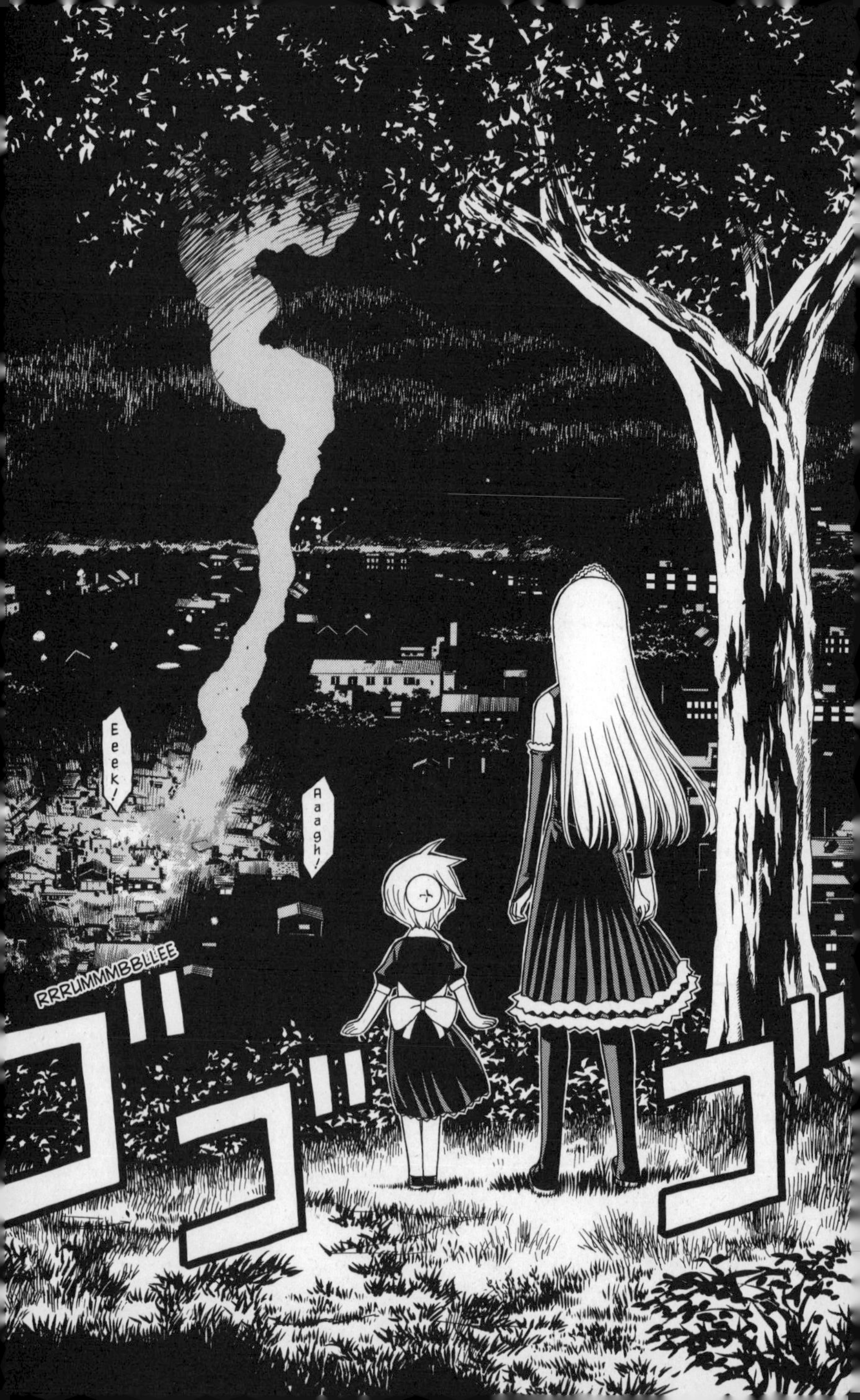
Aaagh!
Eeek!
RRRUMMMBBLLEE
ゴゴゴ

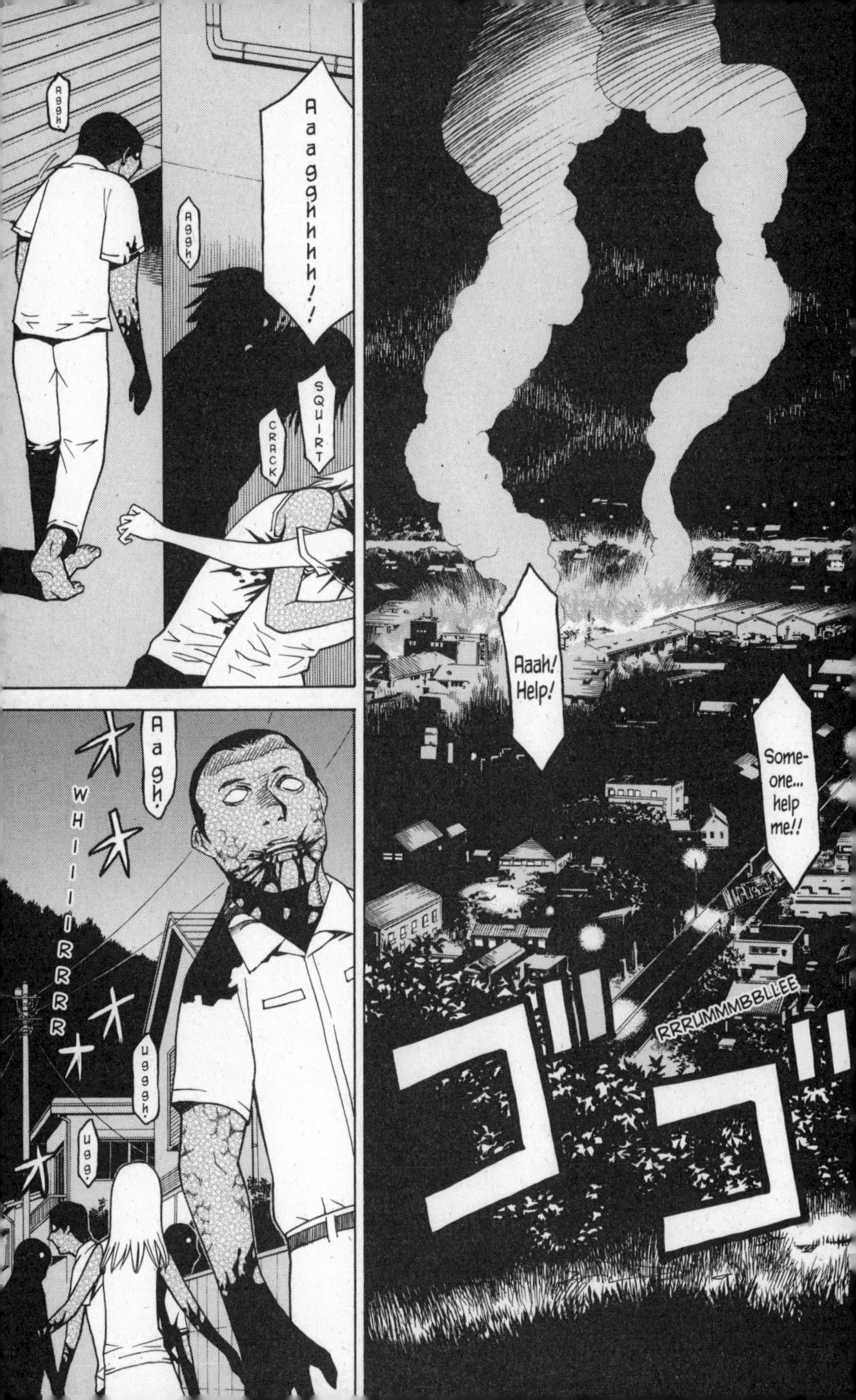
Aaah! Help!
Some-one... help me!!
ゴゴ
RRRUMMMBBLLEE
Aaagghhhhh!!
Aggh.
Aggh.
SQUIRT
CRACK
Aagh.
WHIIIIIRRRR
uggh.
ugg.

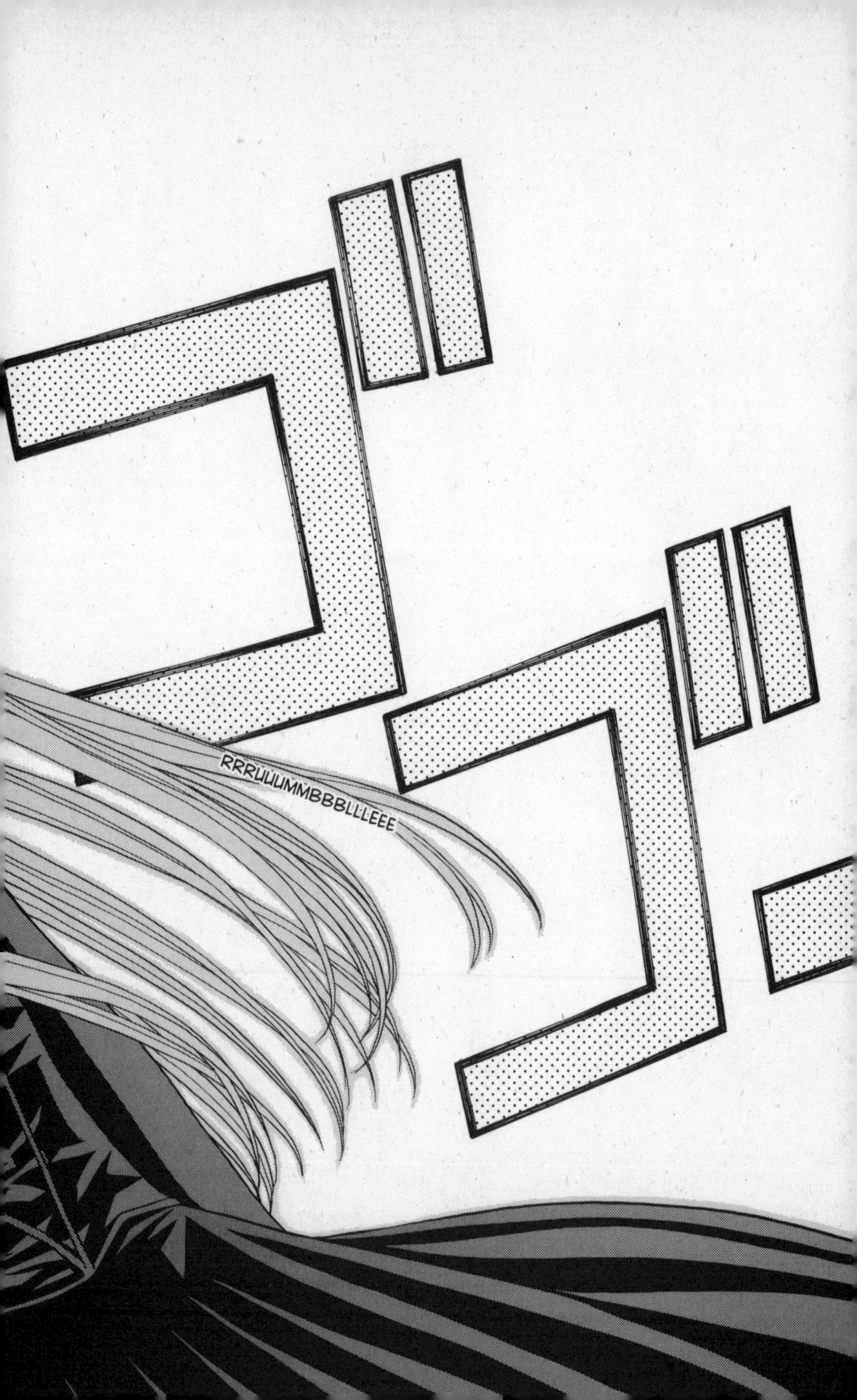
ゴゴー
RRRUUUMMBBBLLLEEE

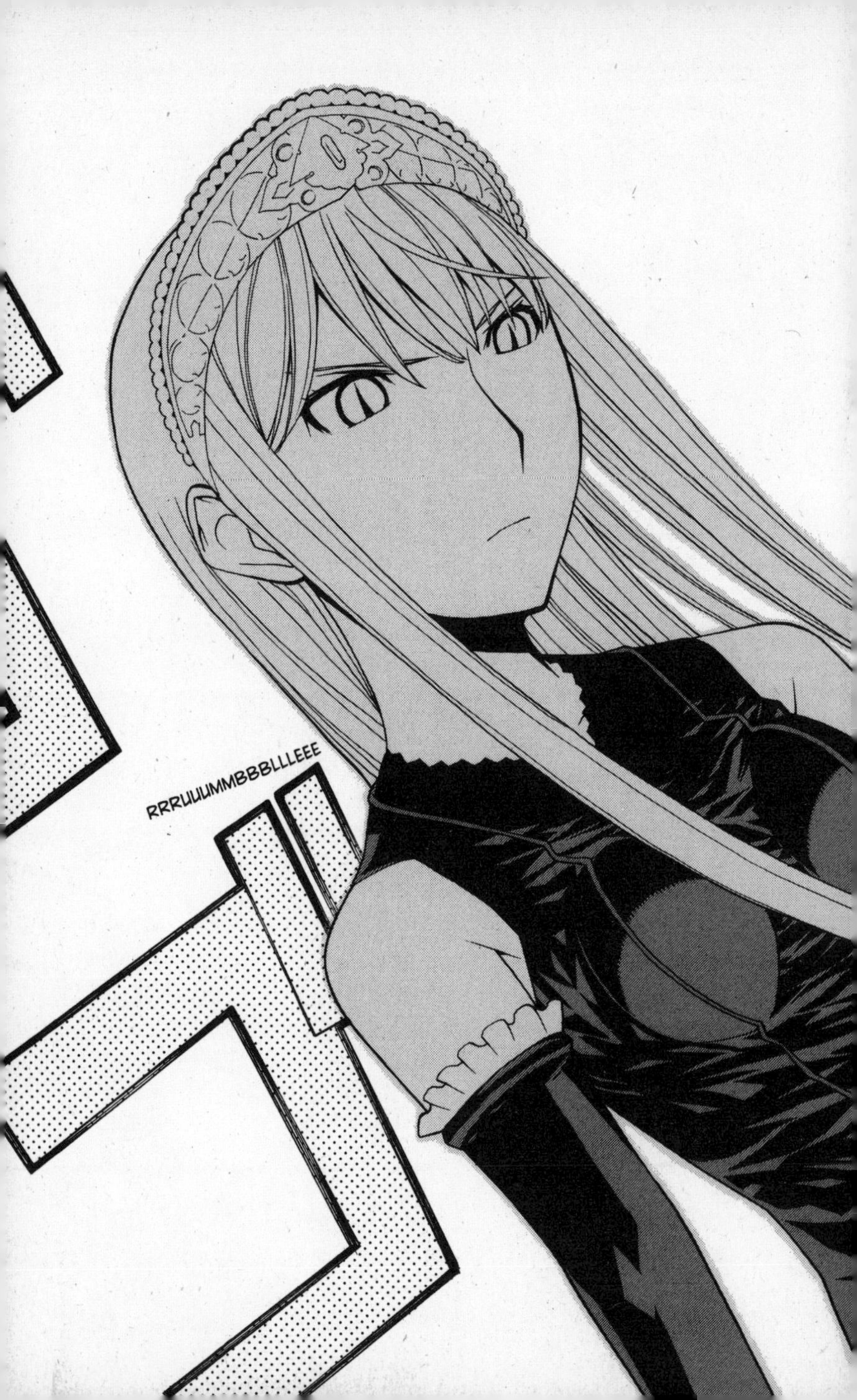
RRRUUUMMBBBLLLEEE

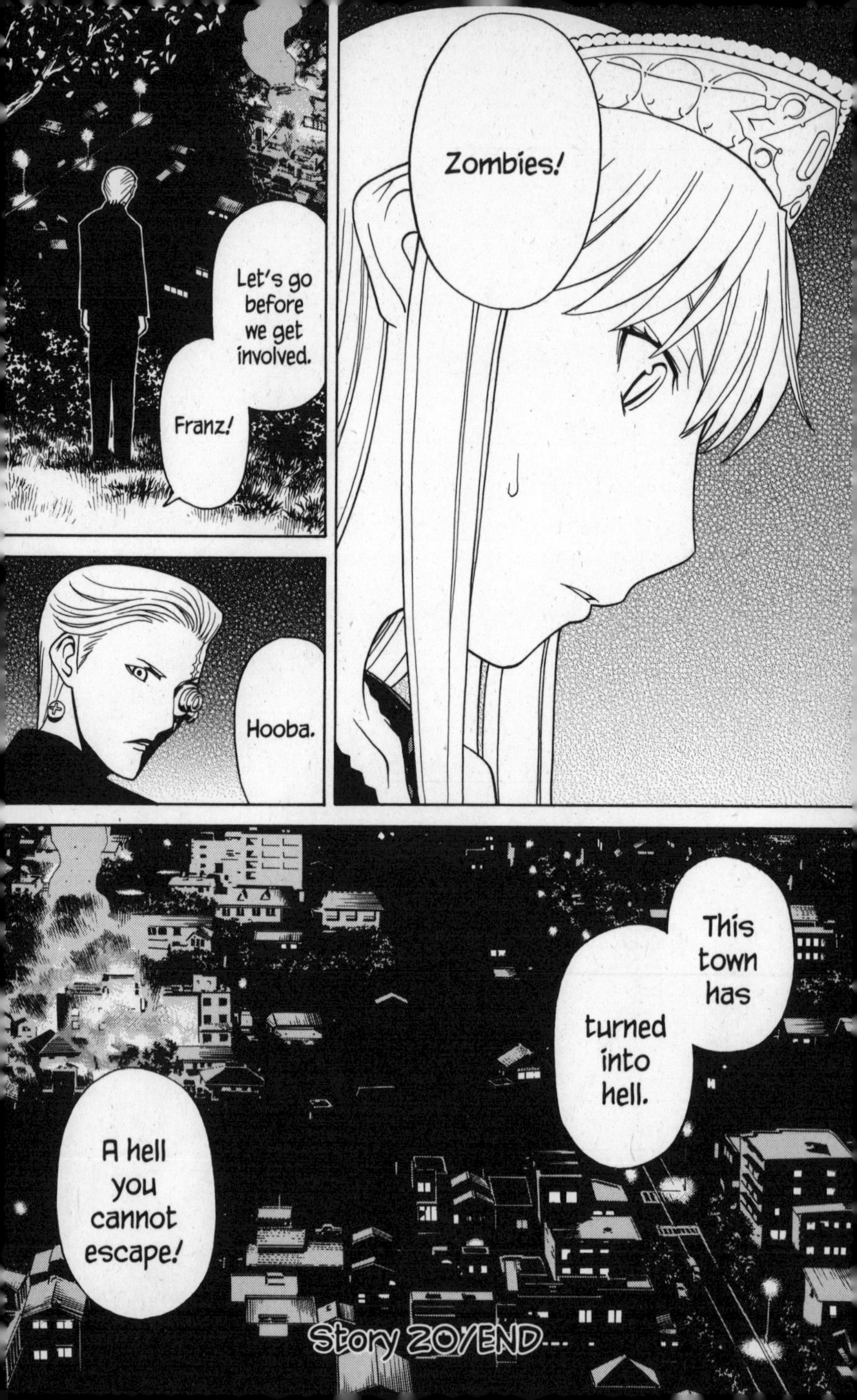
Zombies!
Let's go before we get involved.
Franz!
Hooba.
This town has
turned into hell.
A hell you cannot escape!
Story 20/END...

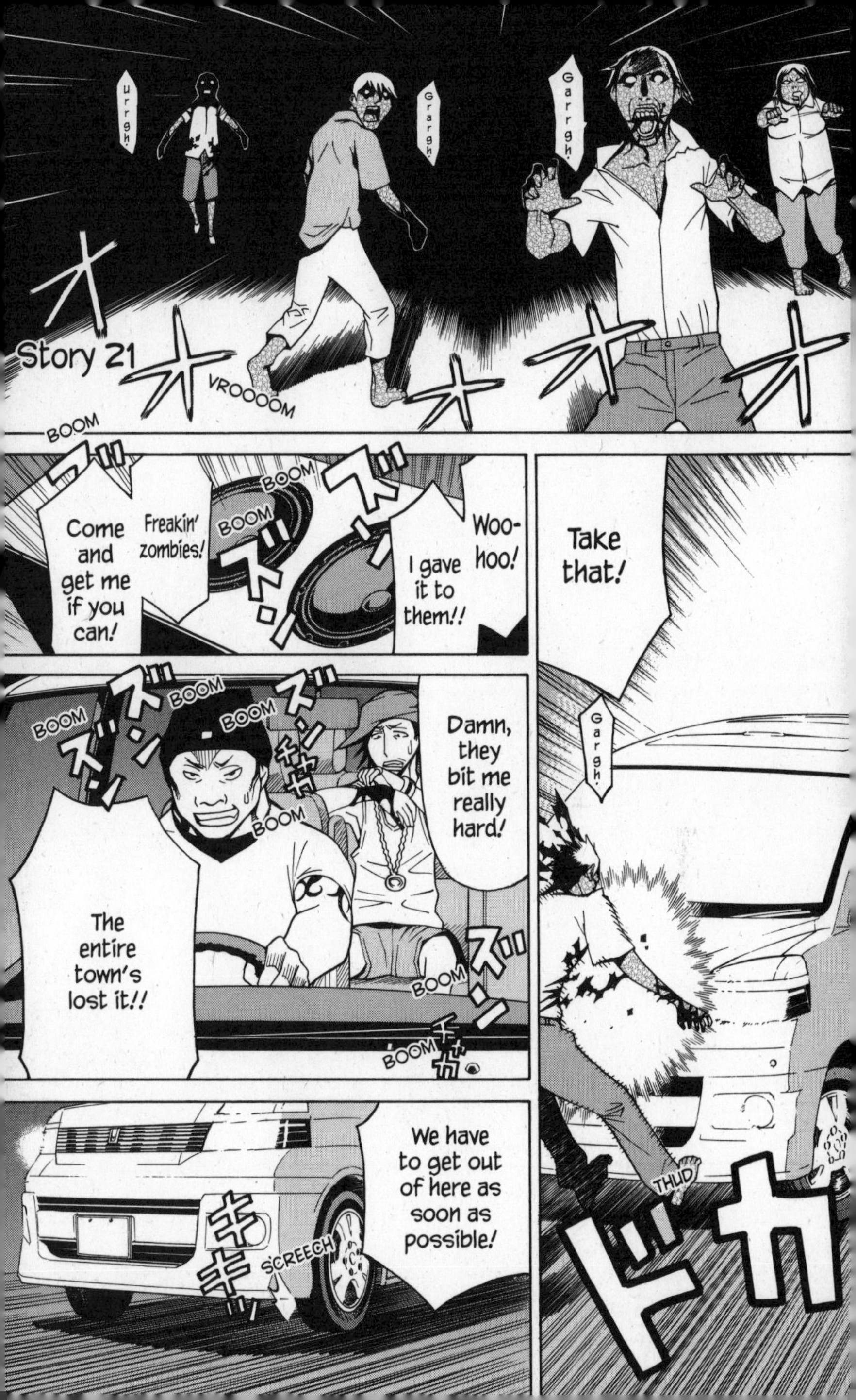
Garrgh.
Grargh.
urrgh.
Story 21
VROOOOM
Take that!
Gargh.
THUD
Woo-hoo!
I gave it to them!!
BOOM
BOOM
BOOM
Freakin' zombies!
Come and get me if you can!
Damn, they bit me really hard!
BOOM
BOOM
BOOM
BOOM
The entire town's lost it!!
BOOM
BOOM
We have to get out of here as soon as possible!
SCREECH

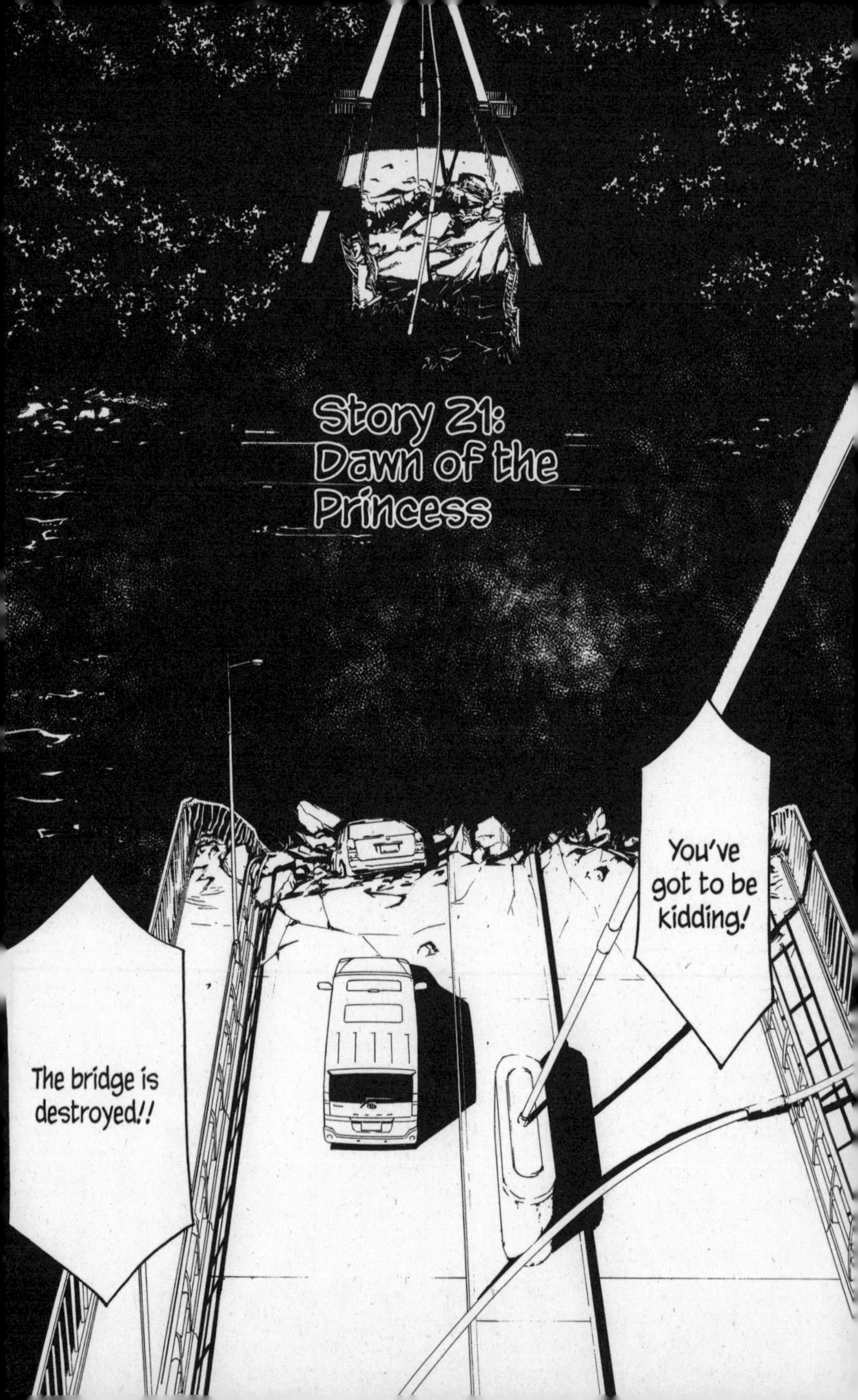
Story 21: Dawn of the Princess
You've got to be kidding!
The bridge is destroyed!!

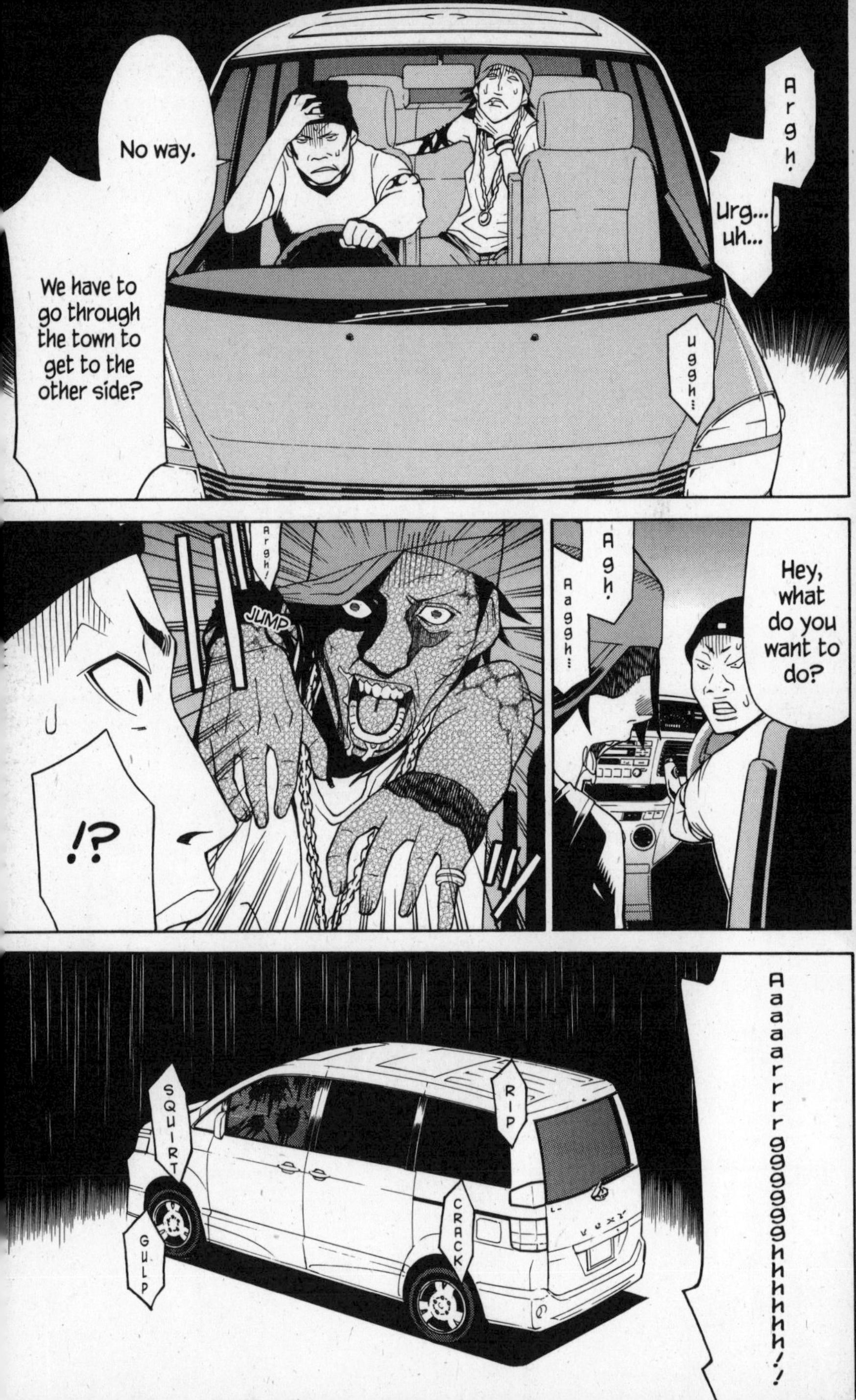

Argh.
Urg... uh...
No way.
ugh...
We have to go through the town to get to the other side?
Hey, what do you want to do?
Agh.
Aaggh...
Argh!
JUMP
!?
Aaaarrrrggggghhhhh!!
RIP
SQUIRT
CRACK
GULP

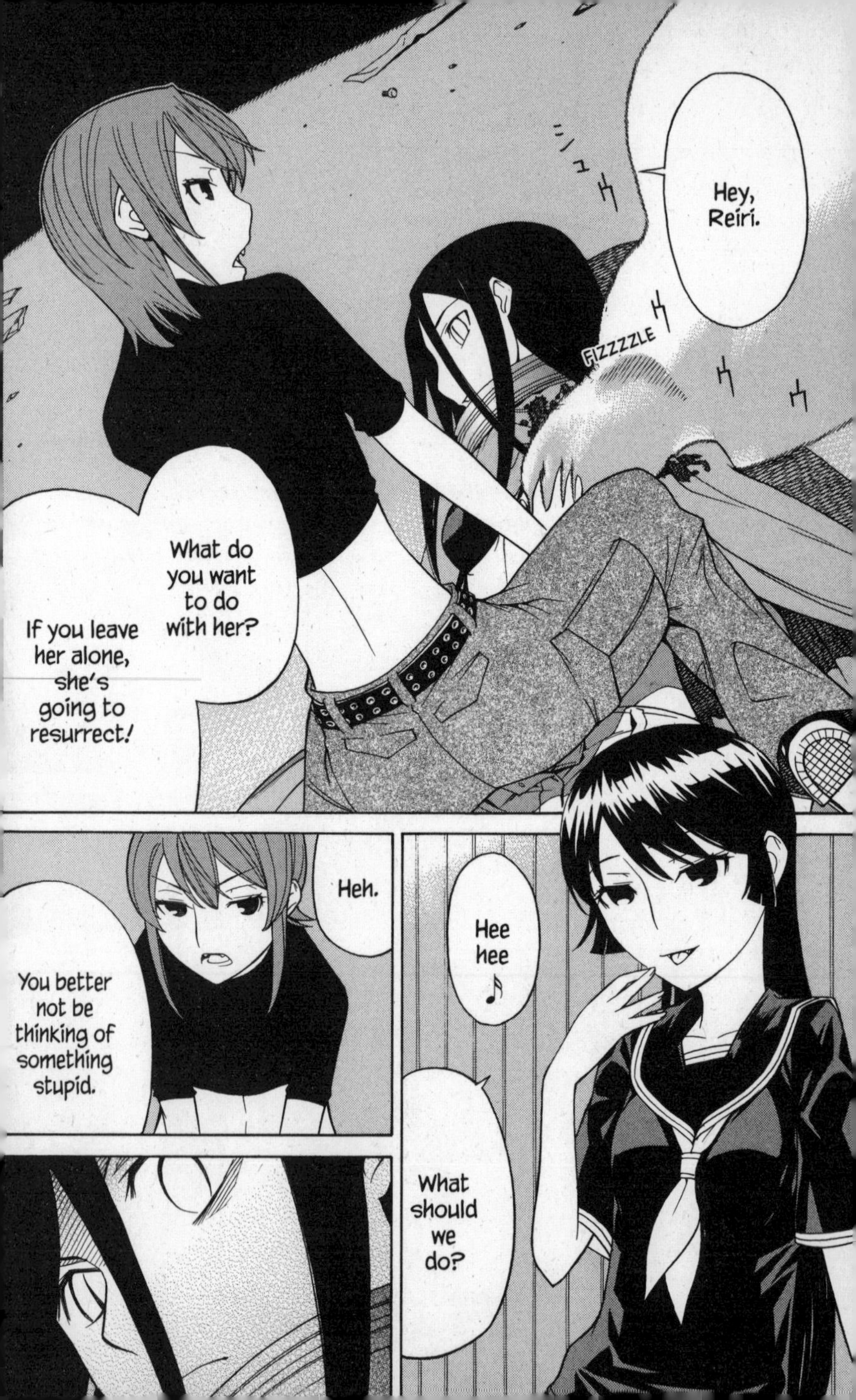
Hey, Reiri.
FIZZZZLE
What do you want to do with her?
If you leave her alone, she's going to resurrect!
Hee hee ♪
What should we do?
Heh.
You better not be thinking of something stupid.

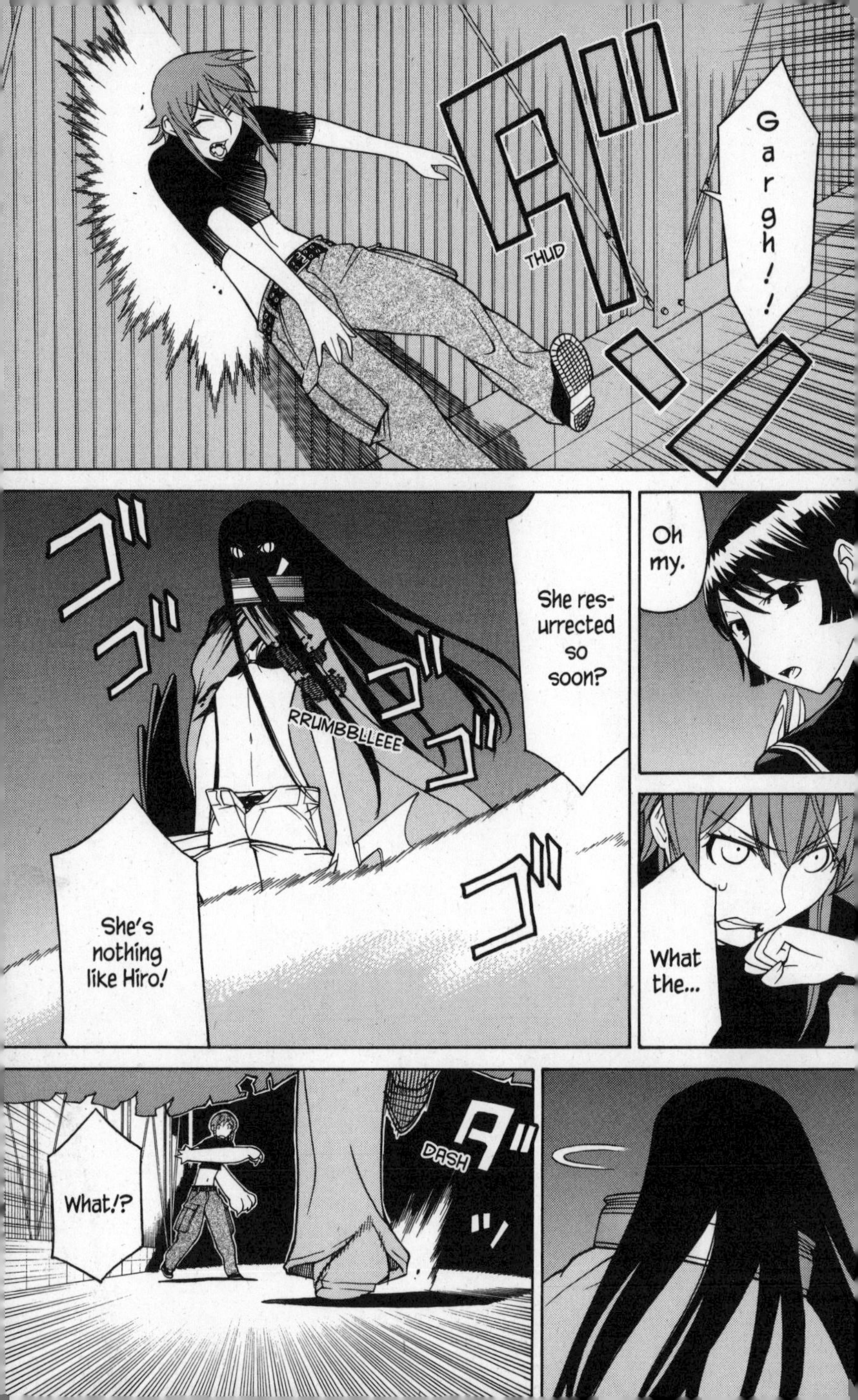
Gargh!!
THUD
Oh my.
What the...
She res-urrected so soon?
RRUMBBLLEEE
She's nothing like Hiro!
DASH
What!?

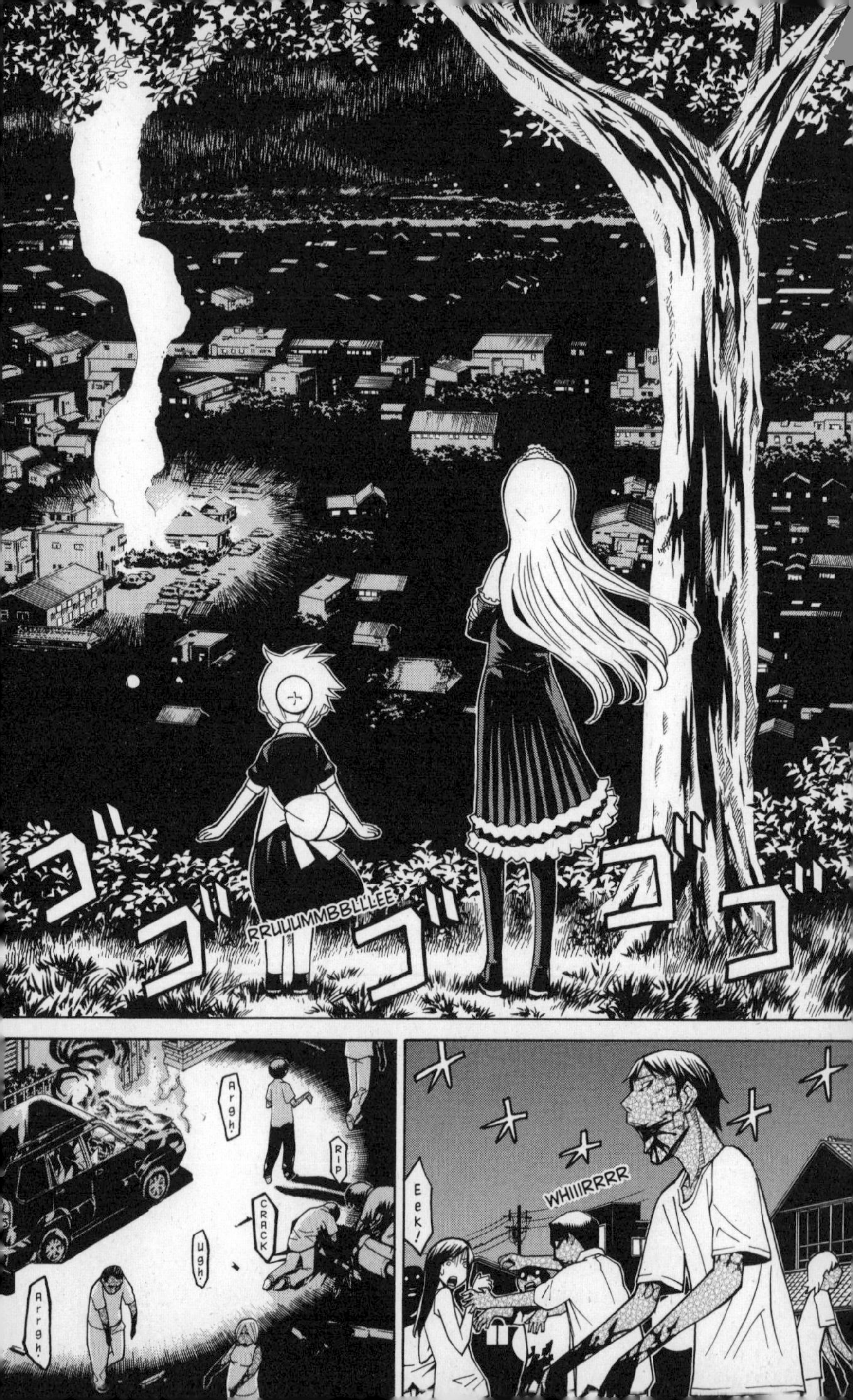
ゴゴゴ
RRUUUMMBBLLLEE
ゴゴ
Eek!
WHIIIRRRR
Argh.
RIP
CRACK
Ugh.
Arrgh.

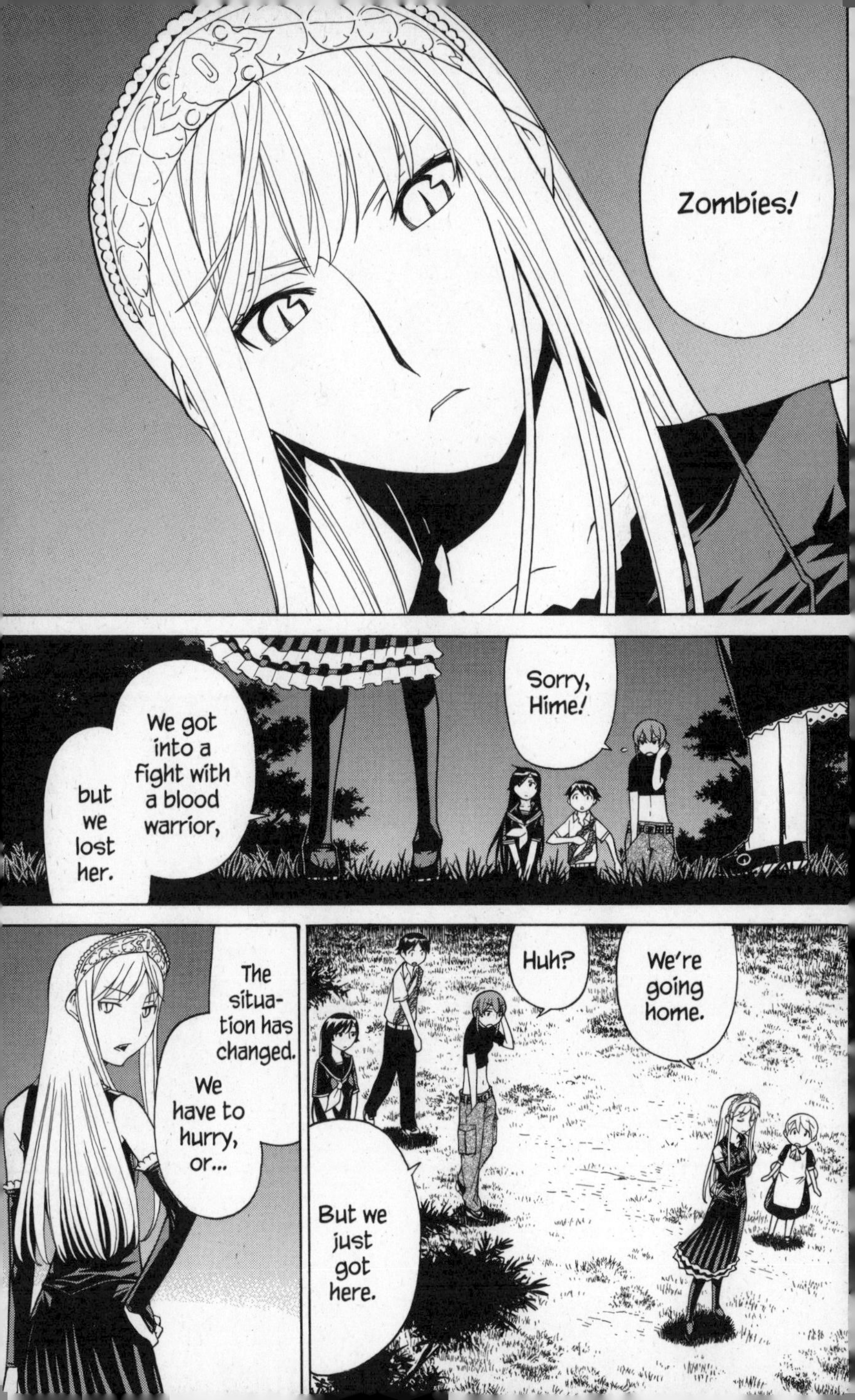
Zombies!
Sorry, Hime!
We got into a fight with a blood warrior,
but we lost her.
We're going home.
Huh?
But we just got here.
The situation has changed.
We have to hurry, or...

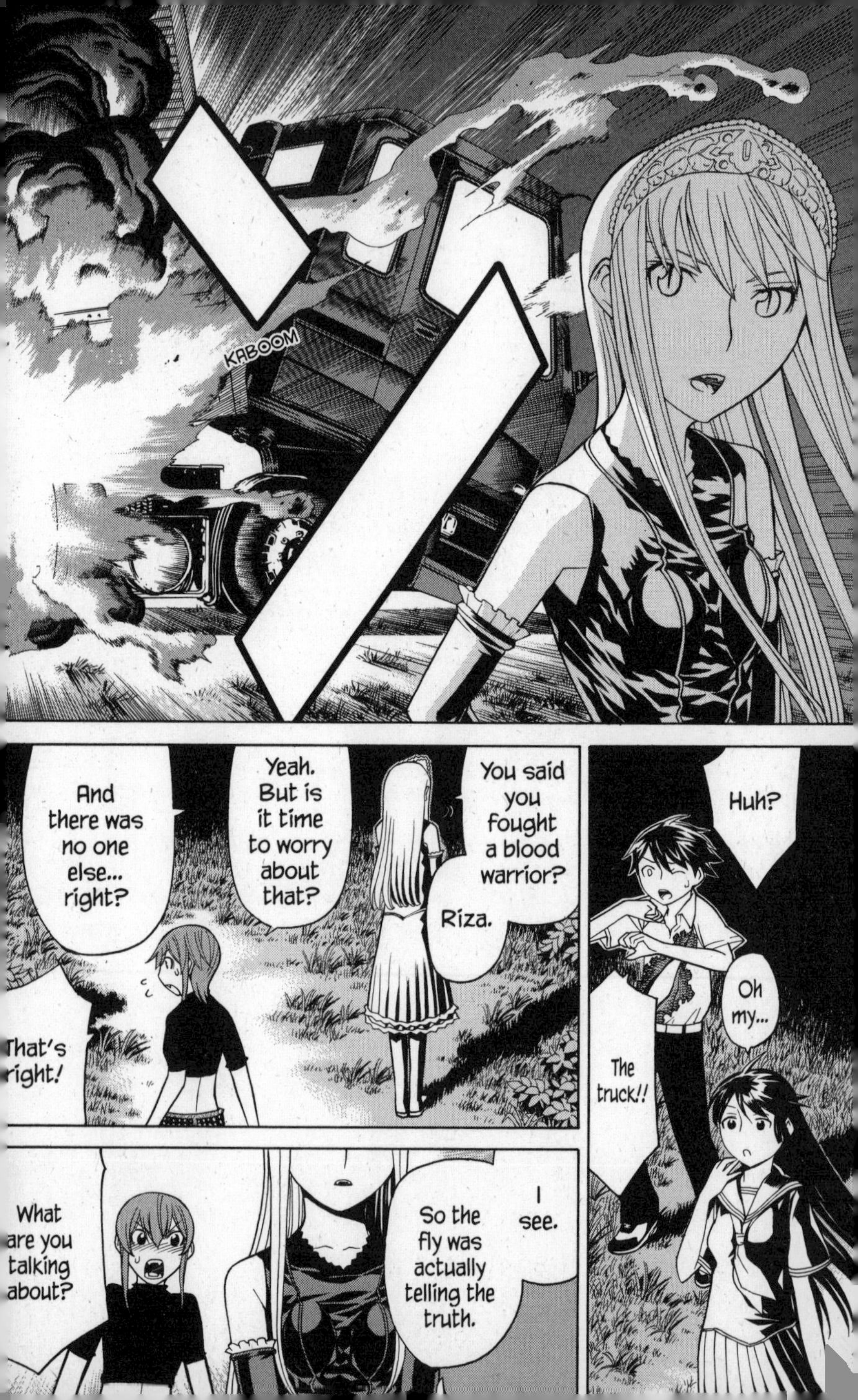
KABOOM
Huh?
Oh my...
The truck!!
You said you fought a blood warrior?
Riza.
Yeah. But is it time to worry about that?
And there was no one else... right?
That's right!
I see.
So the fly was actually telling the truth.
What are you talking about?

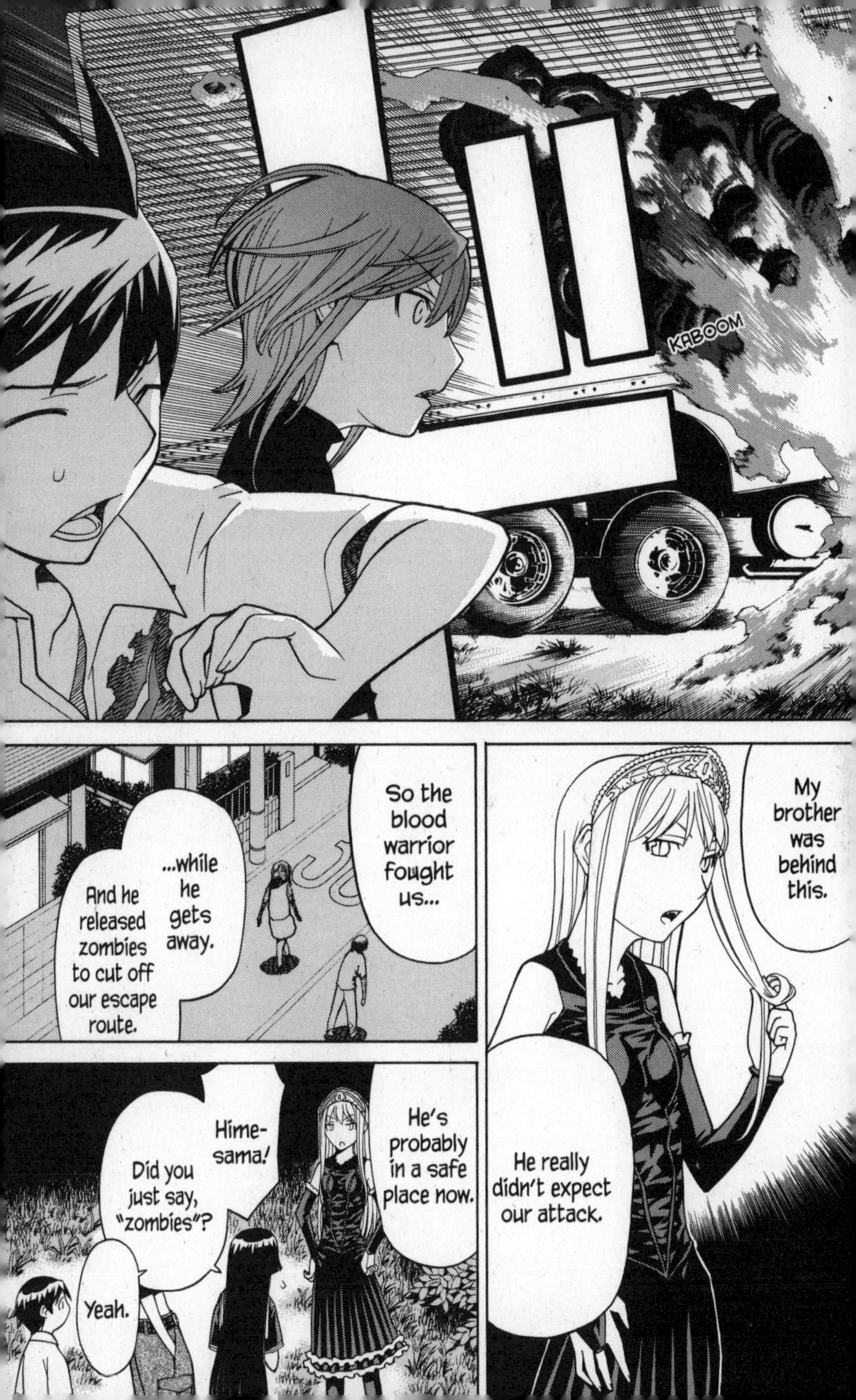
KABOOM
My brother was behind this.
He really didn't expect our attack.
So the blood warrior fought us...
...while he gets away.
And he released zombies to cut off our escape route.
He's probably in a safe place now.
Hime-sama!
Did you just say, "zombies"?
Yeah.

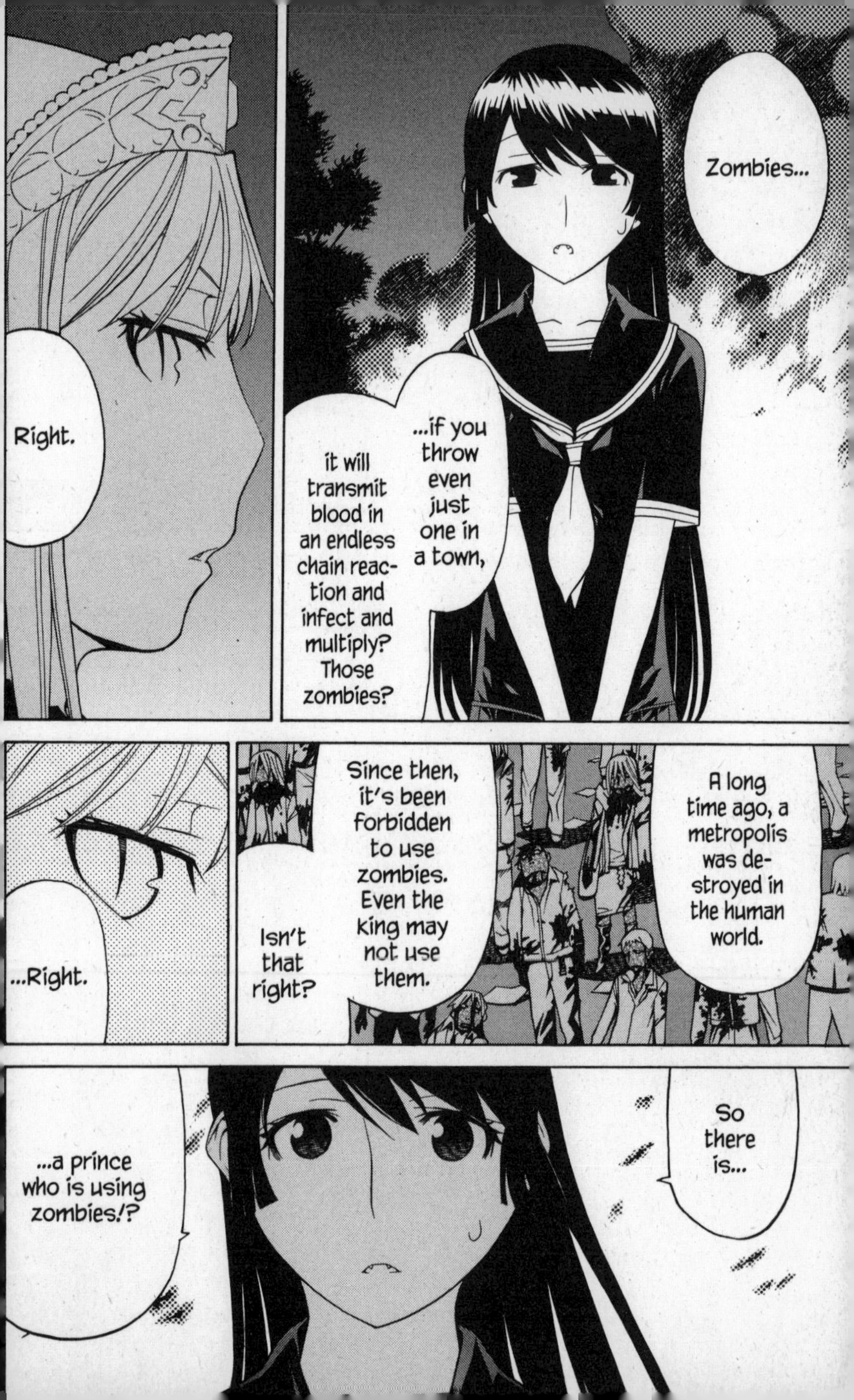
Zombies...
...if you throw even just one in a town,
it will transmit blood in an endless chain reaction and infect and multiply? Those zombies?
Right.
A long time ago, a metropolis was destroyed in the human world.
Since then, it's been forbidden to use zombies. Even the king may not use them.
Isn't that right?
...Right.
So there is...
...a prince who is using zombies!?

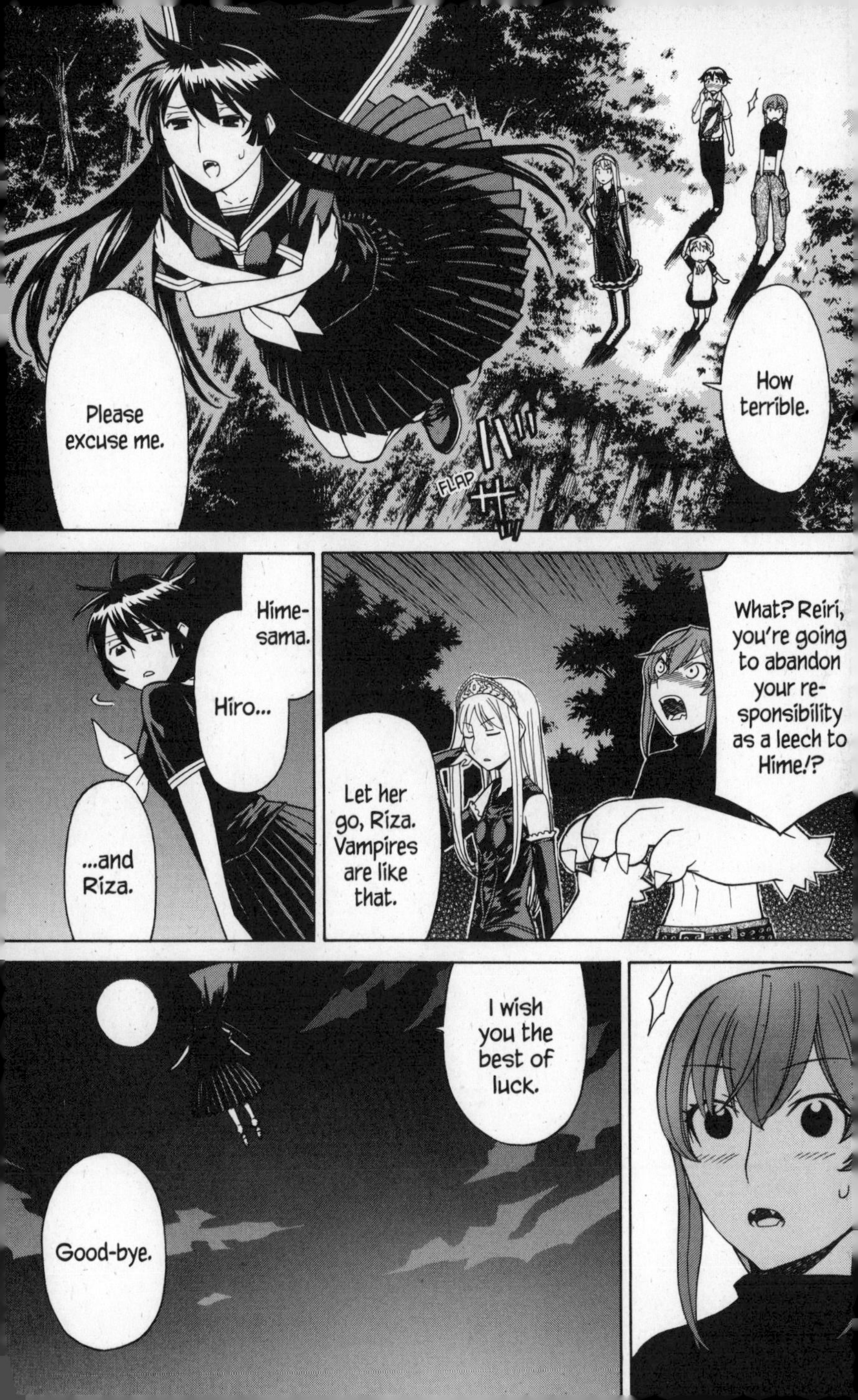
How terrible.
Please excuse me.
FLAP
What? Reiri, you're going to abandon your re-sponsibility as a leech to Hime!?
Let her go, Riza. Vampires are like that.
Hime-sama.
Hiro...
...and Riza.
I wish you the best of luck.
Good-bye.

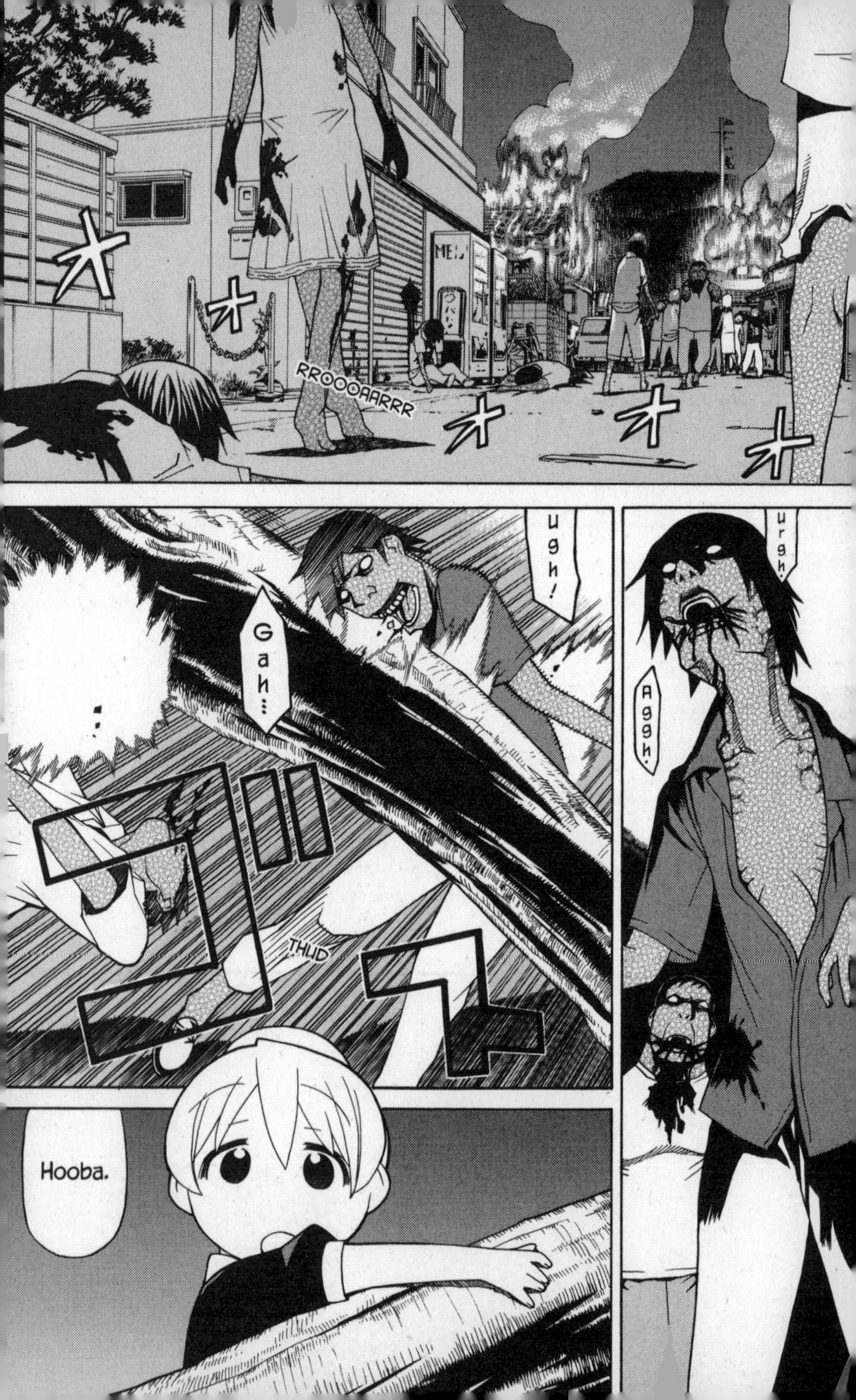
RROOOAARRRR
urgh.
Aggh.
ugh!
Gah...
THUD
Hooba.

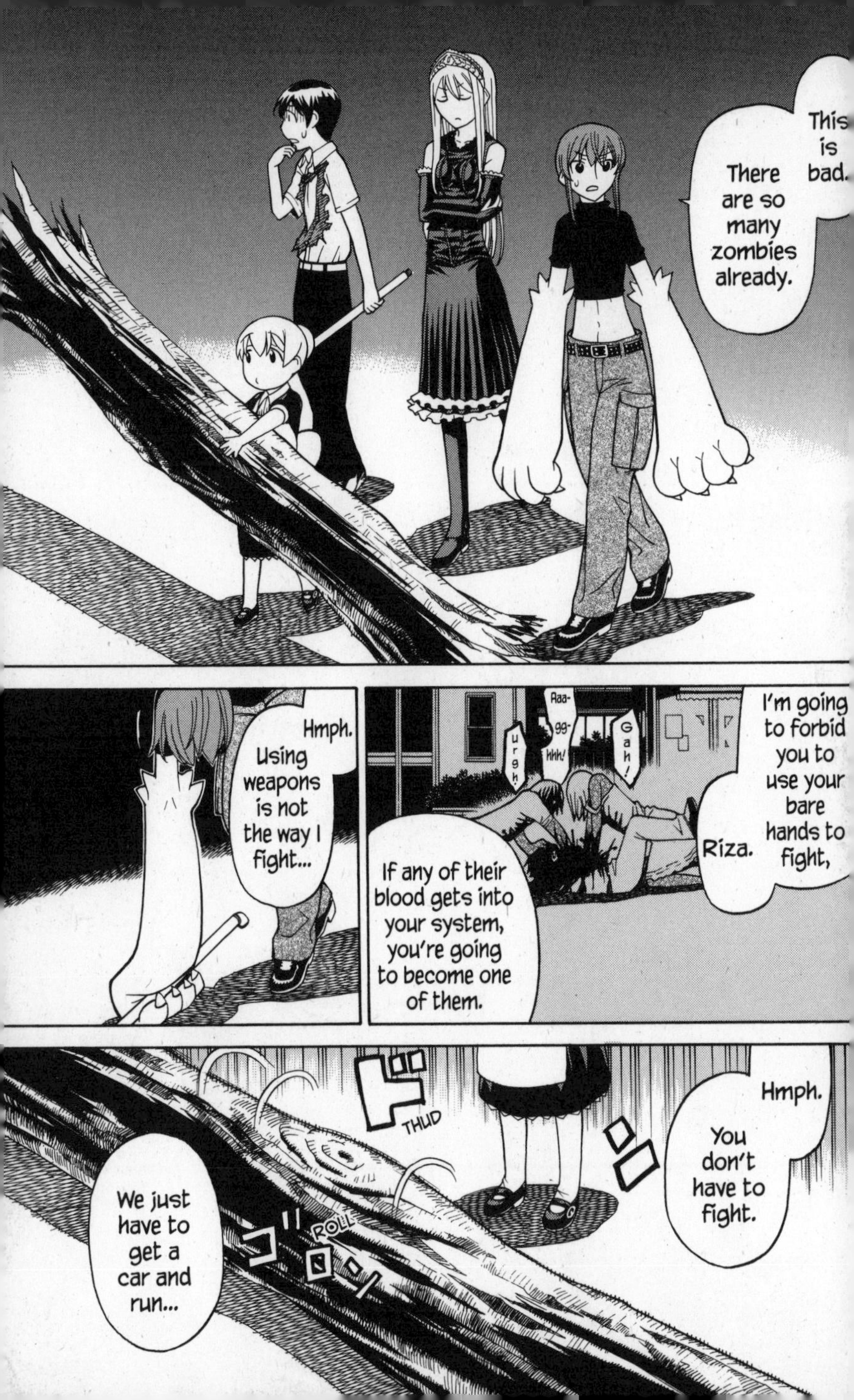
This is bad.
There are so many zombies already.
I'm going to forbid you to use your bare hands to fight,
Riza.
Gah!
Aaa-gg-hhh!
urgh!
If any of their blood gets into your system, you're going to become one of them.
Hmph.
Using weapons is not the way I fight...
Hmph.
You don't have to fight.
THUD
ROLL
We just have to get a car and run...

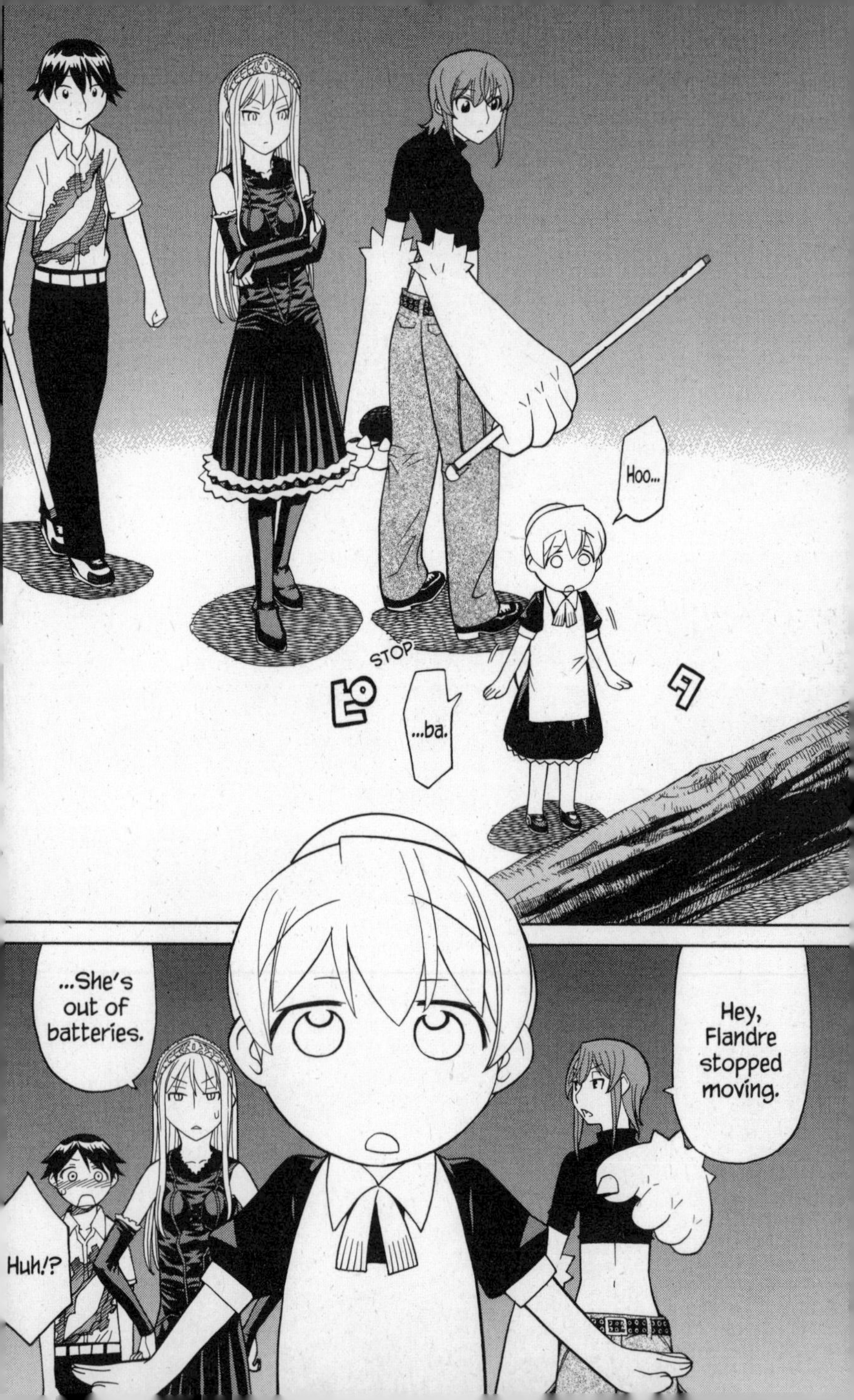
Hoo...
STOP
...ba.
Hey, Flandre stopped moving.
...She's out of batteries.
Huh!?

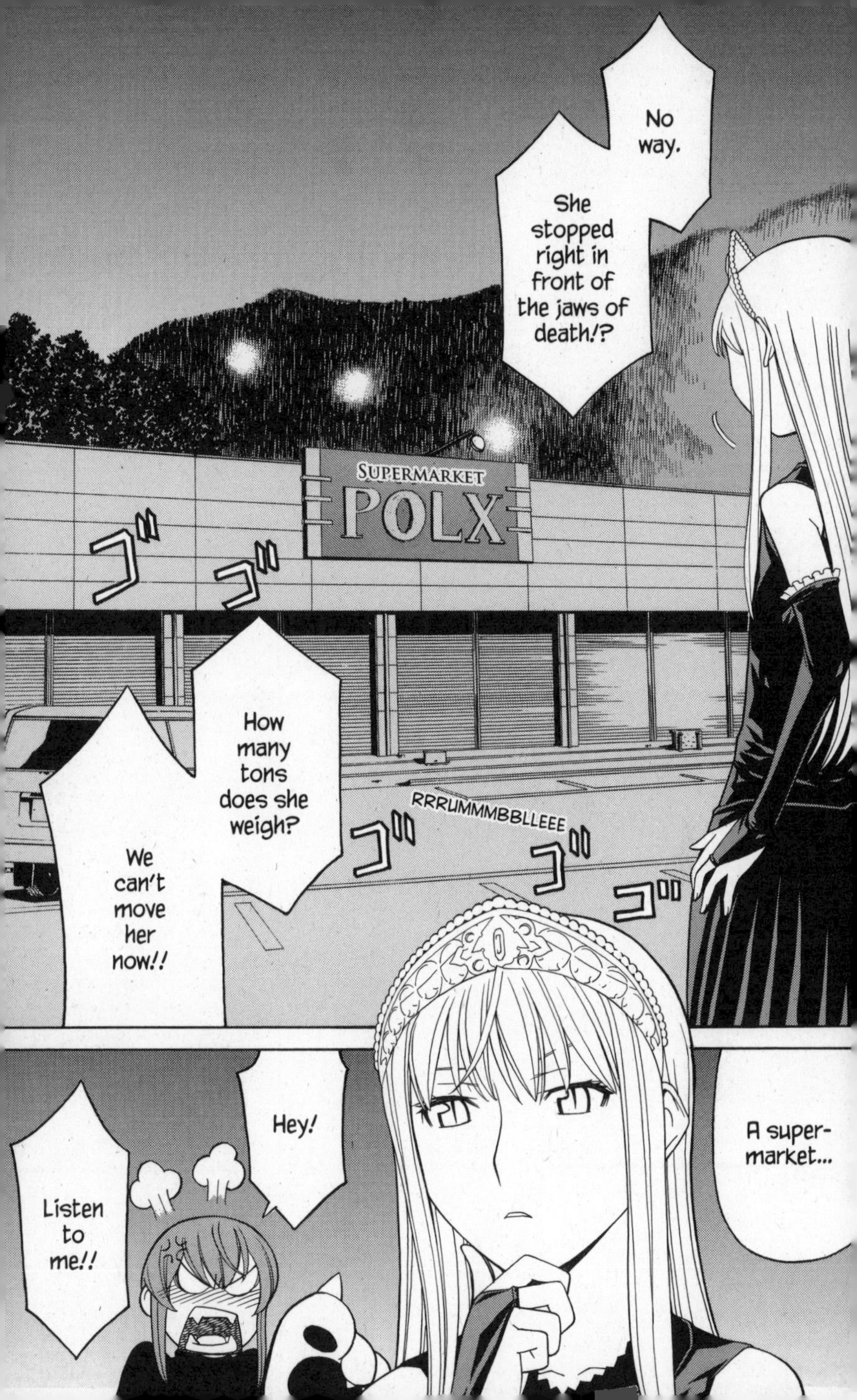
No way.
She stopped right in front of the jaws of death!?
SUPERMARKET POLX
How many tons does she weigh?
We can't move her now!!
RRRUMMMBBLLEEE
A super-market...
Hey!
Listen to me!!

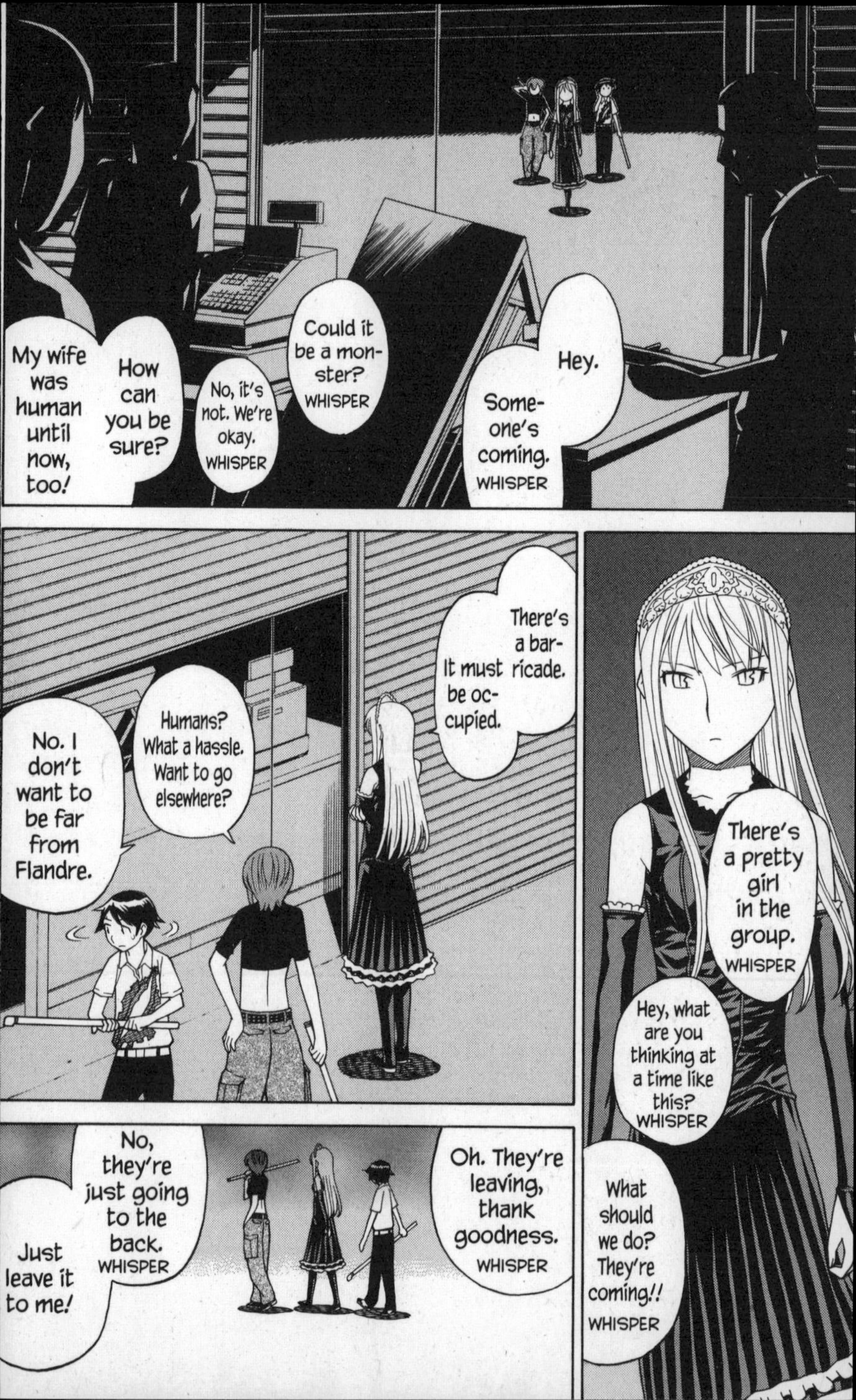
Hey.
Some-one's coming. WHISPER
Could it be a mon-ster? WHISPER
No, it's not. We're okay. WHISPER
How can you be sure?
My wife was human until now, too!
There's a bar-ricade. It must be oc-cupied.
Humans? What a hassle. Want to go elsewhere?
No. I don't want to be far from Flandre.
There's a pretty girl in the group. WHISPER
Hey, what are you thinking at a time like this? WHISPER
What should we do? They're coming!! WHISPER
Oh. They're leaving, thank goodness. WHISPER
No, they're just going to the back. WHISPER
Just leave it to me!

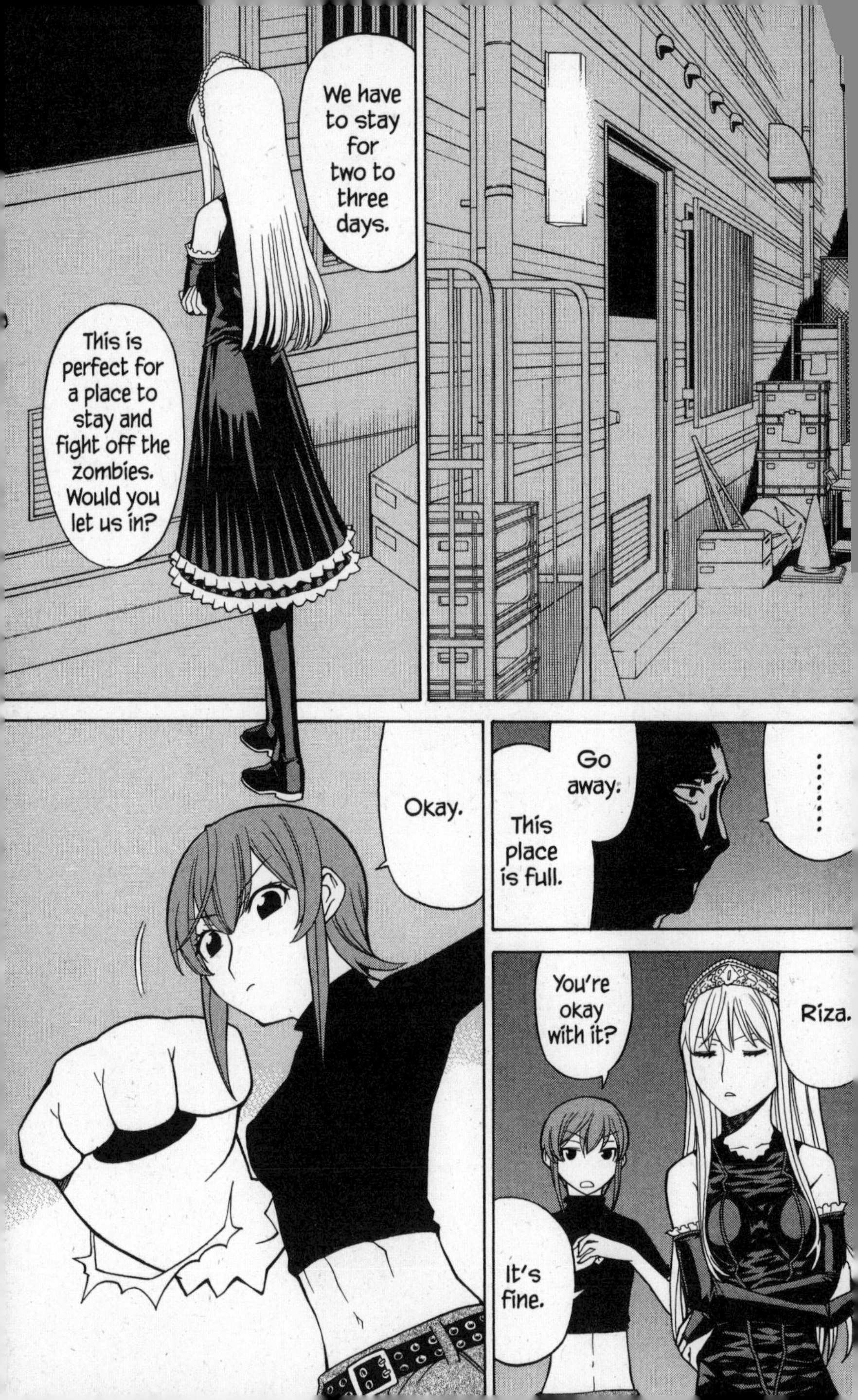
We have to stay for two to three days.
This is perfect for a place to stay and fight off the zombies. Would you let us in?
......
Go away. This place is full.
Riza.
You're okay with it?
It's fine.
Okay.

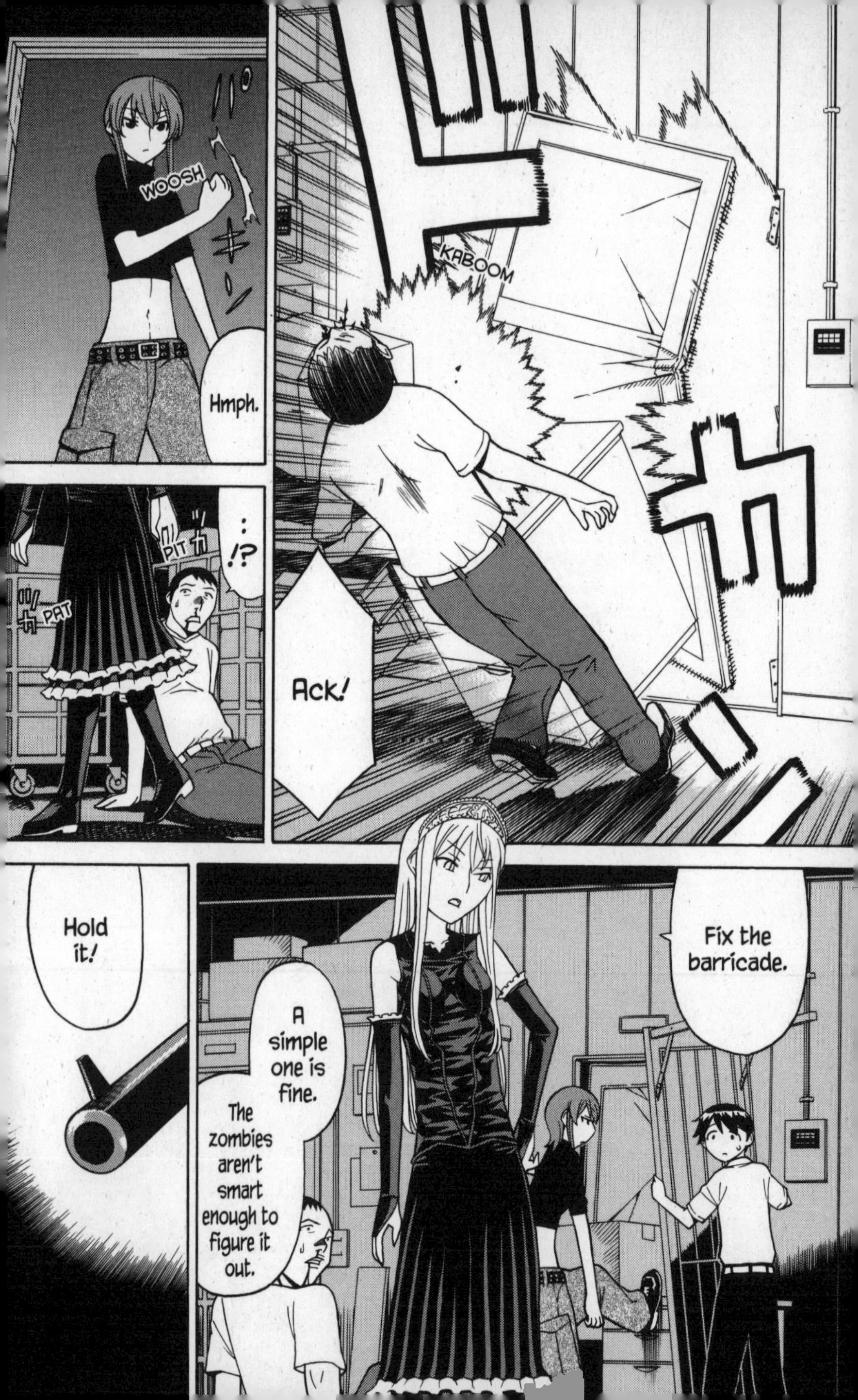
KABOOM
Ack!
WOOSH
Hmph.
...!?
PIT
PAT
Fix the barricade.
A simple one is fine.
The zombies aren't smart enough to figure it out.
Hold it!

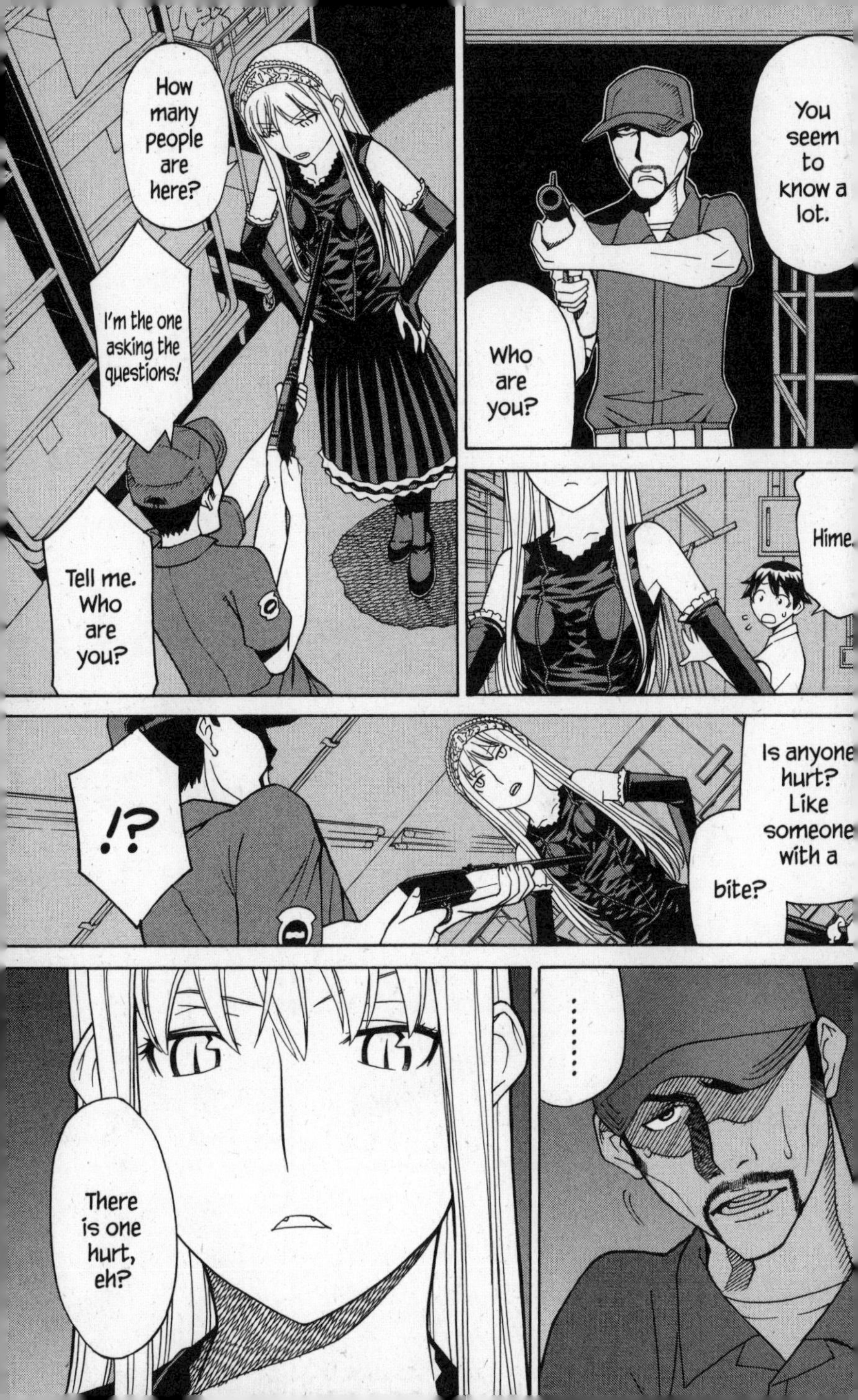
You seem to know a lot.
Who are you?
Hime.
How many people are here?
I'm the one asking the questions!
Tell me. Who are you?
Is anyone hurt? Like someone with a bite?
!?
......
There is one hurt, eh?

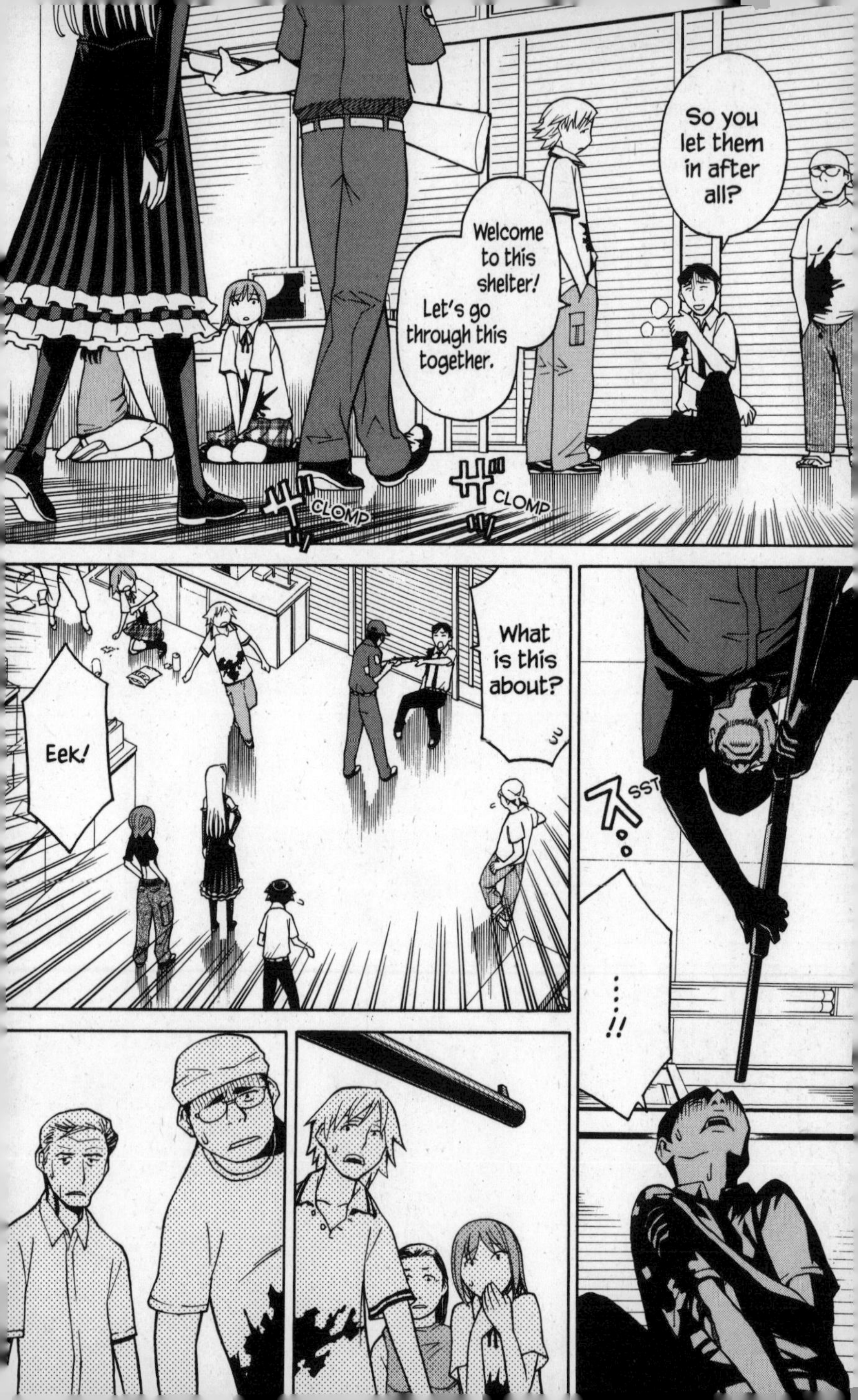
So you let them in after all?
Welcome to this shelter! Let's go through this together.
CLOMP
CLOMP
SST
......!!
What is this about?
Eek!

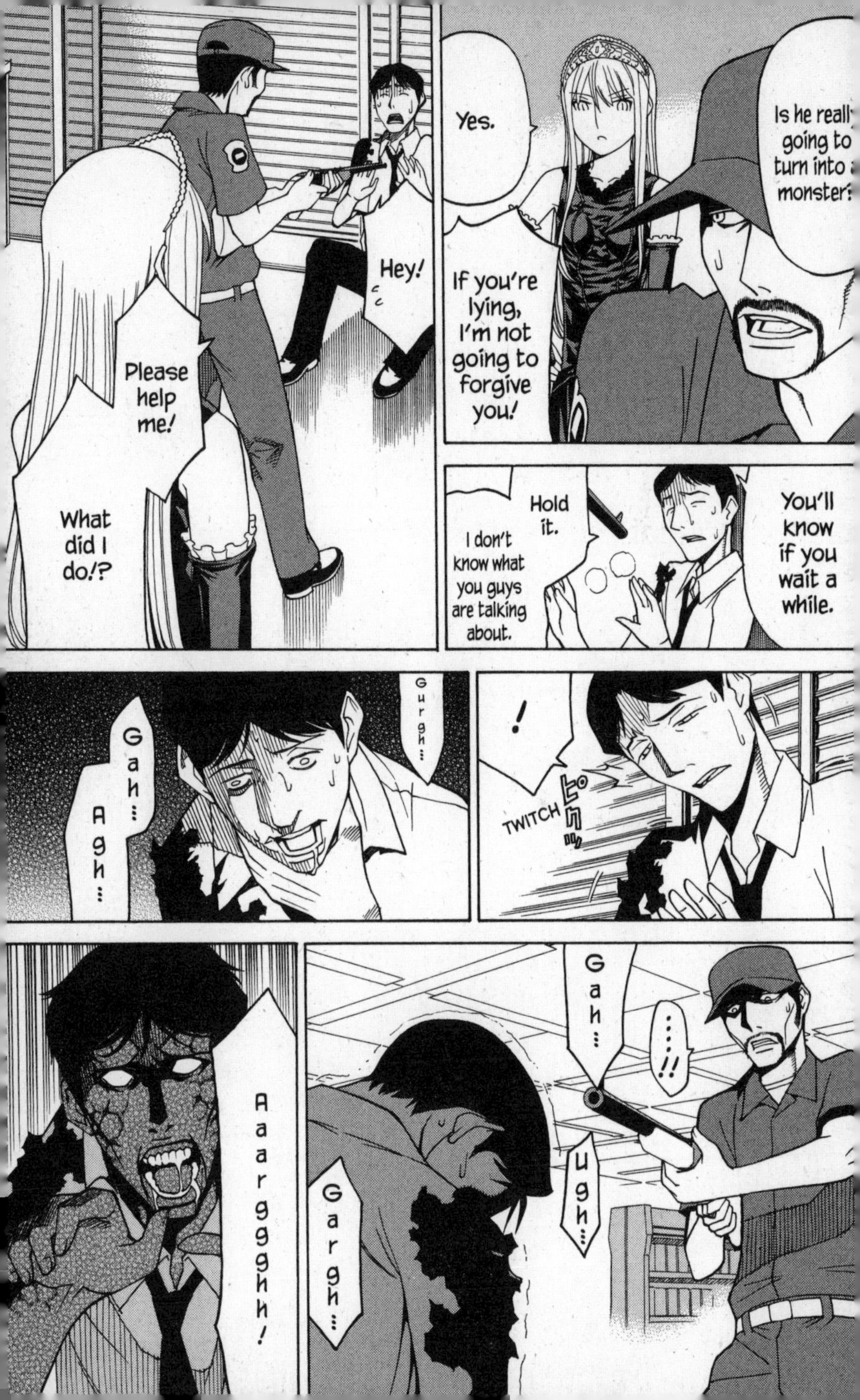

Is he reall going to turn into monster!?
Yes.
If you're lying, I'm not going to forgive you!
Hey!
Please help me!
What did I do!?
You'll know if you wait a while.
Hold it.
I don't know what you guys are talking about.
!
TWITCH
Gurgh...
Gah...
Agh...
Gah...
....!!
Ugh...
Gargh...
Aaargggghh!

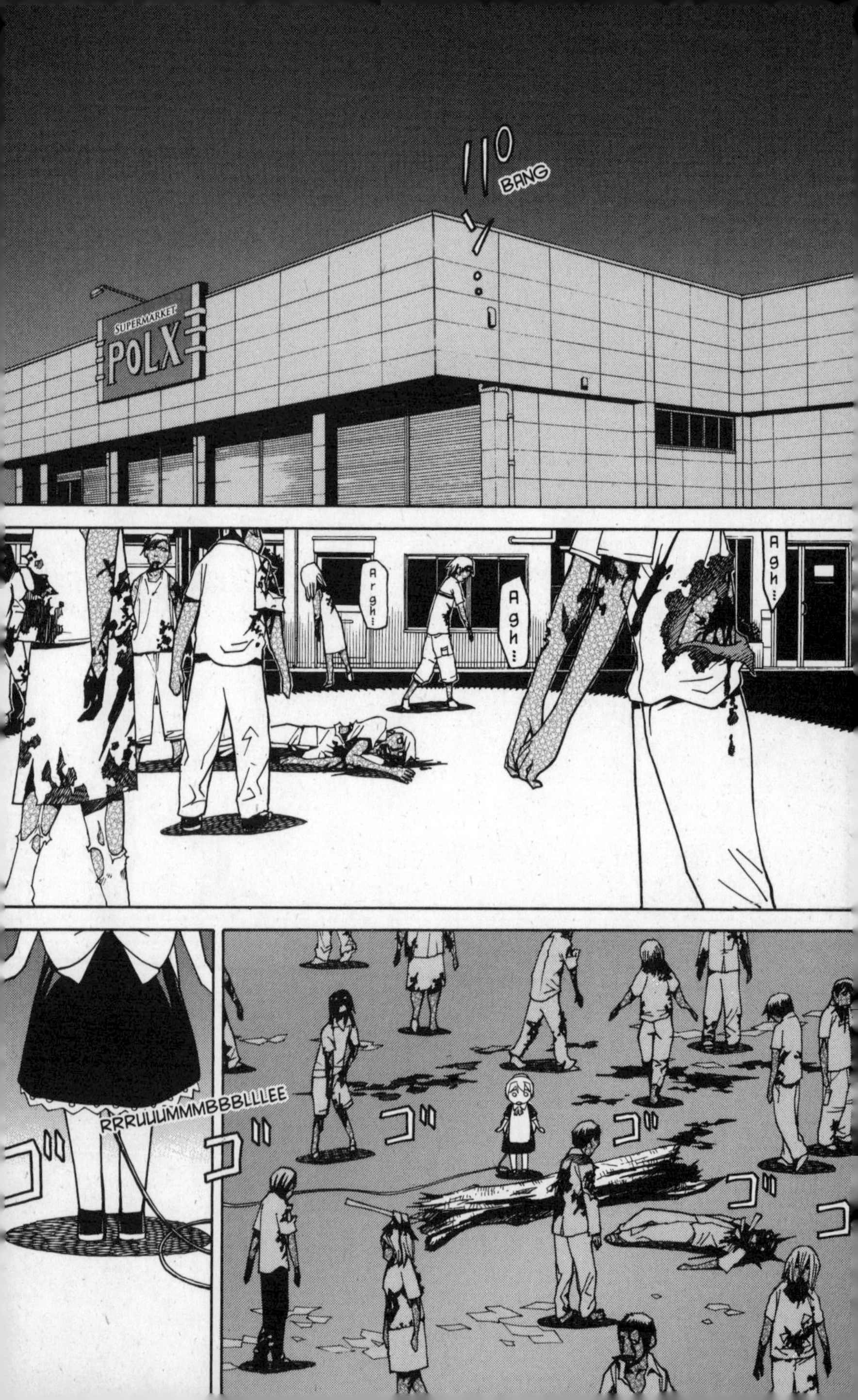

SUPERMARKET
POLX
BANG
Agh…
Agh…
Argh…
RRRUUUMMMBBBLLLEE

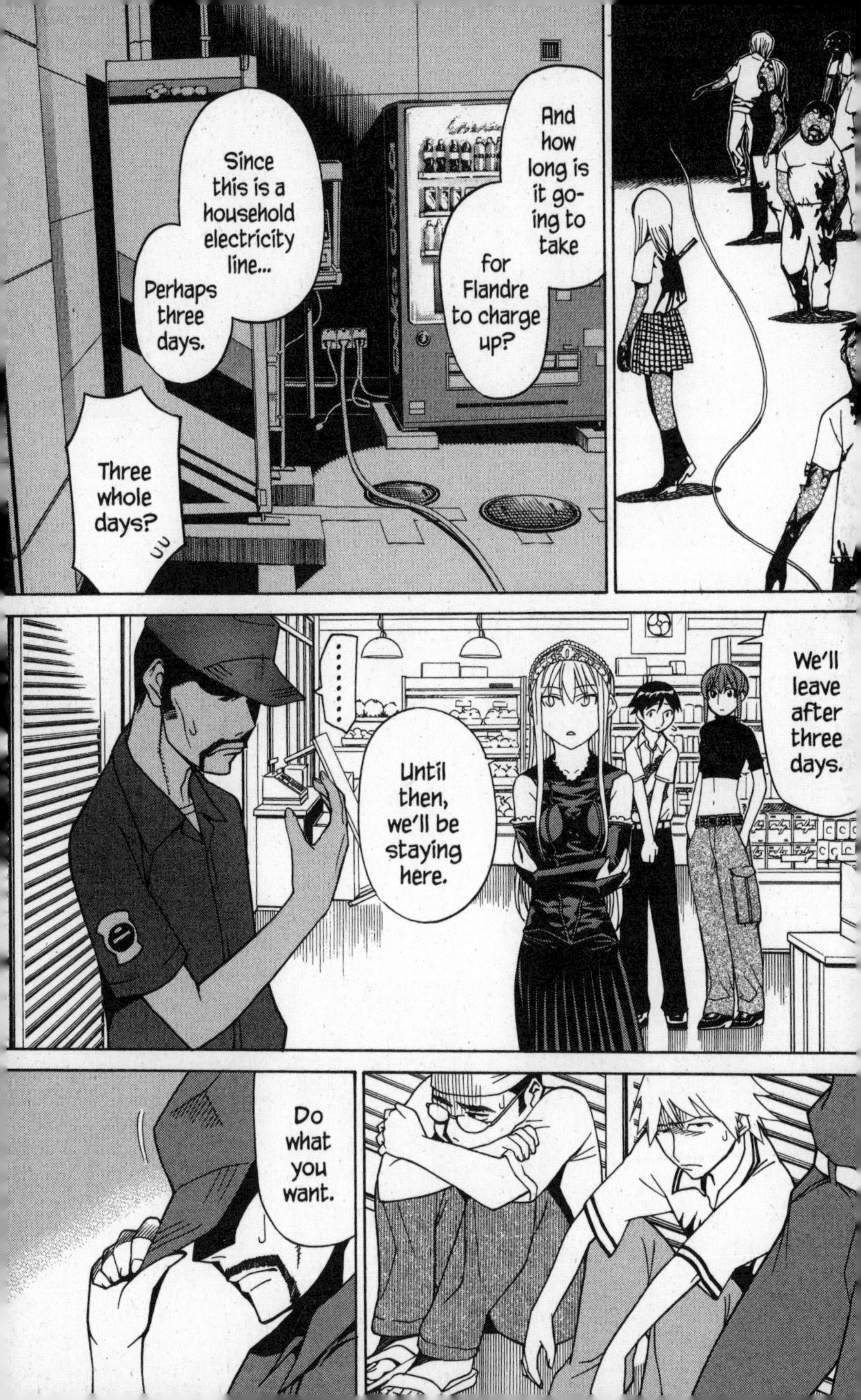

And how long is it going to take for Flandre to charge up?
Since this is a household electricity line...
Perhaps three days.
Three whole days?
We'll leave after three days.
Until then, we'll be staying here.
......
Do what you want.

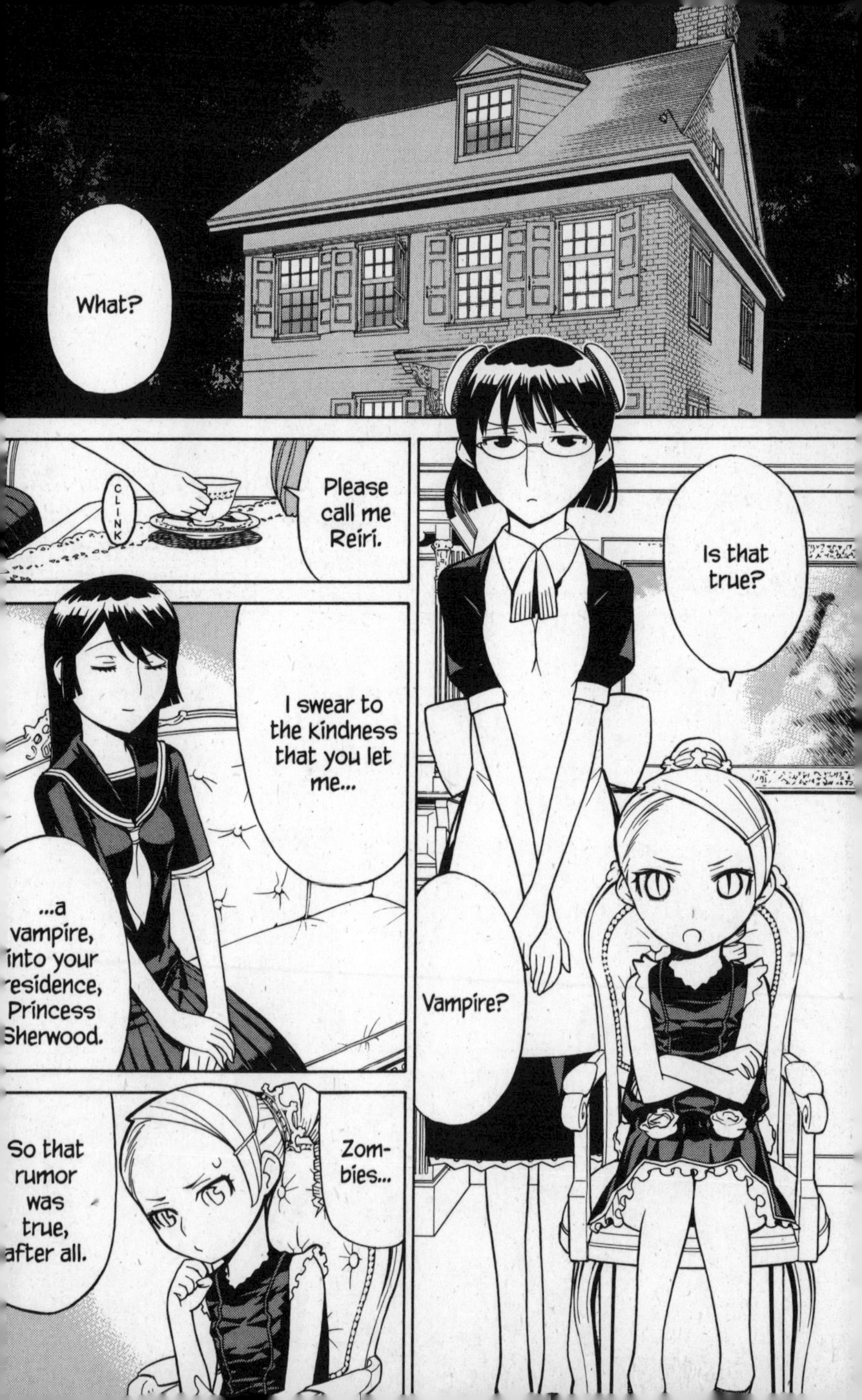
What?
Is that true?
Vampire?
CLINK
Please call me Reiri.
I swear to the kindness that you let me...
...a vampire, into your residence, Princess Sherwood.
Zombies...
So that rumor was true, after all.

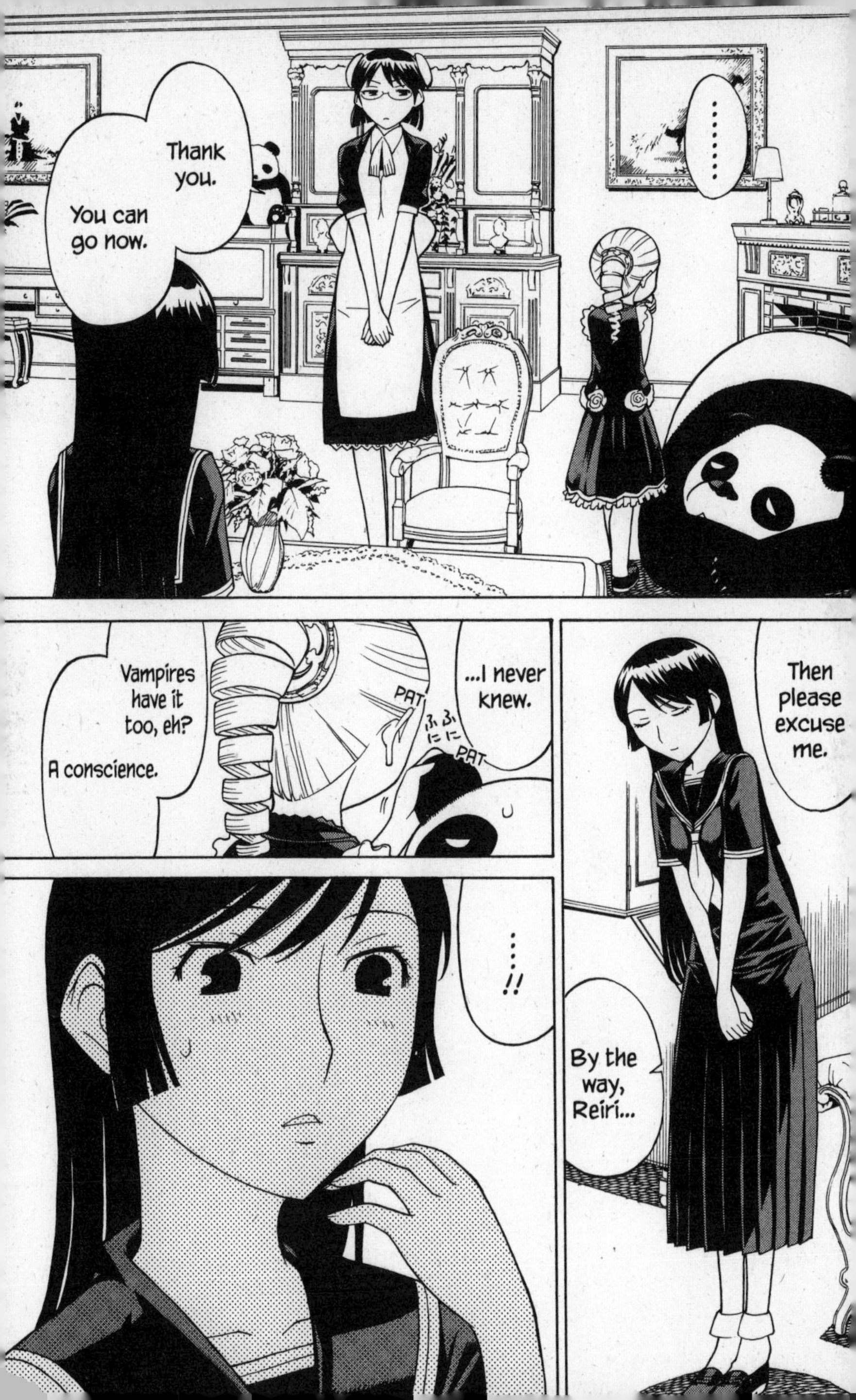
……
Thank you.
You can go now.
Then please excuse me.
By the way, Reiri...
...I never knew.
PAT
ふにふに
PAT
Vampires have it too, eh?
A conscience.
……!!

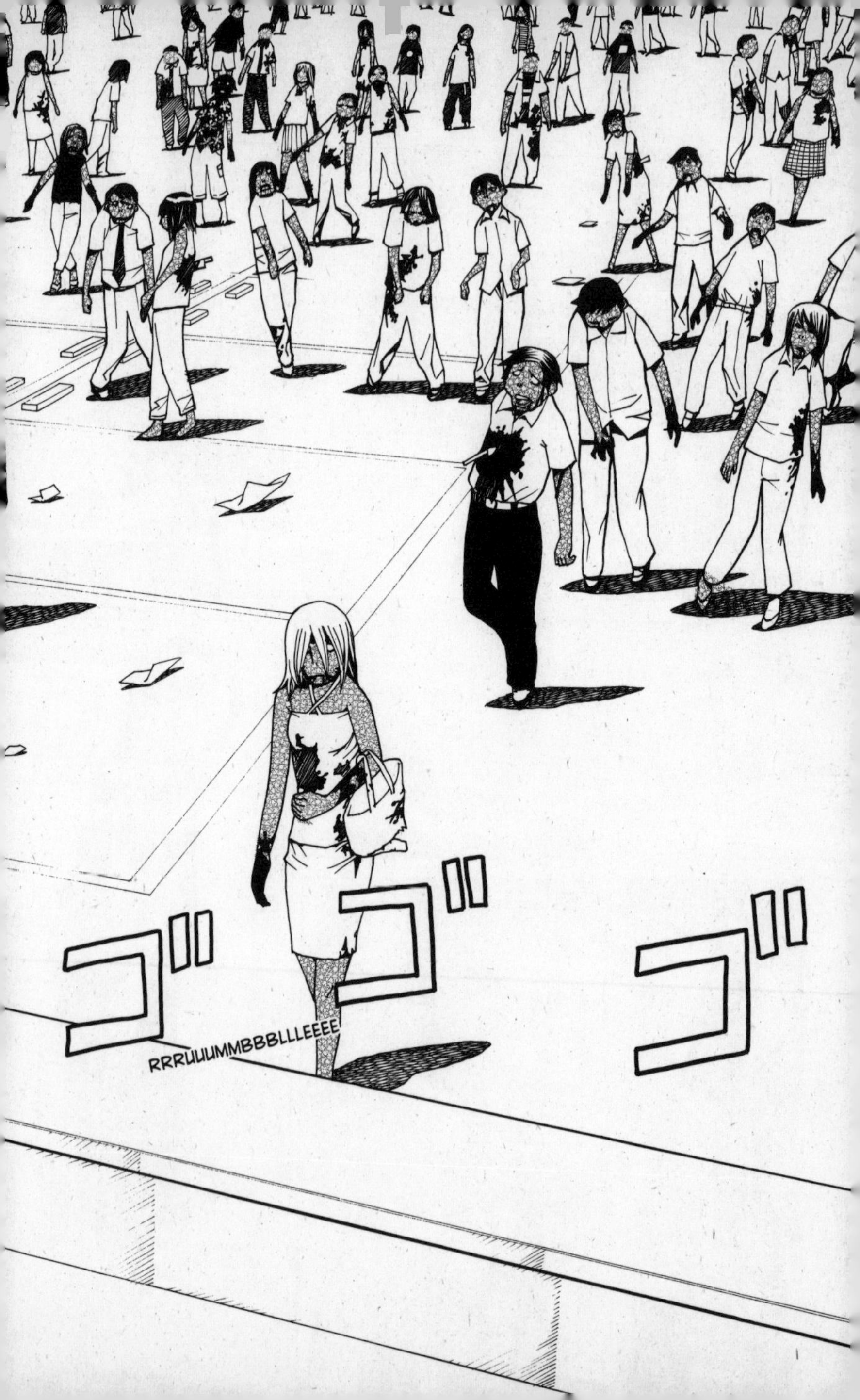

ゴゴゴ
RRRUUUMMBBBLLLEEEE

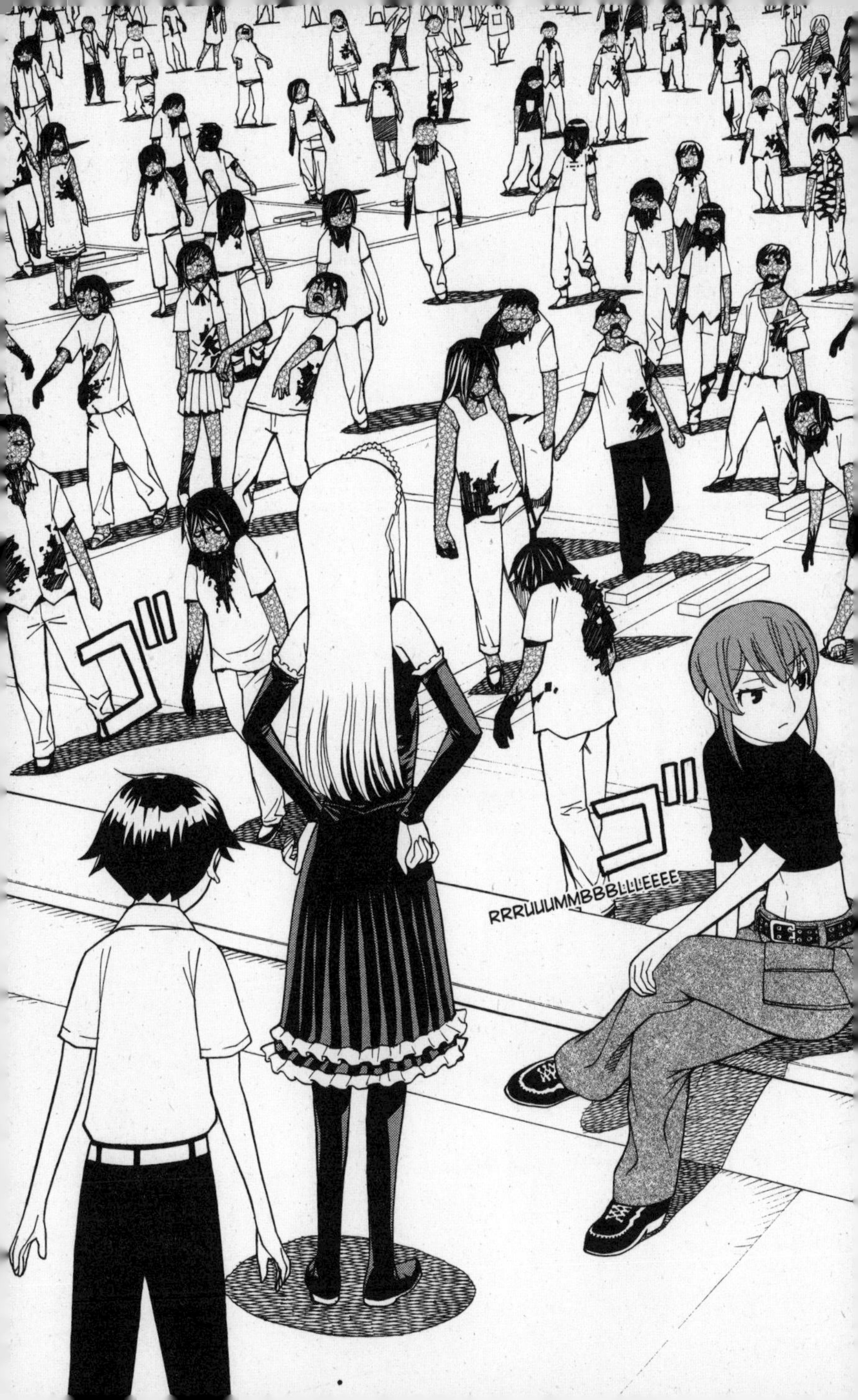
ゴ"
ゴ"
RRRUUUMMBBBLLLEEEE

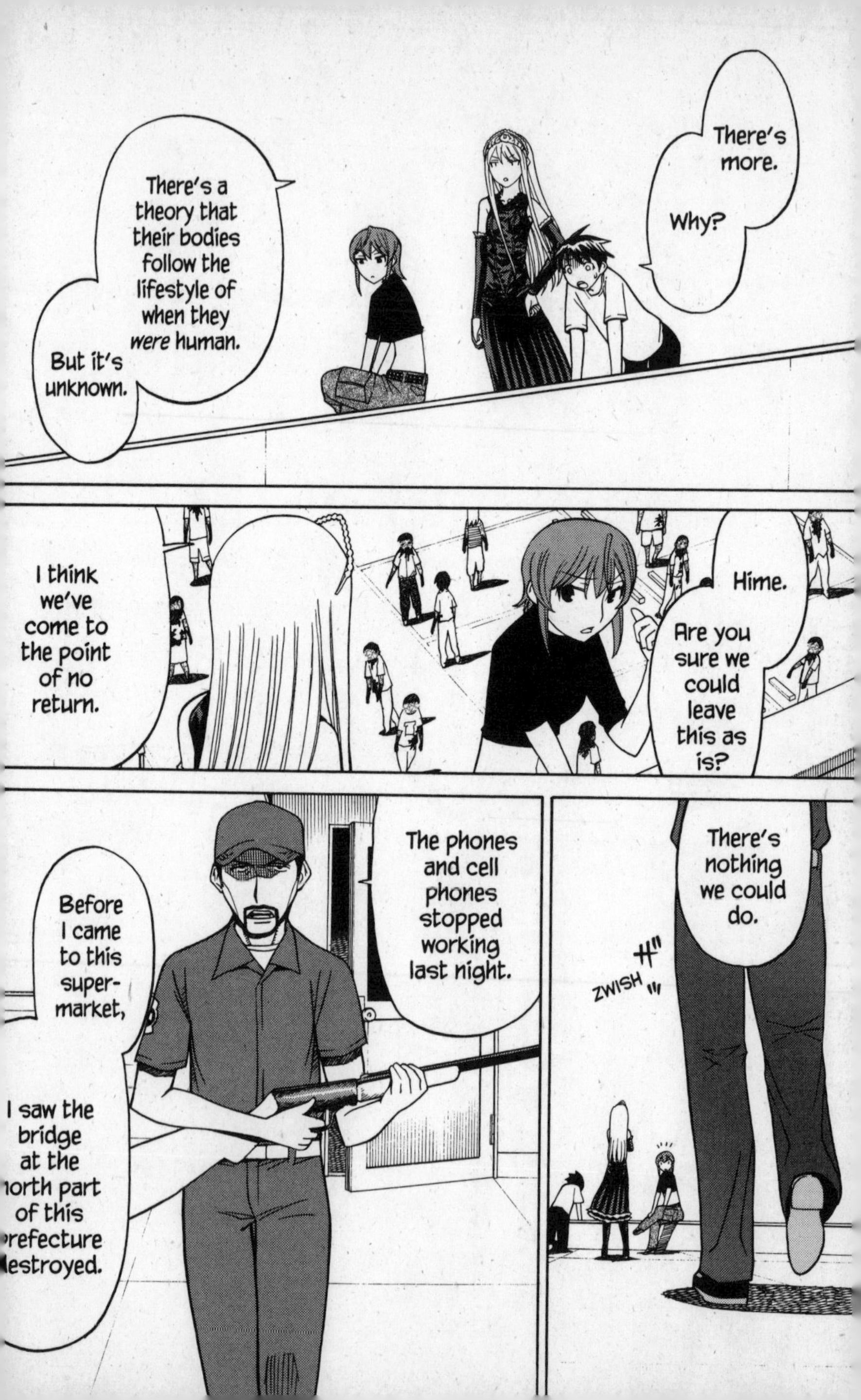
There's more.
Why?
There's a theory that their bodies follow the lifestyle of when they *were* human.
But it's unknown.
Hime.
Are you sure we could leave this as is?
I think we've come to the point of no return.
There's nothing we could do.
ZWISH
The phones and cell phones stopped working last night.
Before I came to this super-market,
I saw the bridge at the orth part of this refecture estroyed.

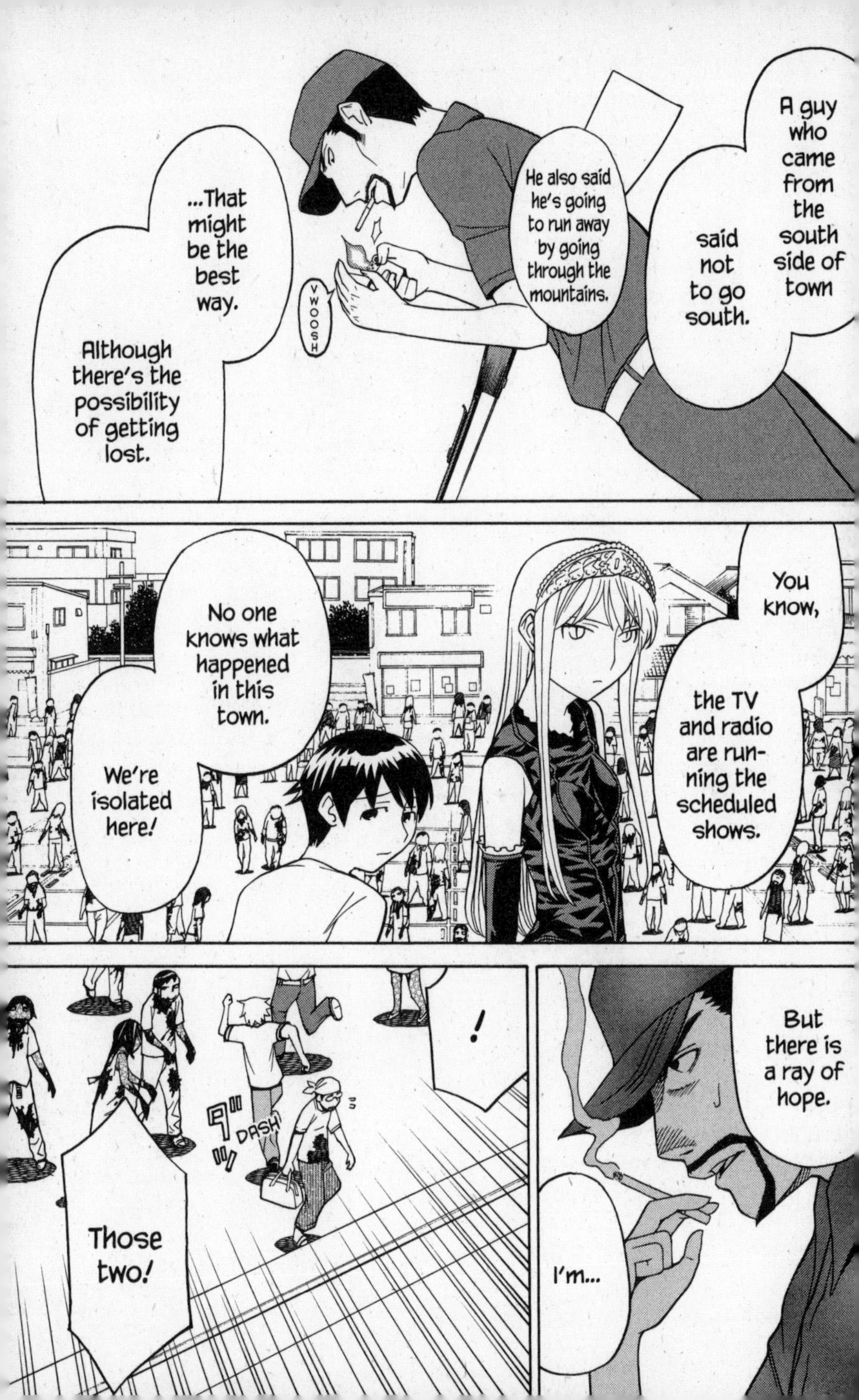
A guy who came from the south side of town said not to go south.
He also said he's going to run away by going through the mountains.
VWOOSH
...That might be the best way.
Although there's the possibility of getting lost.
You know, the TV and radio are running the scheduled shows.
No one knows what happened in this town.
We're isolated here!
But there is a ray of hope.
I'm...
!
DASH
Those two!

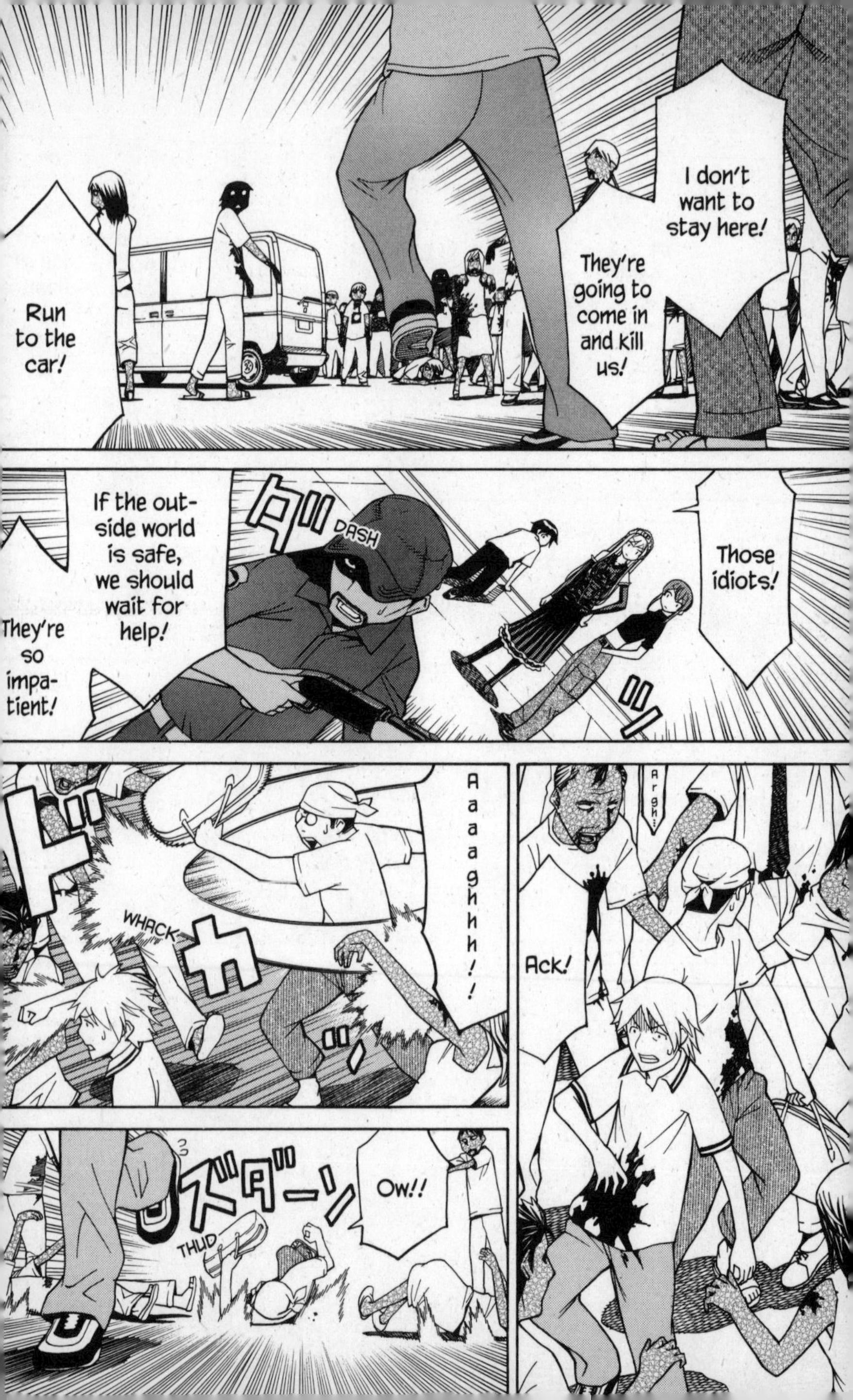
I don't want to stay here!
They're going to come in and kill us!
Run to the car!
Those idiots!
DASH
If the out-side world is safe, we should wait for help!
They're so impa-tient!
Argh...
Ack!
Aaaaghhh!!
WHACK
Ow!!
THUD

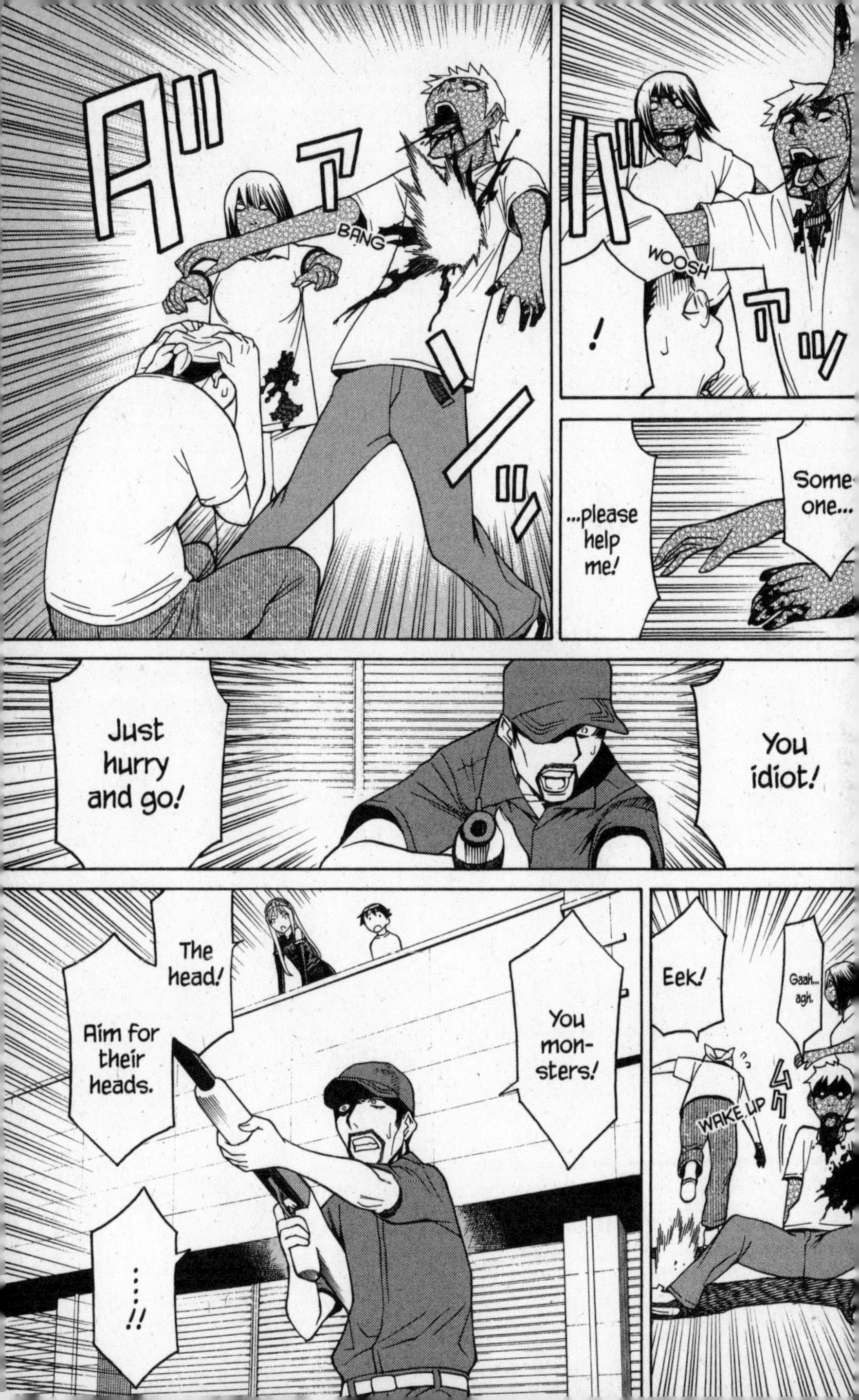

WOOSH
!
Some one...
...please help me!
BANG
You idiot!
Just hurry and go!
Gaah... agh.
Eek!
WAKE UP
You mon- sters!
The head!
Aim for their heads.
......!!

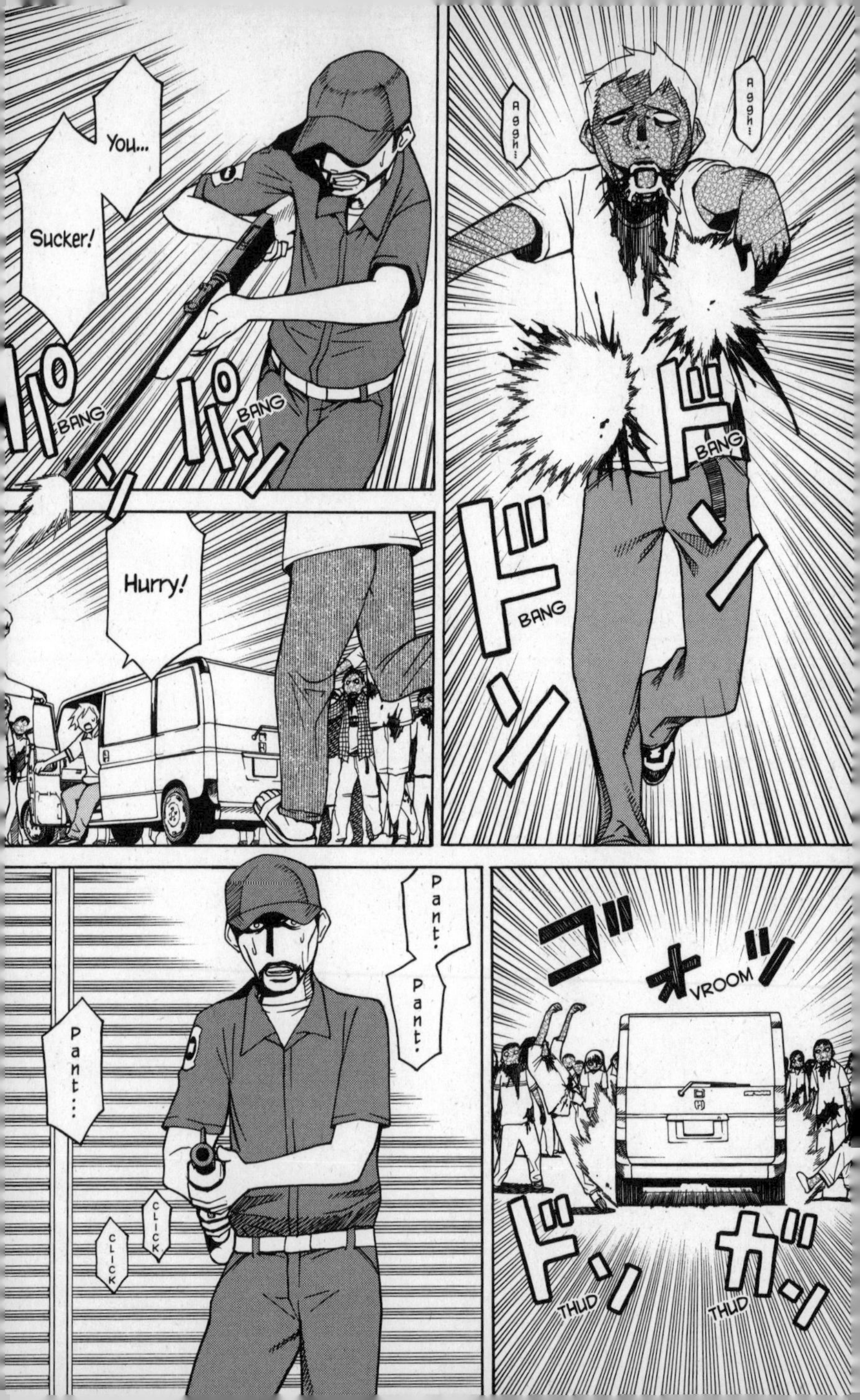
Aggh...
Aggh...
BANG
BANG
You...
Sucker!
BANG
BANG
Hurry!
VROOM
THUD
THUD
Pant. Pant.
Pant...
CLICK
CLICK

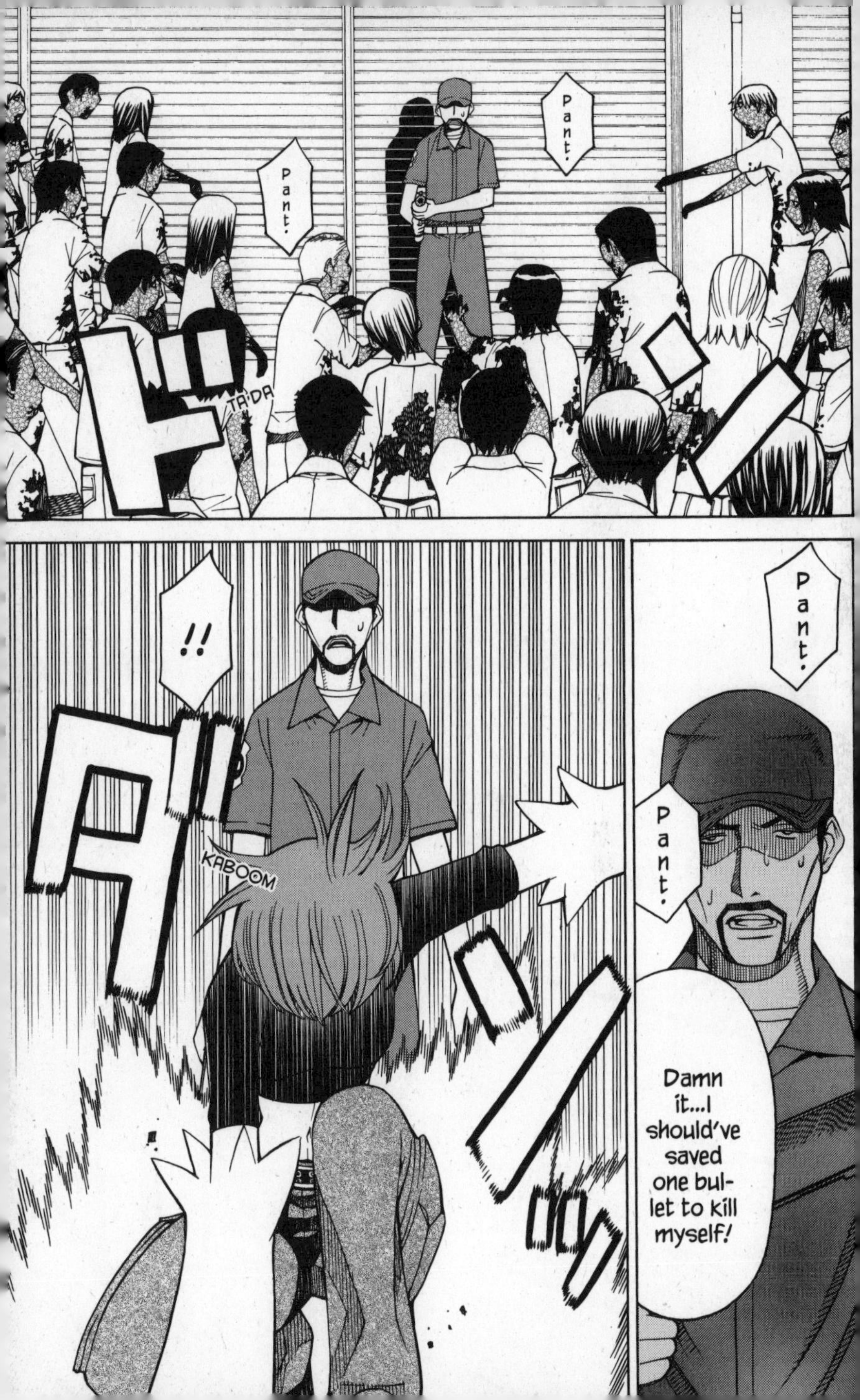
Pant.
Pant.
TA'DA
!!
KABOOM
Pant.
Pant.
Damn it...I should've saved one bullet to kill myself!

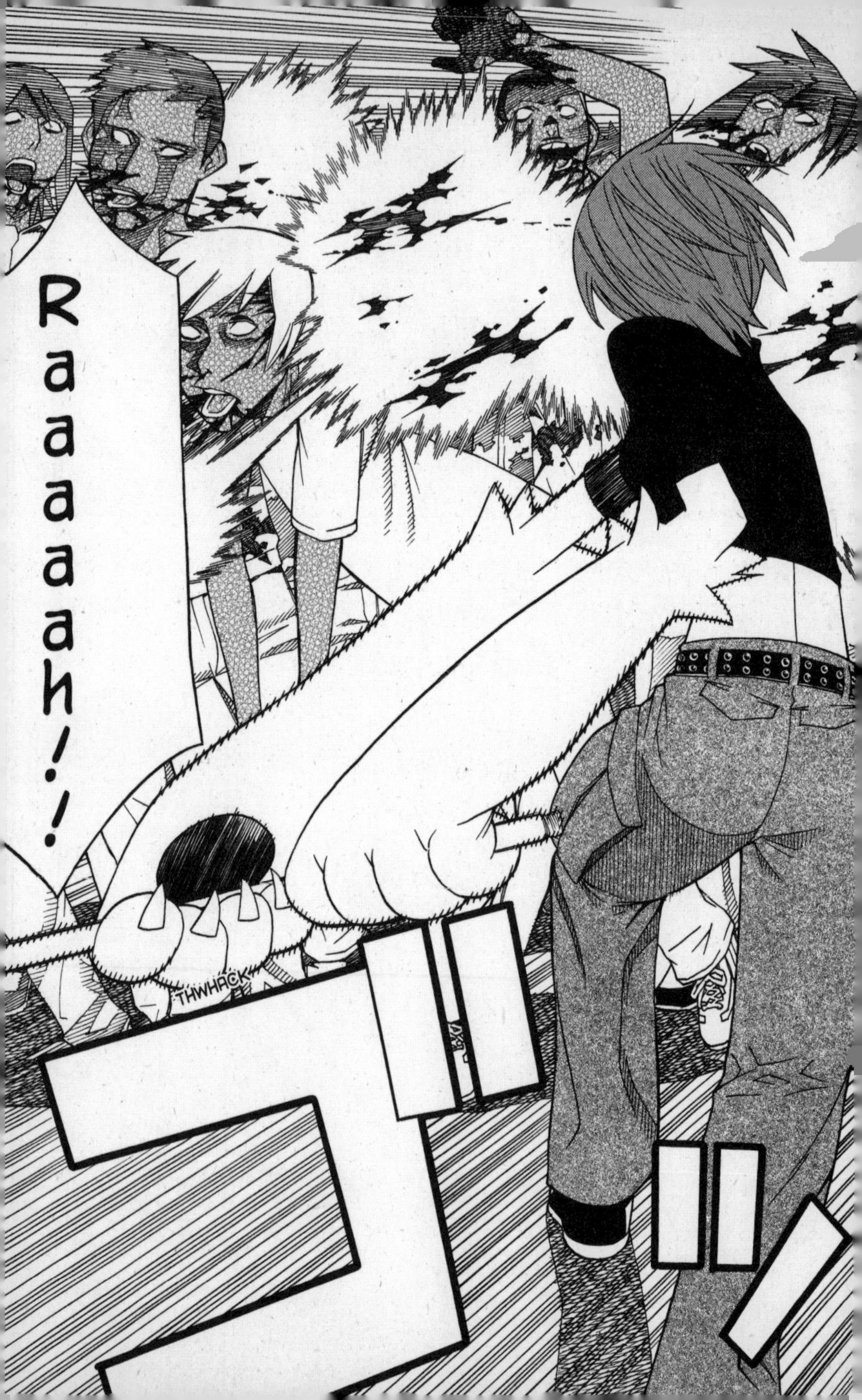
Raaaaah!!
THWHACK

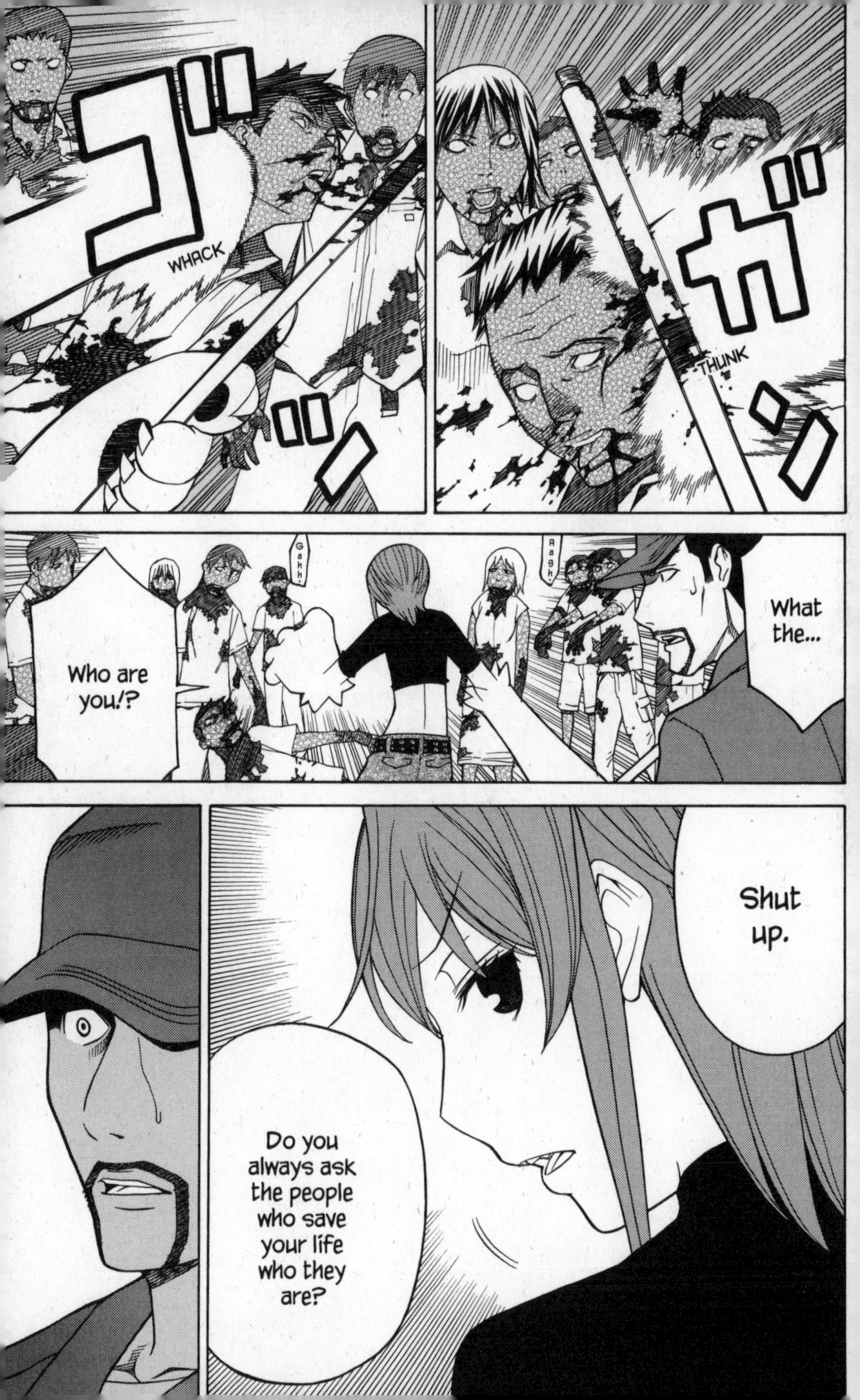
THUNK
WHACK
What the...
Aagh.
Gahh.
Who are you!?
Shut up.
Do you always ask the people who save your life who they are?

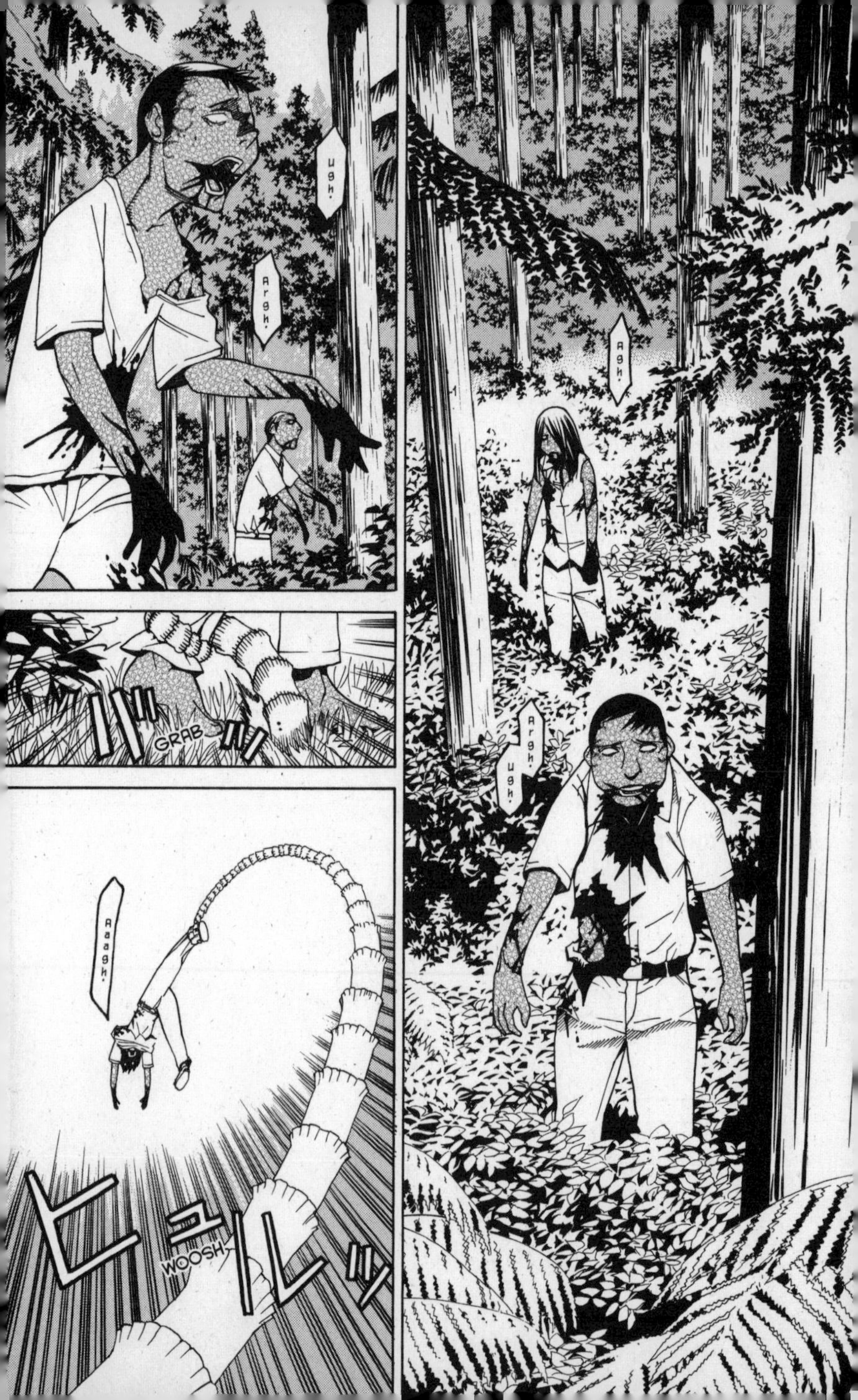
Argh.
Argh.
Ugh.
Ugh.
Argh.
GRAB
Aaagh.
WOOSH

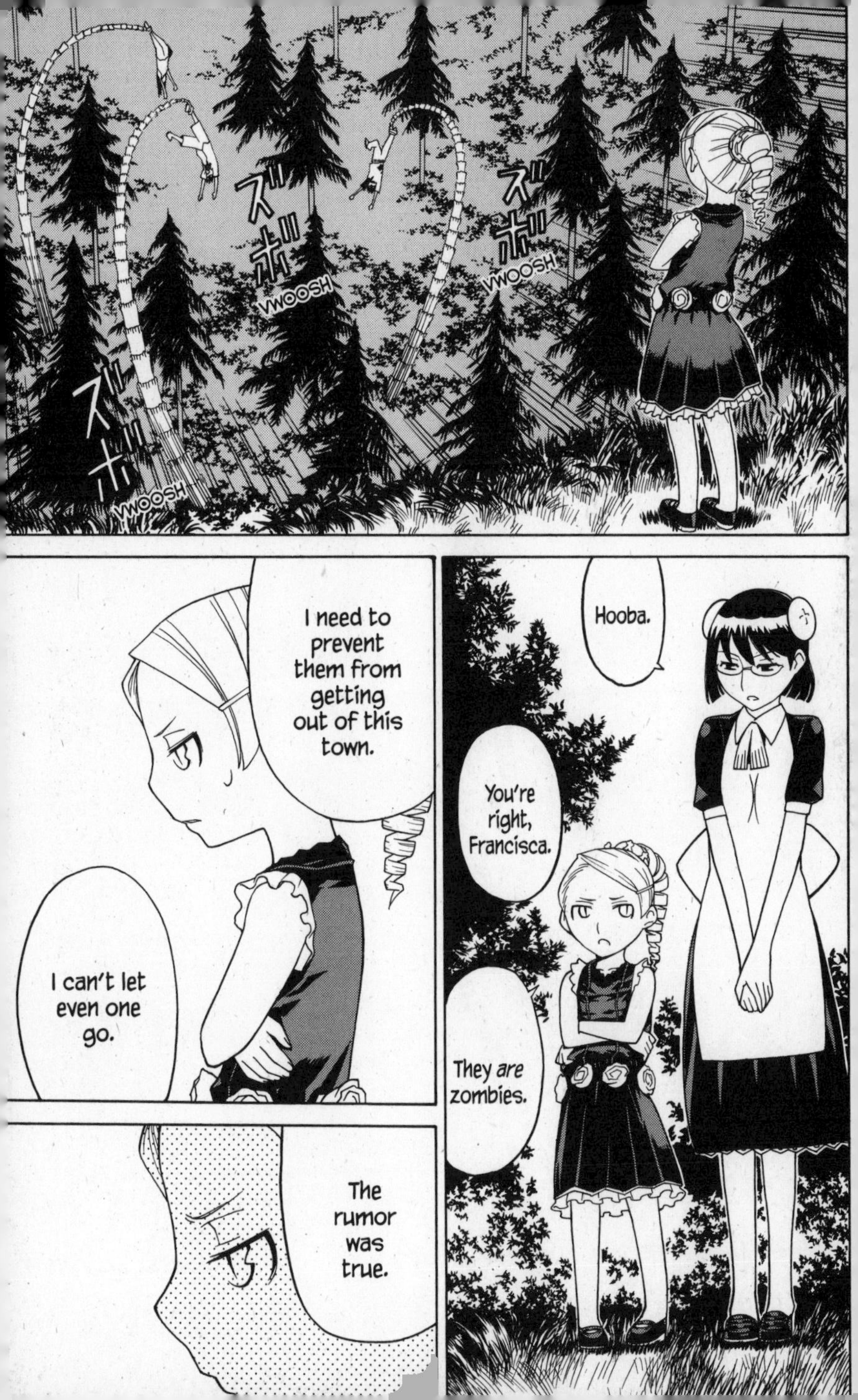
ズボ
VWOOSH
ズボ
VWOOSH
ズボ
VWOOSH
Hooba.
You're right, Francisca.
They are zombies.
I need to prevent them from getting out of this town.
I can't let even one go.
The rumor was true.

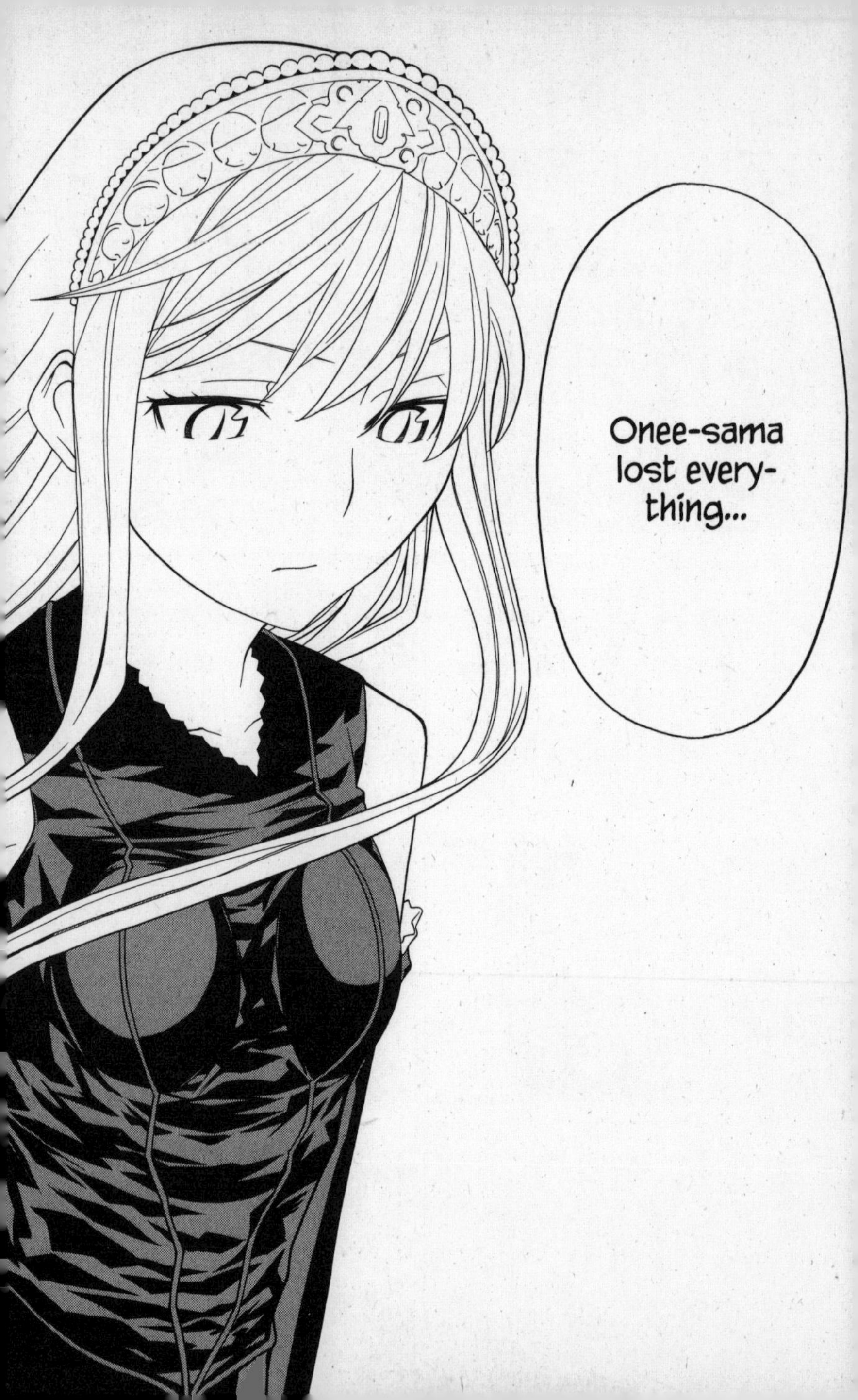
Onee-sama lost every-thing...

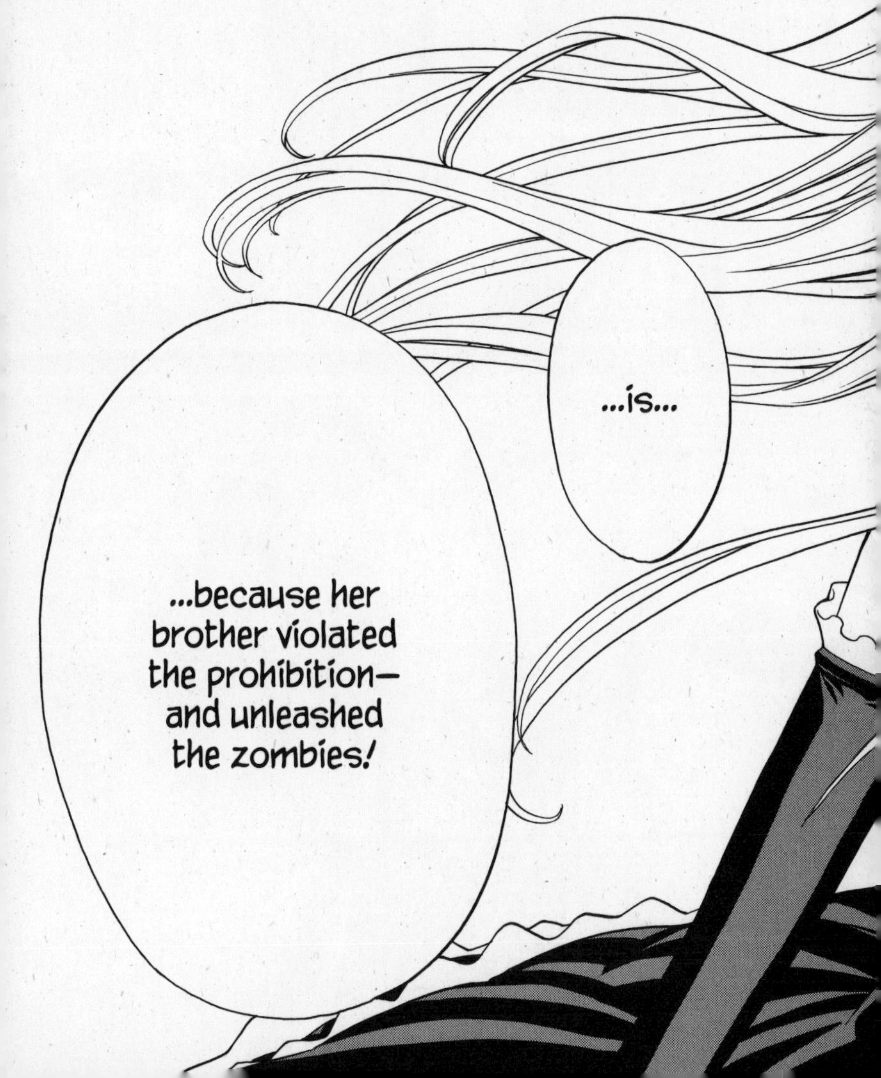
...is...
...because her brother violated the prohibition—and unleashed the zombies!

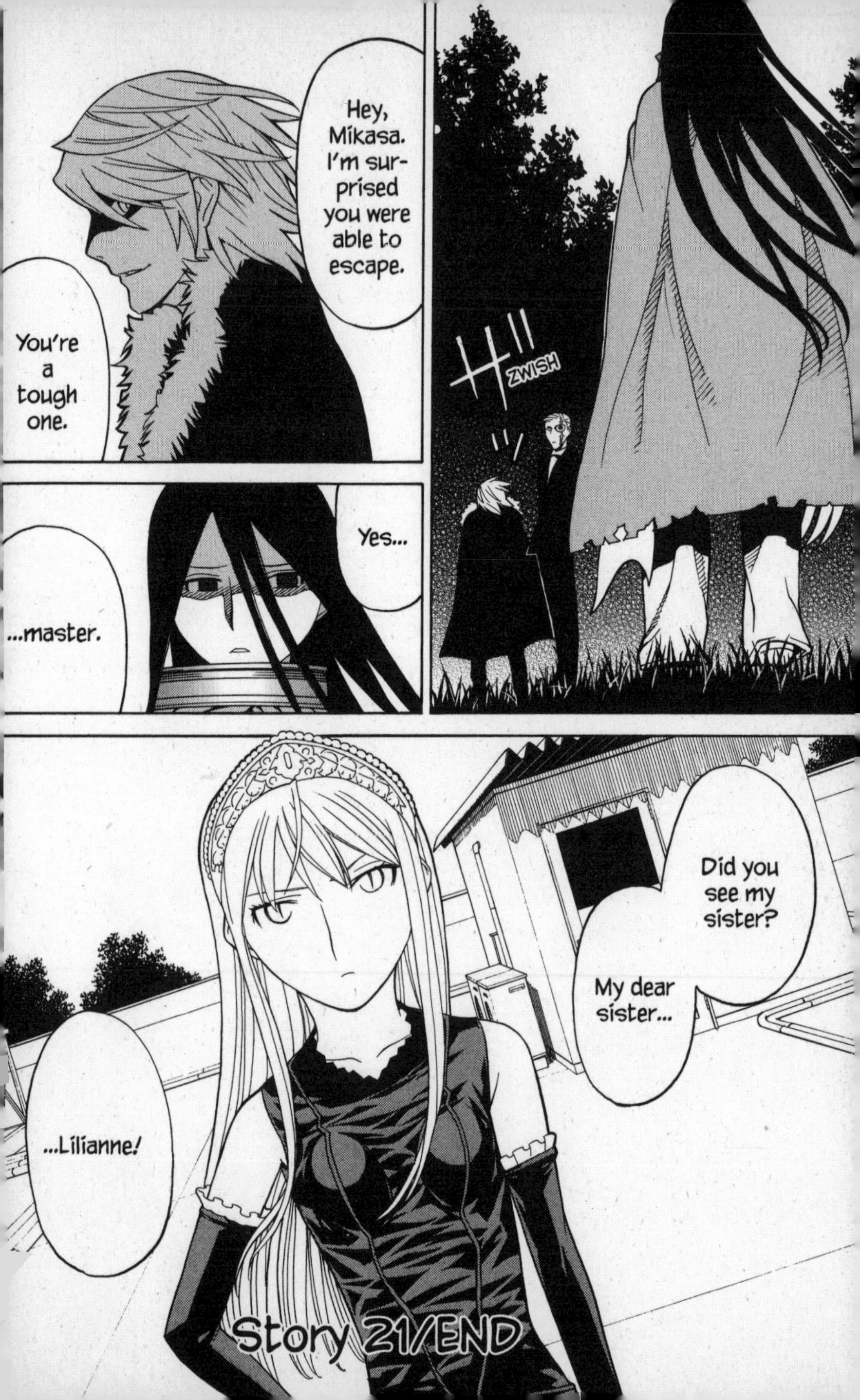
ZWISH
Hey, Mikasa. I'm surprised you were able to escape.
You're a tough one.
Yes...
...master.
Did you see my sister?
My dear sister...
...Lilianne!
Story 21/END

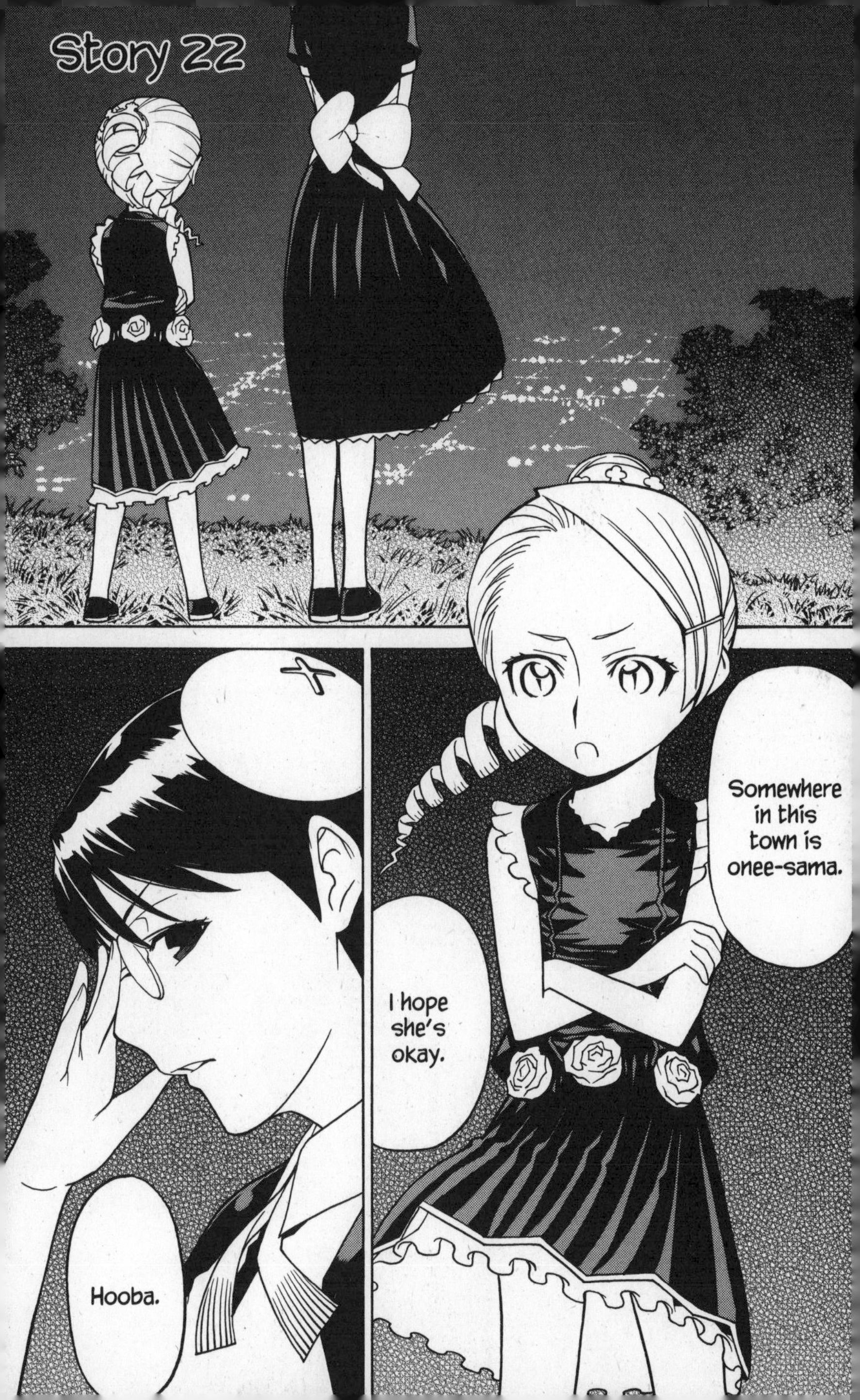
Story 22
Somewhere in this town is onee-sama.
I hope she's okay.
Hooba.

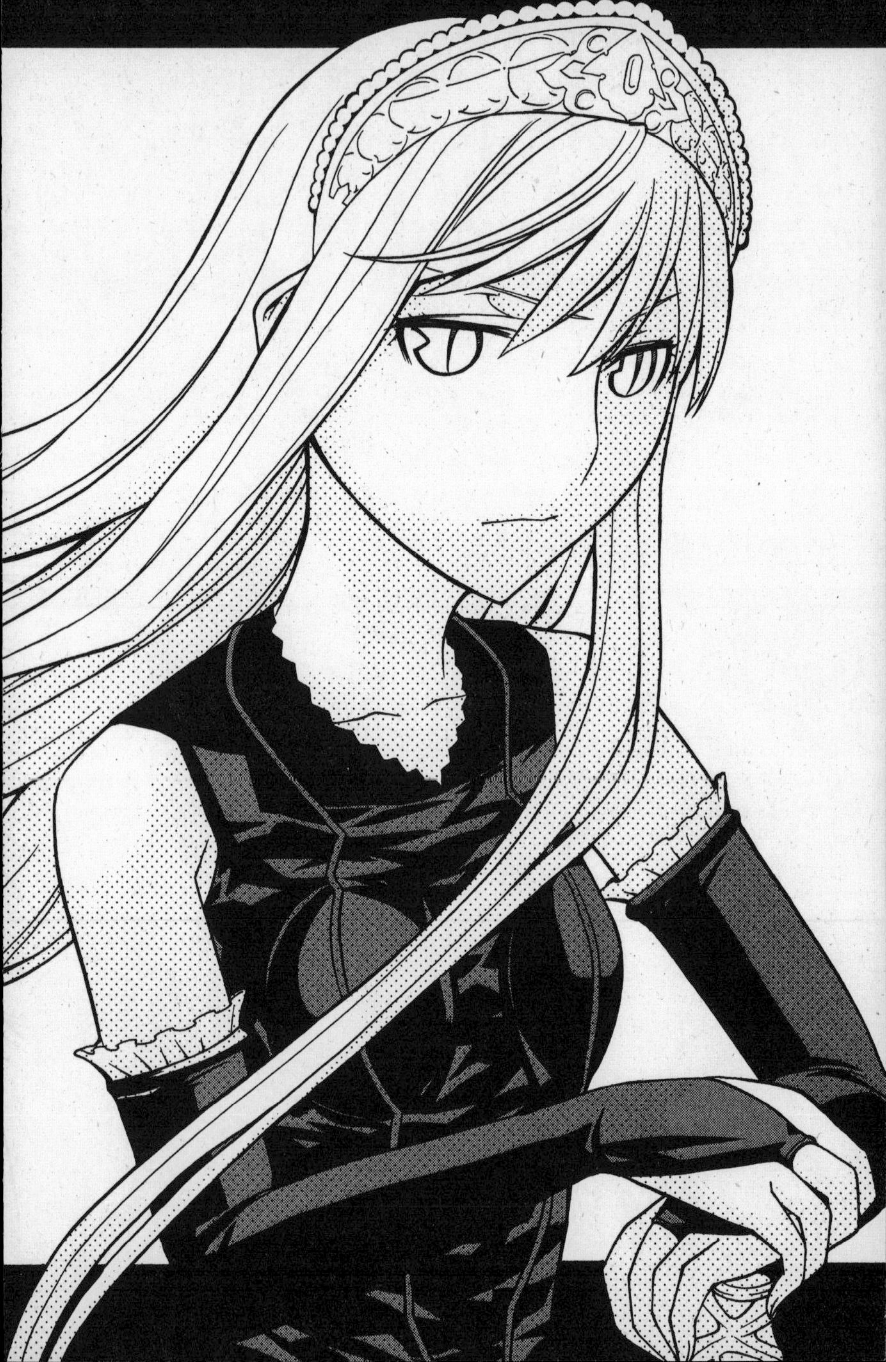

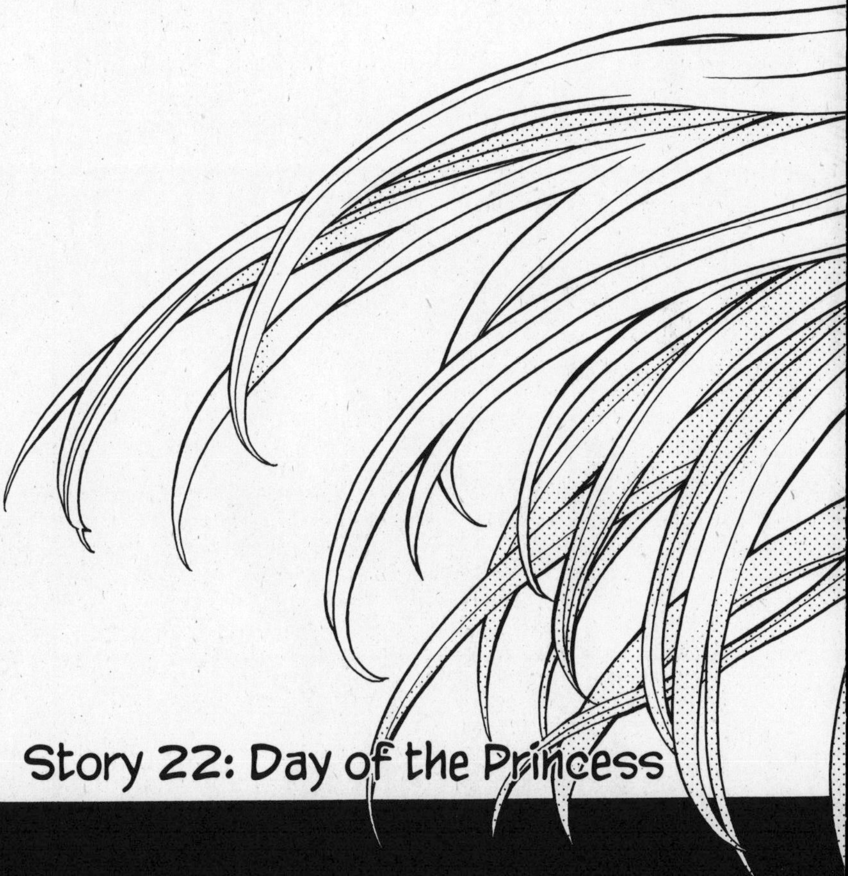

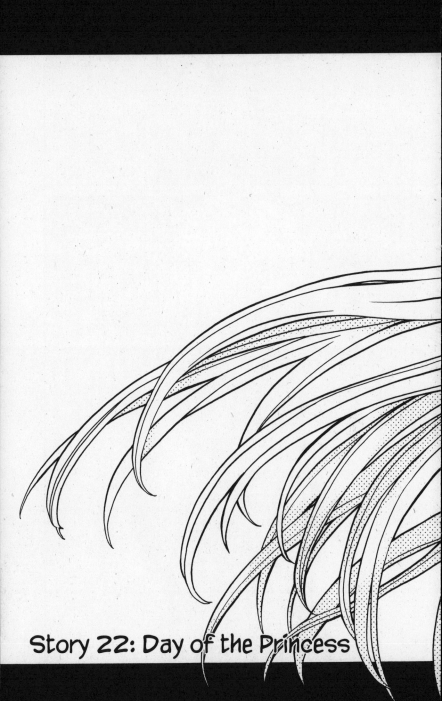

Story 22: Day of the Princess

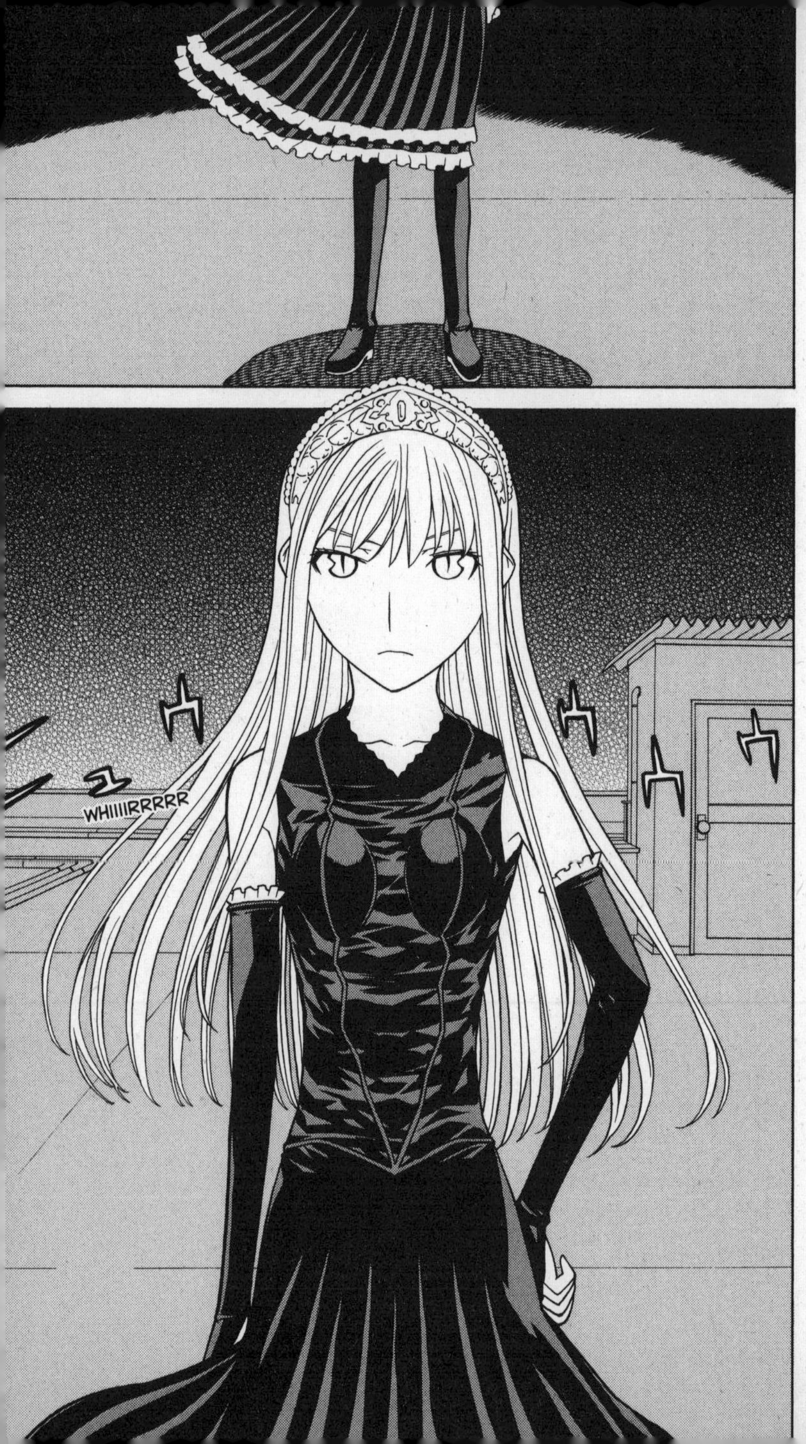
WHIIIIRRRRR

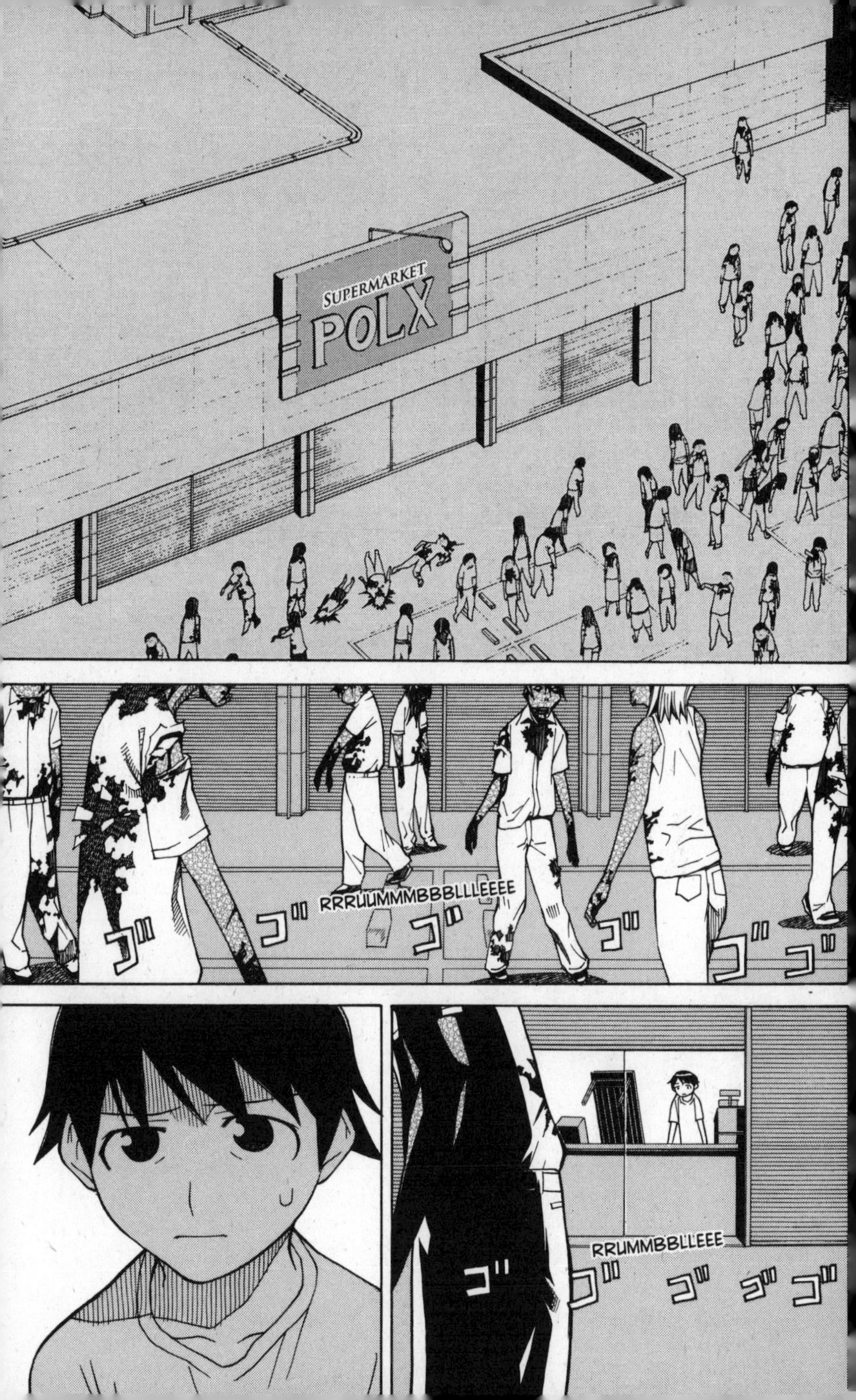
SUPERMARKET
POLX
RRRUUMMMBBBLLLEEEE
ゴゴゴゴゴゴ
RRUMMBBLLEEE
ゴゴゴゴゴ

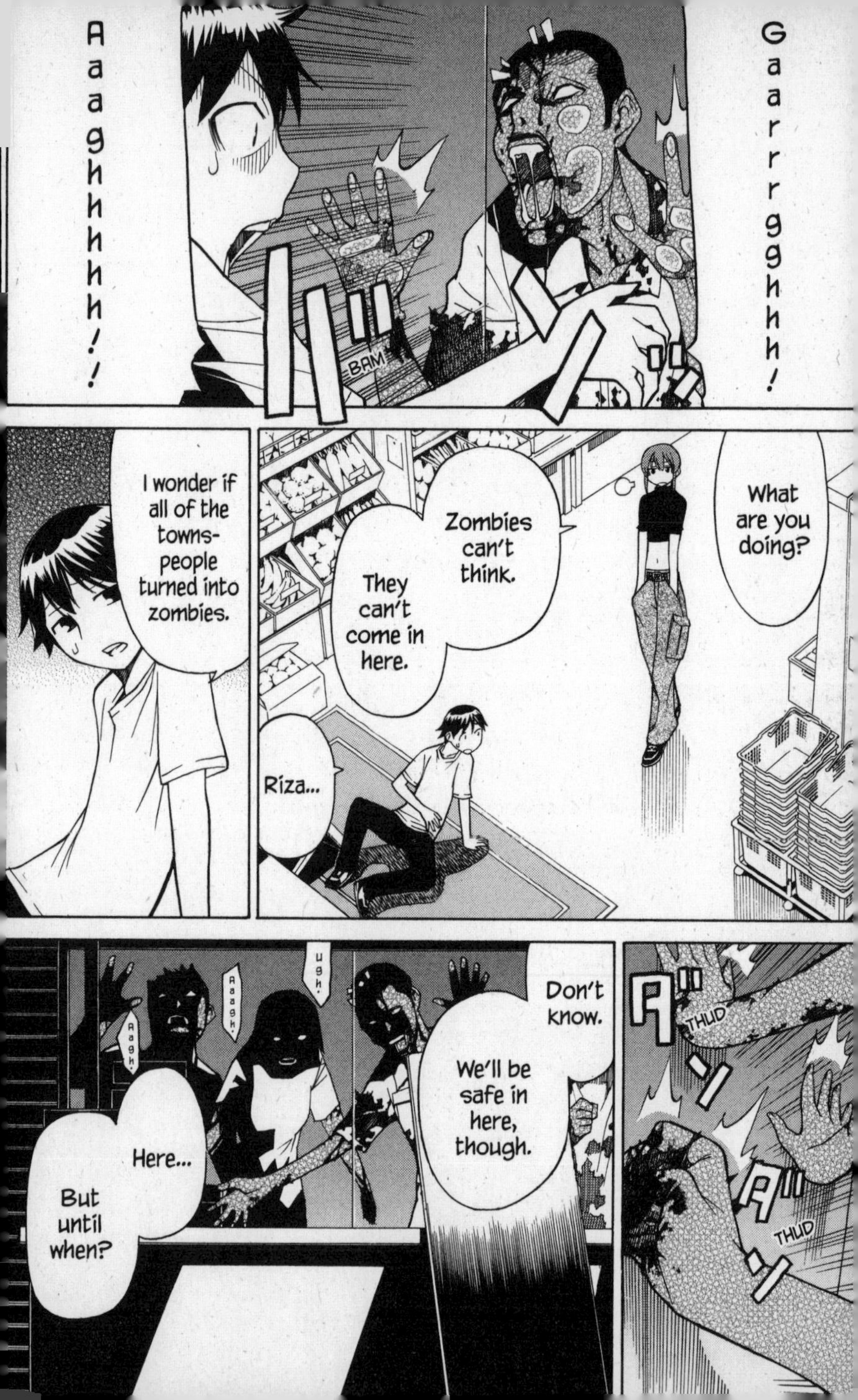
Gaarrrgghhhh!
Aaaghhhhhh!!
BAM
What are you doing?
Zombies can't think.
They can't come in here.
Riza...
I wonder if all of the towns-people turned into zombies.
THUD
THUD
Don't know.
We'll be safe in here, though.
ugh.
Aaagh.
Aagh.
Here...
But until when?

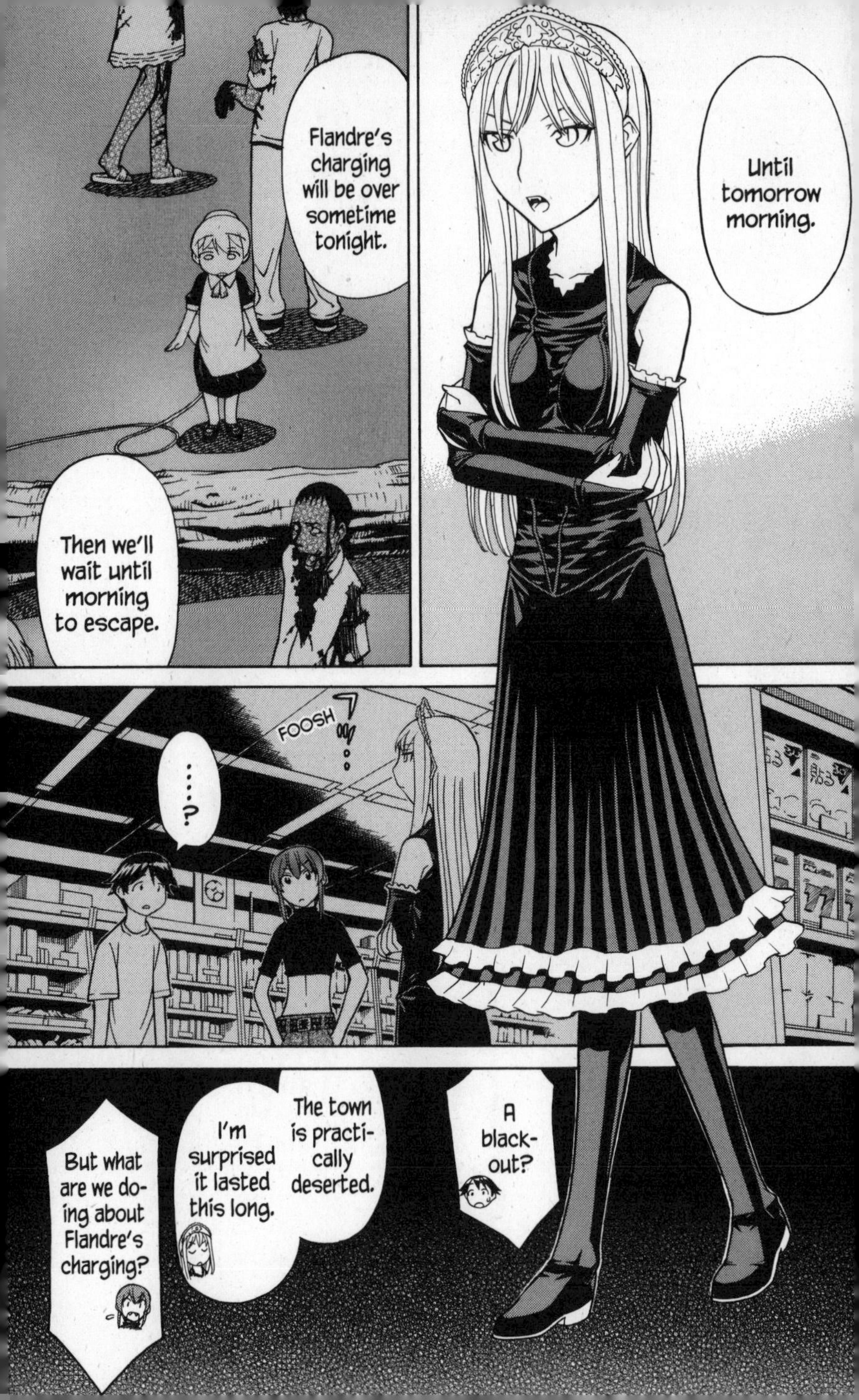

Until tomorrow morning.
Flandre's charging will be over sometime tonight.
Then we'll wait until morning to escape.
FOOSH
...?
A black-out?
The town is practi-cally deserted.
I'm surprised it lasted this long.
But what are we do-ing about Flandre's charging?

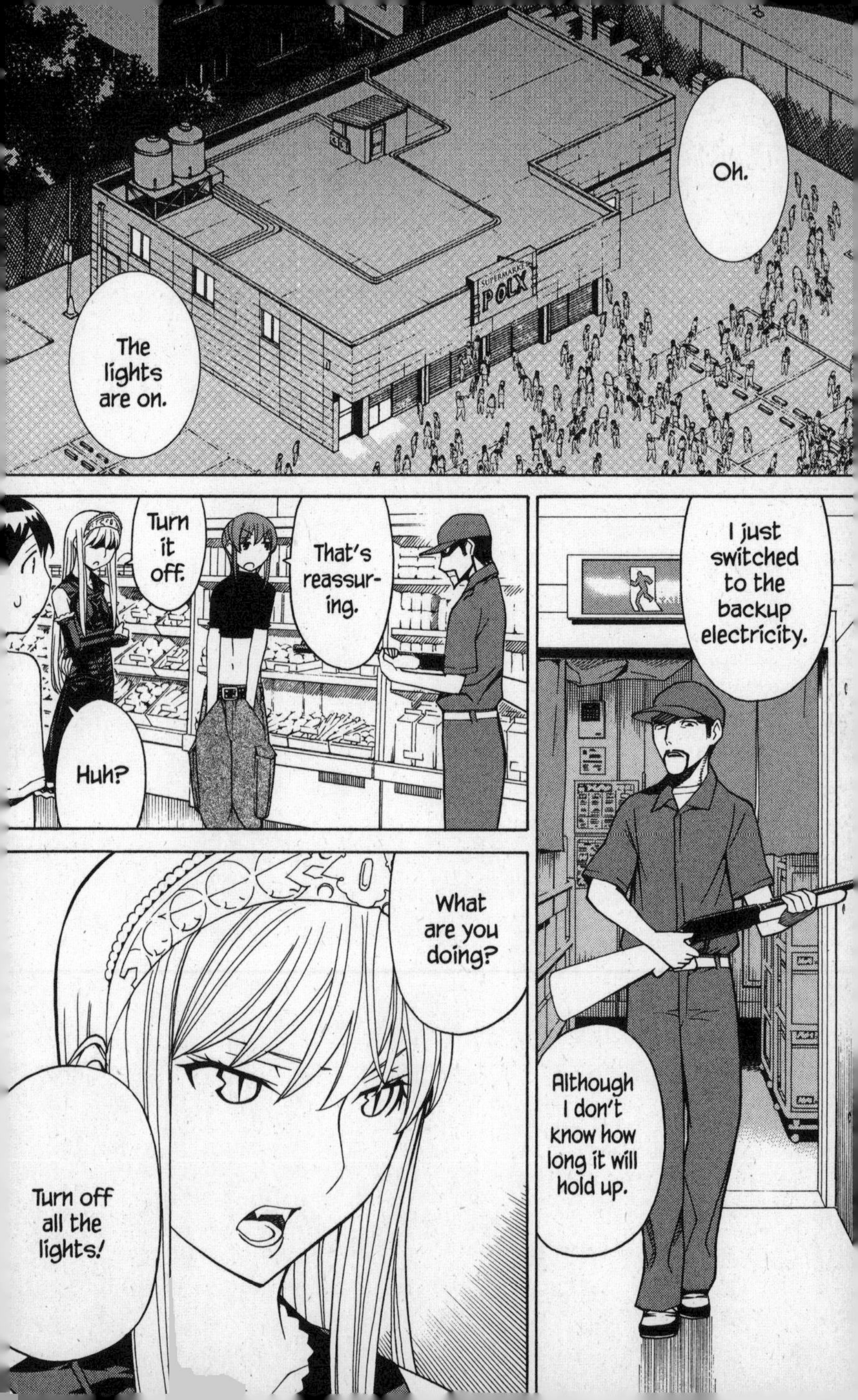
Oh.
The lights are on.
POLX
I just switched to the backup electricity.
Although I don't know how long it will hold up.
That's reassur-ing.
Turn it off.
Huh?
What are you doing?
Turn off all the lights!

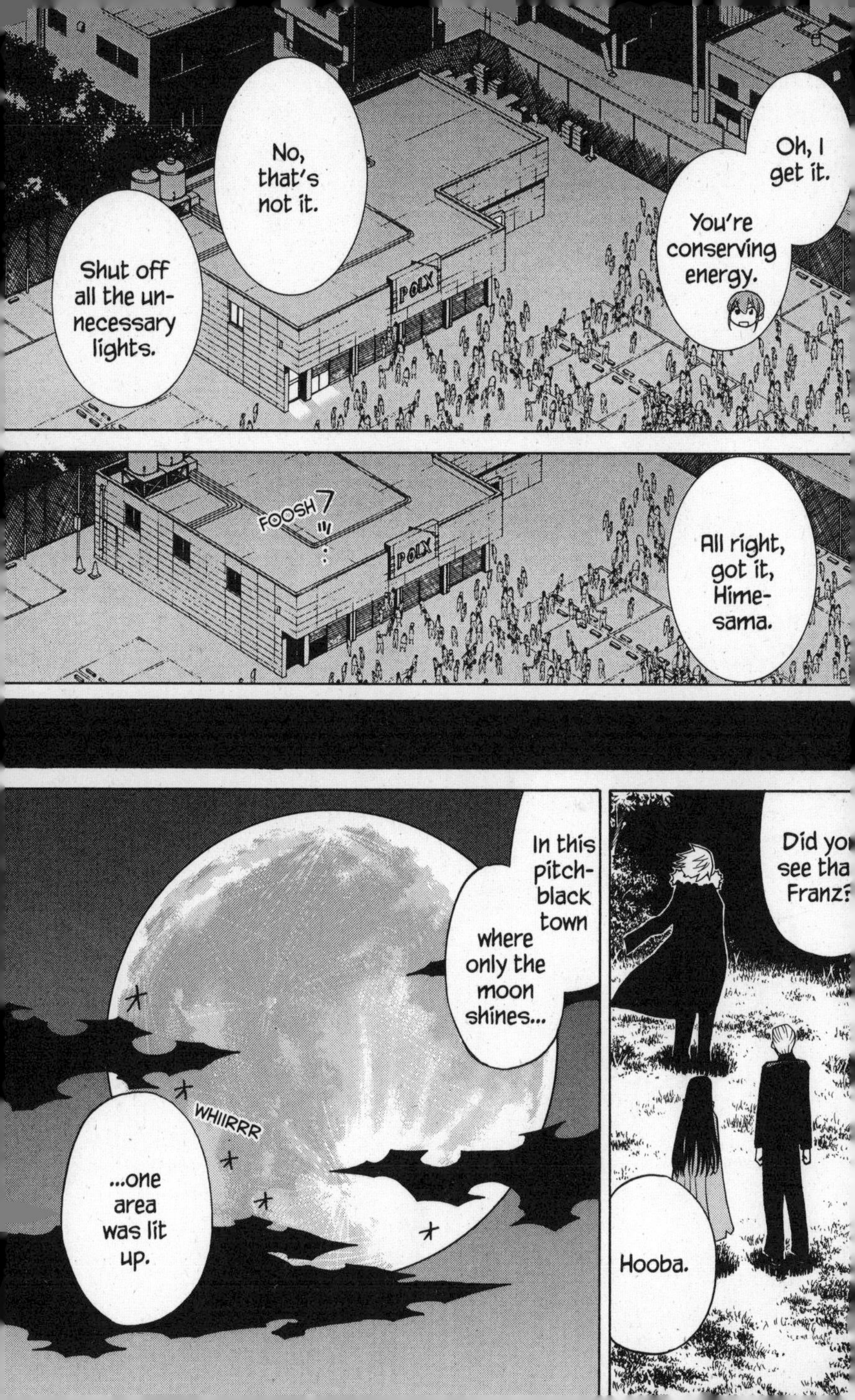
Oh, I get it.
You're conserving energy.
No, that's not it.
Shut off all the un-necessary lights.
All right, got it, Hime-sama.
FOOSH
Did yo see tha Franz?
Hooba.
In this pitch-black town
where only the moon shines...
WHIIRRR
...one area was lit up.

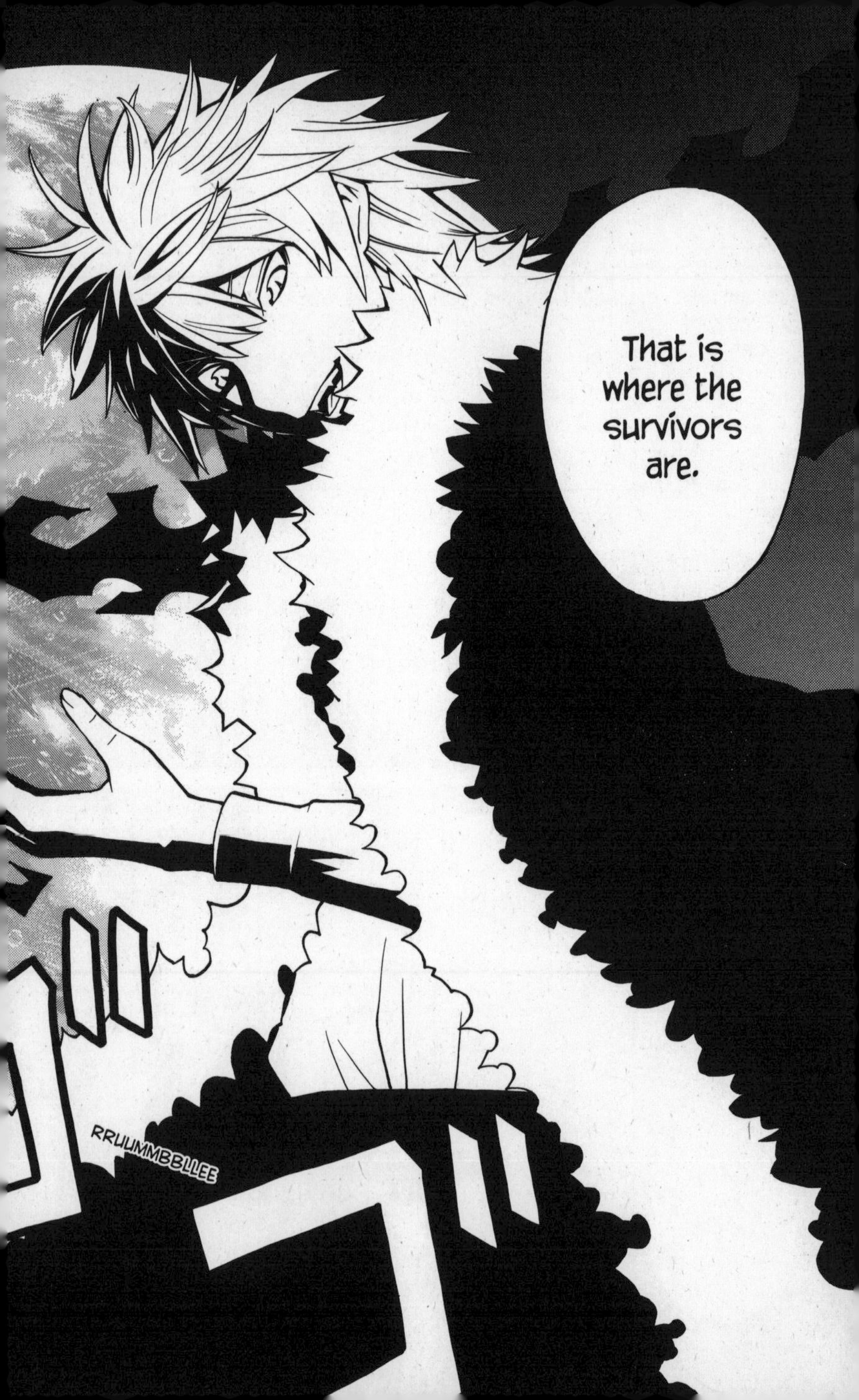
That is where the survivors are.
RRUUMMBBLLEE

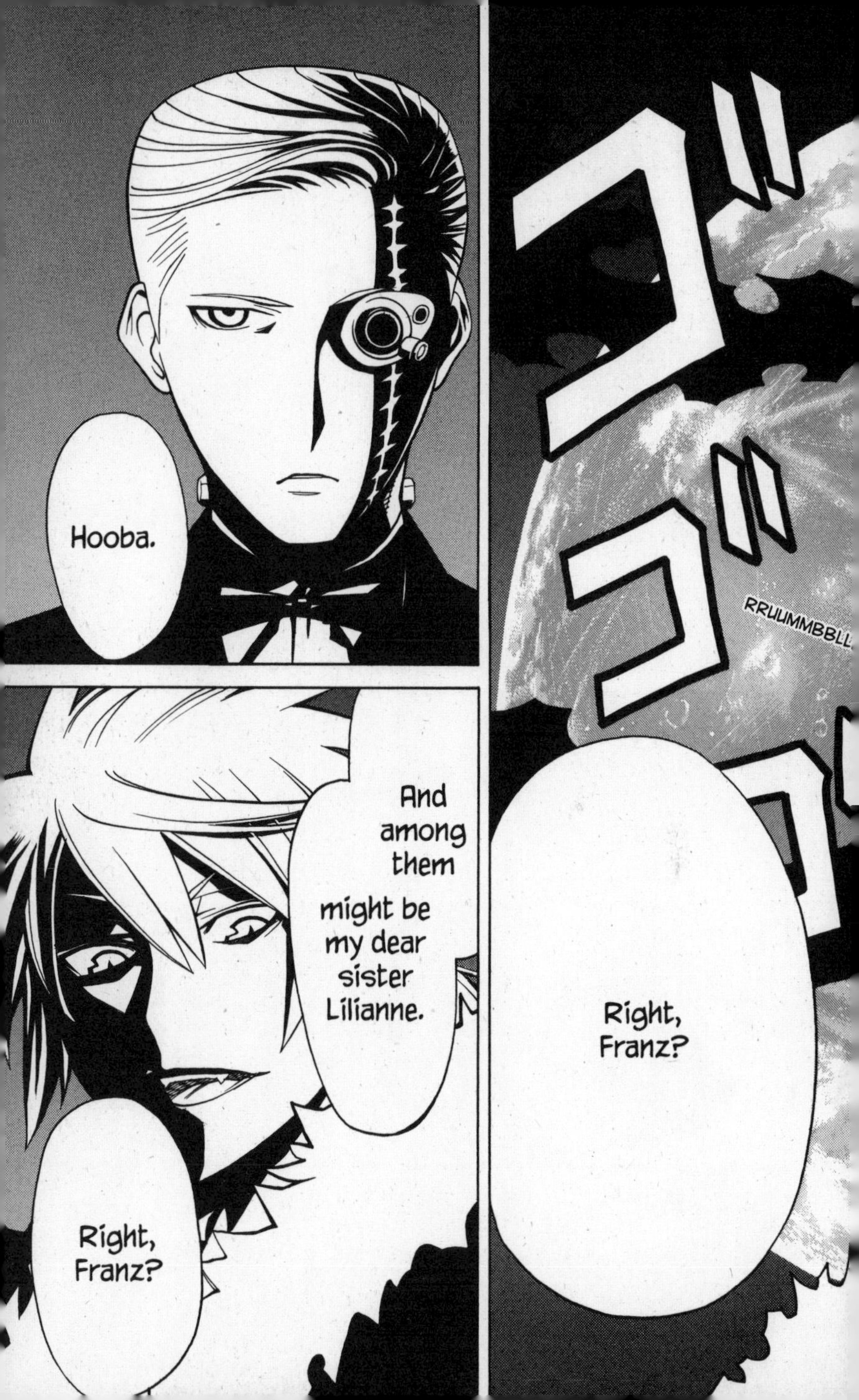
ゴゴゴ
RRUUMMBBLL
Right, Franz?
Hooba.
And among them might be my dear sister Lilianne.
Right, Franz?

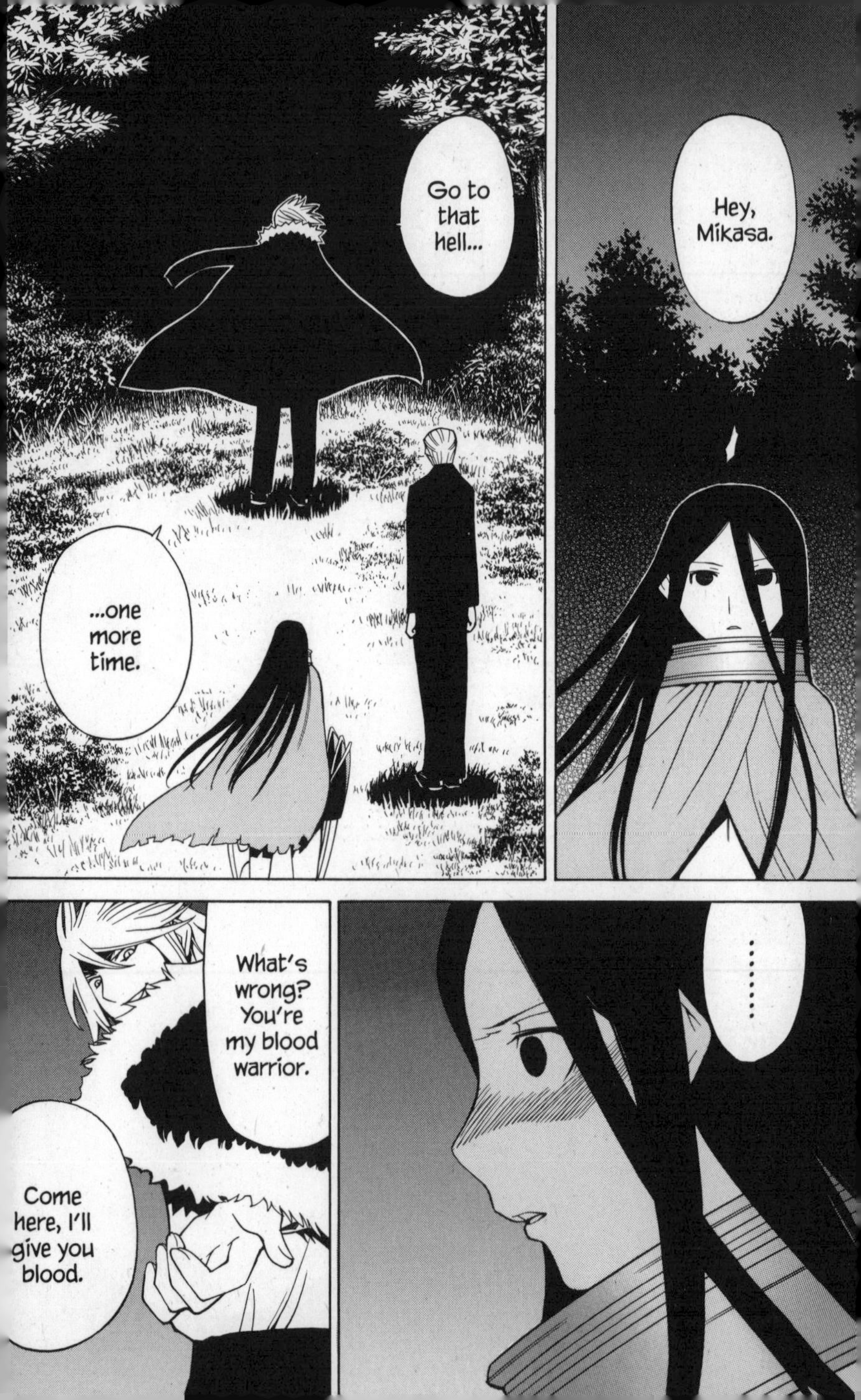
Hey, Mikasa.
Go to that hell...
...one more time.
....
What's wrong? You're my blood warrior.
Come here, I'll give you blood.

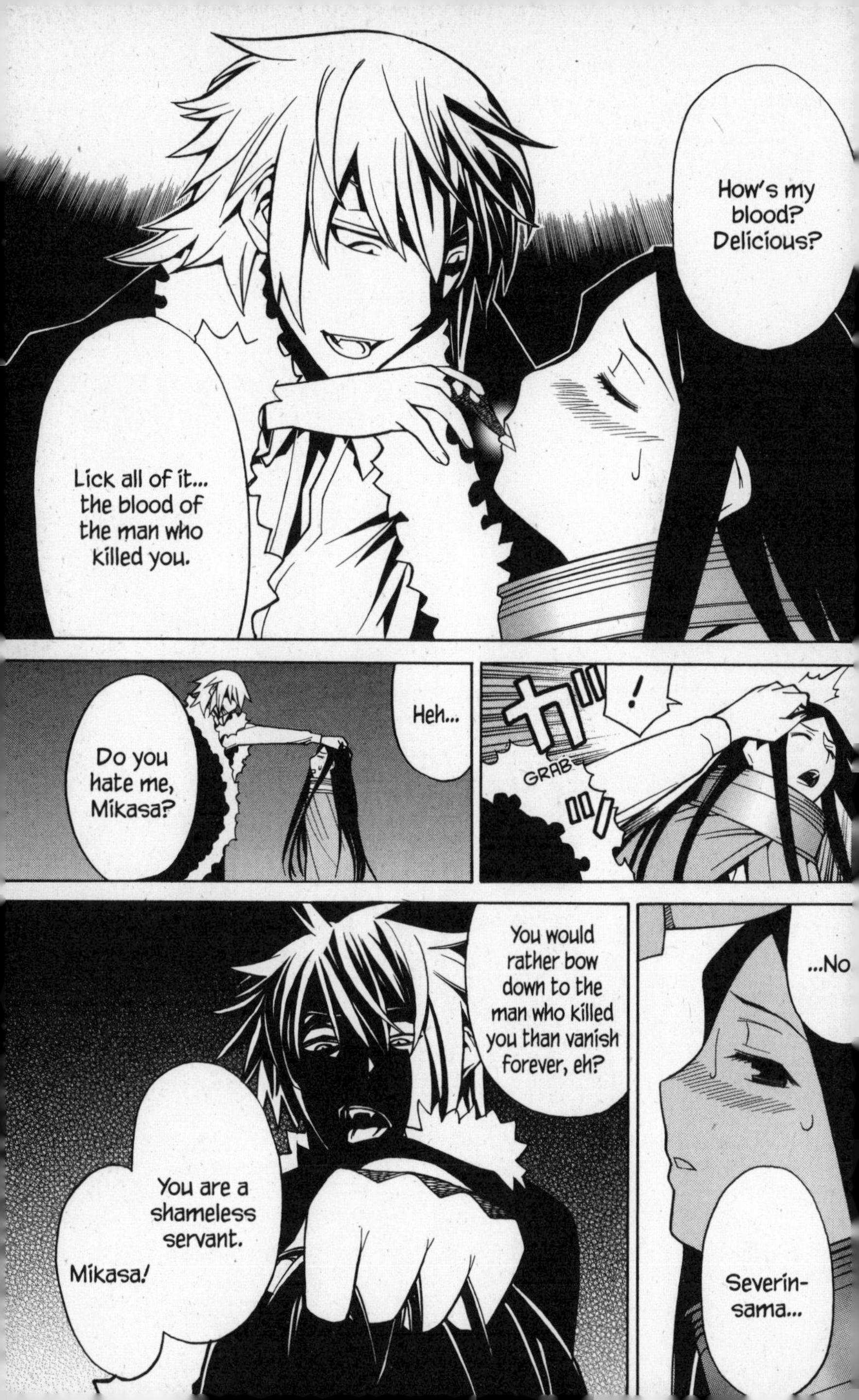
How's my blood? Delicious?
Lick all of it... the blood of the man who killed you.
!
ガッ
GRAB
Heh...
Do you hate me, Mikasa?
...No
Severin-sama...
You would rather bow down to the man who killed you than vanish forever, eh?
You are a shameless servant.
Mikasa!

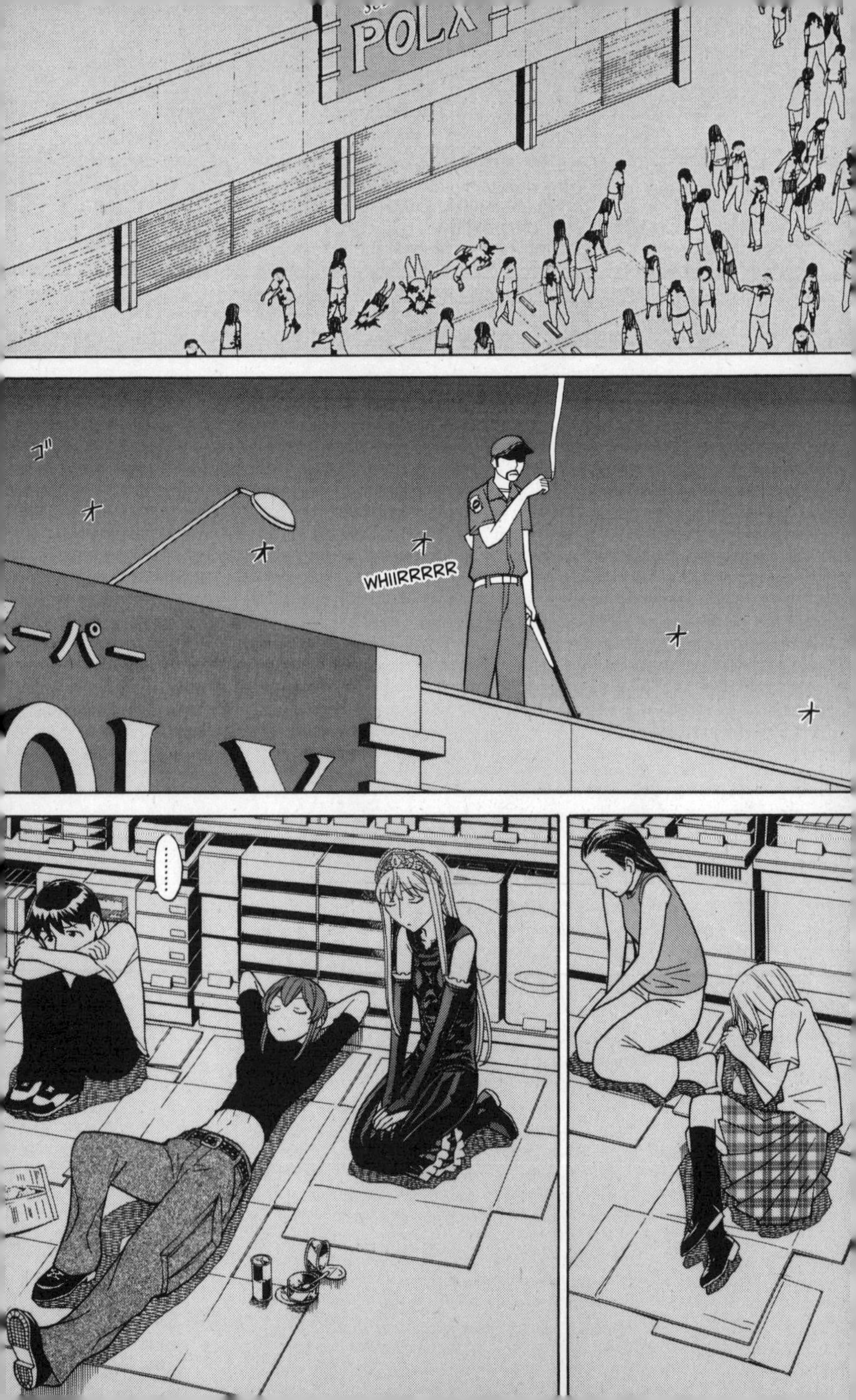

POLX
ゴオオオオオ
WHIIRRRRR
スーパー
......

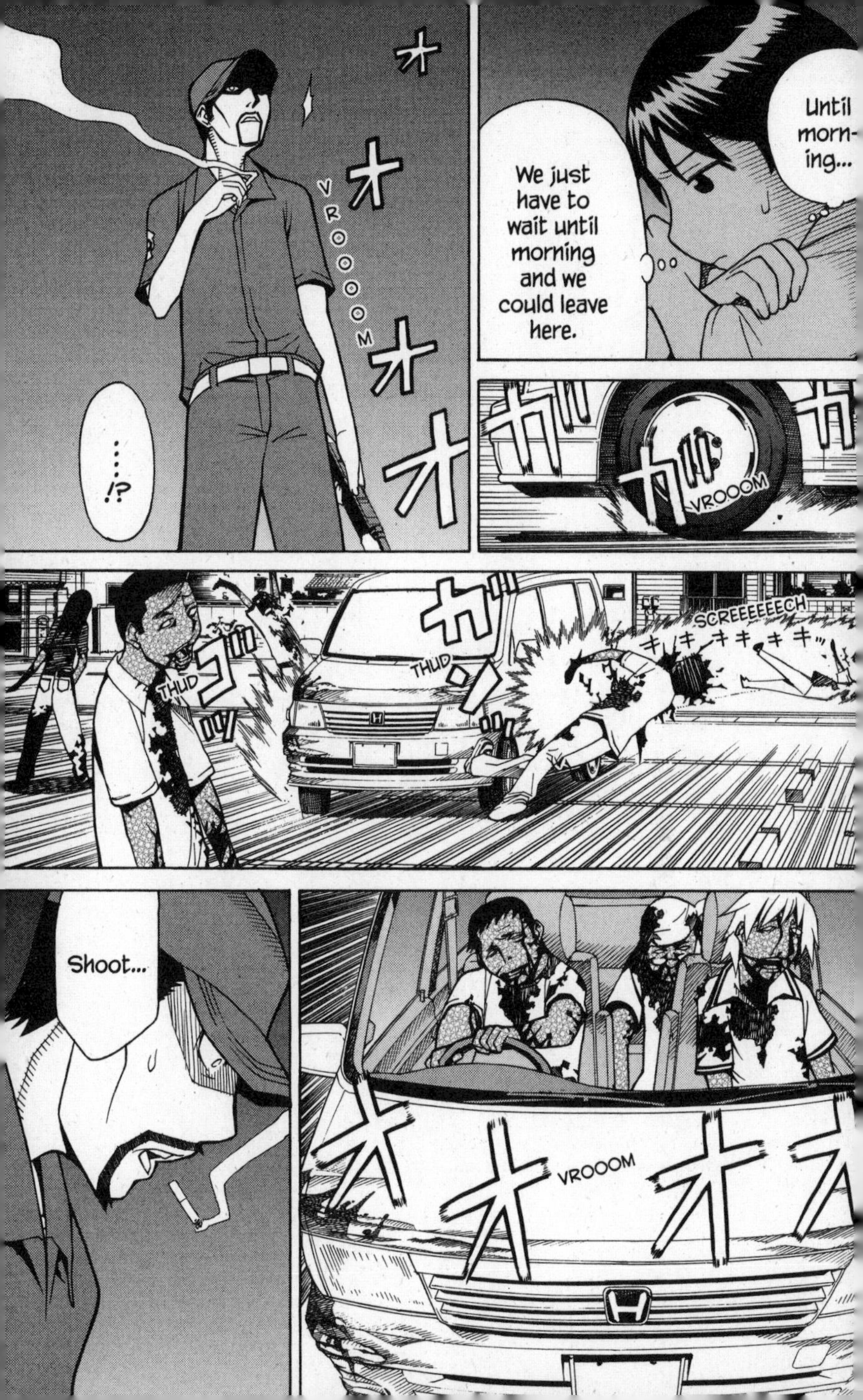
Until morning...
We just have to wait until morning and we could leave here.
VROOOM
VROOOOOM
....!?
SCREEEEEECH
THUD
THUD
VROOOM
Shoot...

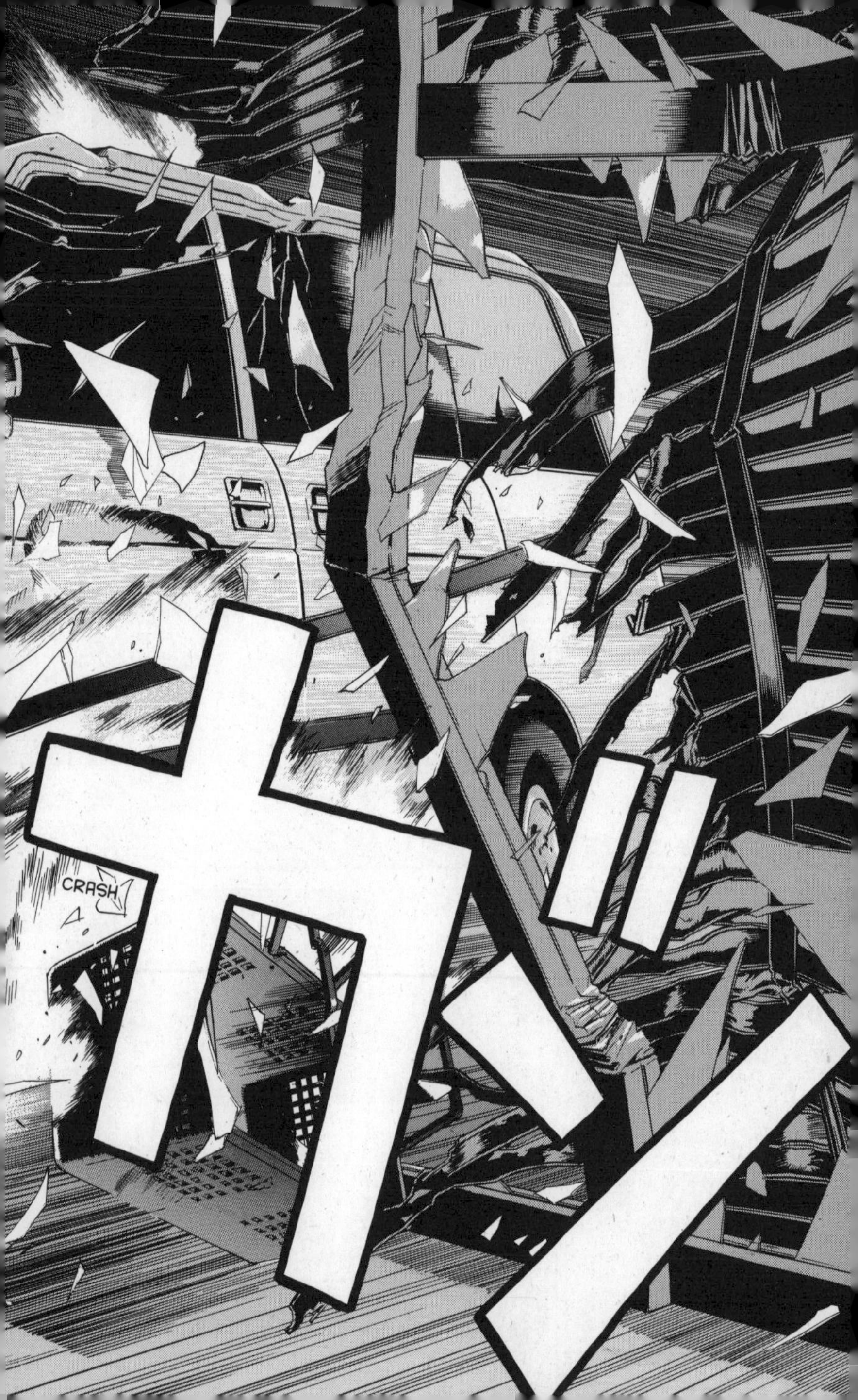
ガッ
CRASH

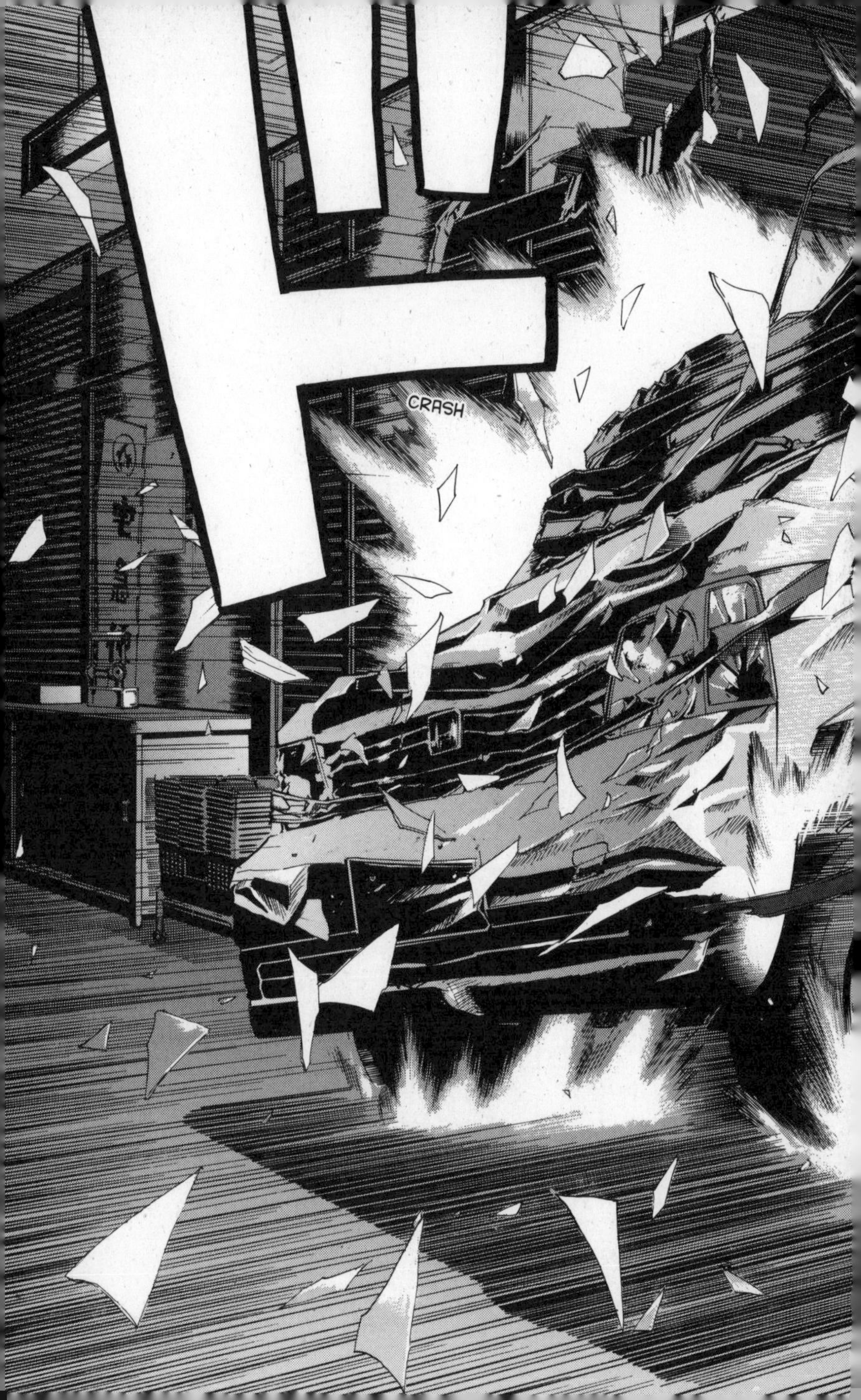
CRASH

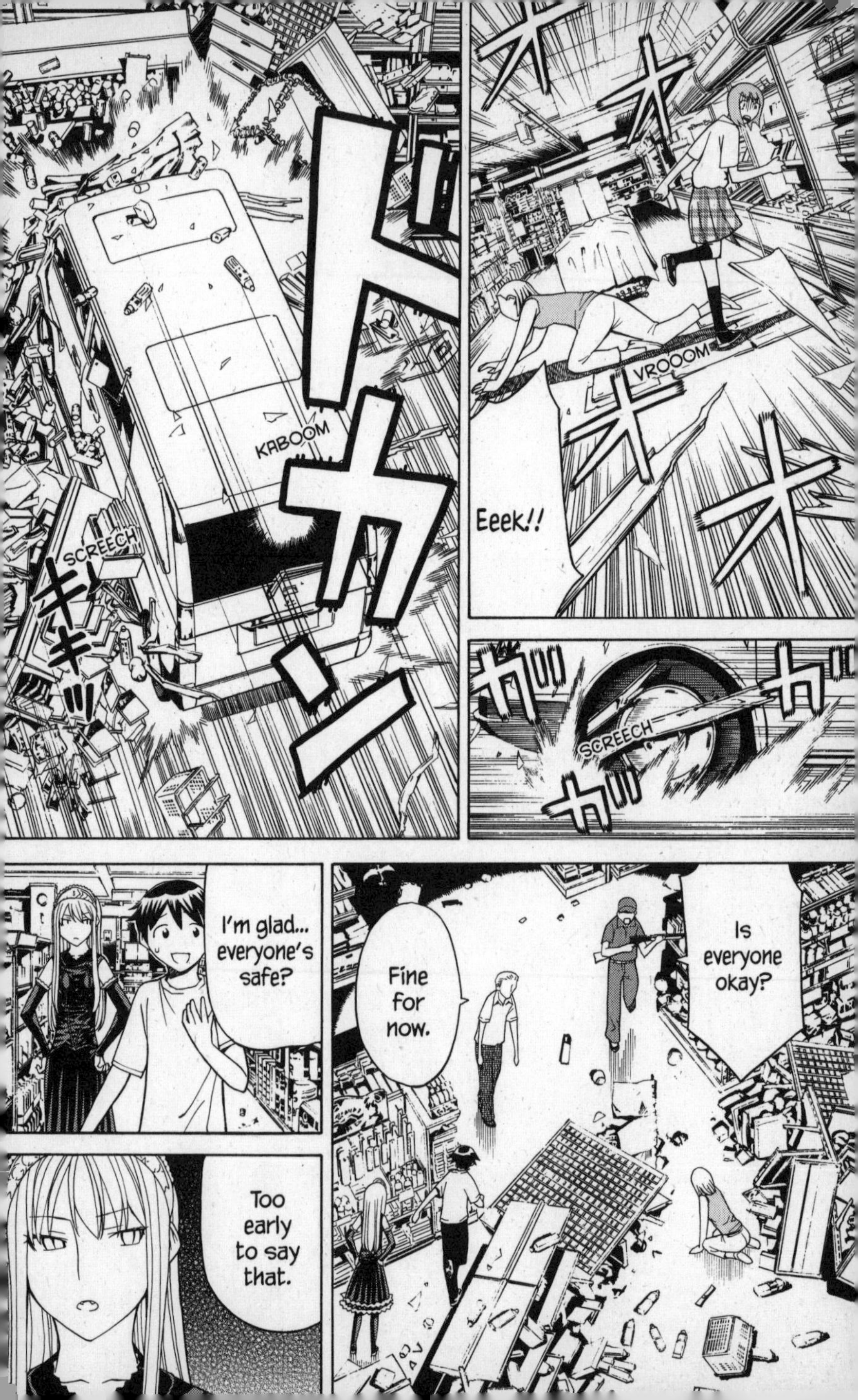
VROOOM
Eeek!!
SCREECH
KABOOM
SCREECH
Is everyone okay?
Fine for now.
I'm glad... everyone's safe?
Too early to say that.

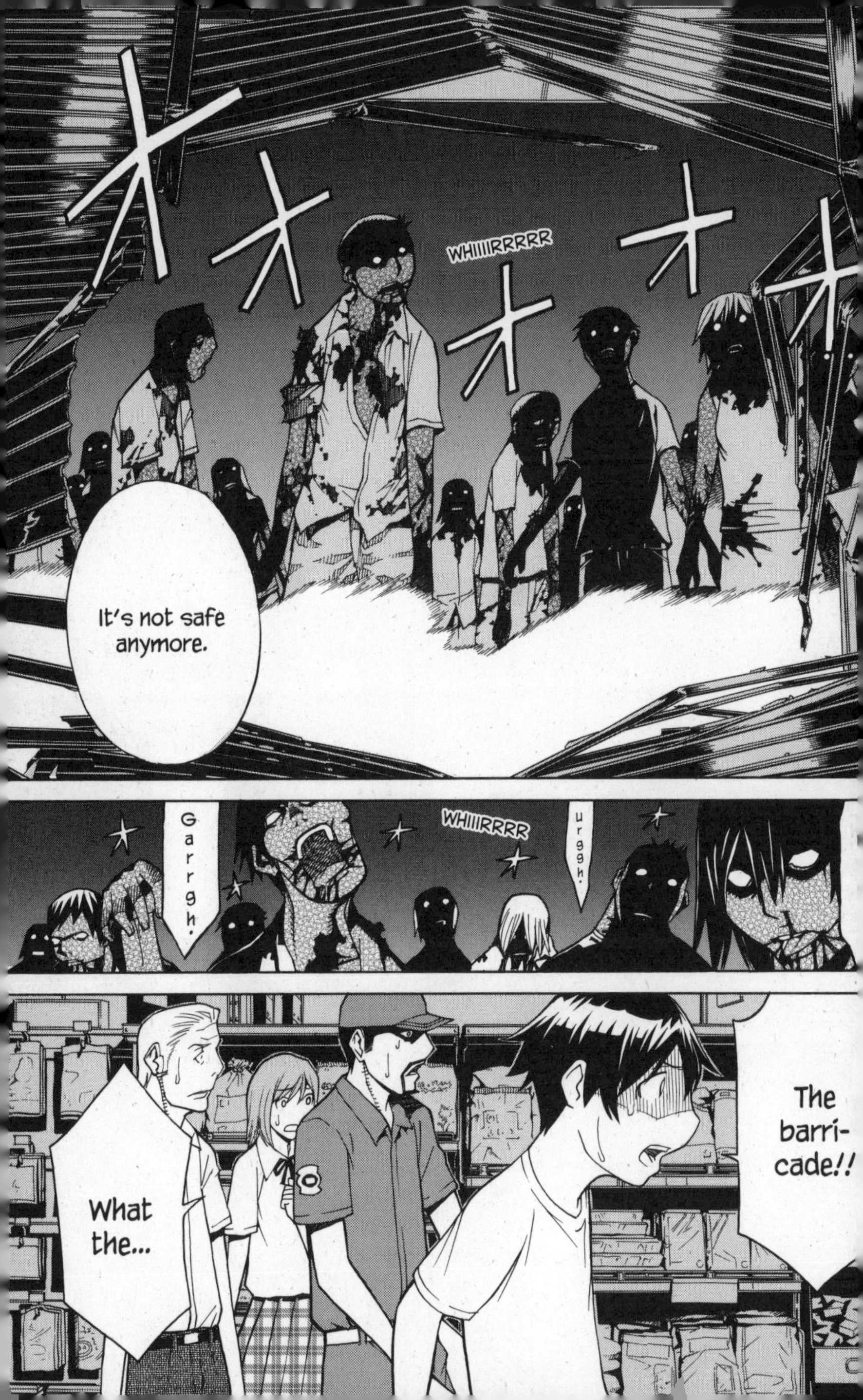
WHIIIIRRRRR
It's not safe anymore.
urggh.
WHIIIRRRR
Garrgh.
The barri-cade!!
What the...

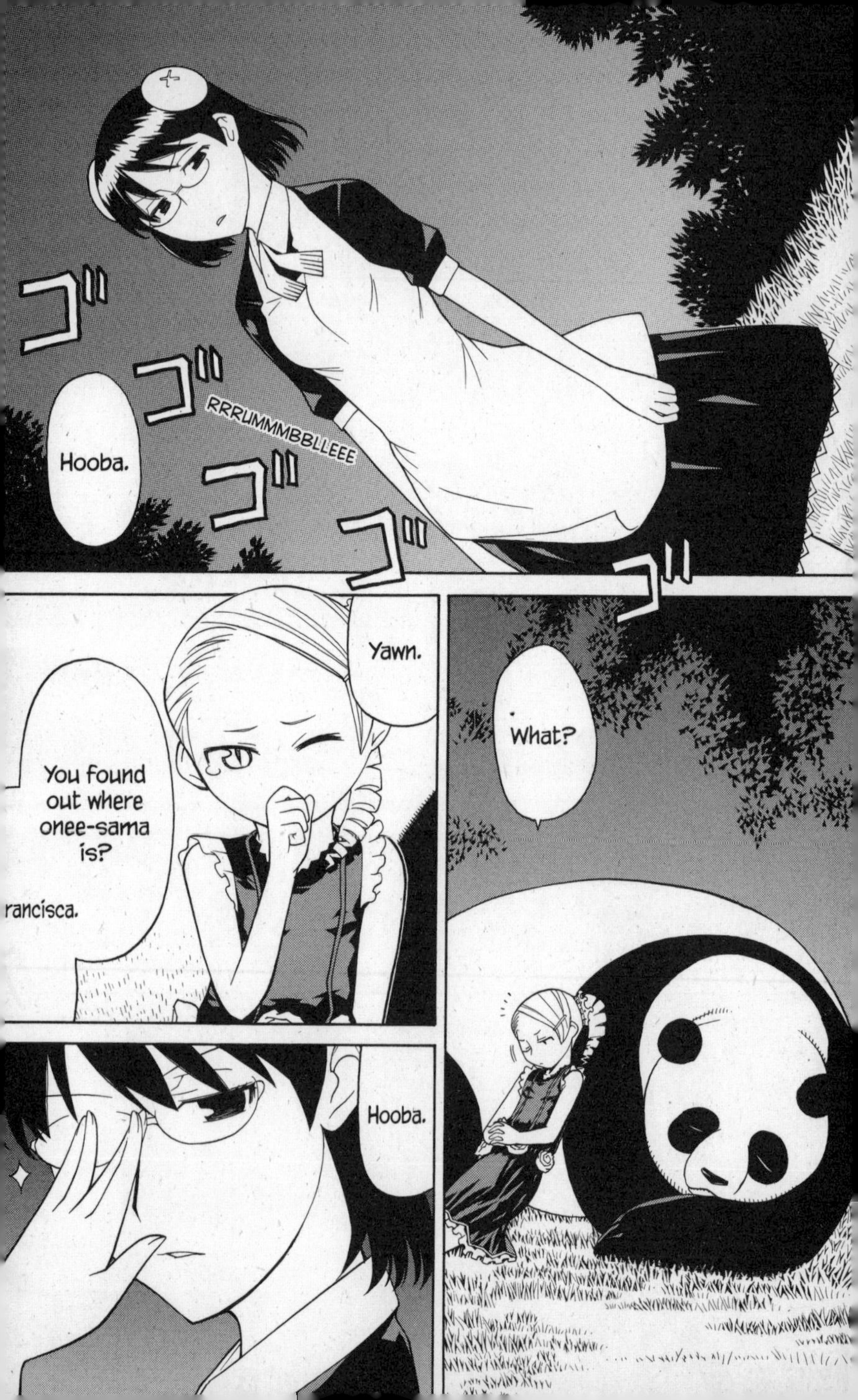
ゴ ゴ ゴ ゴ ゴ ゴ
RRRUMMMBBLLEEE
Hooba.
What?
Yawn.
You found out where onee-sama is?
rancisca.
Hooba.

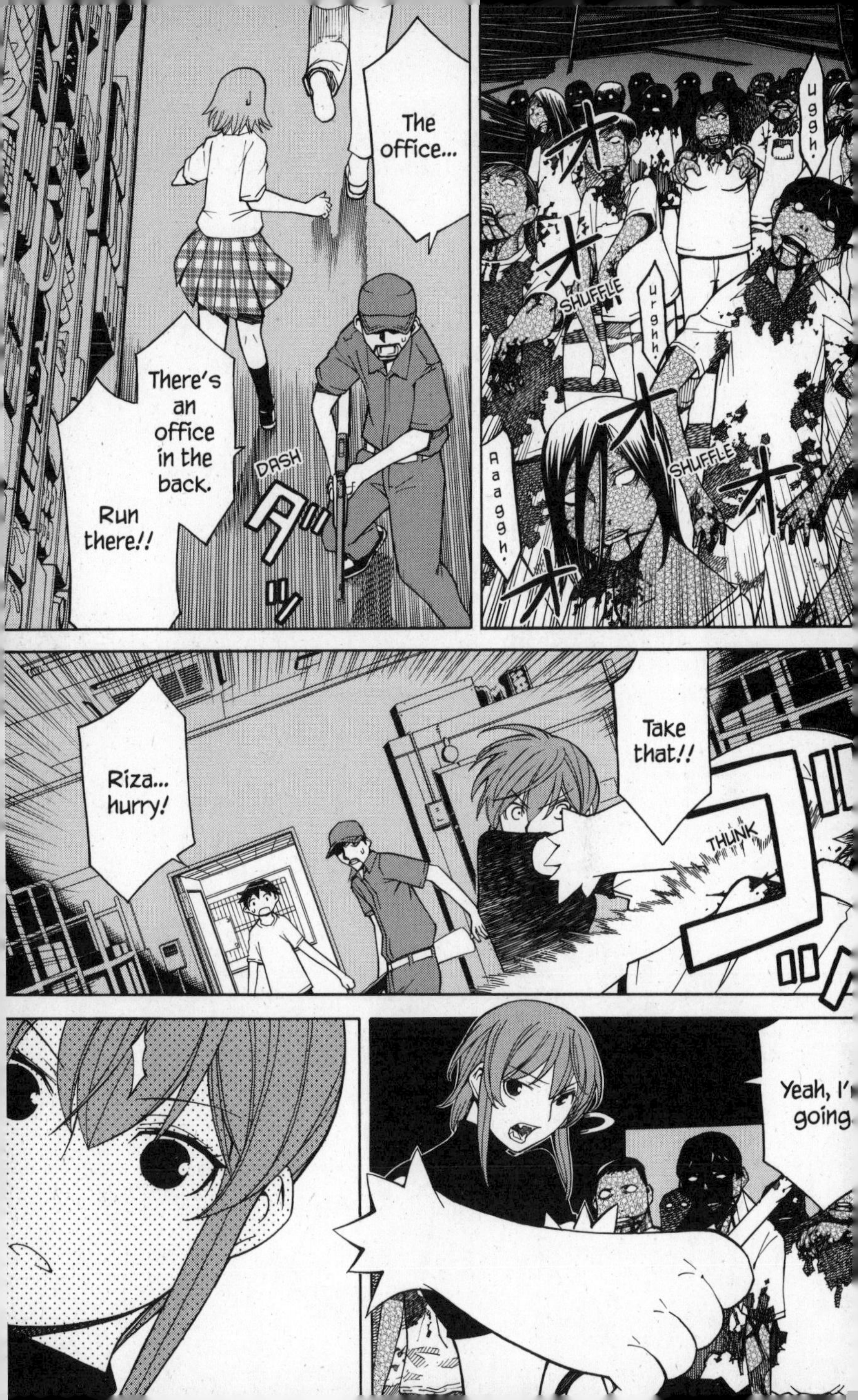
Uggh.
SHUFFLE
urghh.
Aaaggh.
SHUFFLE
The office...
There's an office in the back.
Run there!!
DASH
Take that!!
THUNK
Riza... hurry!
Yeah, I' going

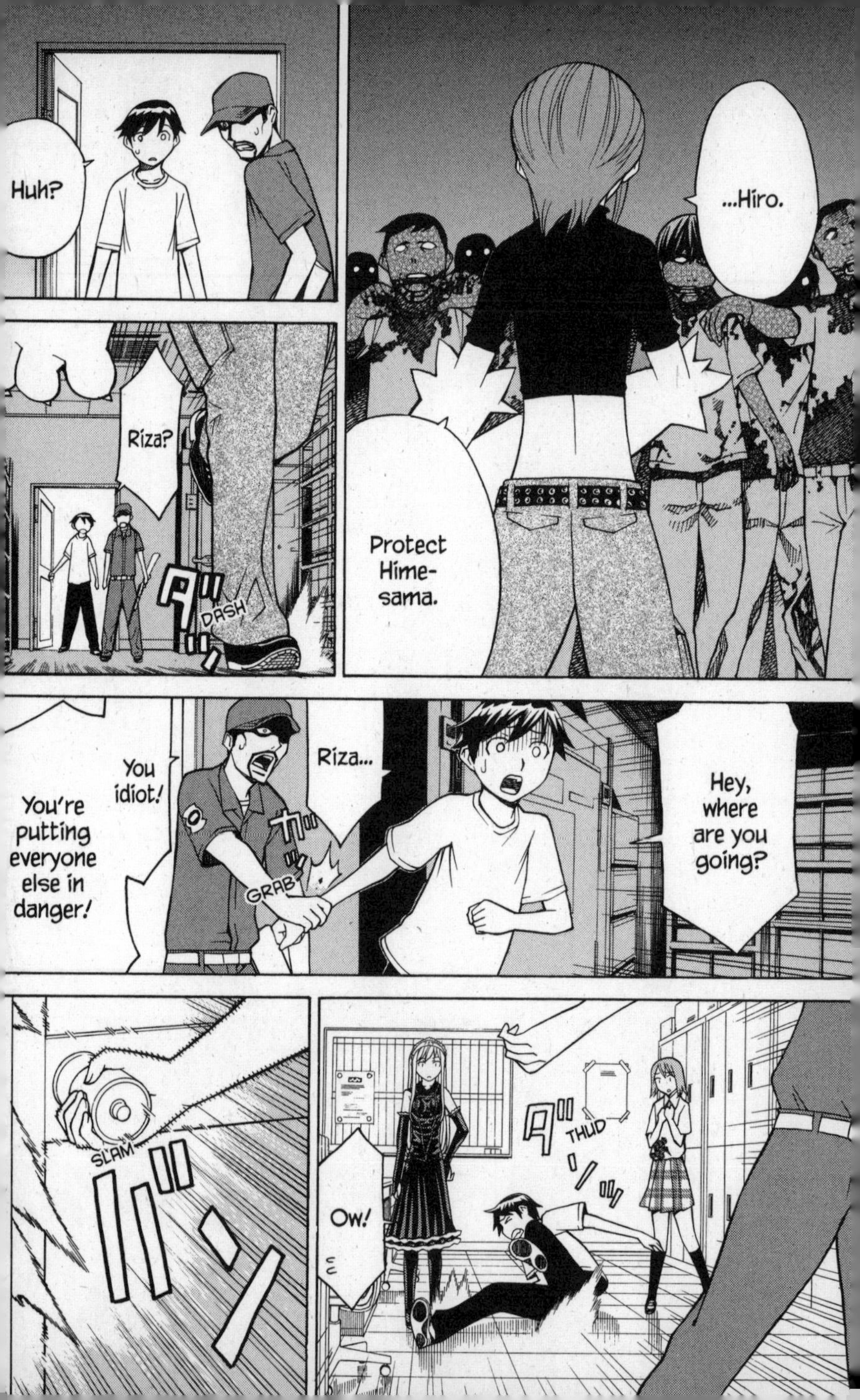
...Hiro.
Protect Hime-sama.
Huh?
Riza?
DASH
Hey, where are you going?
Riza...
You idiot!
GRAB
You're putting everyone else in danger!
THUD
Ow!
SLAM

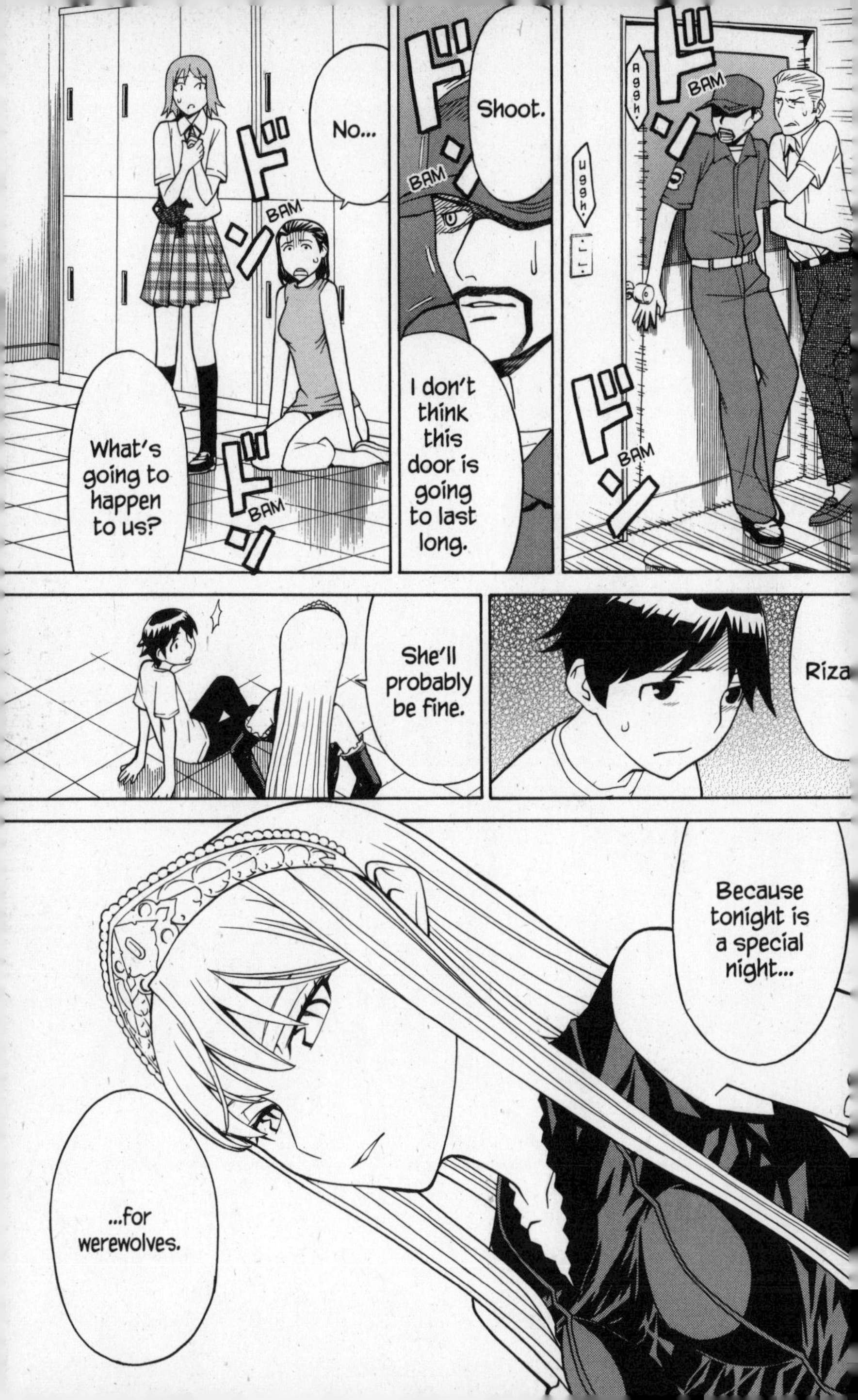
Aggh.
Uggh.
BAM
BAM
Shoot.
BAM
I don't think this door is going to last long.
No...
BAM
BAM
What's going to happen to us?
Riza
She'll probably be fine.
Because tonight is a special night...
...for werewolves.

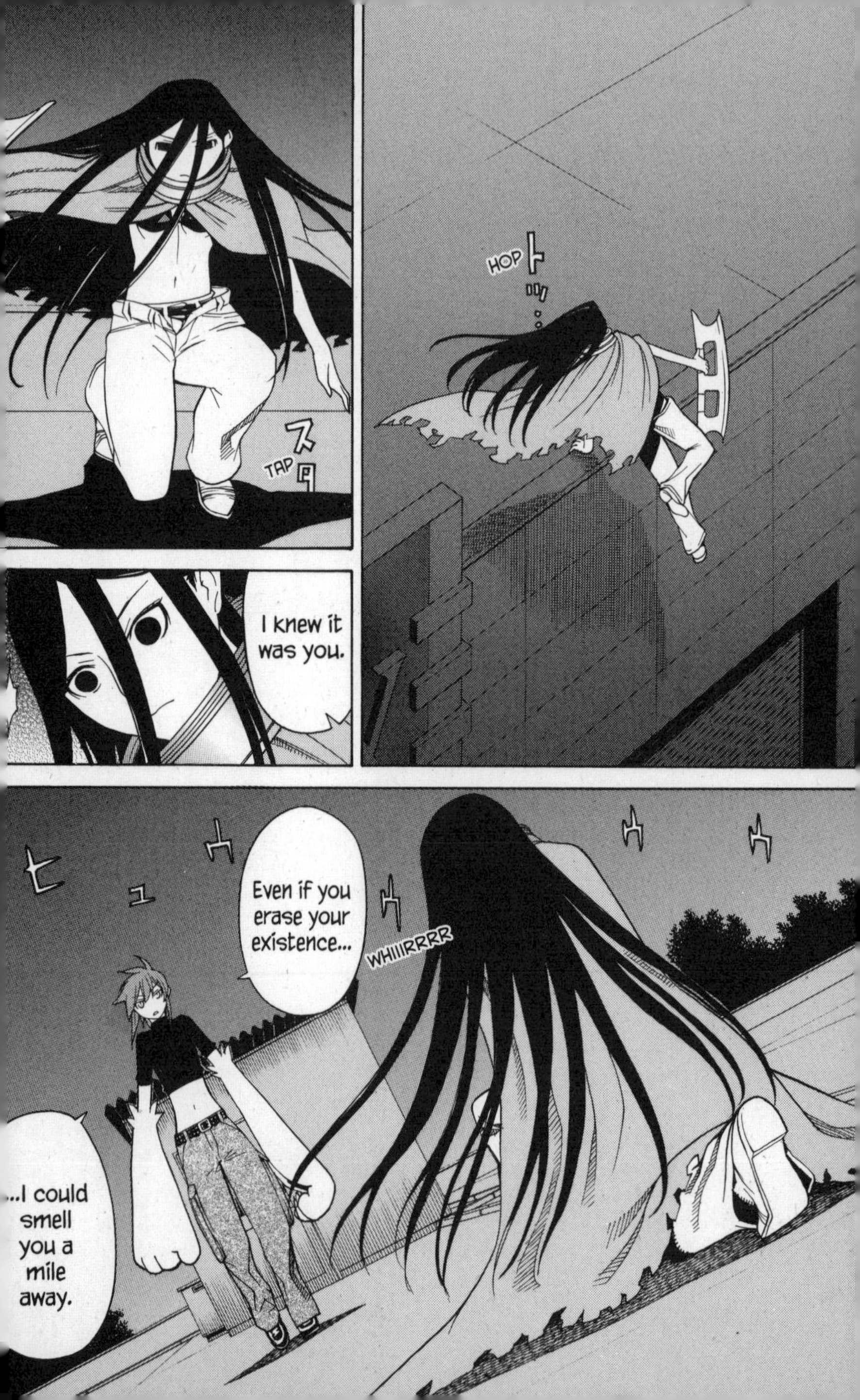
HOP
トッ
TAP
スタ
I knew it was you.
Even if you erase your existence...
WHIIIRRRR
...I could smell you a mile away.

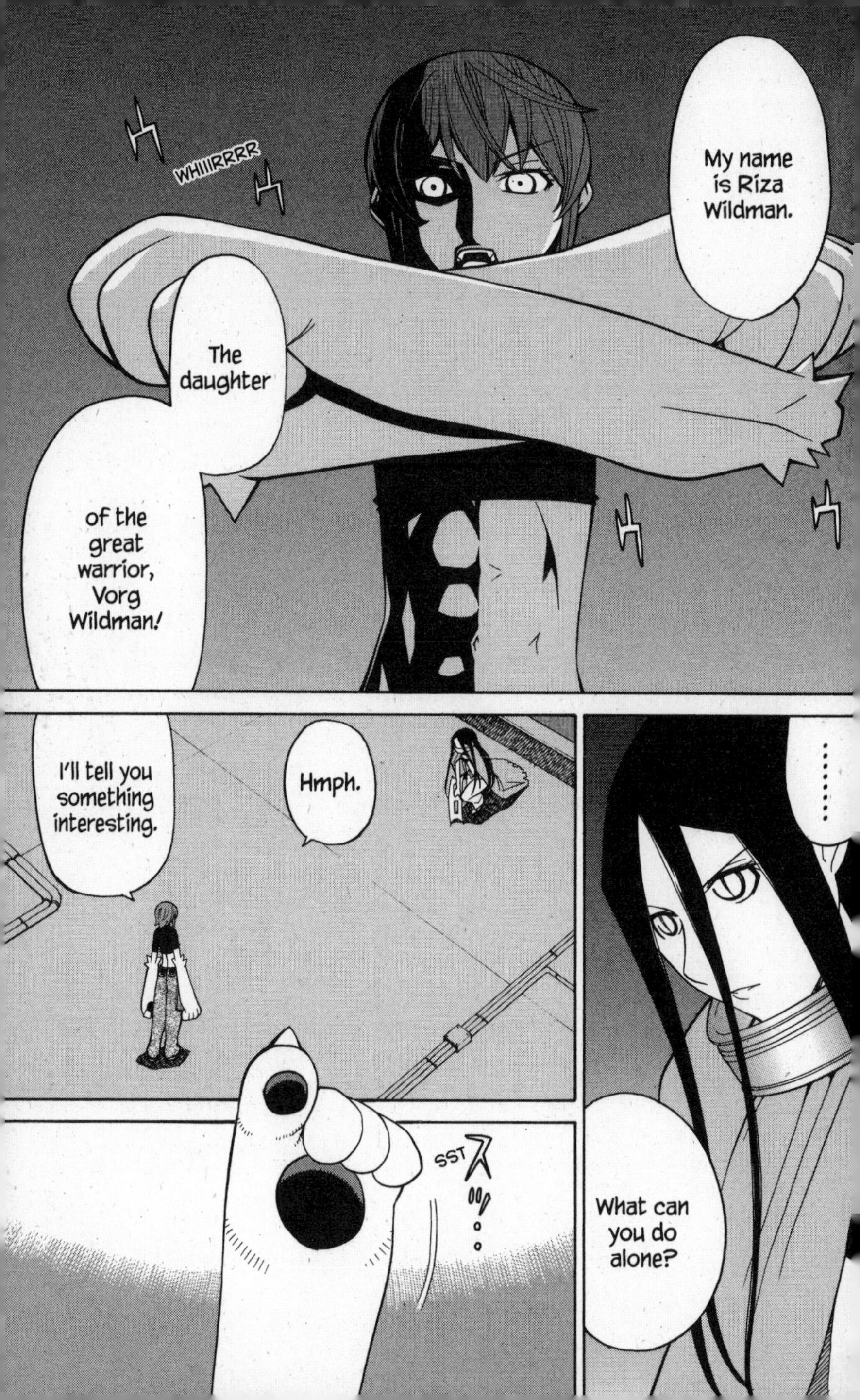
My name is Riza Wildman.
WHIIIRRRR
The daughter of the great warrior, Vorg Wildman!
......
What can you do alone?
Hmph.
I'll tell you something interesting.
SST

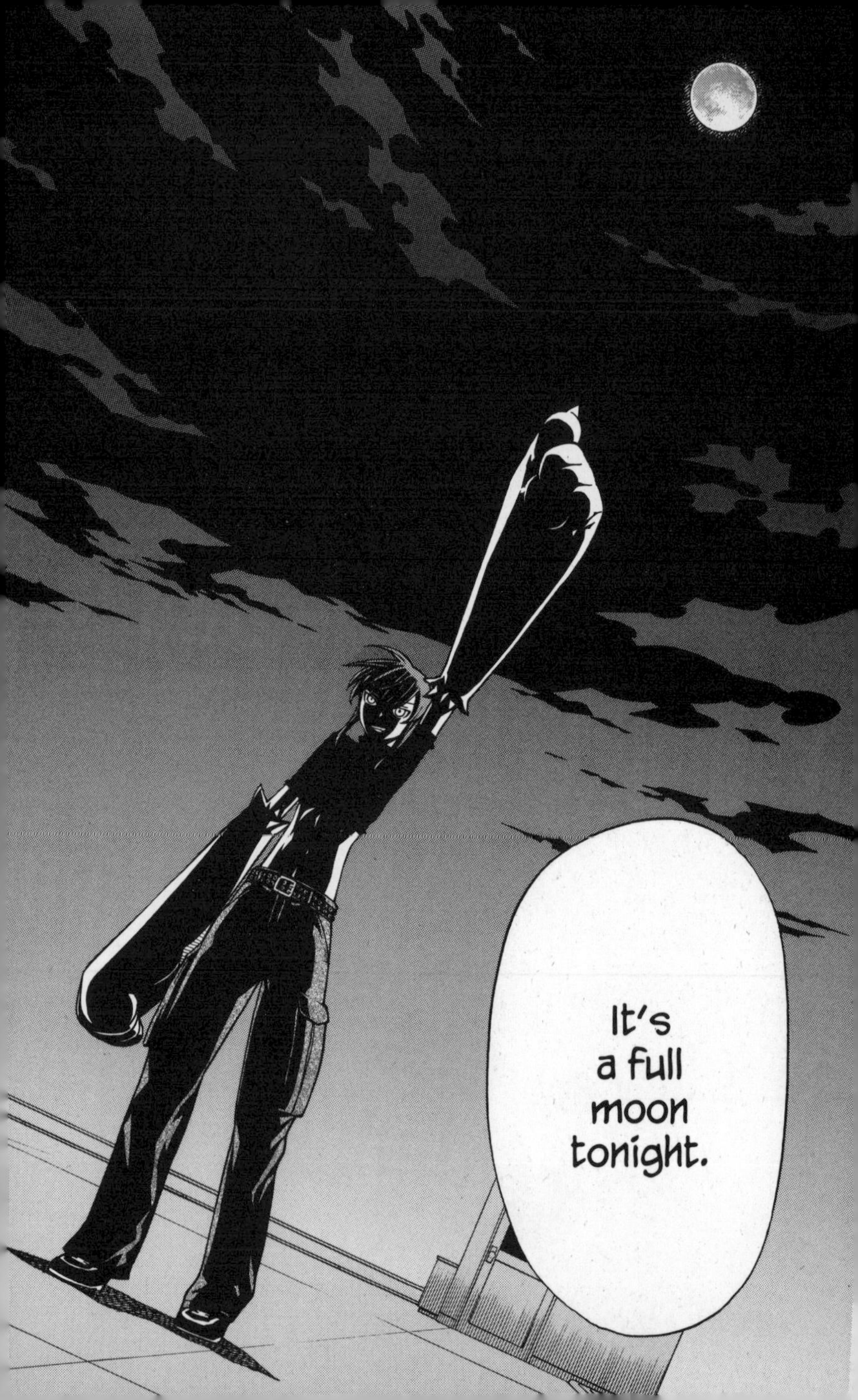
It's a full moon tonight.

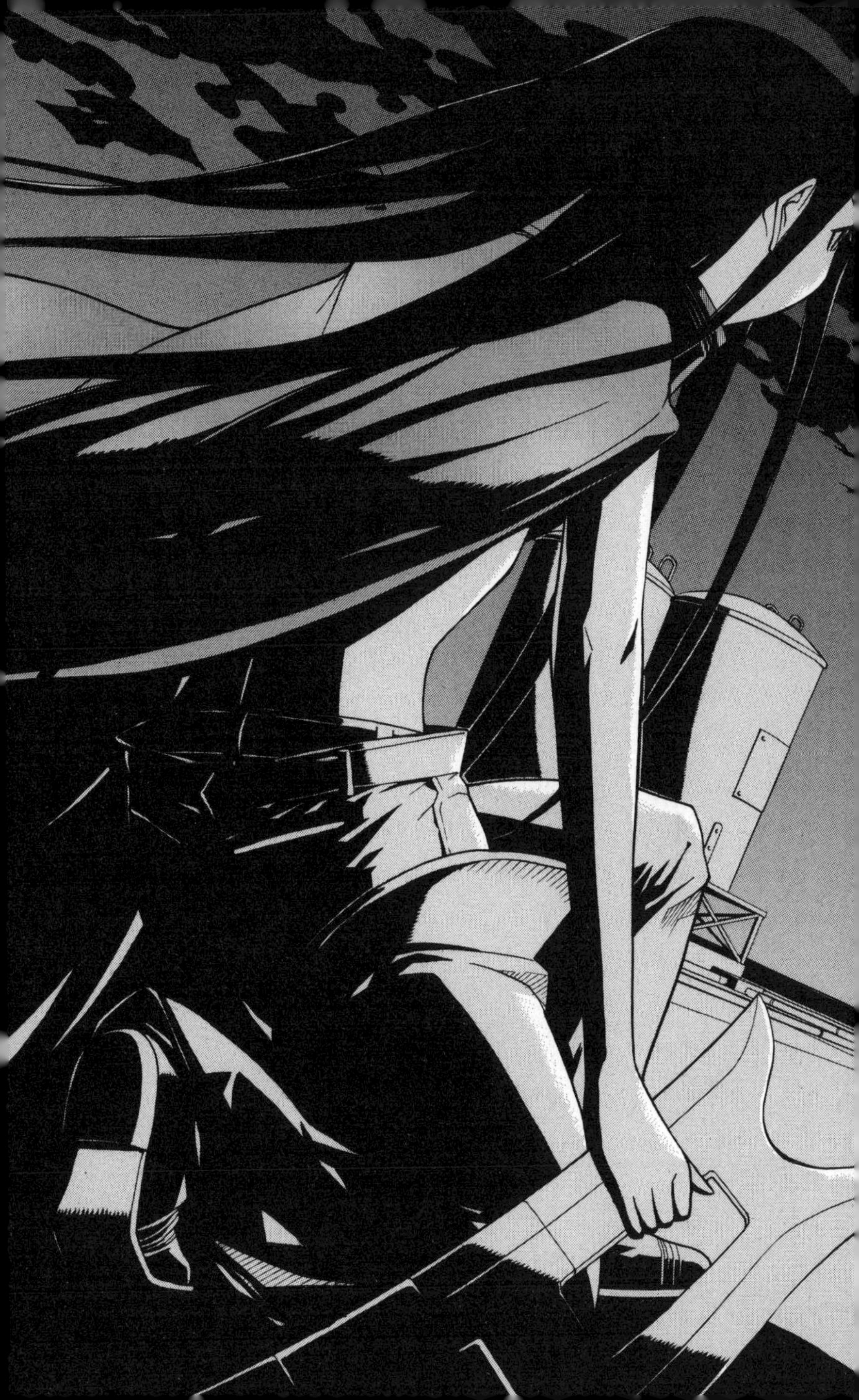

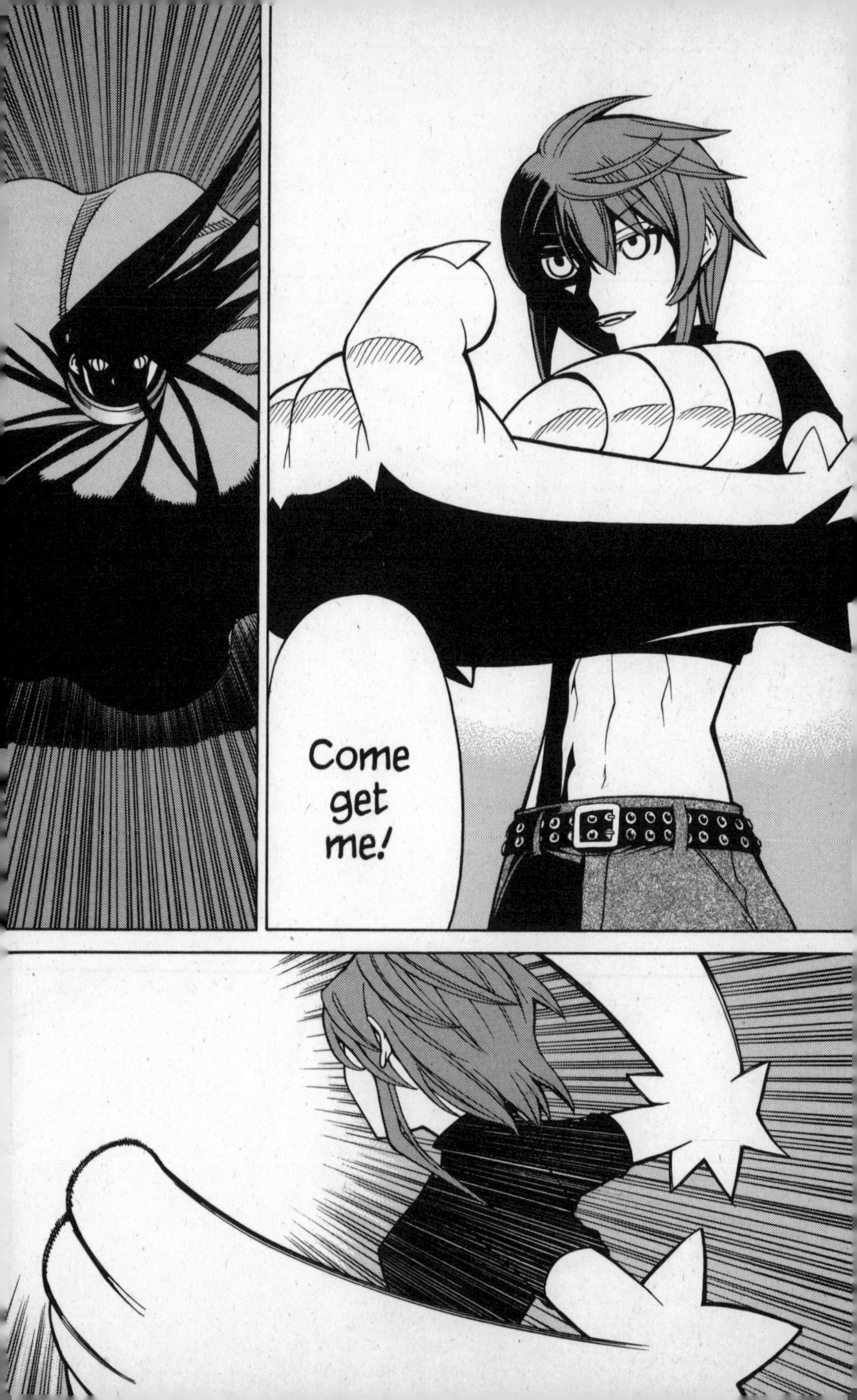
Come get me!

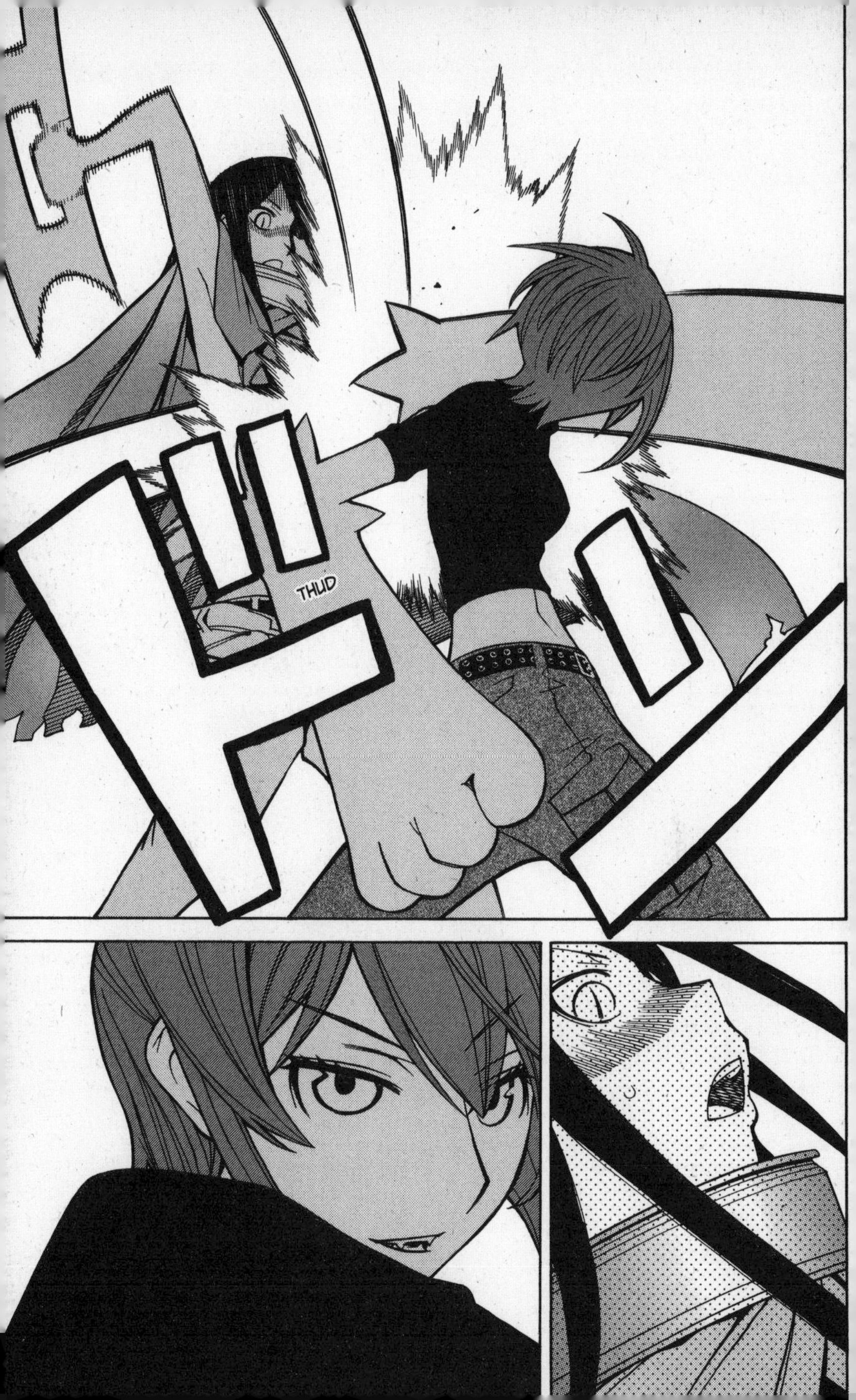
THUD

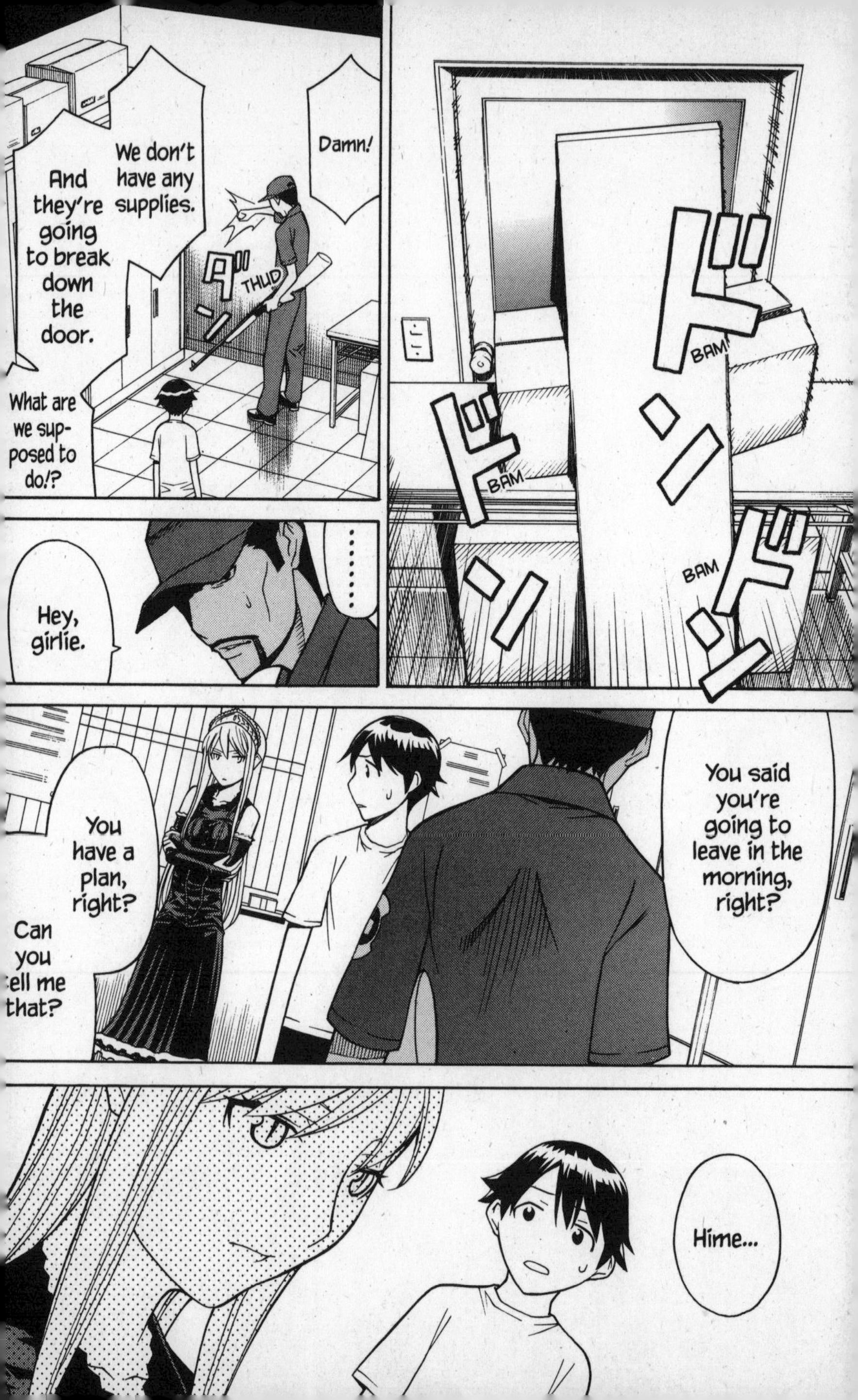
BAM
BAM
BAM
Damn!
We don't have any supplies.
And they're going to break down the door.
THUD
What are we supposed to do!?
......
Hey, girlie.
You said you're going to leave in the morning, right?
You have a plan, right?
Can you
ell me that?
Hime...

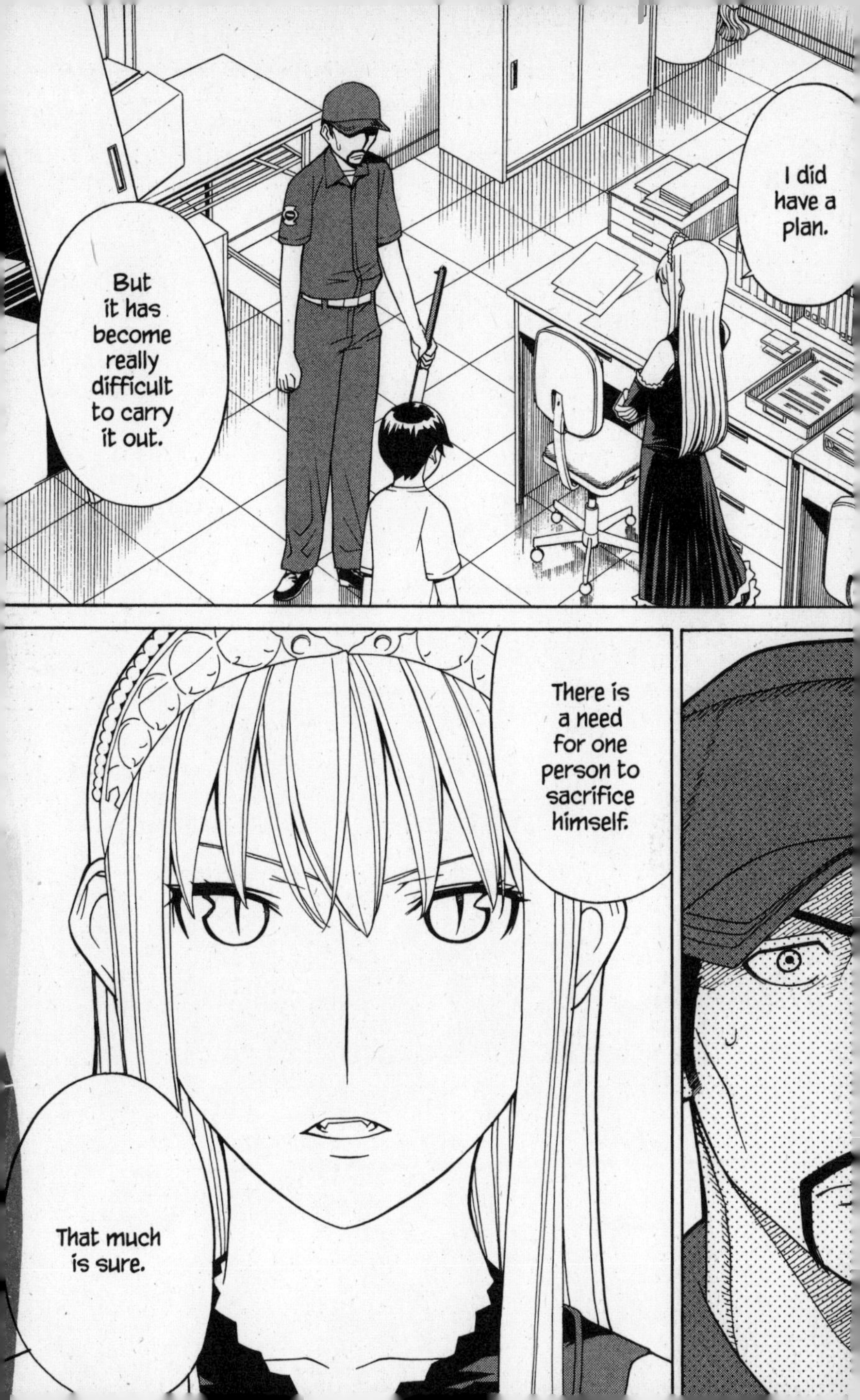
I did have a plan.
But it has become really difficult to carry it out.
There is a need for one person to sacrifice himself.
That much is sure.

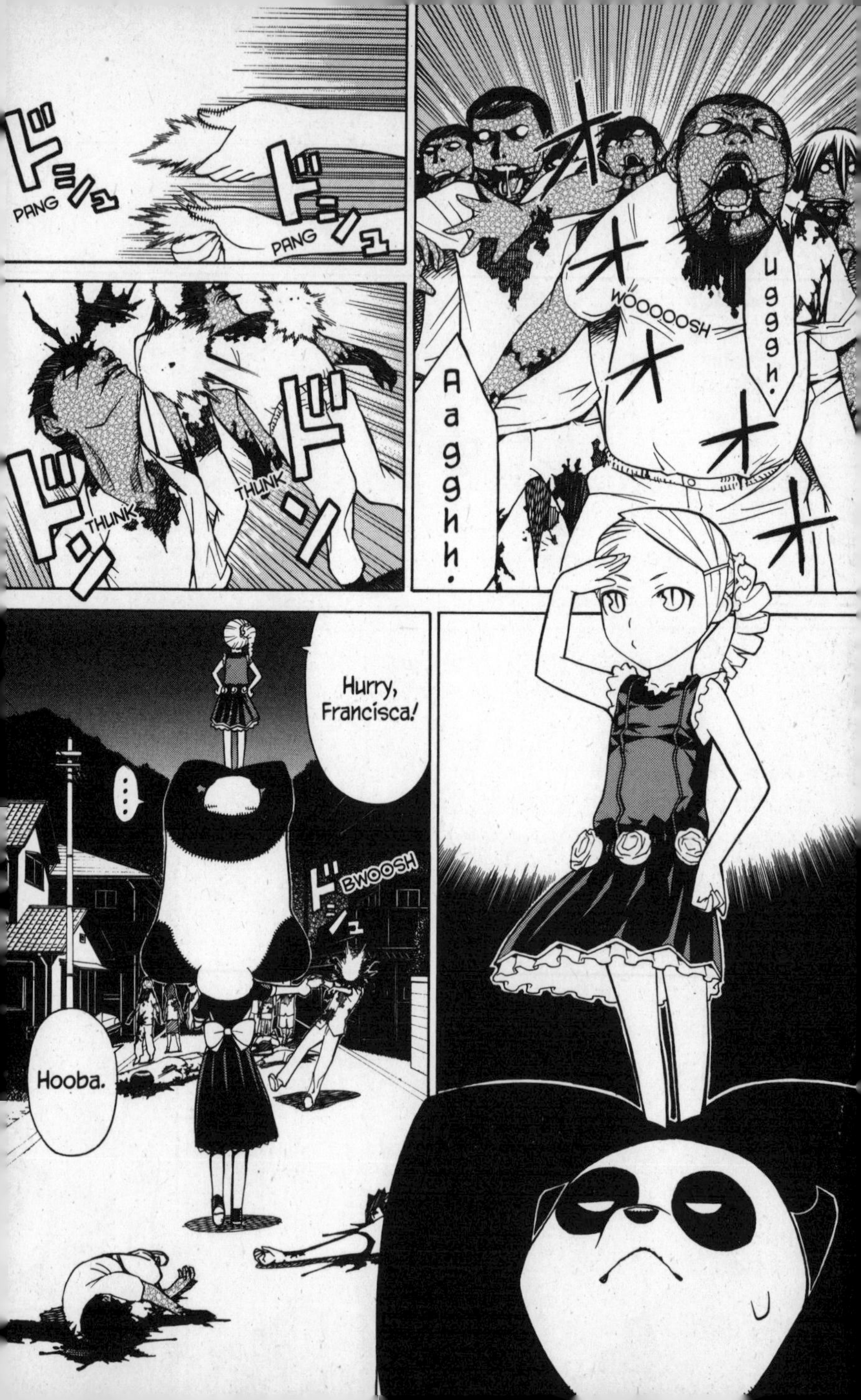

オオオオオ
WOOOOOSH
Ugggh.
Aagghh.
ドシュ
PANG
ドシュ
PANG
ドッ
THUNK
ドッ
THUNK
Hurry, Francisca!
...
ドシュ
BWOOSH
Hooba.

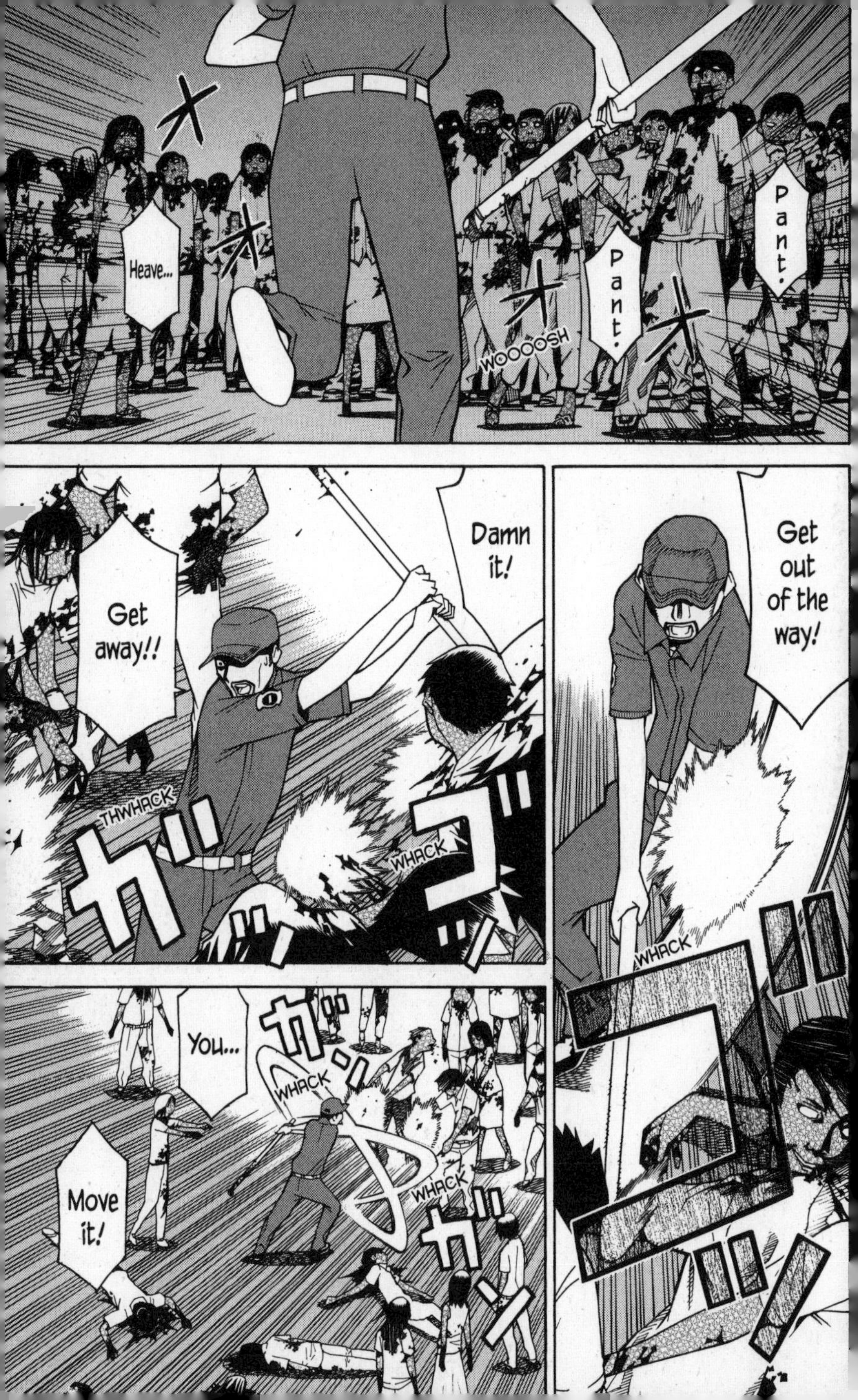
Pant.
Pant.
WOOOOSH
Heave...
Get out of the way!
WHACK
Damn it!
Get away!!
WHACK
THWHACK
You...
WHACK
WHACK
Move it!

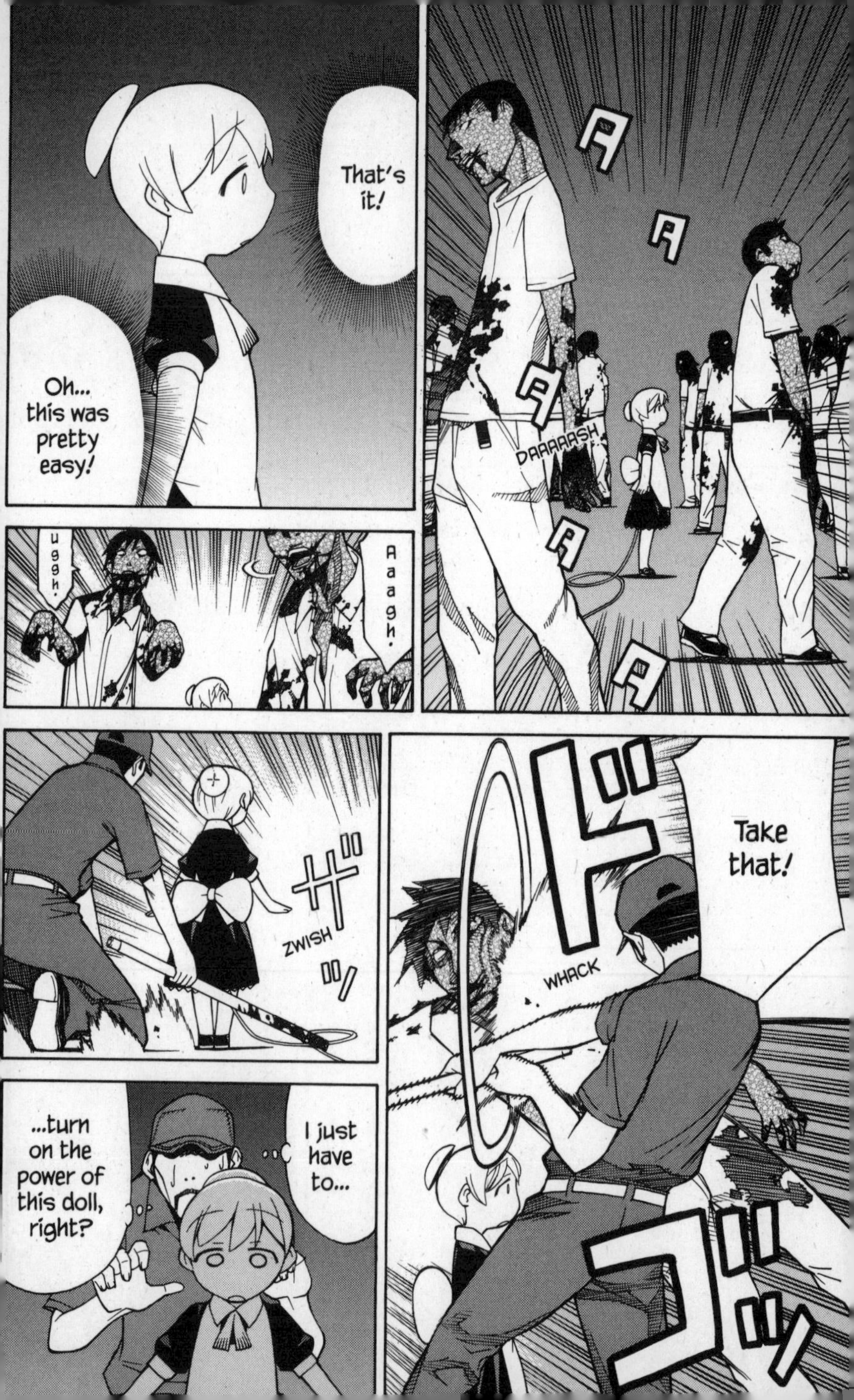

A
A
A
A
A
DAAAAASH
That's it!
Oh... this was pretty easy!
Aaagh.
ugggh.
ド
WHACK
Take that!
ゴッ
ザッ
ZWISH
I just have to...
...turn on the power of this doll, right?

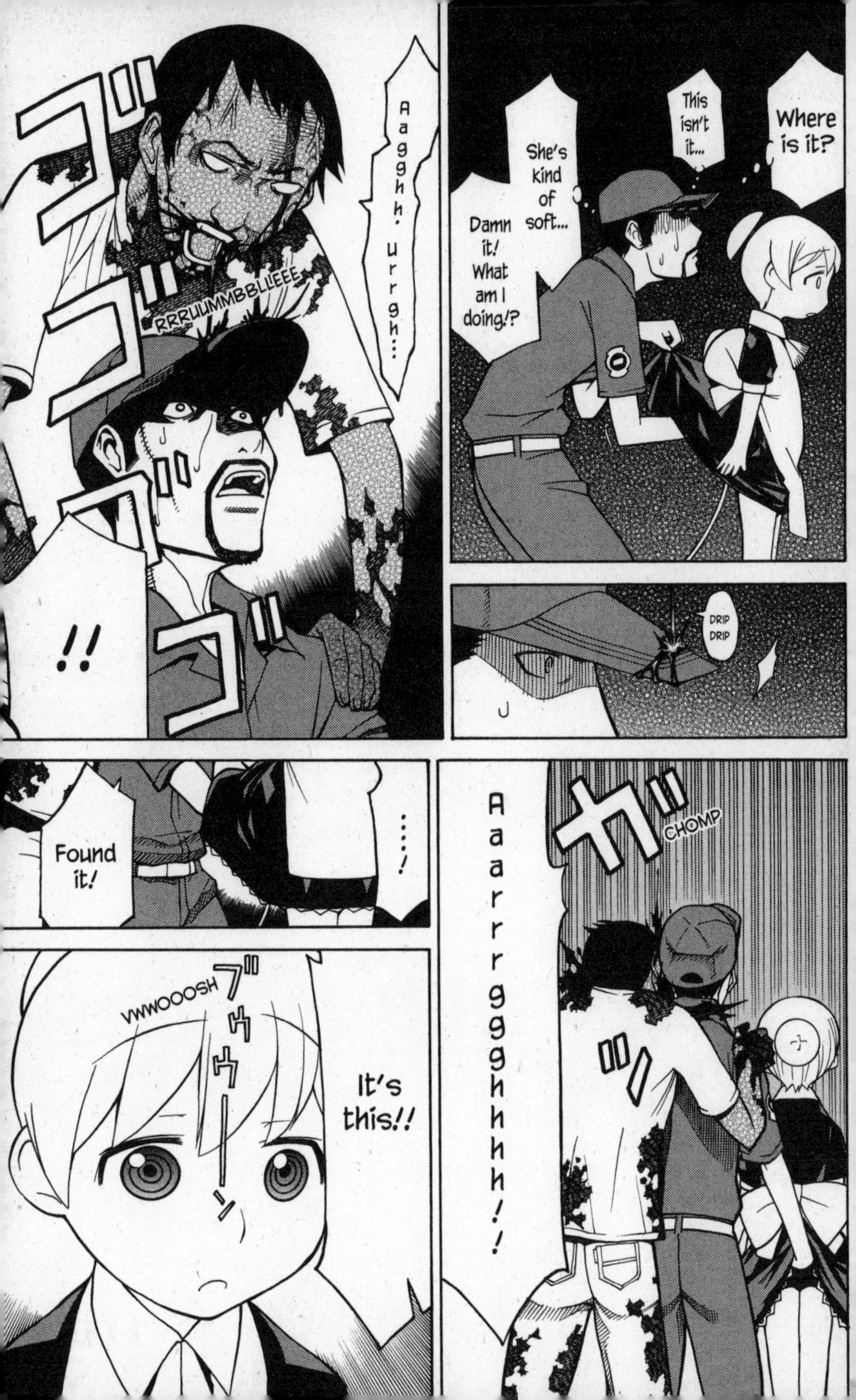
Where is it?
This isn't it...
She's kind of soft...
Damn it! What am I doing!?
DRIP DRIP
Aagghh. Urrgh...
RRRUUMMBBLLIEEE
!!
CHOMP
Aaarrrggghhhhh!!
...!
Found it!
It's this!!
VWWOOOSH

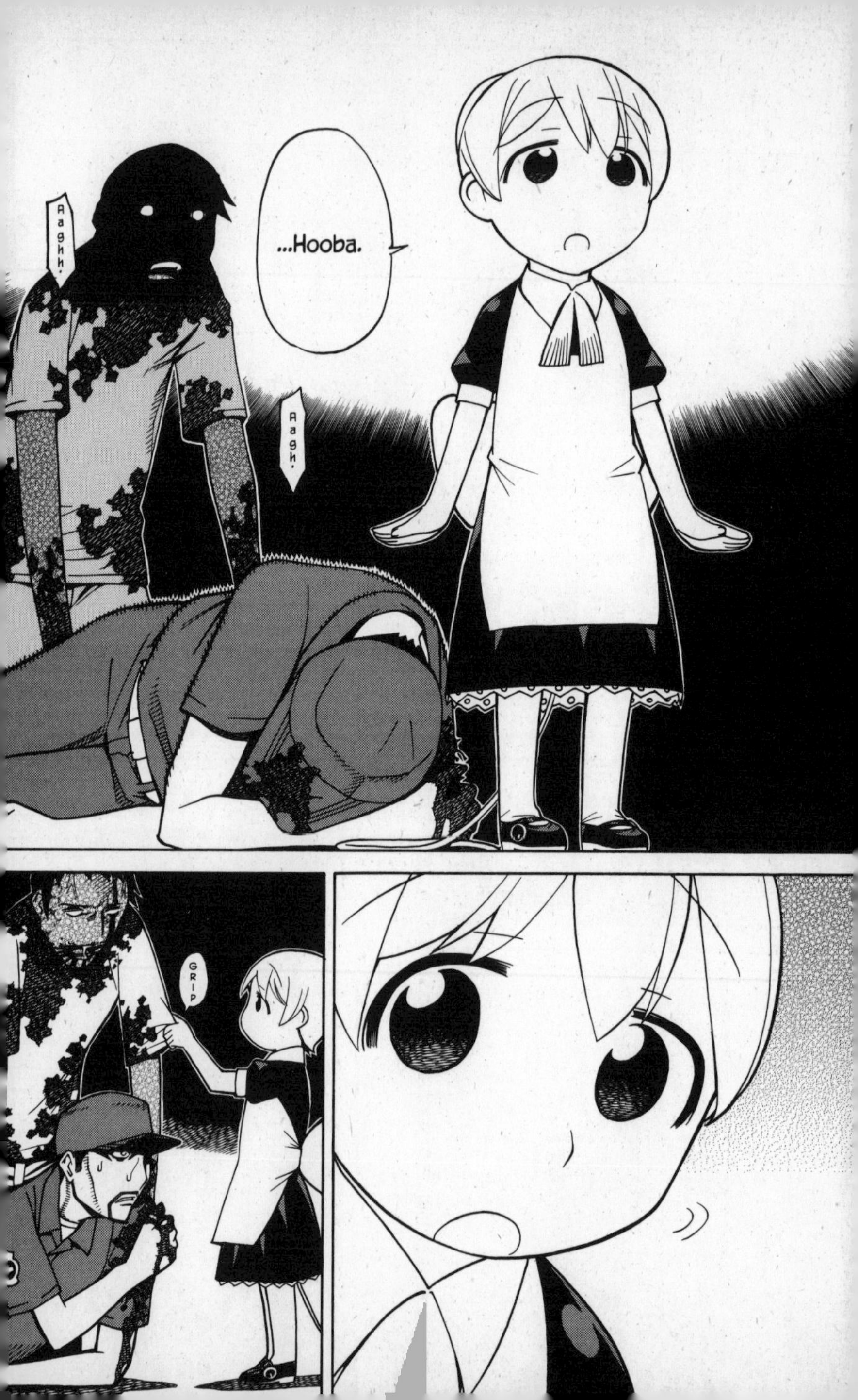
...Hooba.
Aagh.
Aagh.
GRIP

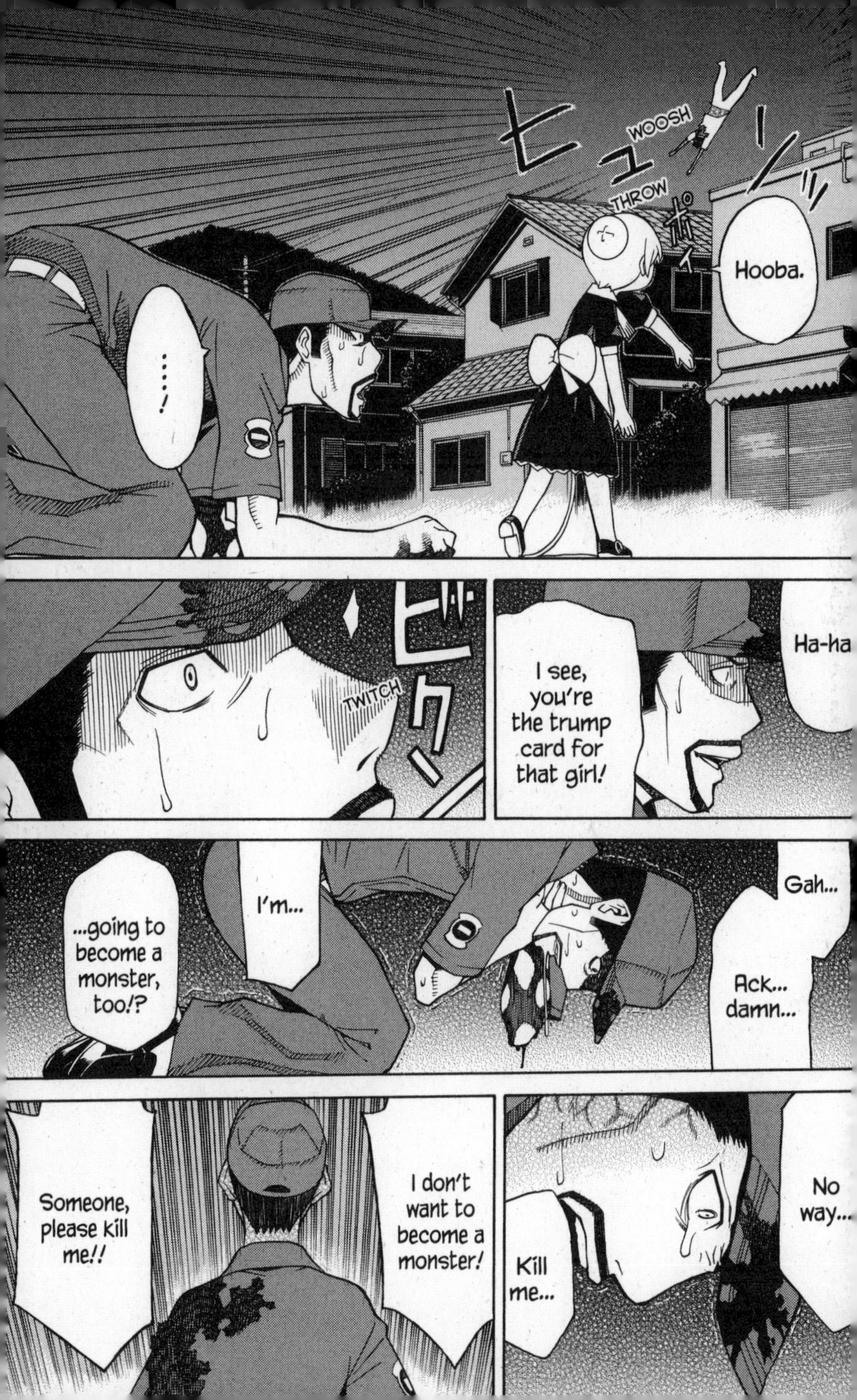
WOOSH
THROW
Hooba.
.....!
Ha-ha
I see, you're the trump card for that girl!
TWITCH
Gah...
Ack... damn...
I'm...
...going to become a monster, too!?
No way...
Kill me...
I don't want to become a monster!
Someone, please kill me!!

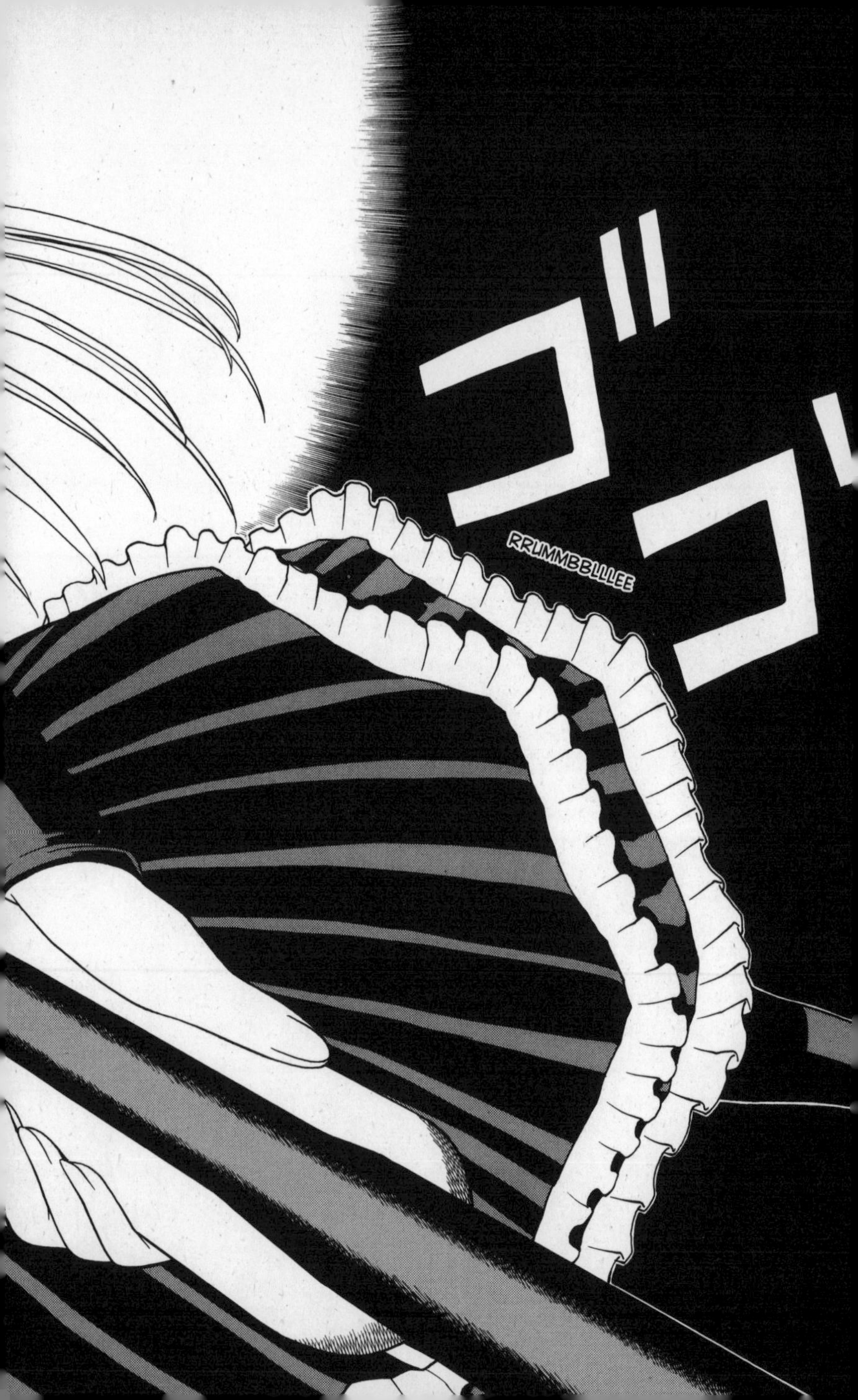
ゴゴ
RRUMMBBLLLEE

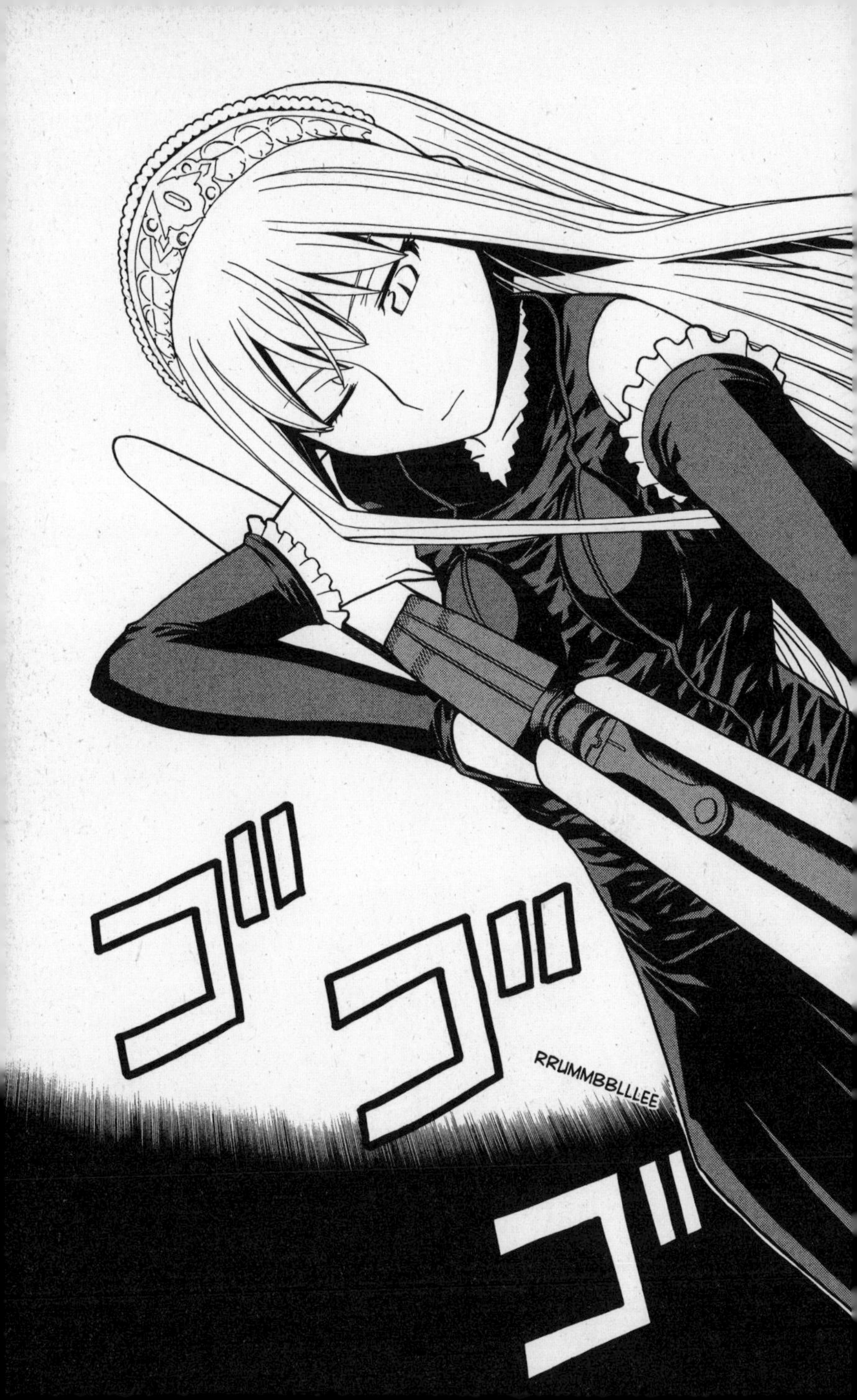
ゴゴゴ
RRUMMBBLLLEE

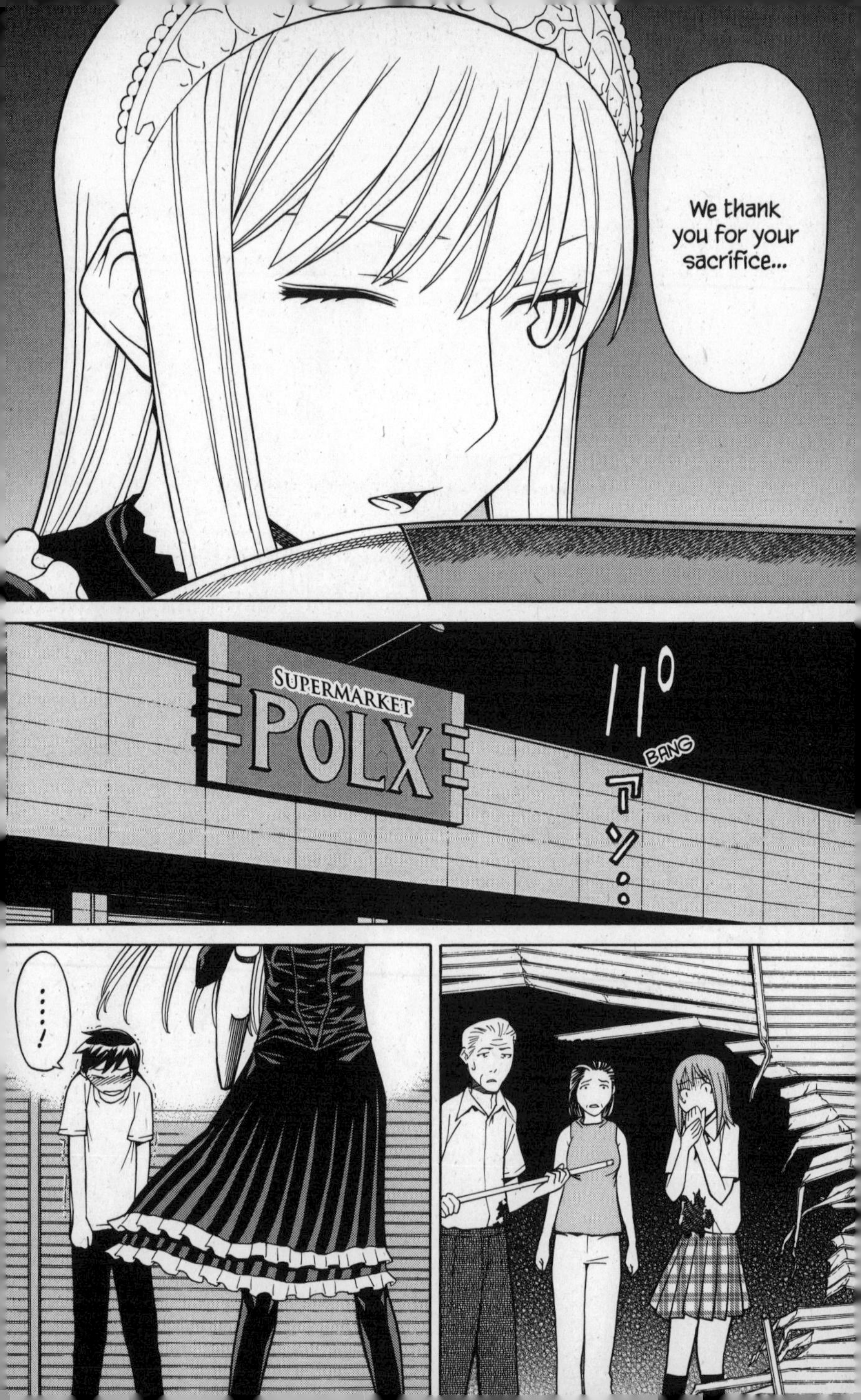
We thank you for your sacrifice...
SUPERMARKET POLX
BANG
....!

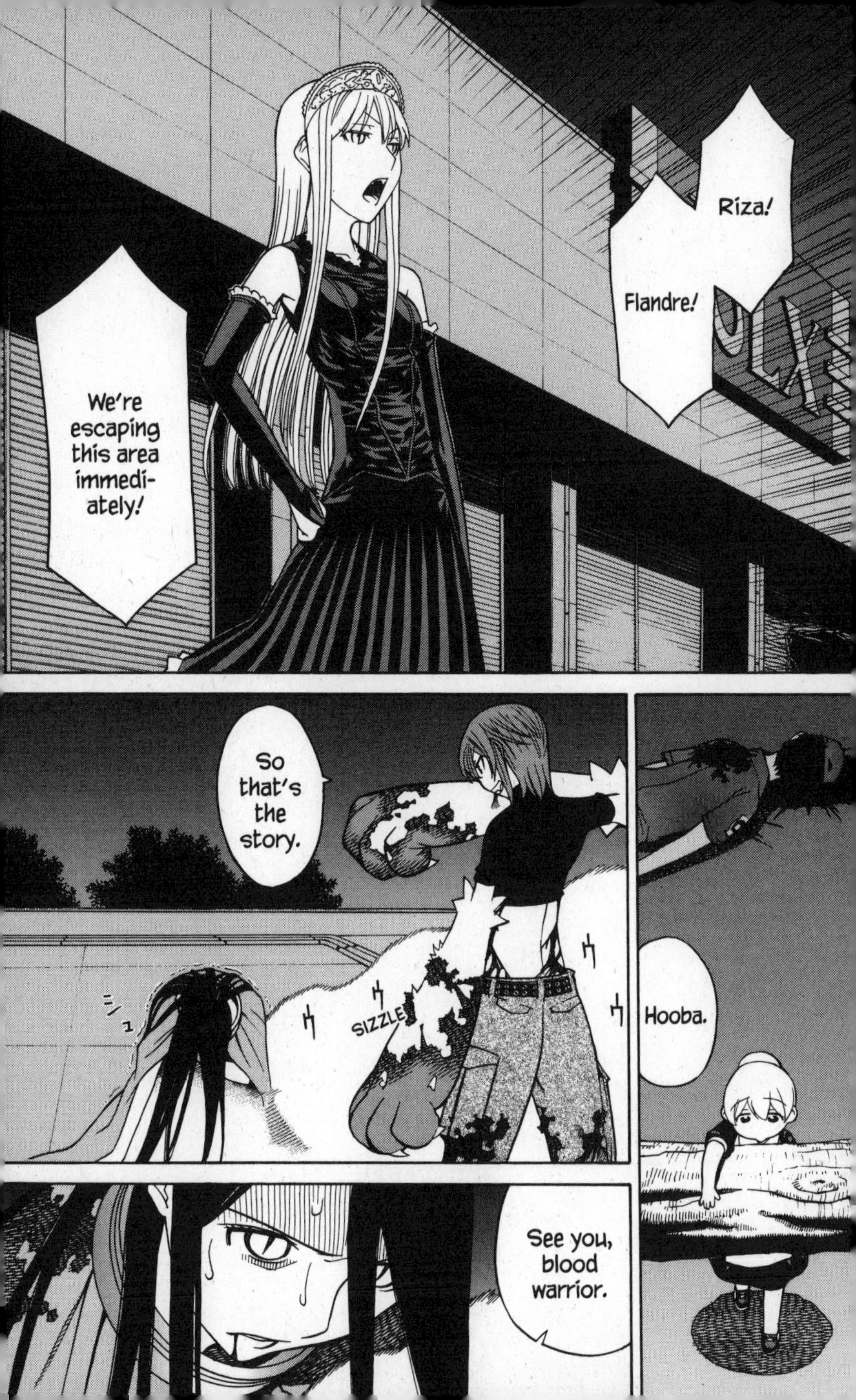
Riza!
Flandre!
We're escaping this area immedi-ately!
Hooba.
So that's the story.
SIZZLE
See you, blood warrior.

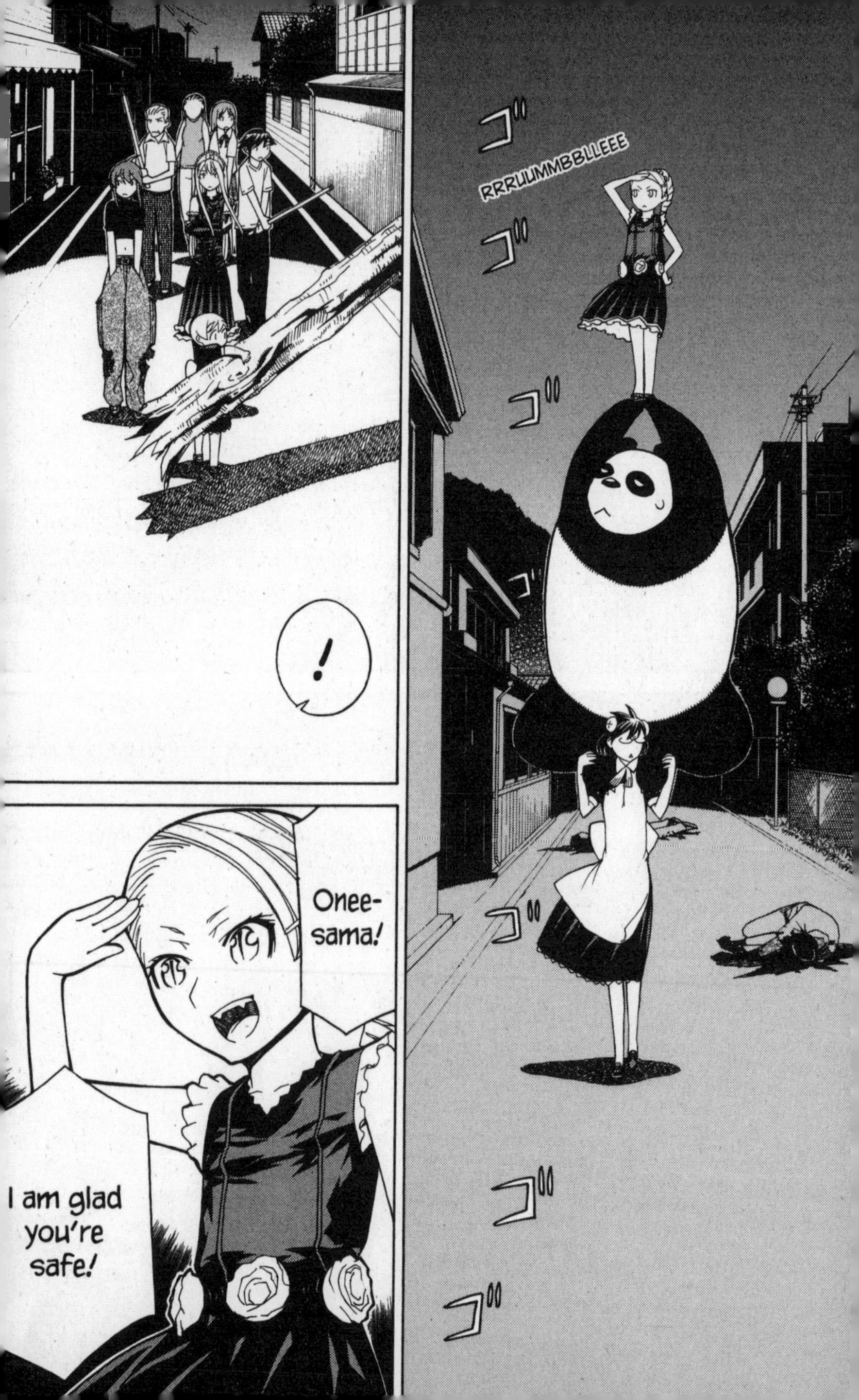

ゴ
RRRUUMMBBLLEEE
ゴ
ゴ
ゴ
ゴ
ゴ
ゴ
!
Onee-sama!
I am glad you're safe!

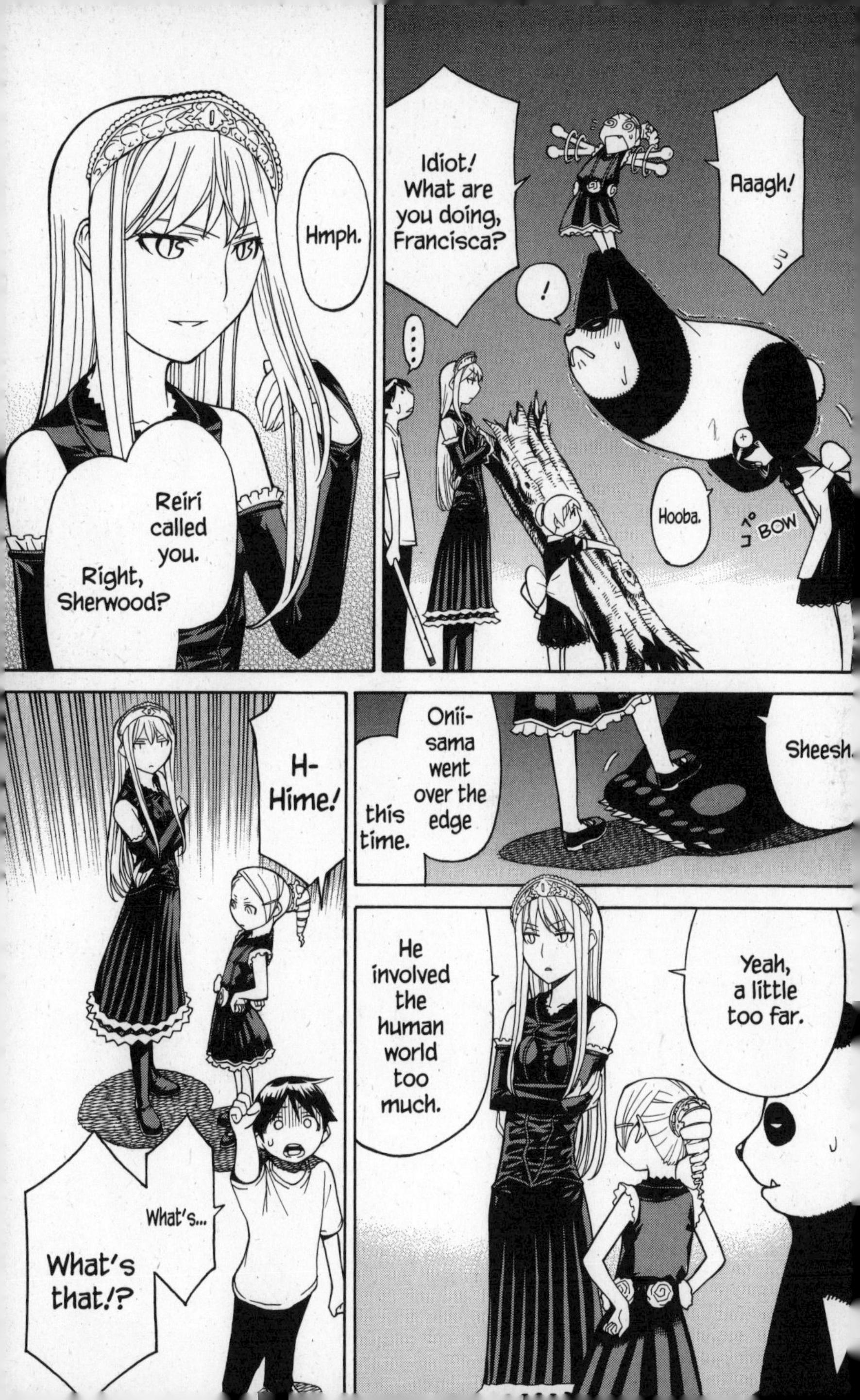
Aaagh!
Idiot! What are you doing, Francisca?
!
...
BOW
ペコ
Hooba.
Hmph.
Reiri called you. Right, Sherwood?
Sheesh.
Onii-sama went over the edge this time.
Yeah, a little too far.
He involved the human world too much.
H-Hime!
What's...
What's that!?

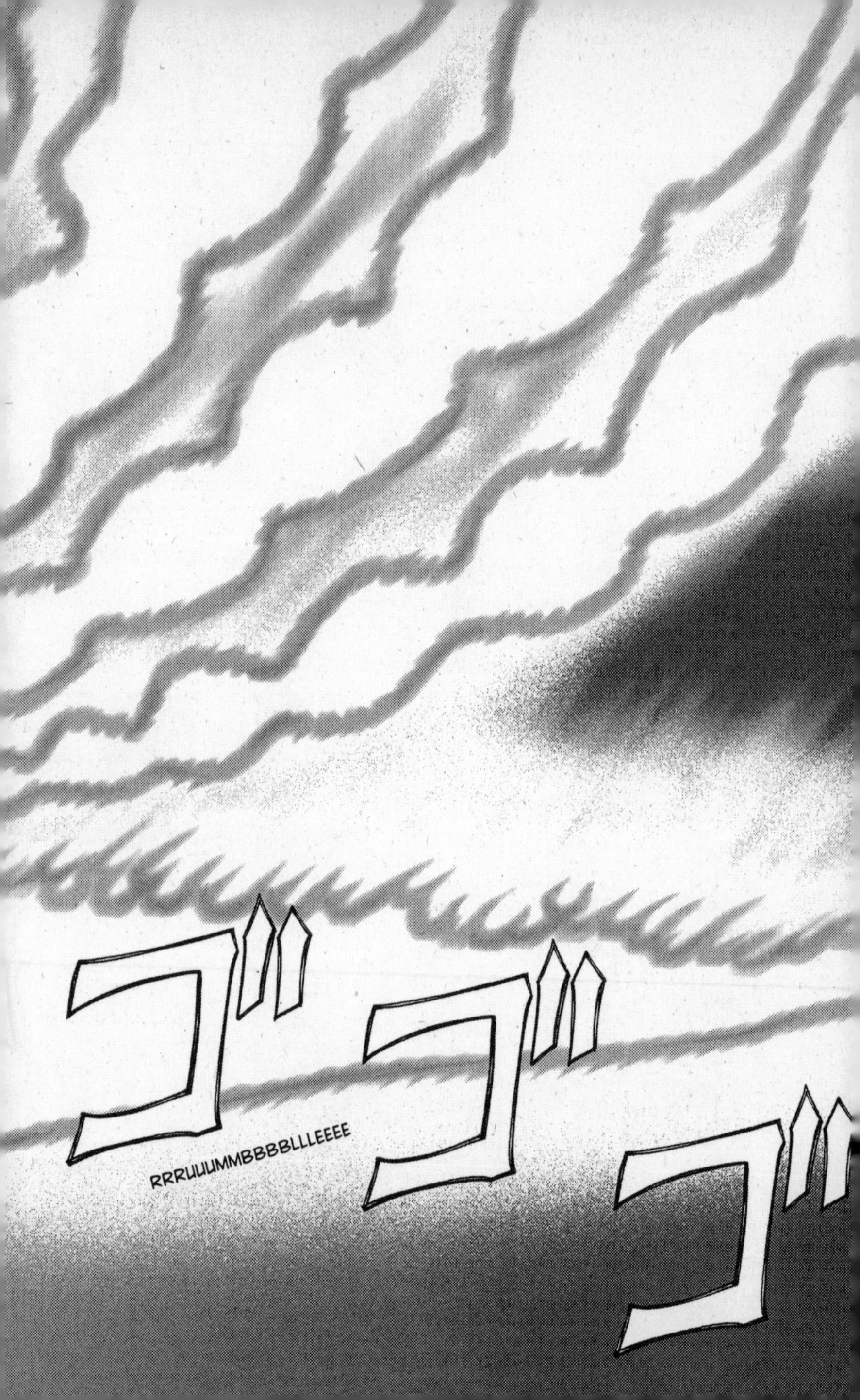
ゴゴゴ
RRRUUUMMBBBBLLLEEEE

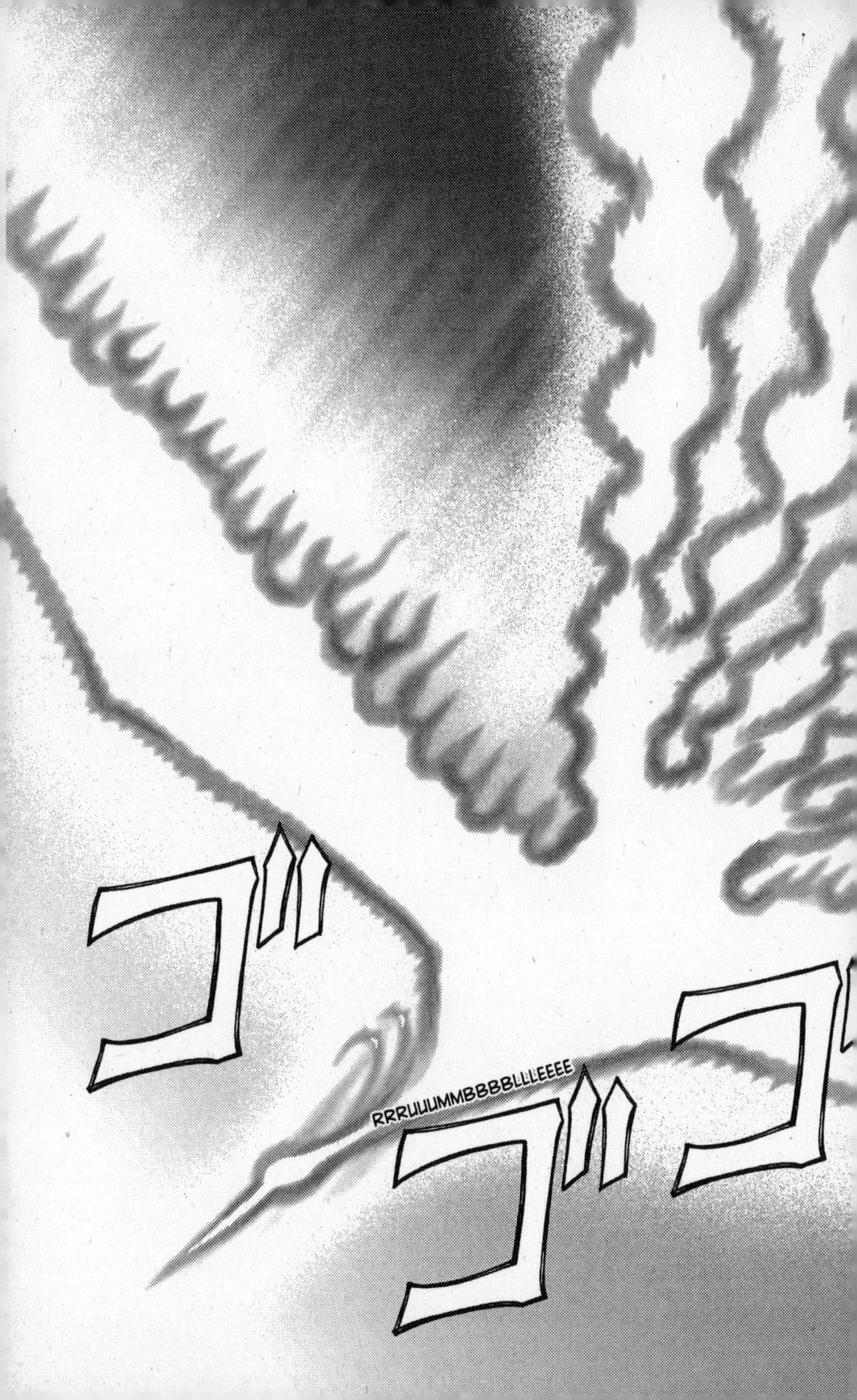
ゴゴゴ
RRRUUUMMBBBBLLLEEEE

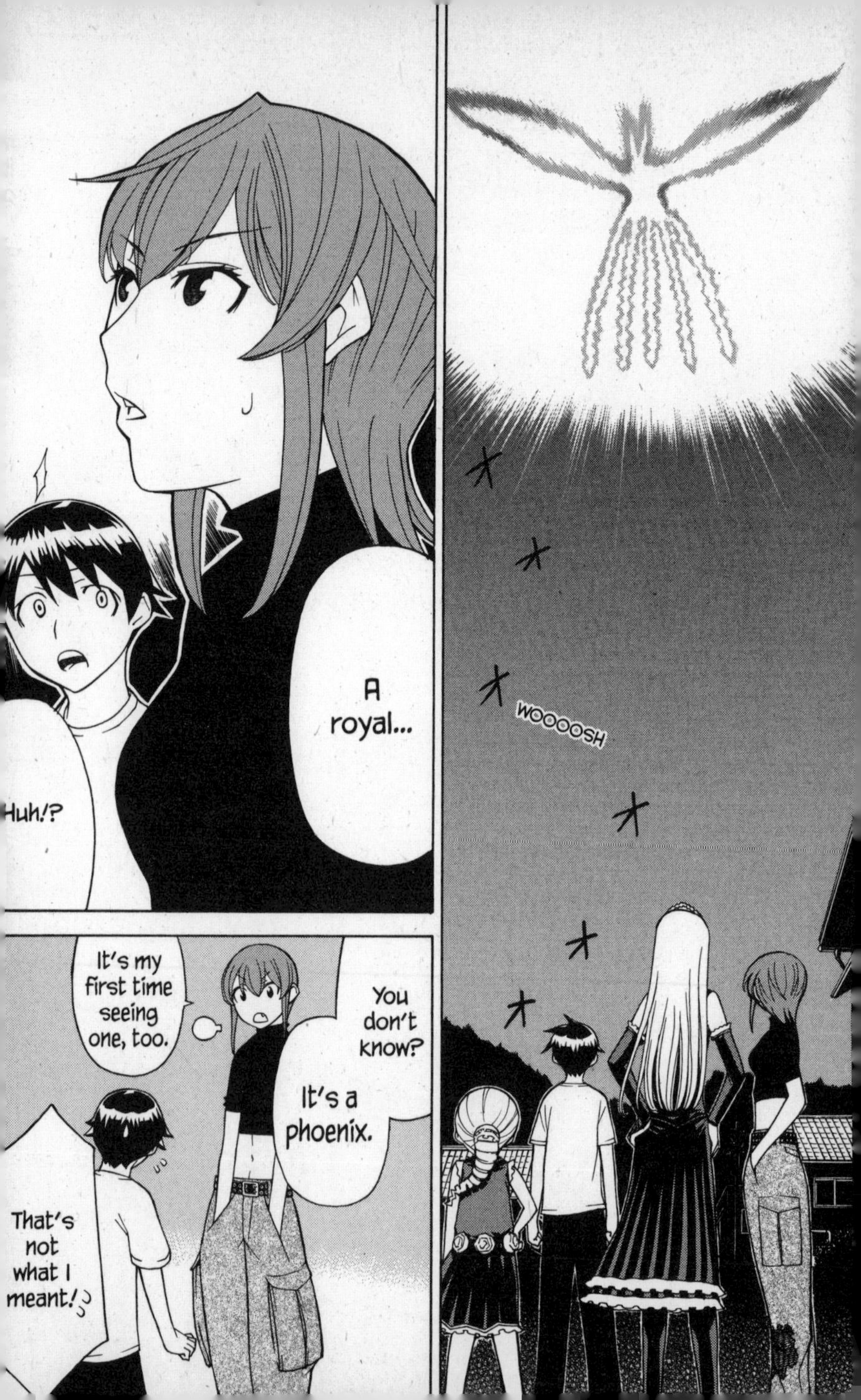
WOOOOSH
A royal...
Huh!?
You don't know?
It's a phoenix.
It's my first time seeing one, too.
That's not what I meant!

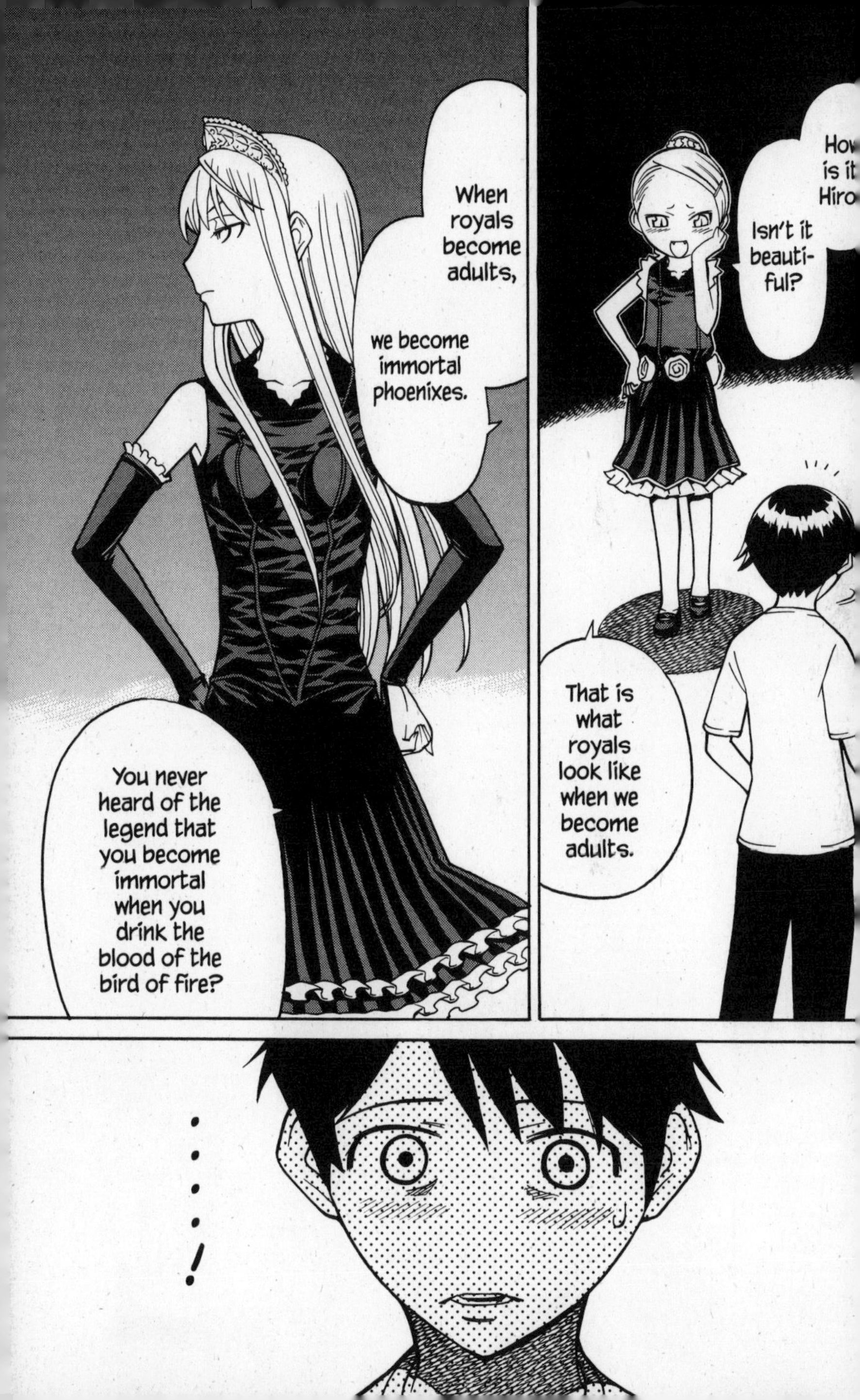
Ho is it Hiro
Isn't it beauti-ful?
That is what royals look like when we become adults.
When royals become adults,
we become immortal phoenixes.
You never heard of the legend that you become immortal when you drink the blood of the bird of fire?
....!

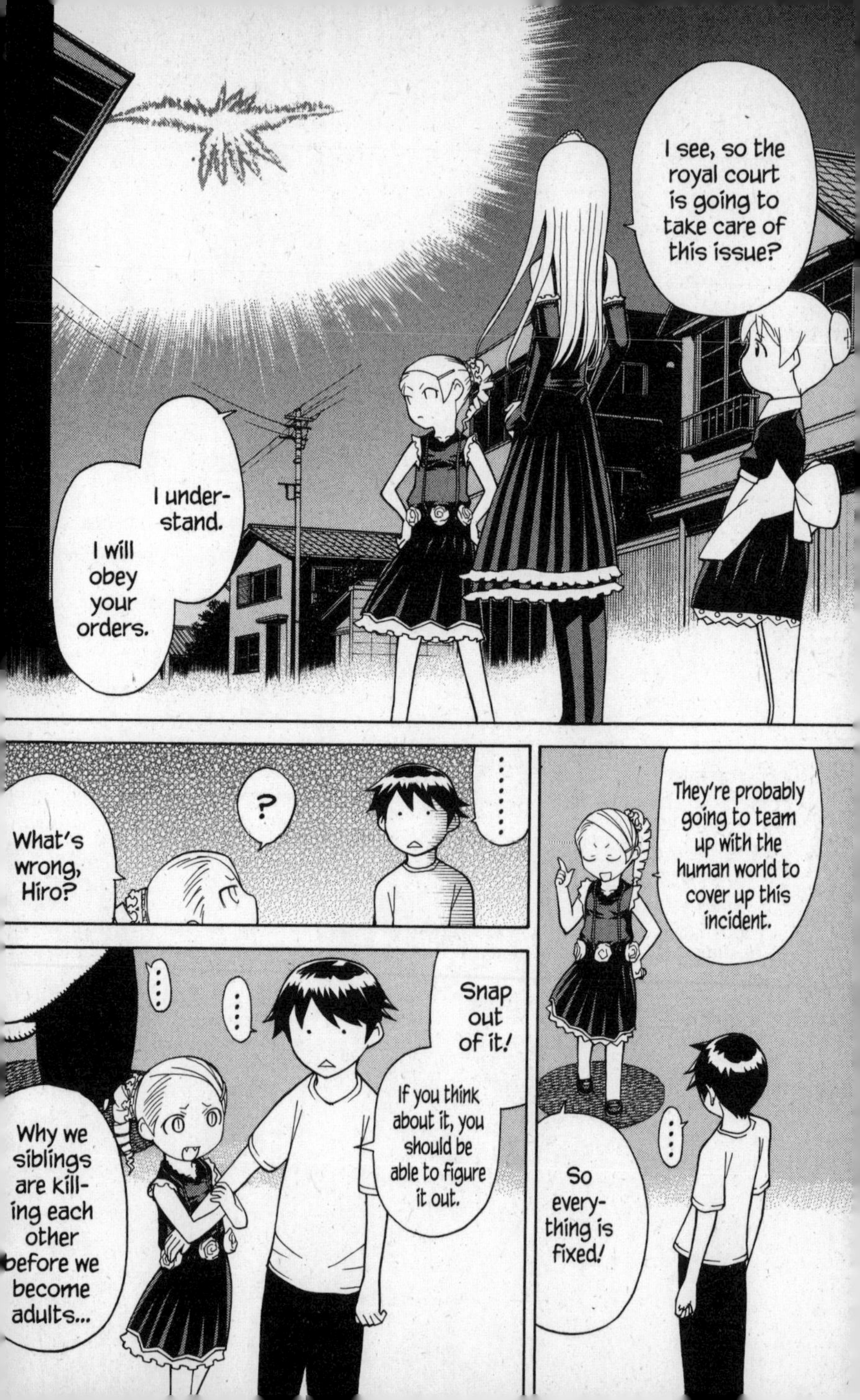
I see, so the royal court is going to take care of this issue?
I under-stand. I will obey your orders.
They're probably going to team up with the human world to cover up this incident.
...
So every-thing is fixed!
......
?
What's wrong, Hiro?
Snap out of it!
If you think about it, you should be able to figure it out.
...
...
Why we siblings are kill-ing each other before we become adults...

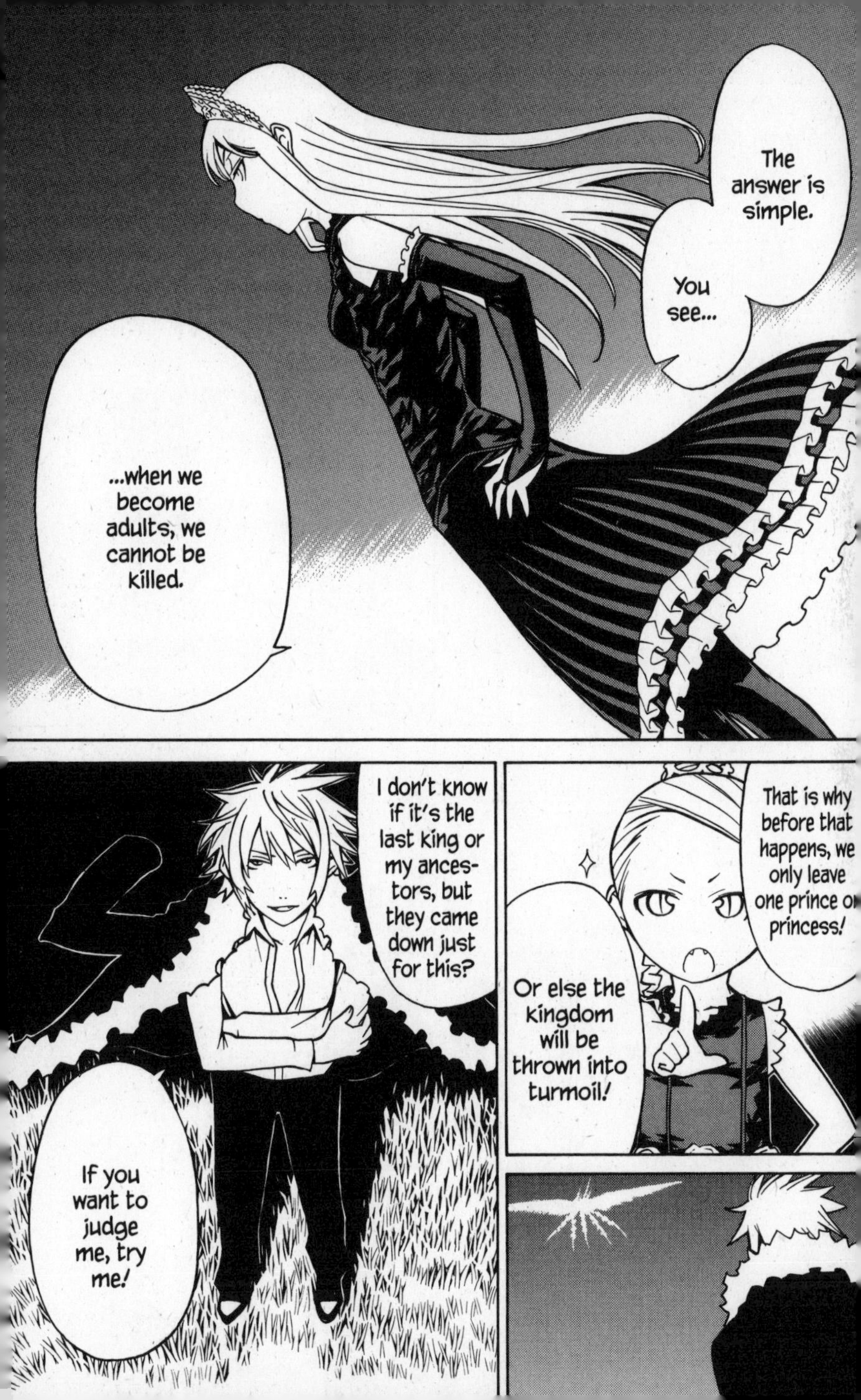
The answer is simple.
You see...
...when we become adults, we cannot be killed.
That is why before that happens, we only leave one prince or princess!
Or else the kingdom will be thrown into turmoil!
I don't know if it's the last king or my ancestors, but they came down just for this?
If you want to judge me, try me!

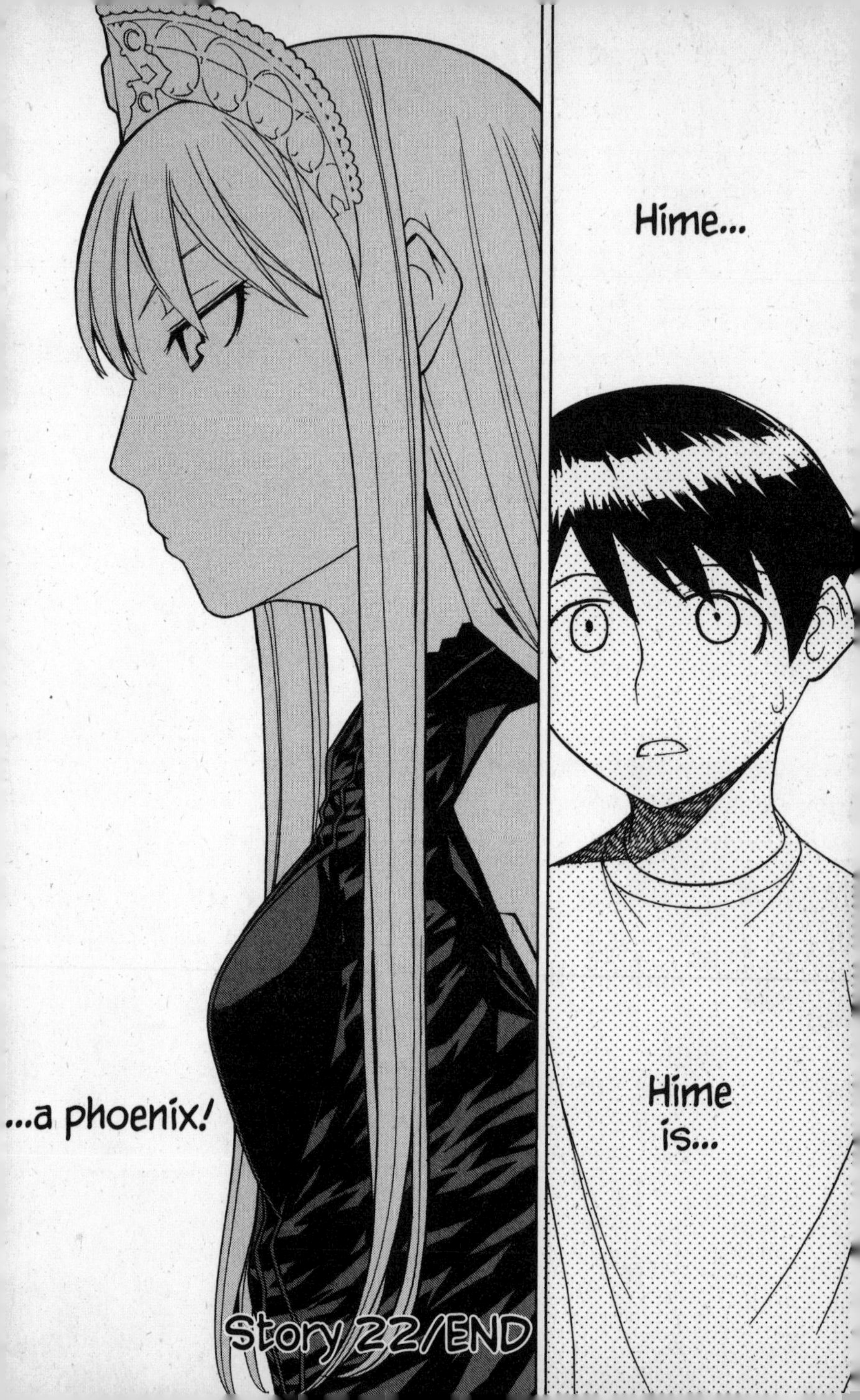
Hime...
Hime is...
...a phoenix!
Story 22/END

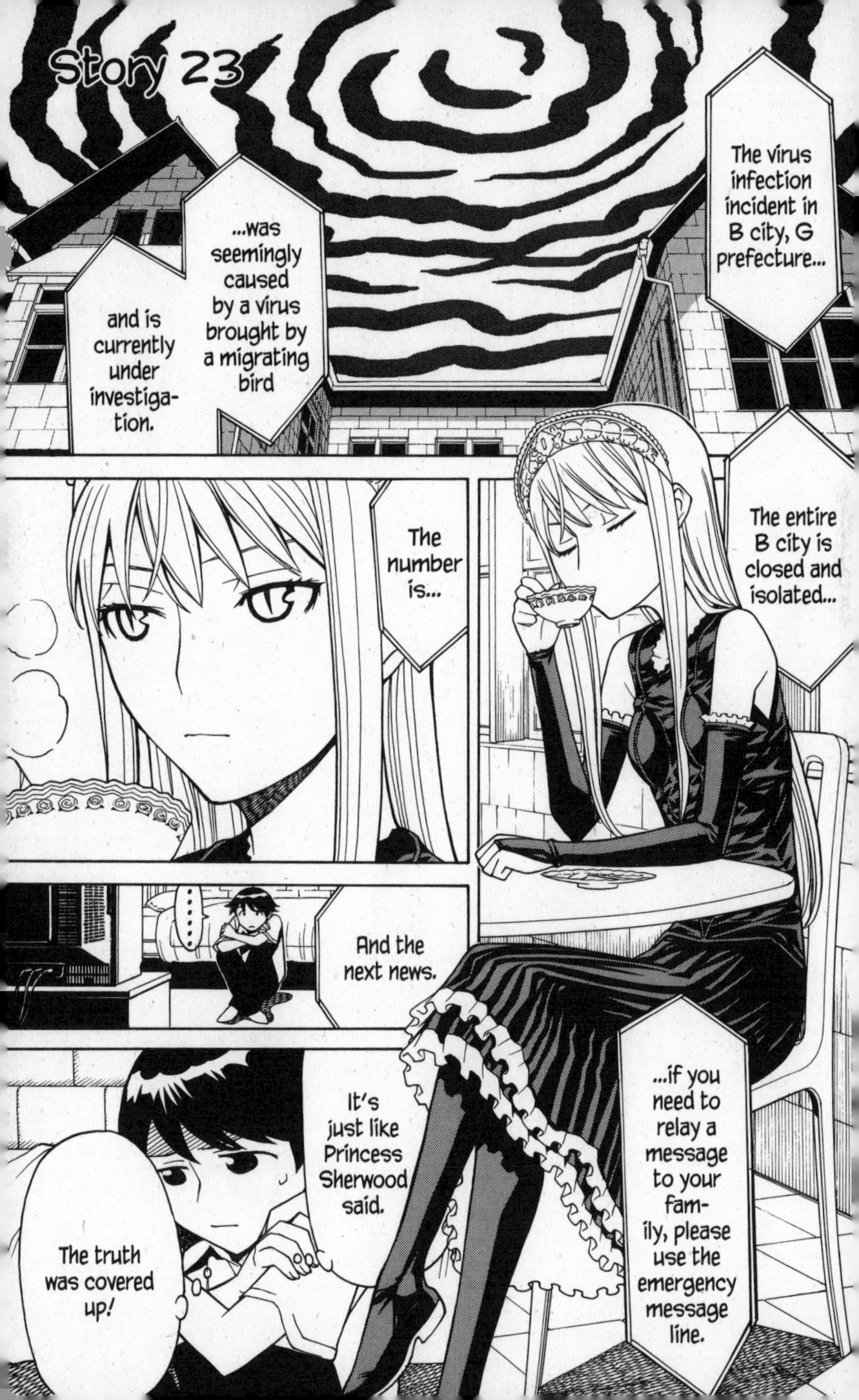
Story 23
The virus infection incident in B city, G prefecture...
...was seemingly caused by a virus brought by a migrating bird
and is currently under investigation.
The entire B city is closed and isolated...
...if you need to relay a message to your family, please use the emergency message line.
The number is...
And the next news.
It's just like Princess Sherwood said.
The truth was covered up!

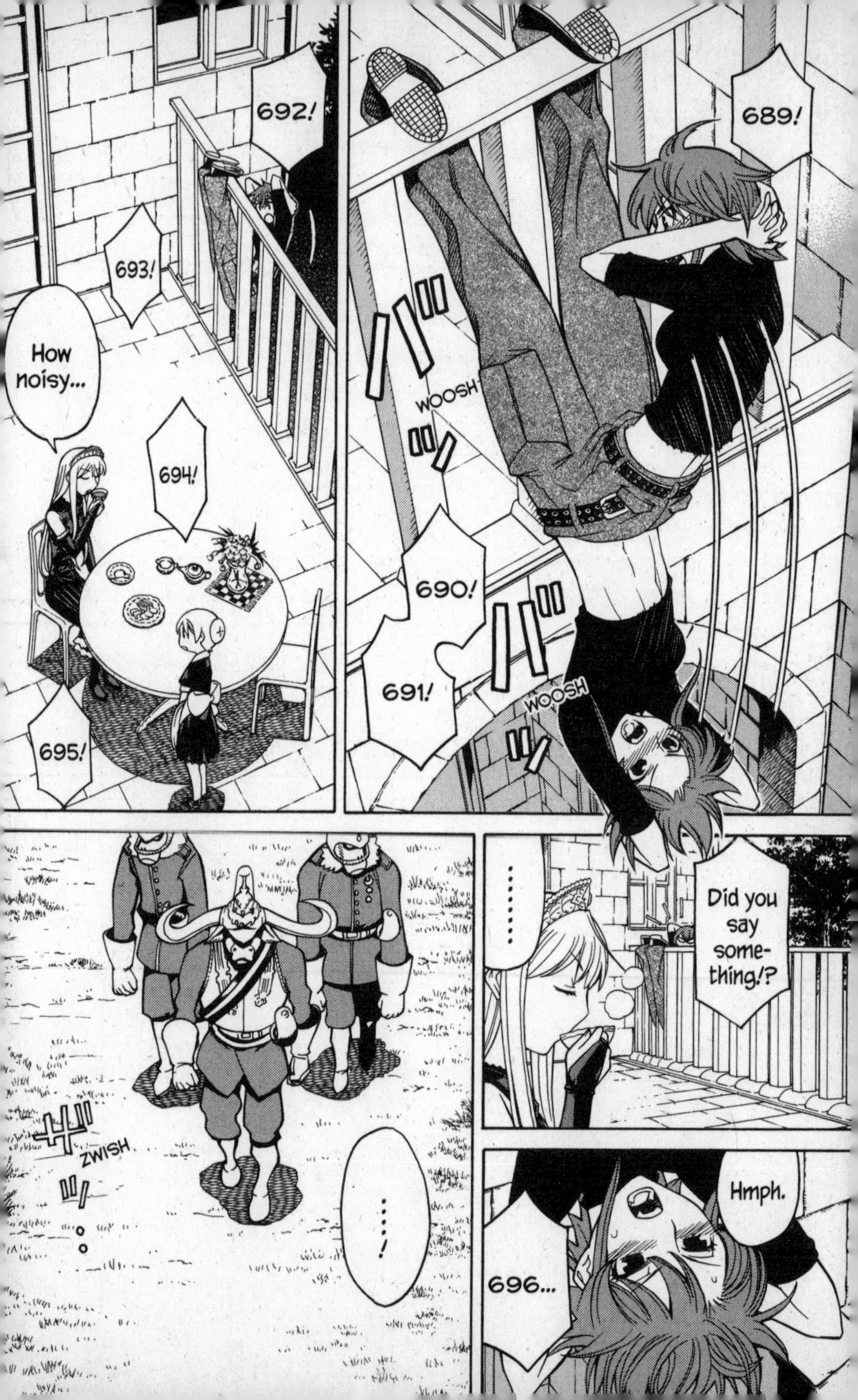
689!
WOOSH
690!
691!
WOOSH
692!
693!
How noisy...
694!
695!
Did you say some-thing!?
......
Hmph.
696...
ZWISH
....!

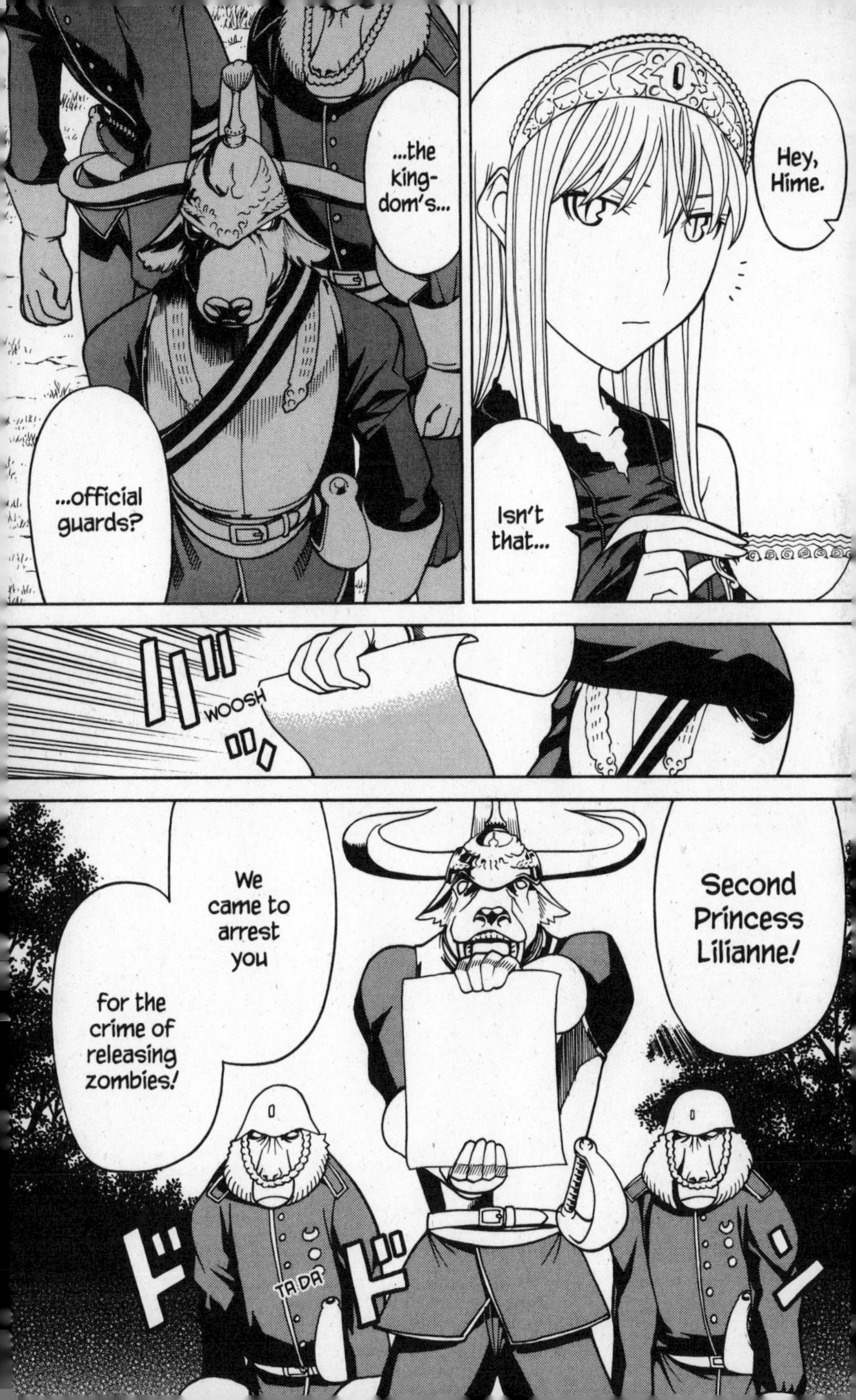
Hey, Hime.
Isn't that...
...the king-dom's...
...official guards?
WOOSH
Second Princess Lilianne!
We came to arrest you
for the crime of releasing zombies!
TA DA

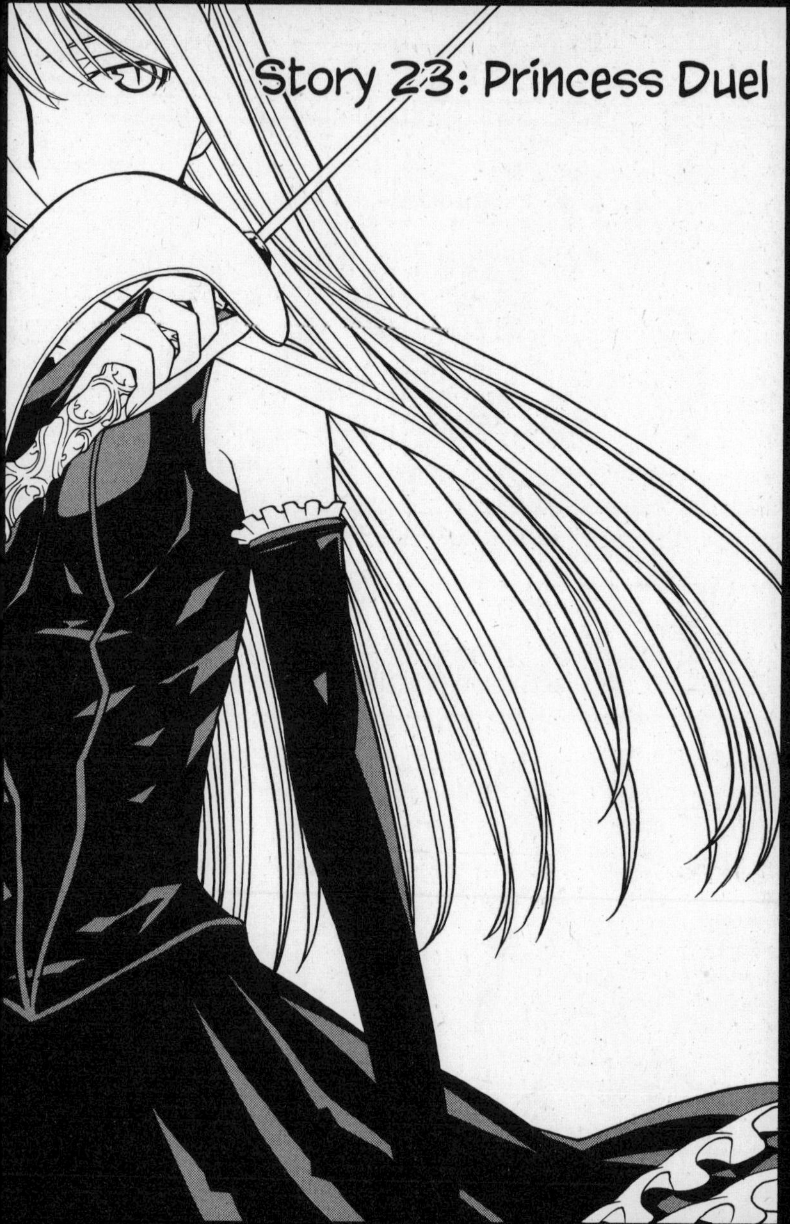
Story 23: Princess Duel

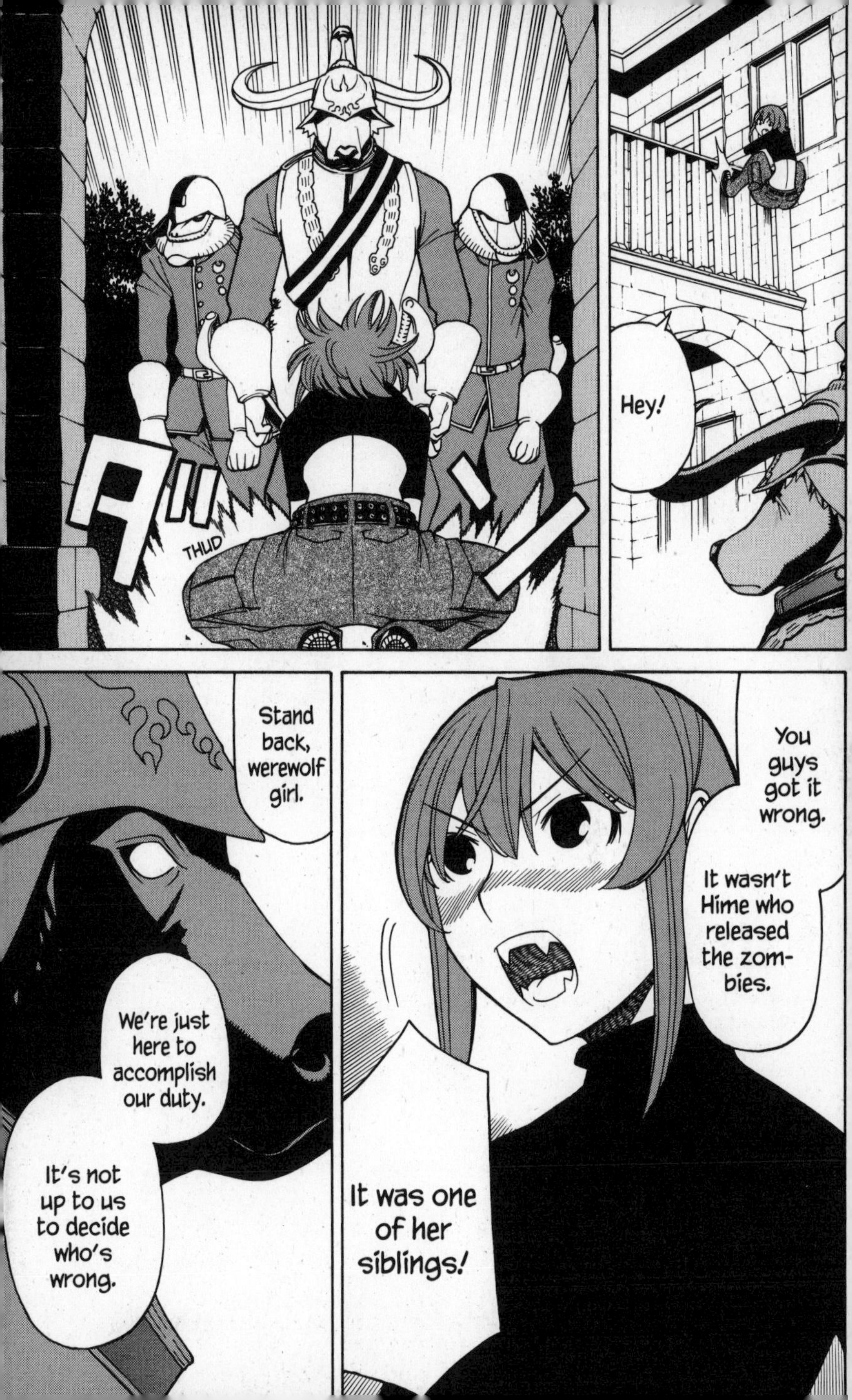
Hey!
THUD
You guys got it wrong.
It wasn't Hime who released the zom-bies.
It was one of her siblings!
Stand back, werewolf girl.
We're just here to accomplish our duty.
It's not up to us to decide who's wrong.

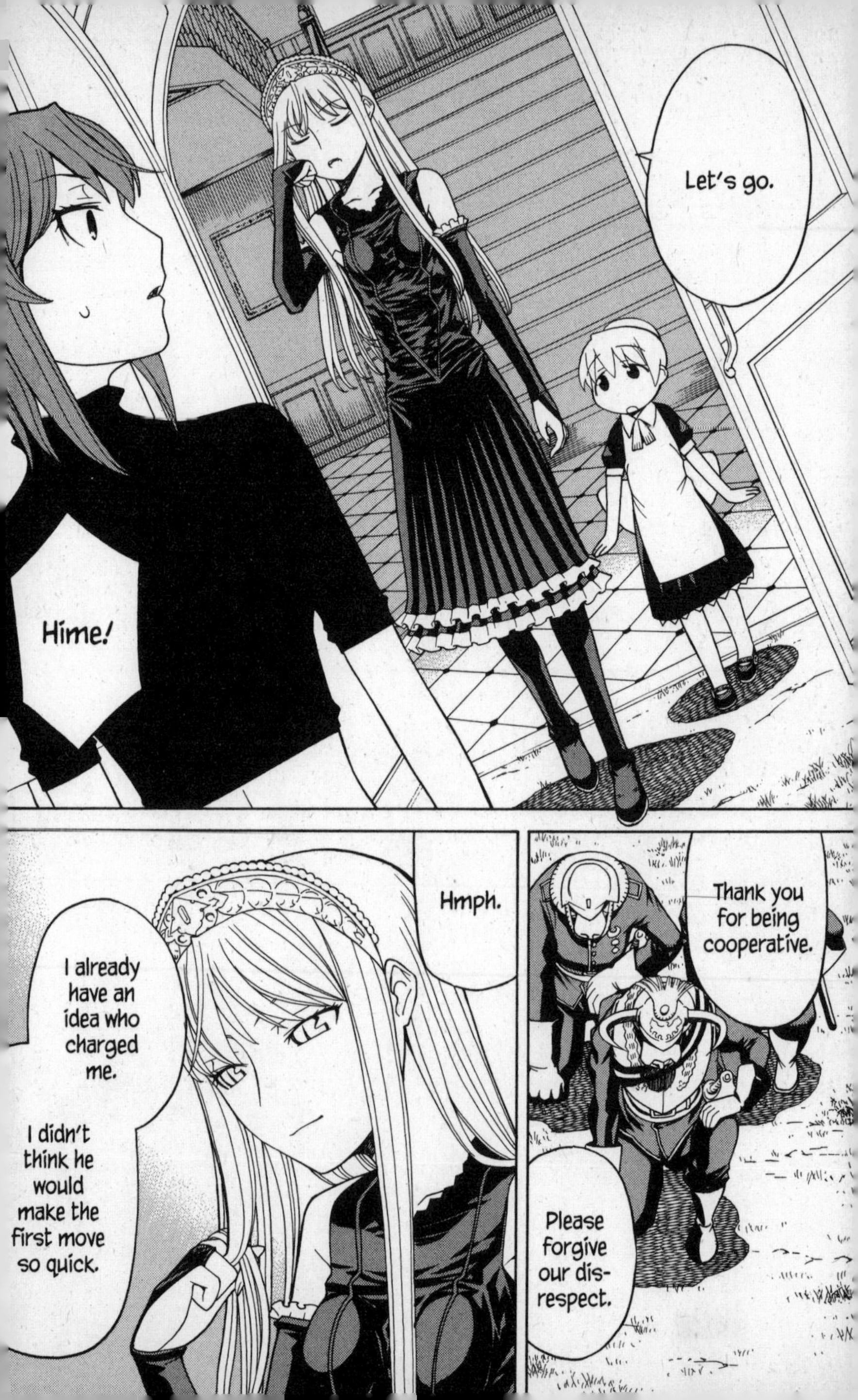
Let's go.
Hime!
Thank you for being cooperative.
Please forgive our dis-respect.
Hmph.
I already have an idea who charged me.
I didn't think he would make the first move so quick.

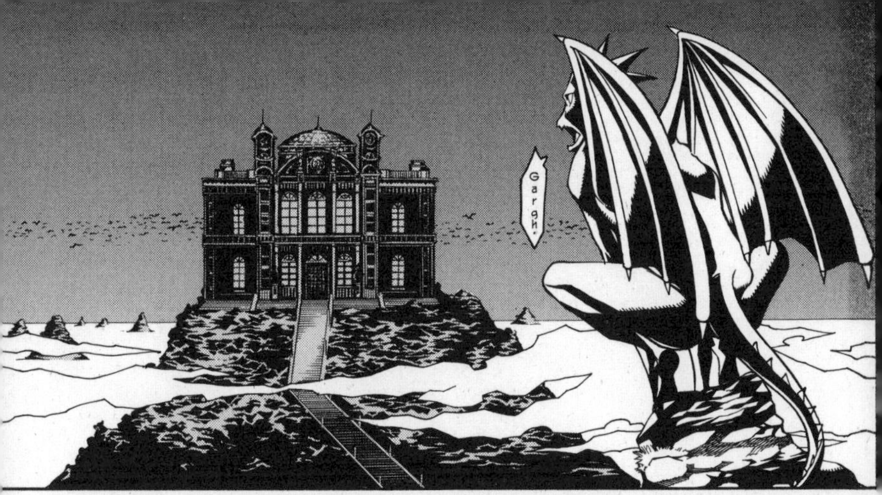
Gargh.

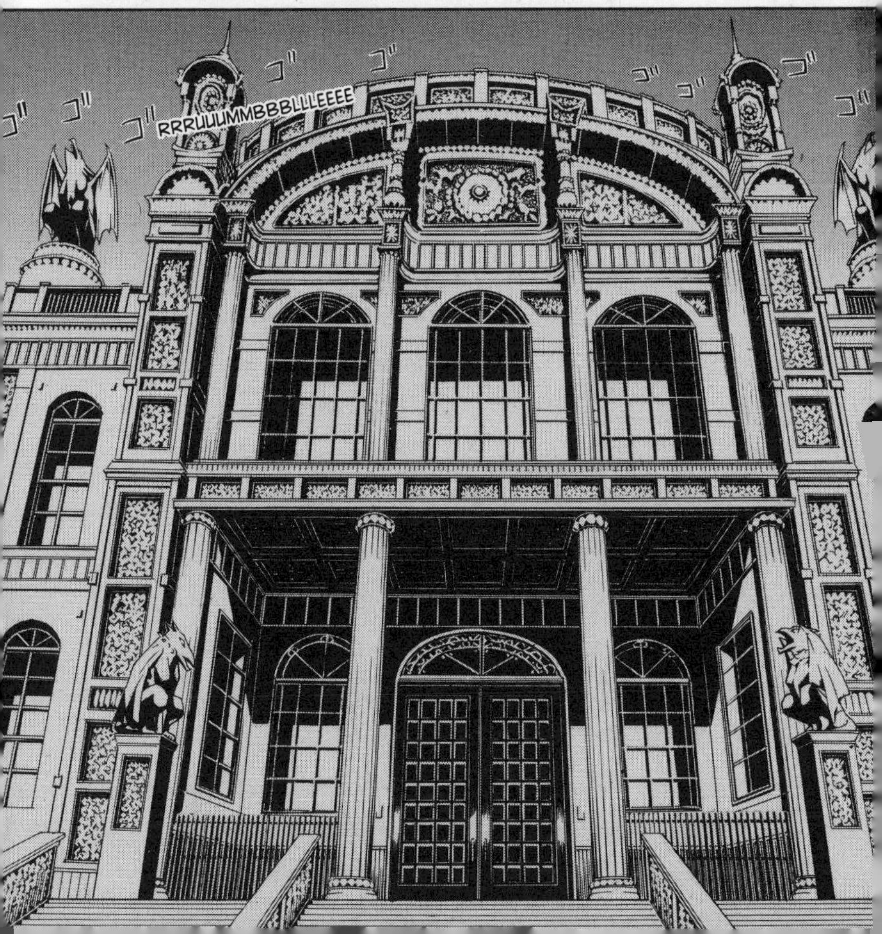
ゴゴゴゴゴゴゴゴゴ
RRRUUUMMBBBLLLEEEE

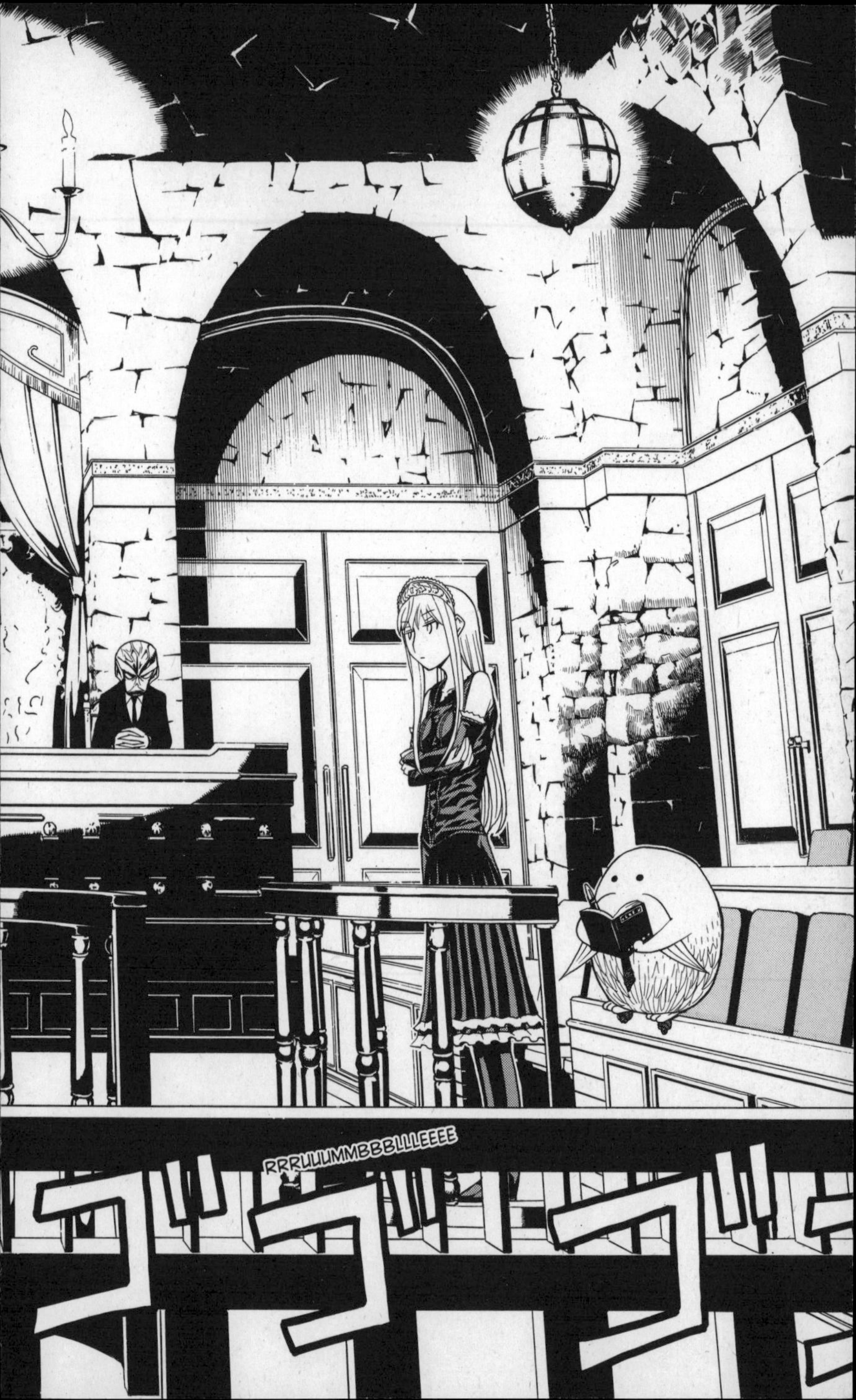
RRRUUUMMBBBLLLEEEE

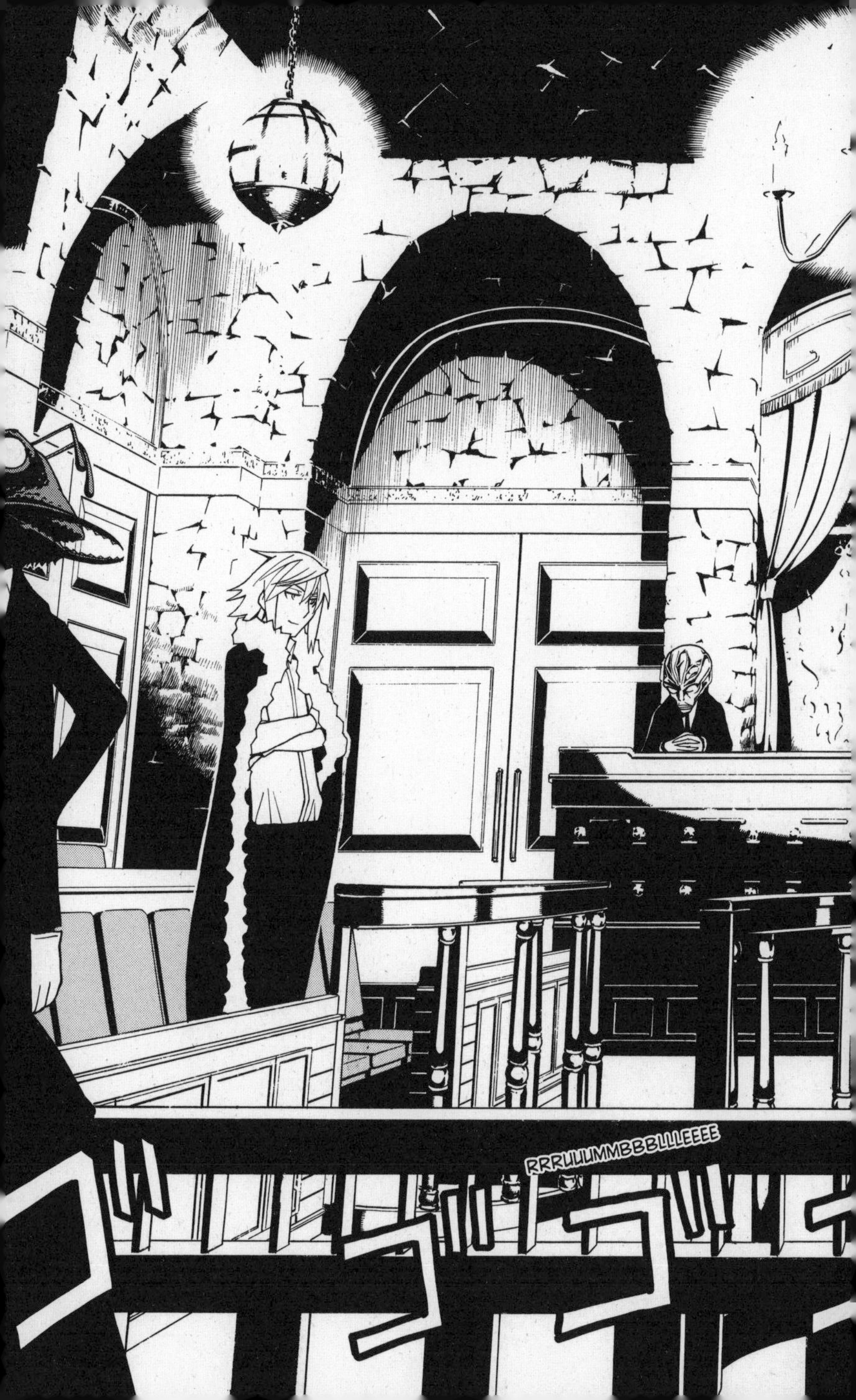
RRRUUUMMBBBLLLEEEE

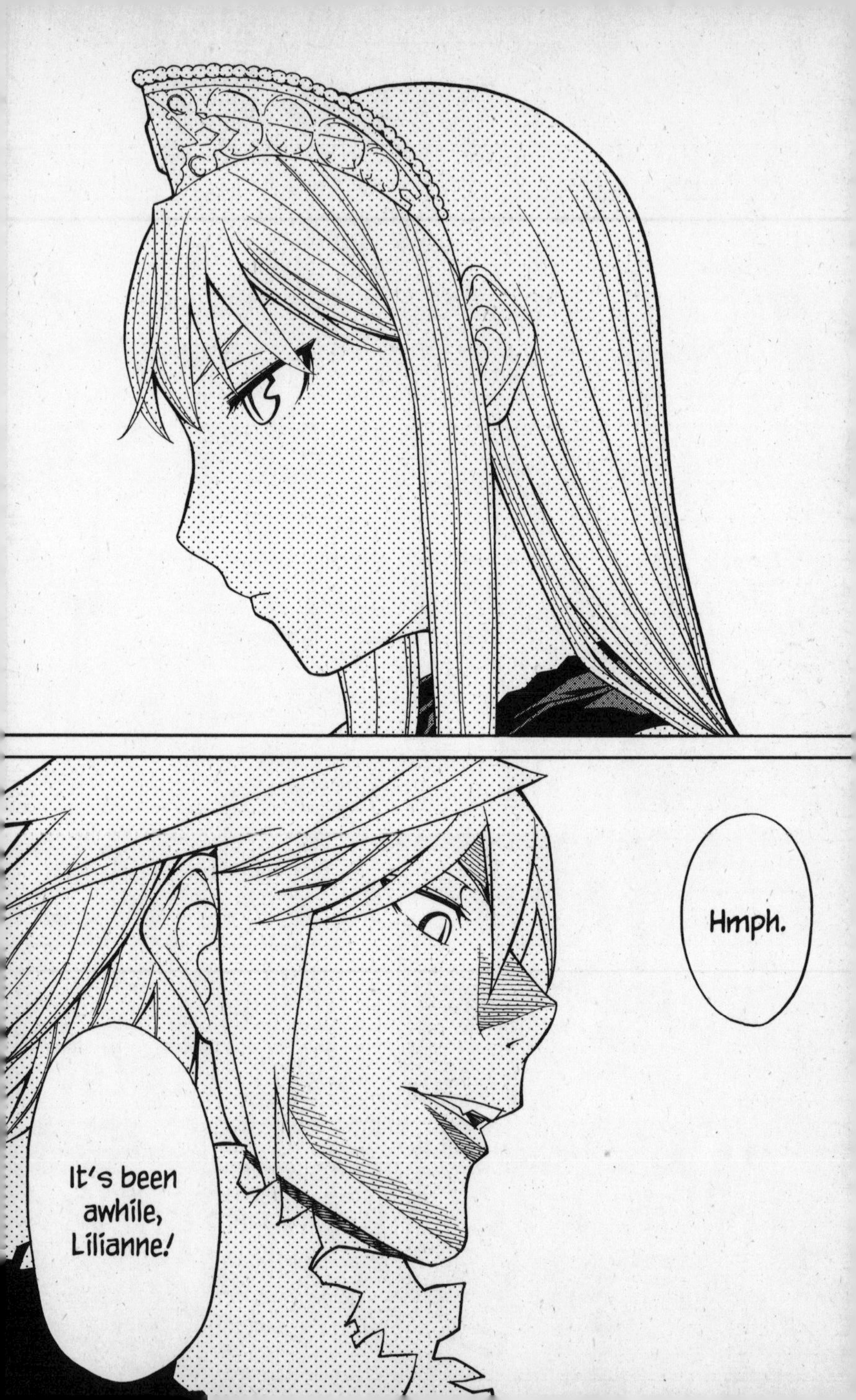
Hmph.
It's been awhile, Lilianne!

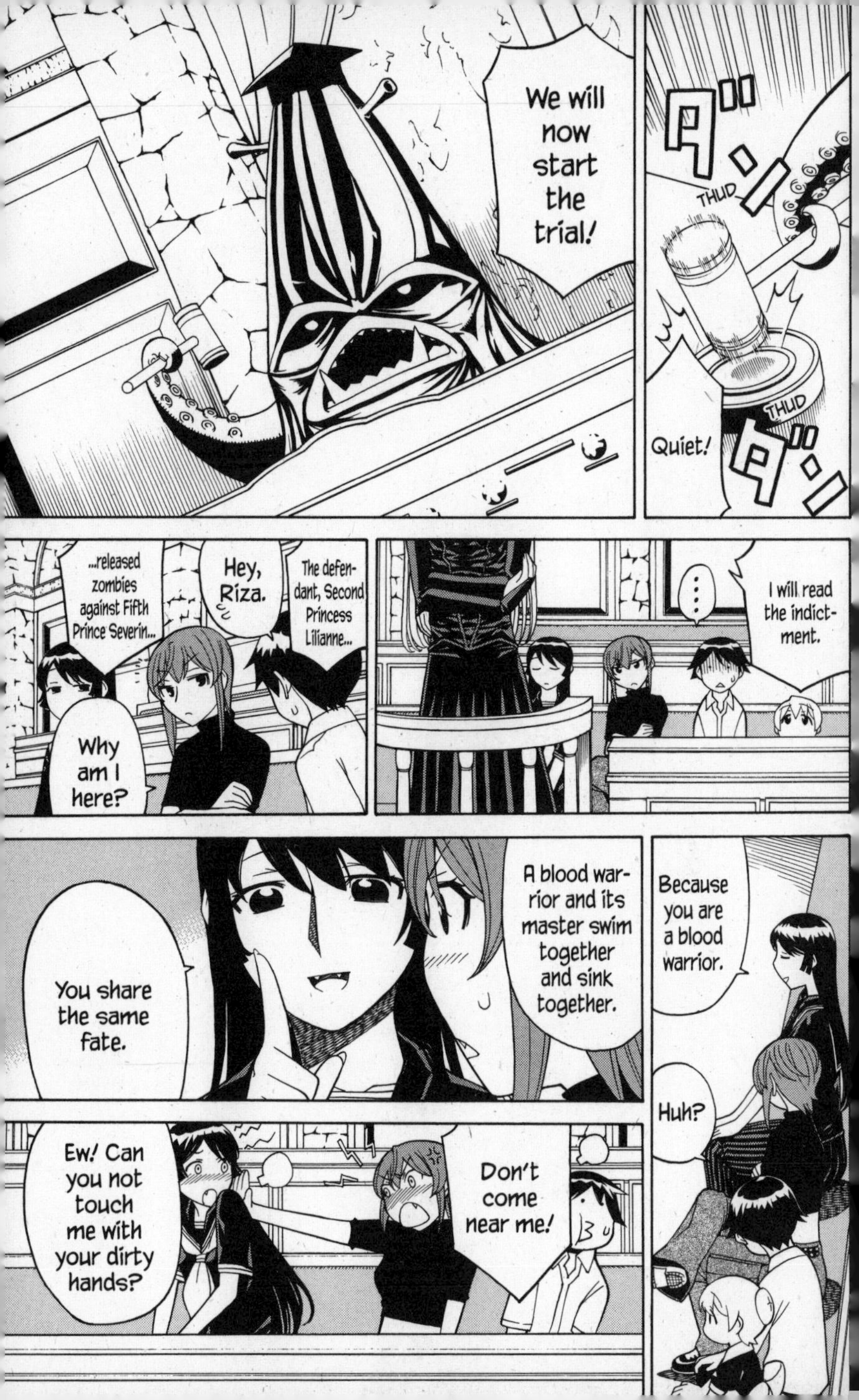
THUD
THUD
Quiet!
We will now start the trial!
I will read the indictment.
...
The defendant, Second Princess Lilianne...
Hey, Riza.
...released zombies against Fifth Prince Severin...
Why am I here?
Because you are a blood warrior.
Huh?
A blood warrior and its master swim together and sink together.
You share the same fate.
Don't come near me!
Ew! Can you not touch me with your dirty hands?

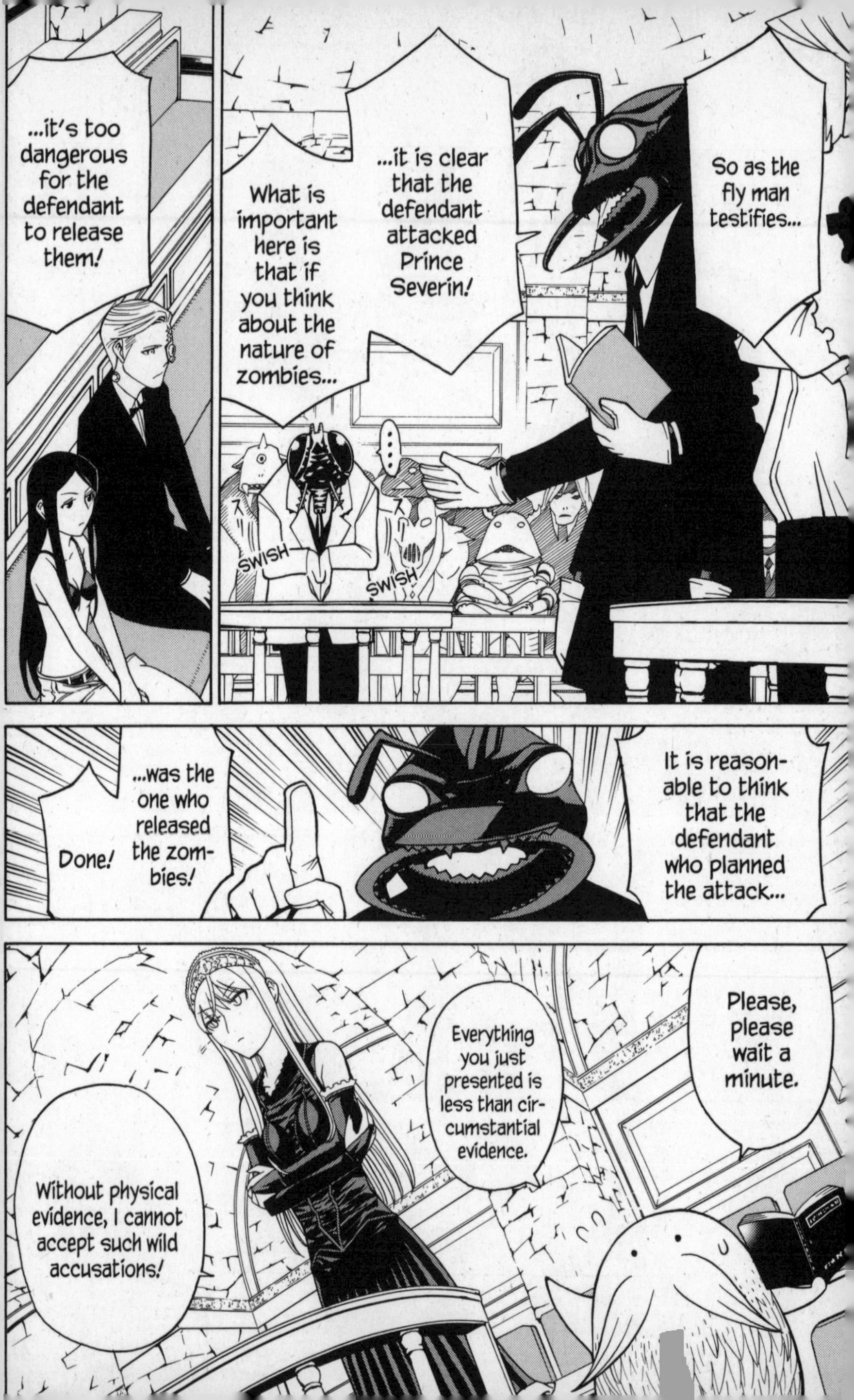
So as the fly man testifies...
...it is clear that the defendant attacked Prince Severin!
What is important here is that if you think about the nature of zombies...
...
SWISH
SWISH
...it's too dangerous for the defendant to release them!
It is reasonable to think that the defendant who planned the attack...
...was the one who released the zombies!
Done!
Please, please wait a minute.
Everything you just presented is less than circumstantial evidence.
Without physical evidence, I cannot accept such wild accusations!

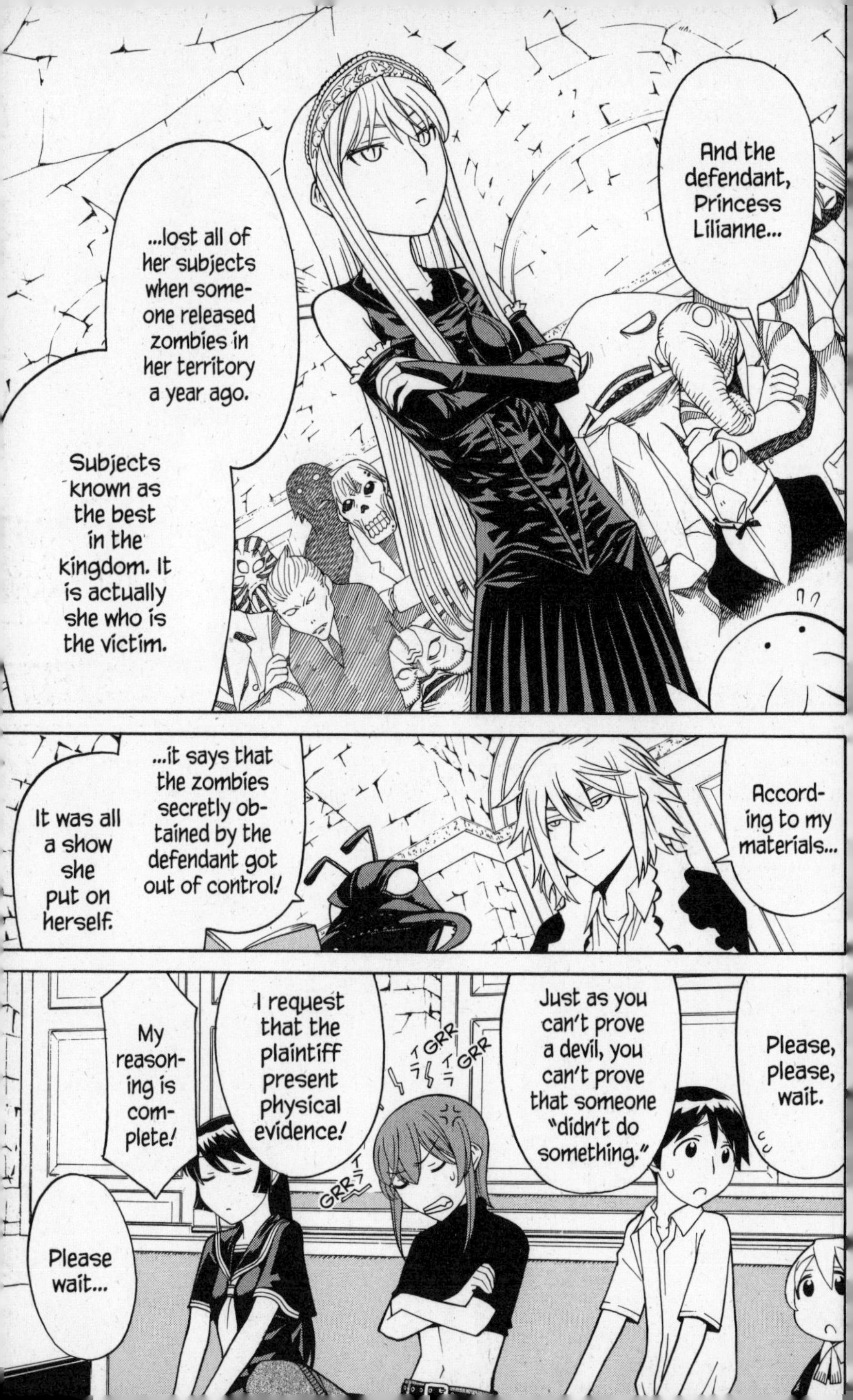
And the defendant, Princess Lilianne...
...lost all of her subjects when someone released zombies in her territory a year ago.
Subjects known as the best in the kingdom. It is actually she who is the victim.
According to my materials...
...it says that the zombies secretly obtained by the defendant got out of control!
It was all a show she put on herself.
Please, please, wait.
Just as you can't prove a devil, you can't prove that someone "didn't do something."
GRR GRR
I request that the plaintiff present physical evidence!
GRR
My reasoning is complete!
Please wait...

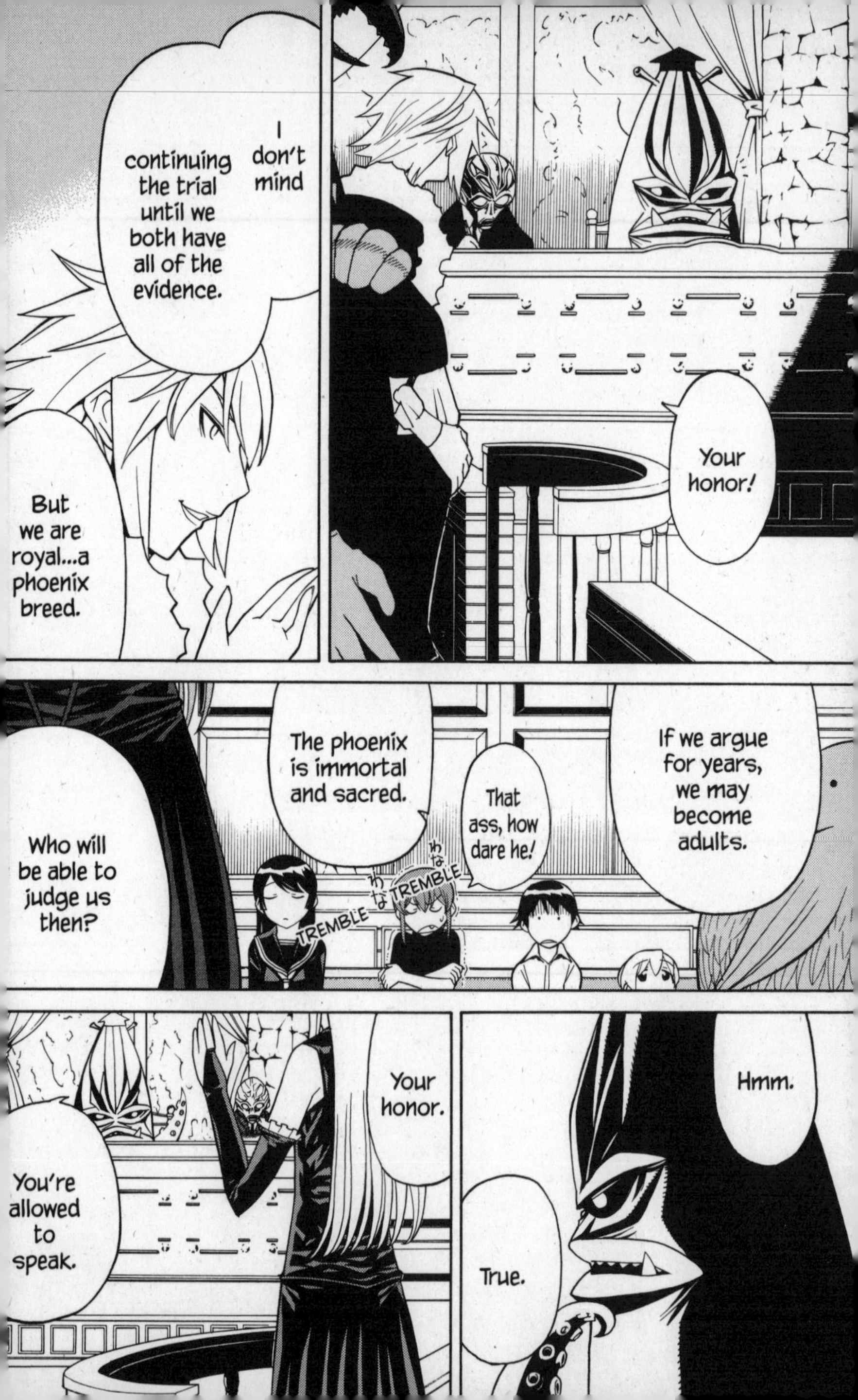
Your honor!
I don't mind continuing the trial until we both have all of the evidence.
But we are royal...a phoenix breed.
If we argue for years, we may become adults.
That ass, how dare he!
TREMBLE
TREMBLE
The phoenix is immortal and sacred.
Who will be able to judge us then?
Hmm.
True.
Your honor.
You're allowed to speak.

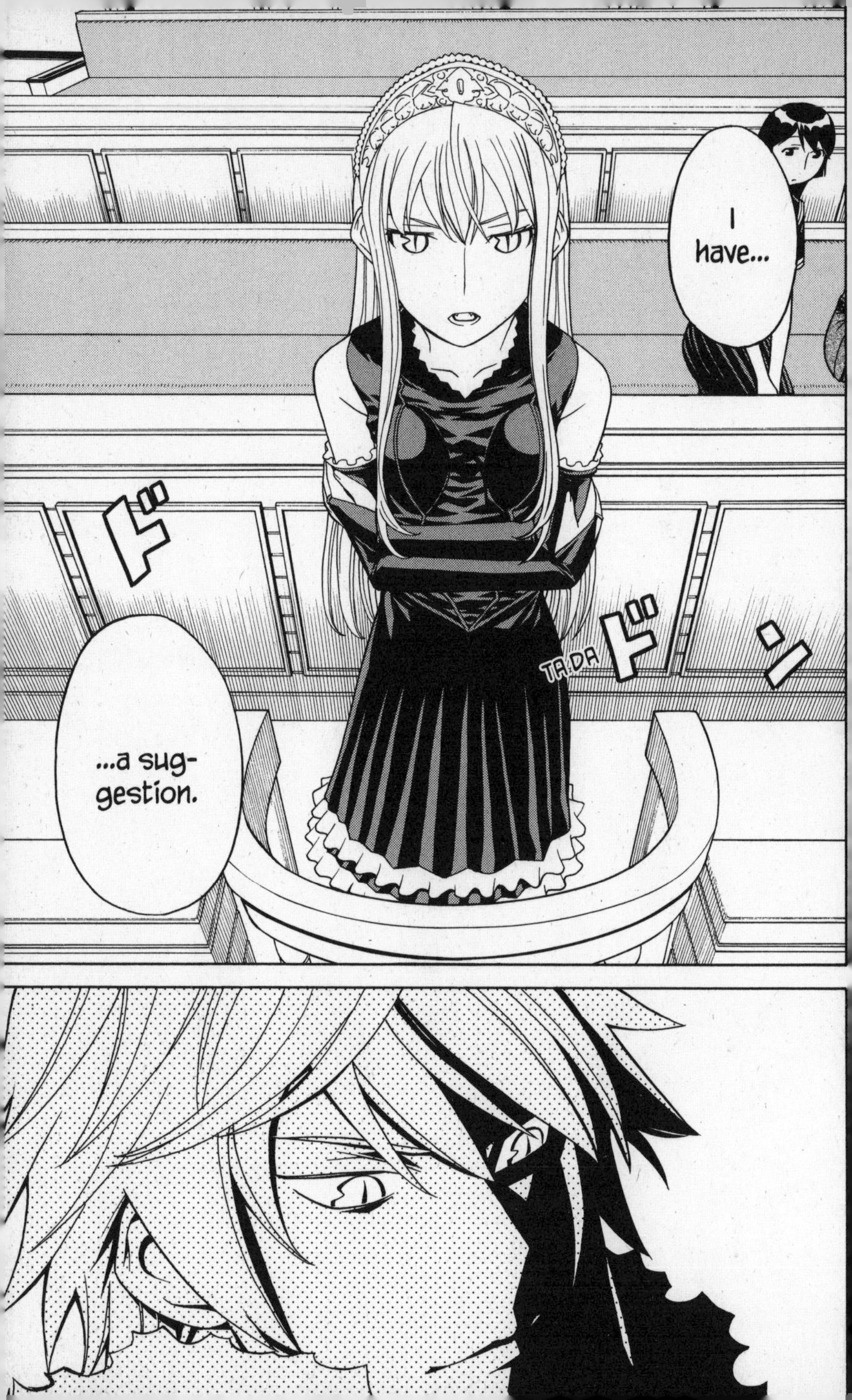
I have...
TA-DA
ドドン
...a sug-gestion.

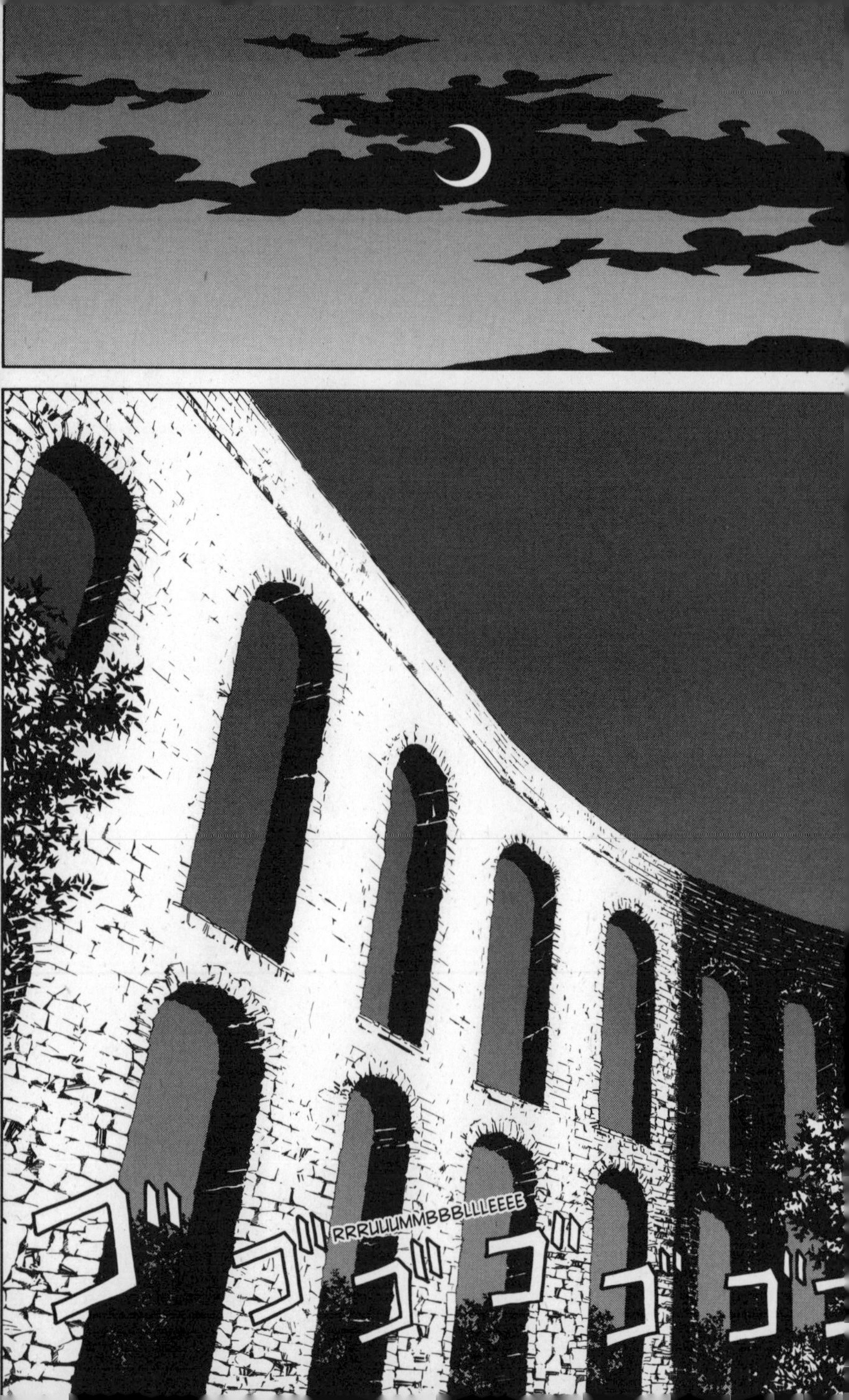
ゴゴゴゴゴゴ
RRRUUUMMBBBLLLEEEE

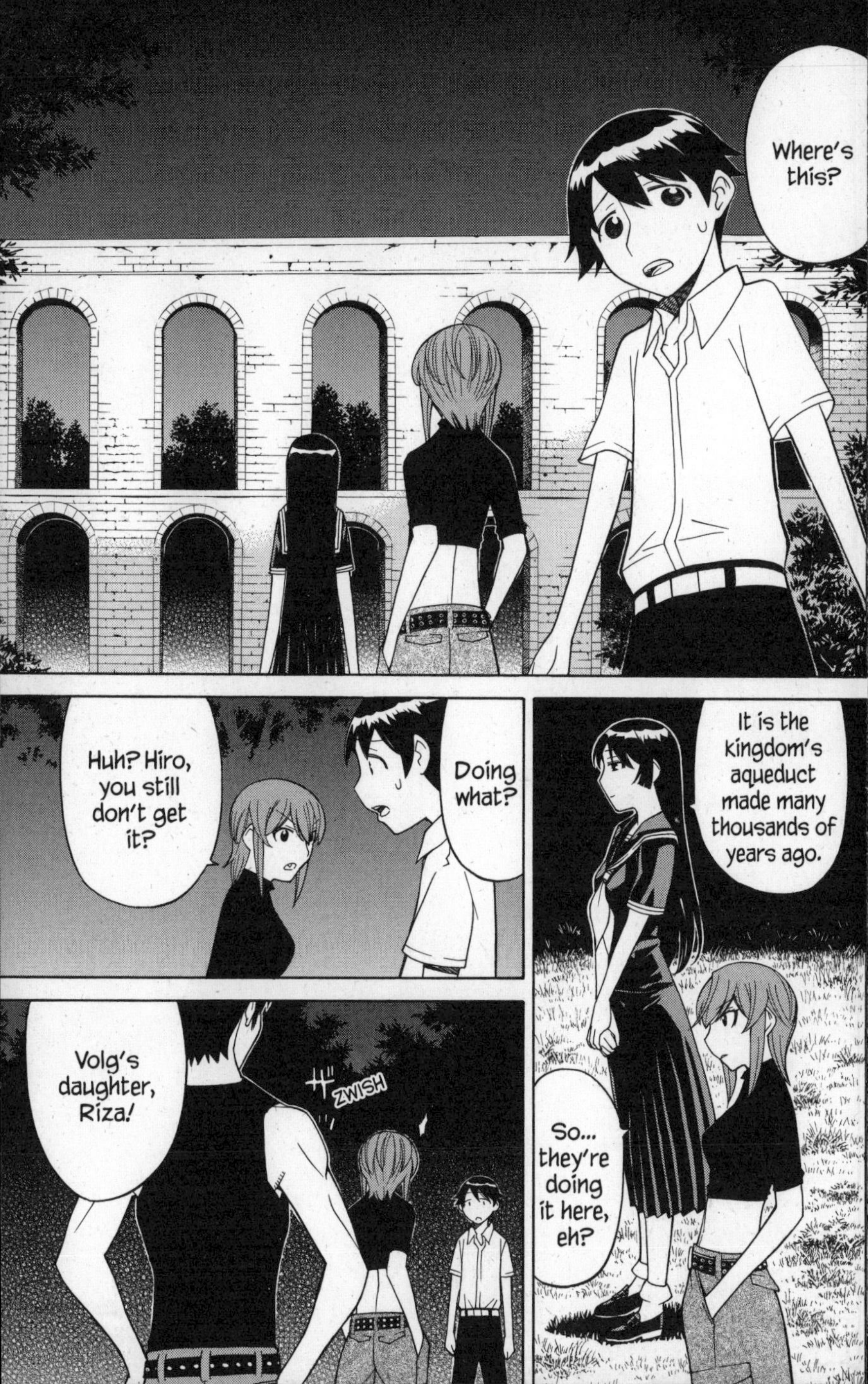
Where's this?
It is the kingdom's aqueduct made many thousands of years ago.
So... they're doing it here, eh?
Doing what?
Huh? Hiro, you still don't get it?
Volg's daughter, Riza!
ZWISH

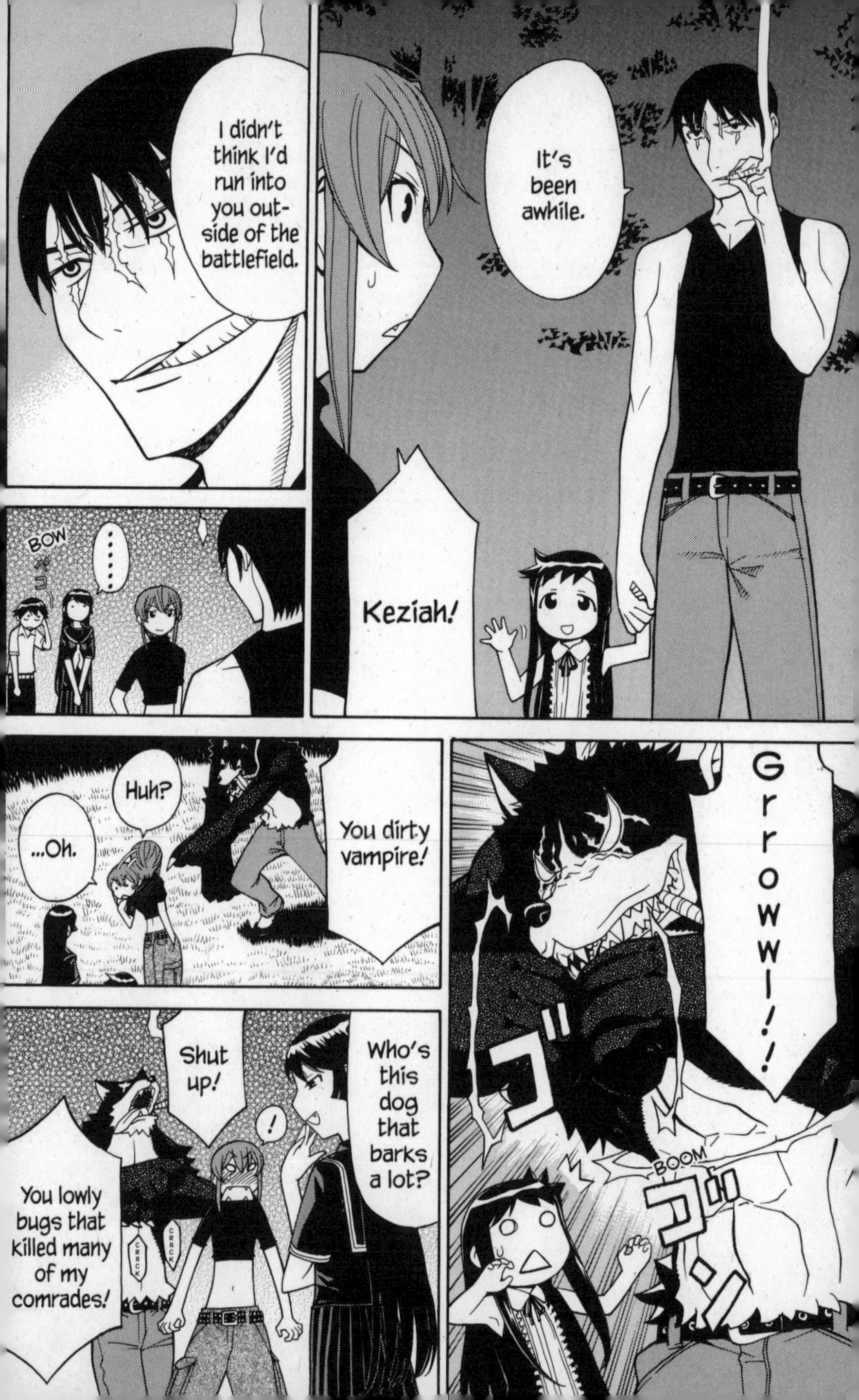

It's been awhile.
Keziah!
I didn't think I'd run into you outside of the battlefield.
BOW
......
Grrowl!!
BOOM
You dirty vampire!
Huh?
...Oh.
Who's this dog that barks a lot?
!
Shut up!
You lowly bugs that killed many of my comrades!
CRACK
CRACK

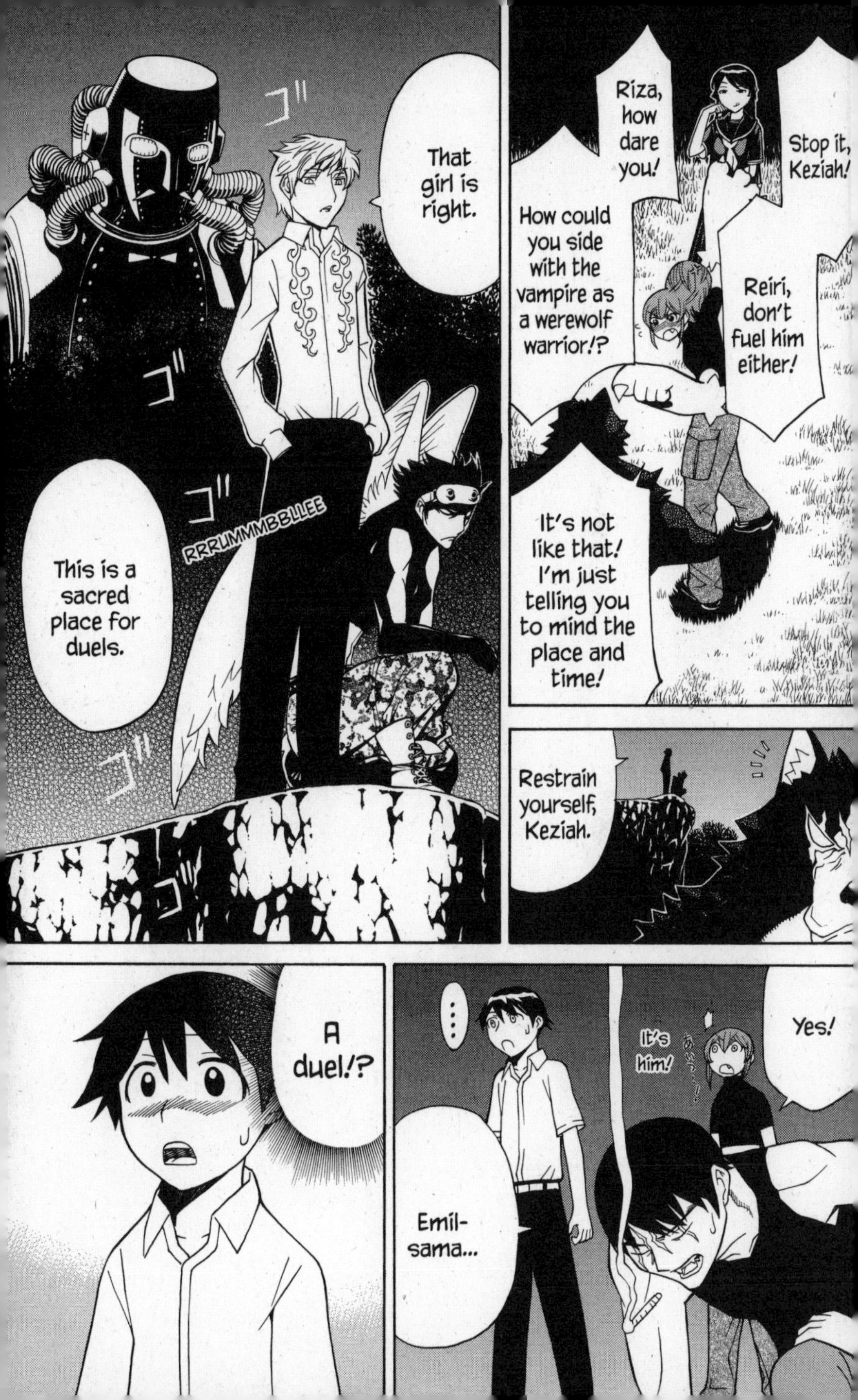

Stop it, Keziah!
Riza, how dare you!
Reiri, don't fuel him either!
How could you side with the vampire as a werewolf warrior!?
It's not like that! I'm just telling you to mind the place and time!
Restrain yourself, Keziah.
That girl is right.
ゴ゛
ゴ゛
RRRUMMMBBLLEE
ゴ゛
This is a sacred place for duels.
ゴ゛
ゴ゛
Yes!
It's him!
あいつ…!
....
Emil-sama...
A duel!?

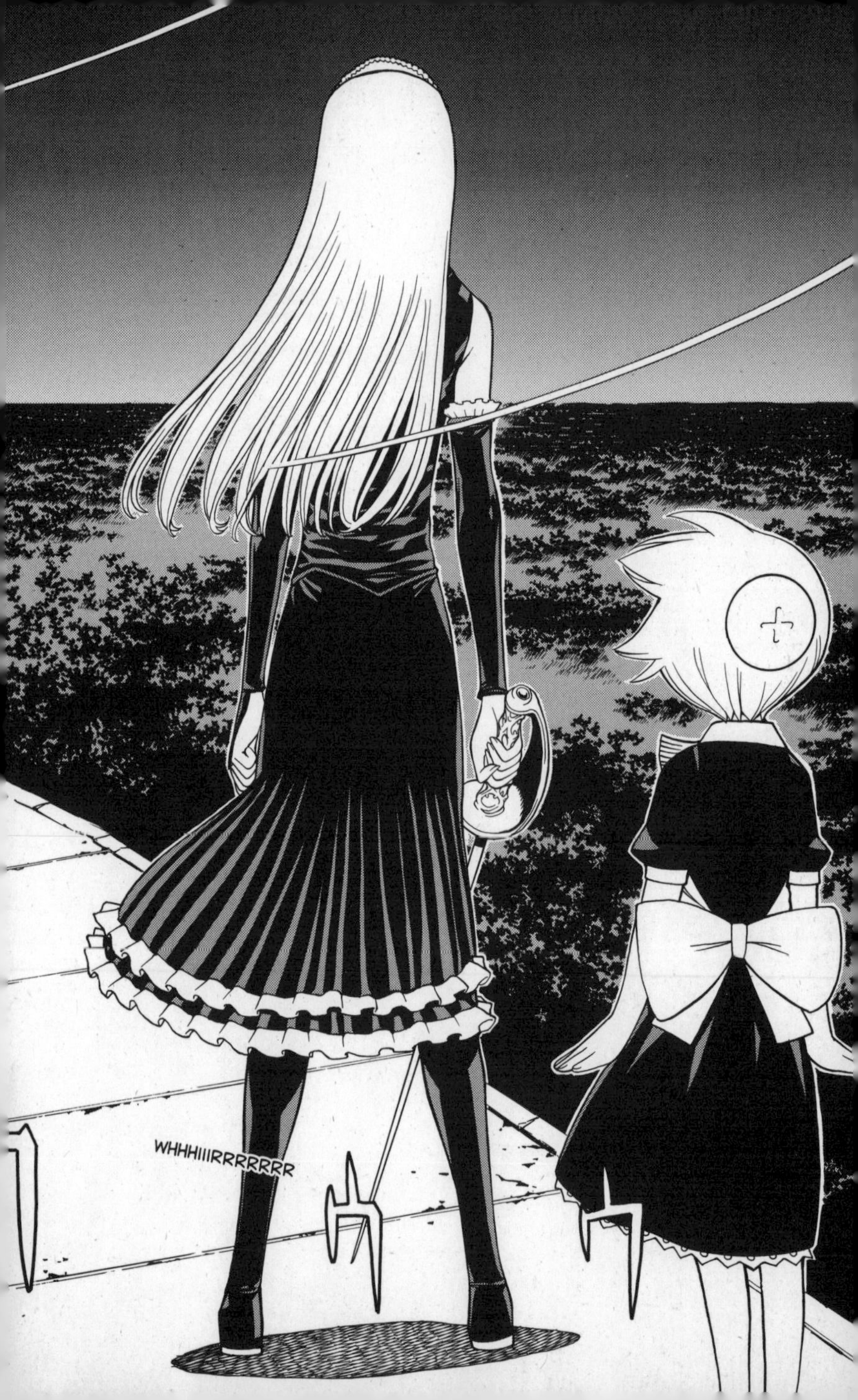
WHHHIIIRRRRRRR

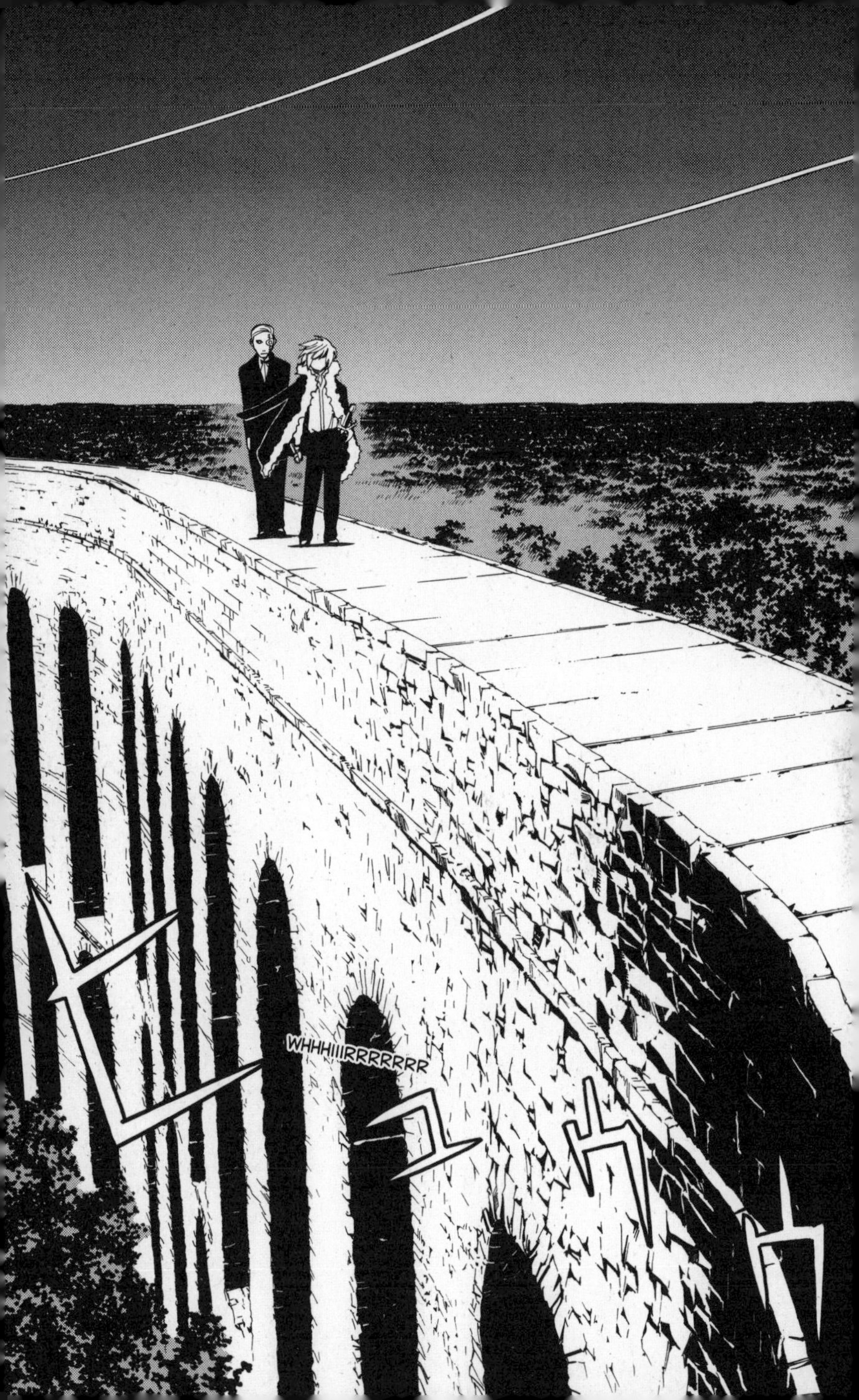
WHHHIIIRRRRRRR

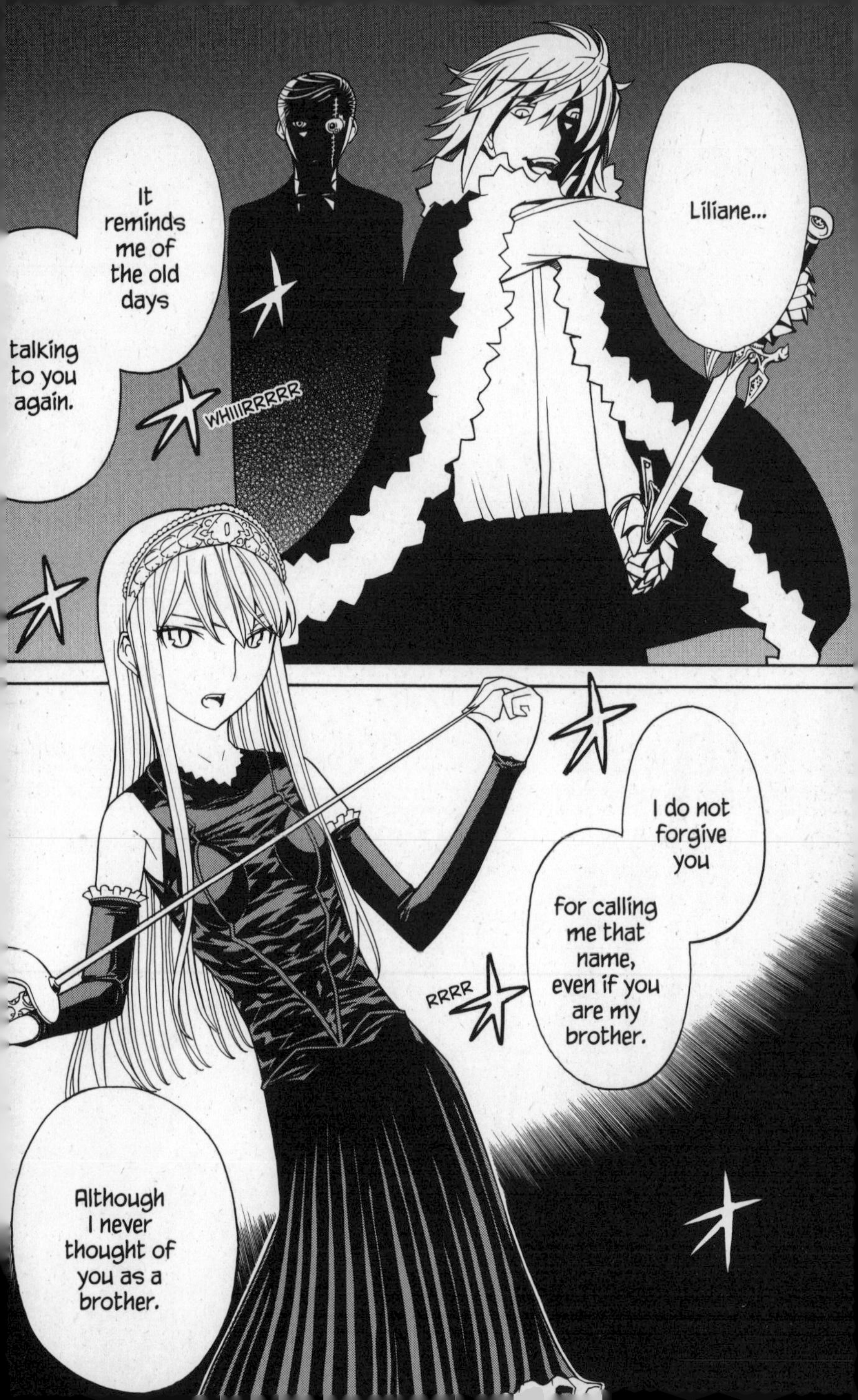
Liliane...
It reminds me of the old days
talking to you again.
WHIIIRRRRR
I do not forgive you
for calling me that name, even if you are my brother.
RRRR
Although I never thought of you as a brother.

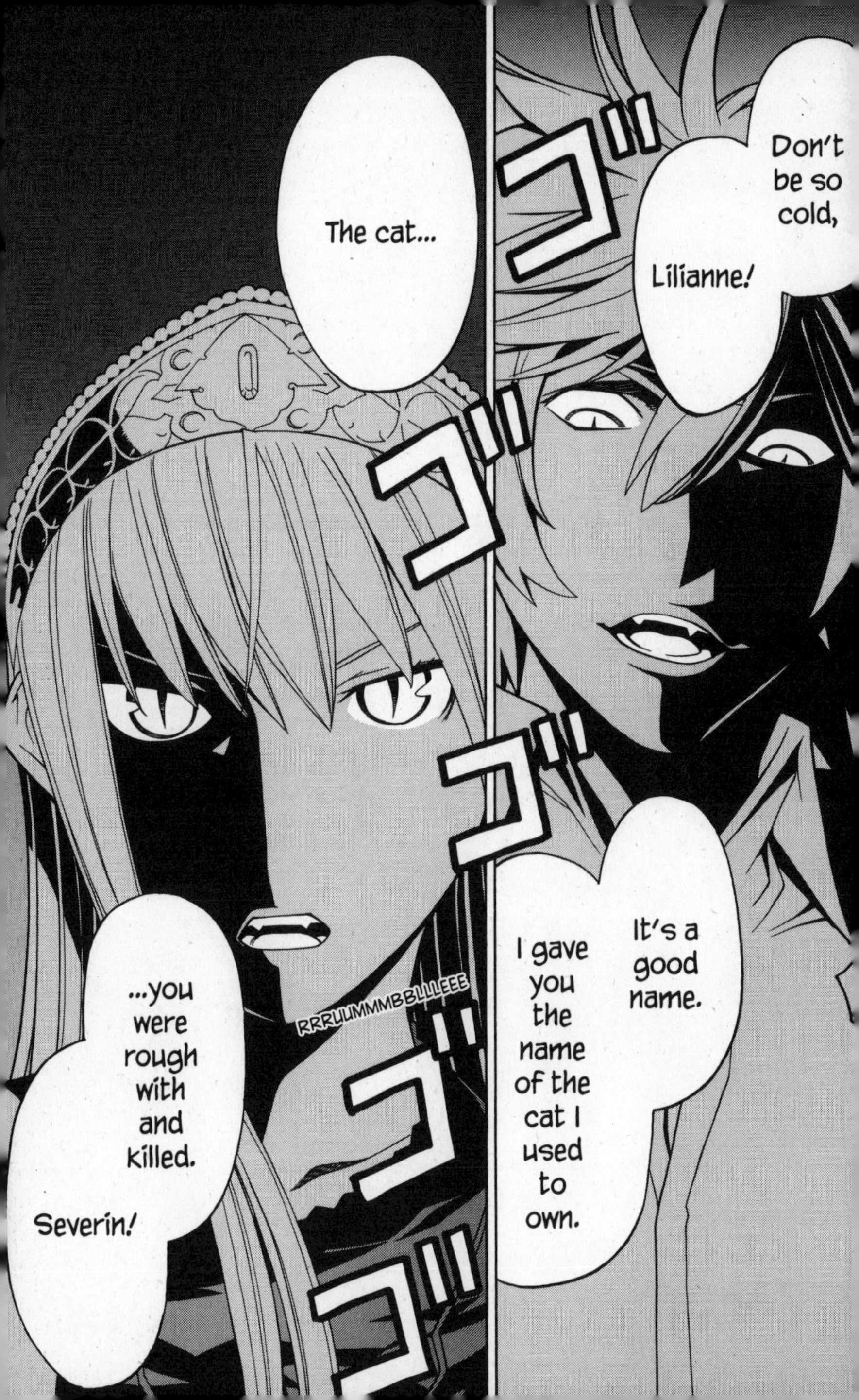
Don't be so cold,
Lilianne!
ゴゴゴゴゴ
It's a good name.
I gave you the name of the cat I used to own.
The cat...
RRRUUMMMBBLLLEEE
...you were rough with and killed.
Severin!

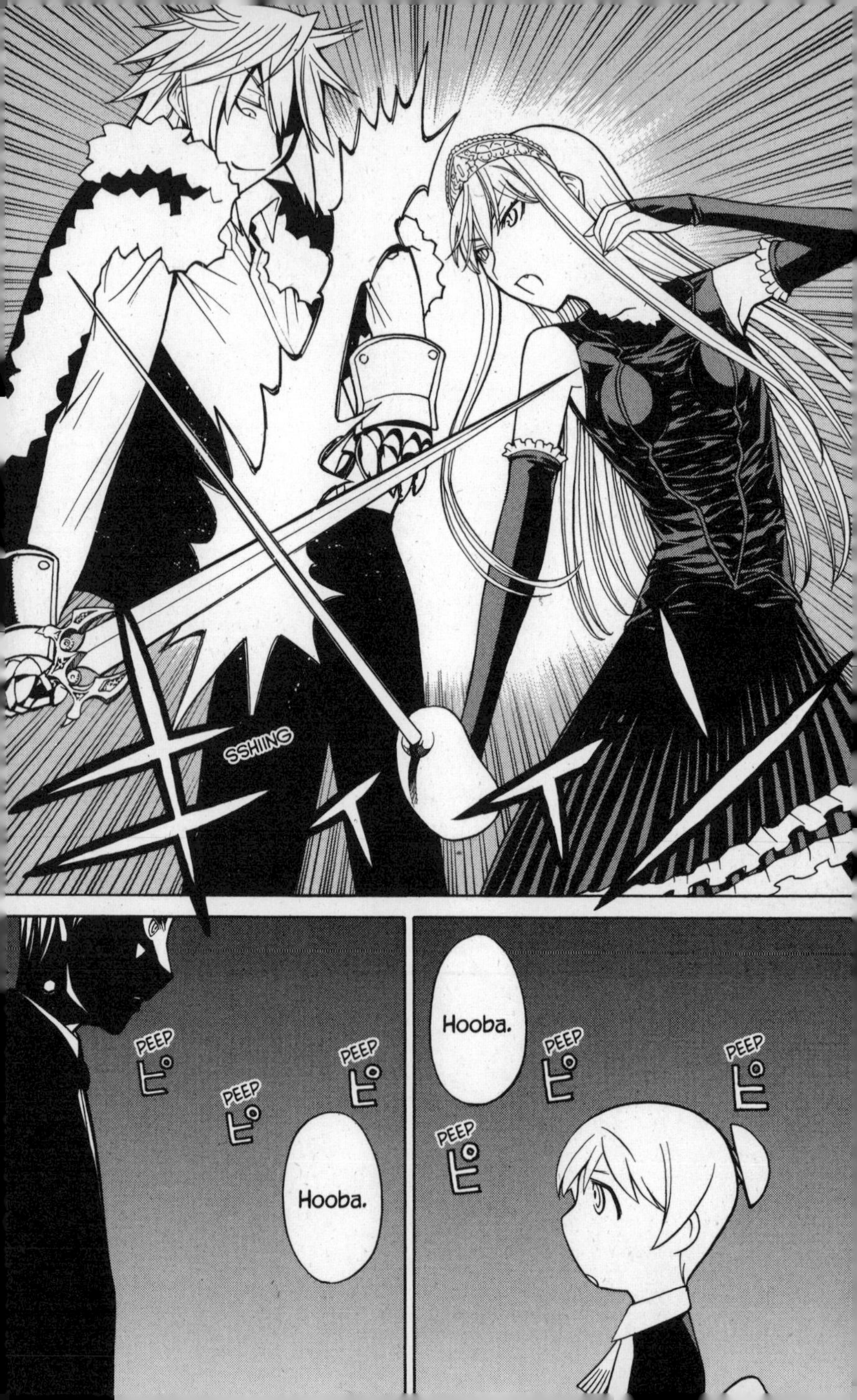
SSHIING
Hooba.
PEEP ピ
PEEP ピ
PEEP ピ
PEEP ピ
PEEP ピ
PEEP ピ
Hooba.

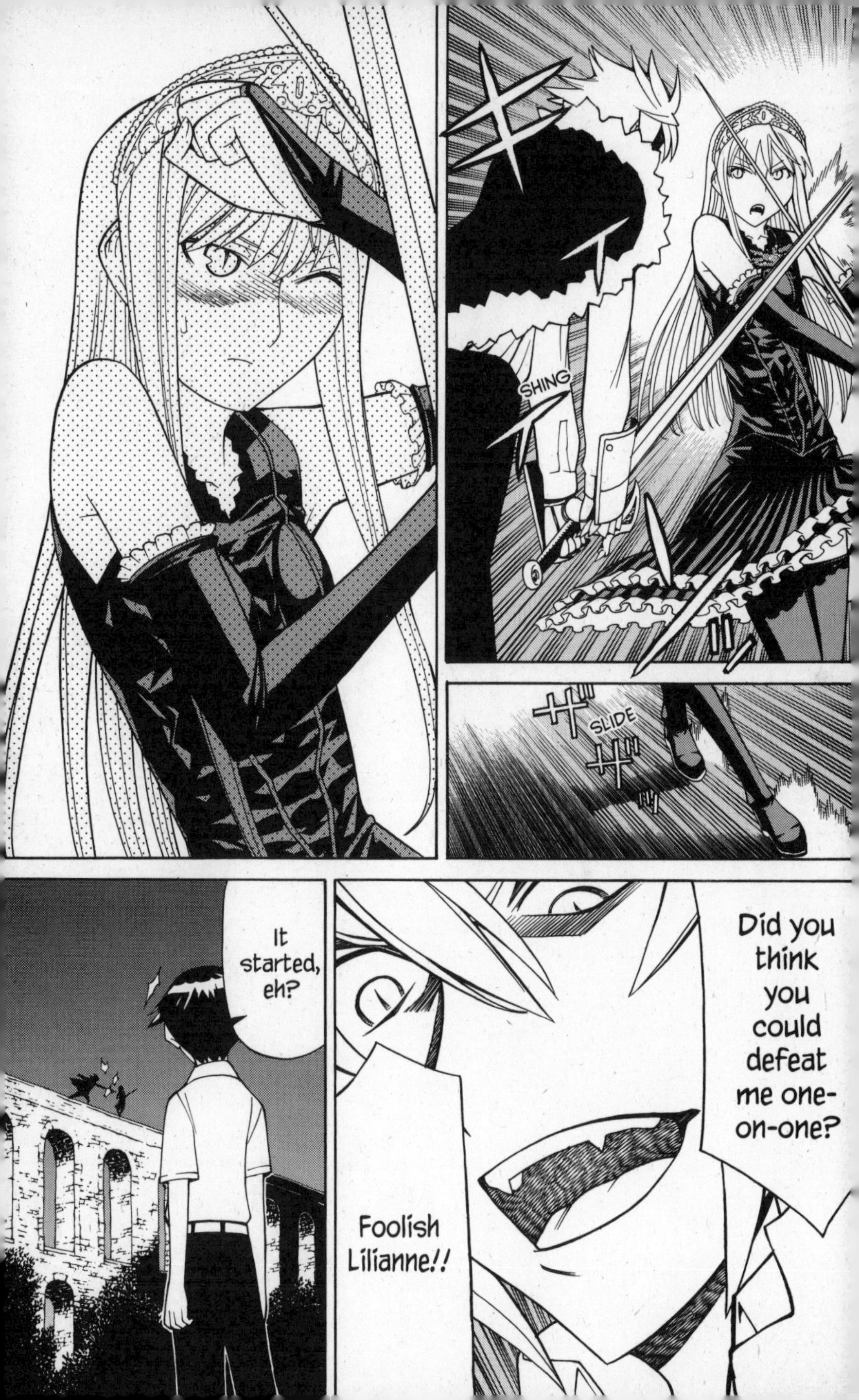
SHING
SLIDE
Did you think you could defeat me one-on-one?
Foolish Lilianne!!
It started, eh?

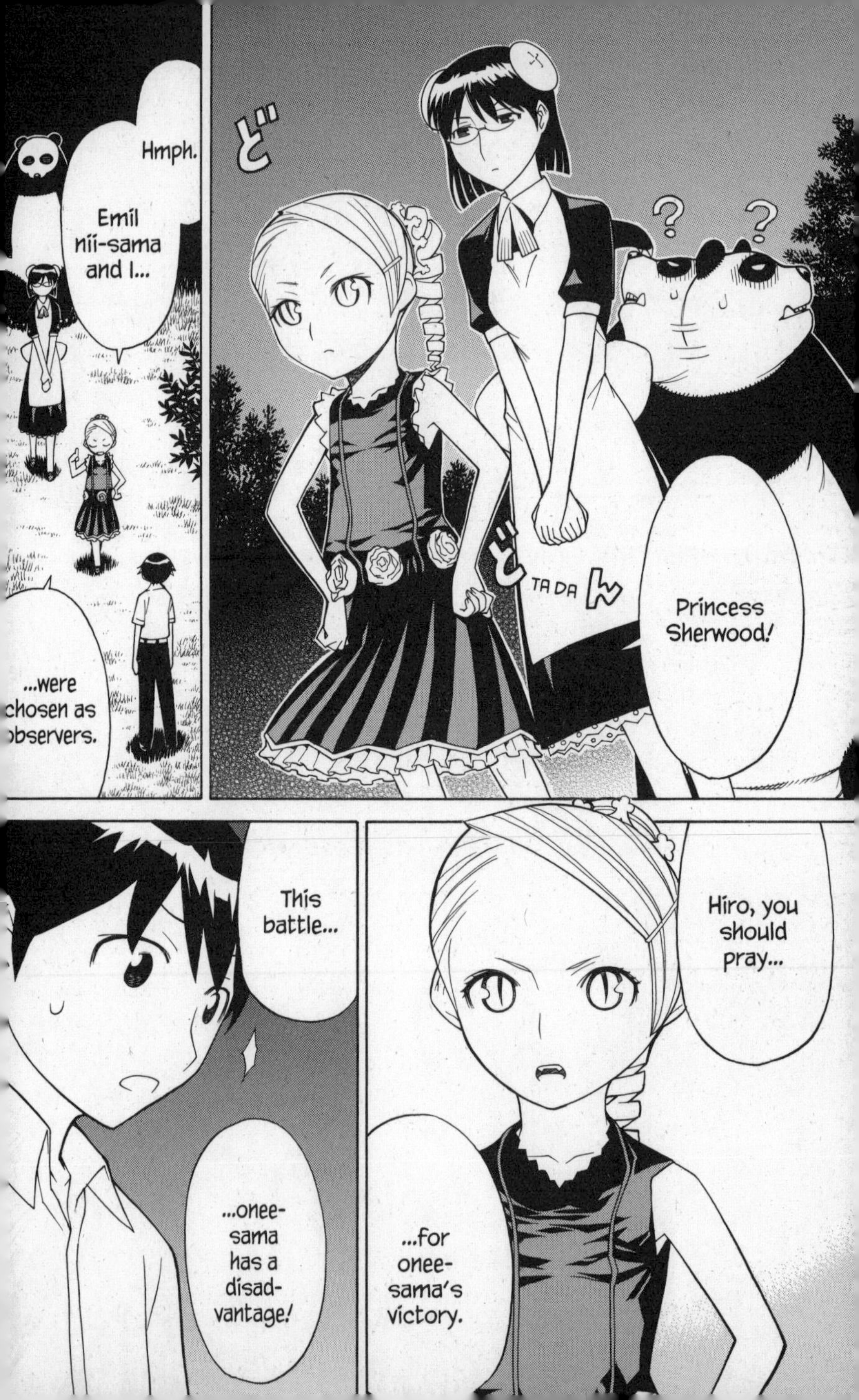

ど
ど TA DA ん
Princess Sherwood!
Hmph.
Emil nii-sama and I...
...were chosen as observers.
Hiro, you should pray...
...for onee-sama's victory.
This battle...
...onee-sama has a disadvantage!

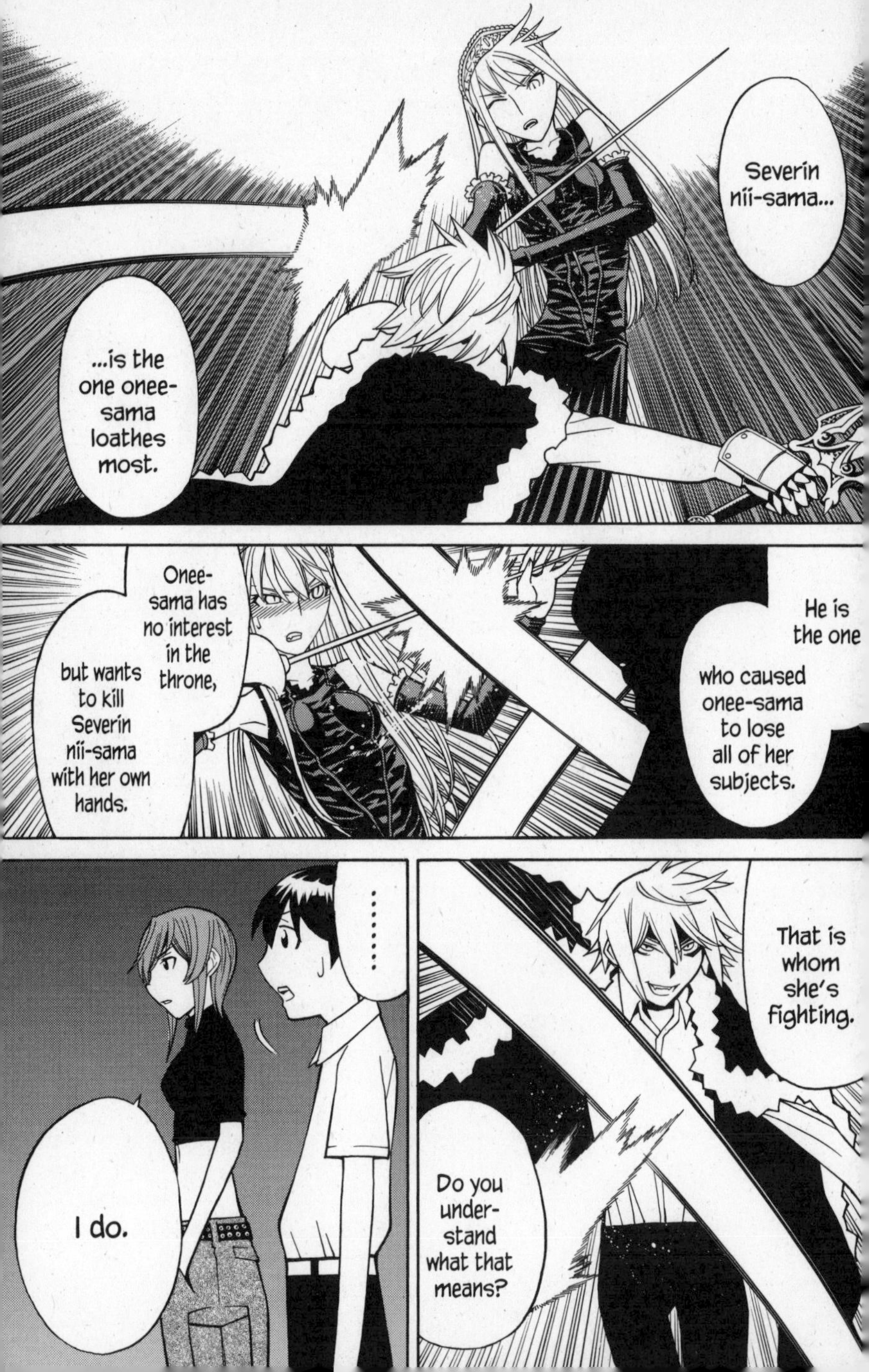
Severin nii-sama...
...is the one onee-sama loathes most.
He is the one who caused onee-sama to lose all of her subjects.
Onee-sama has no interest in the throne,
but wants to kill Severin nii-sama with her own hands.
That is whom she's fighting.
Do you understand what that means?
......
I do.

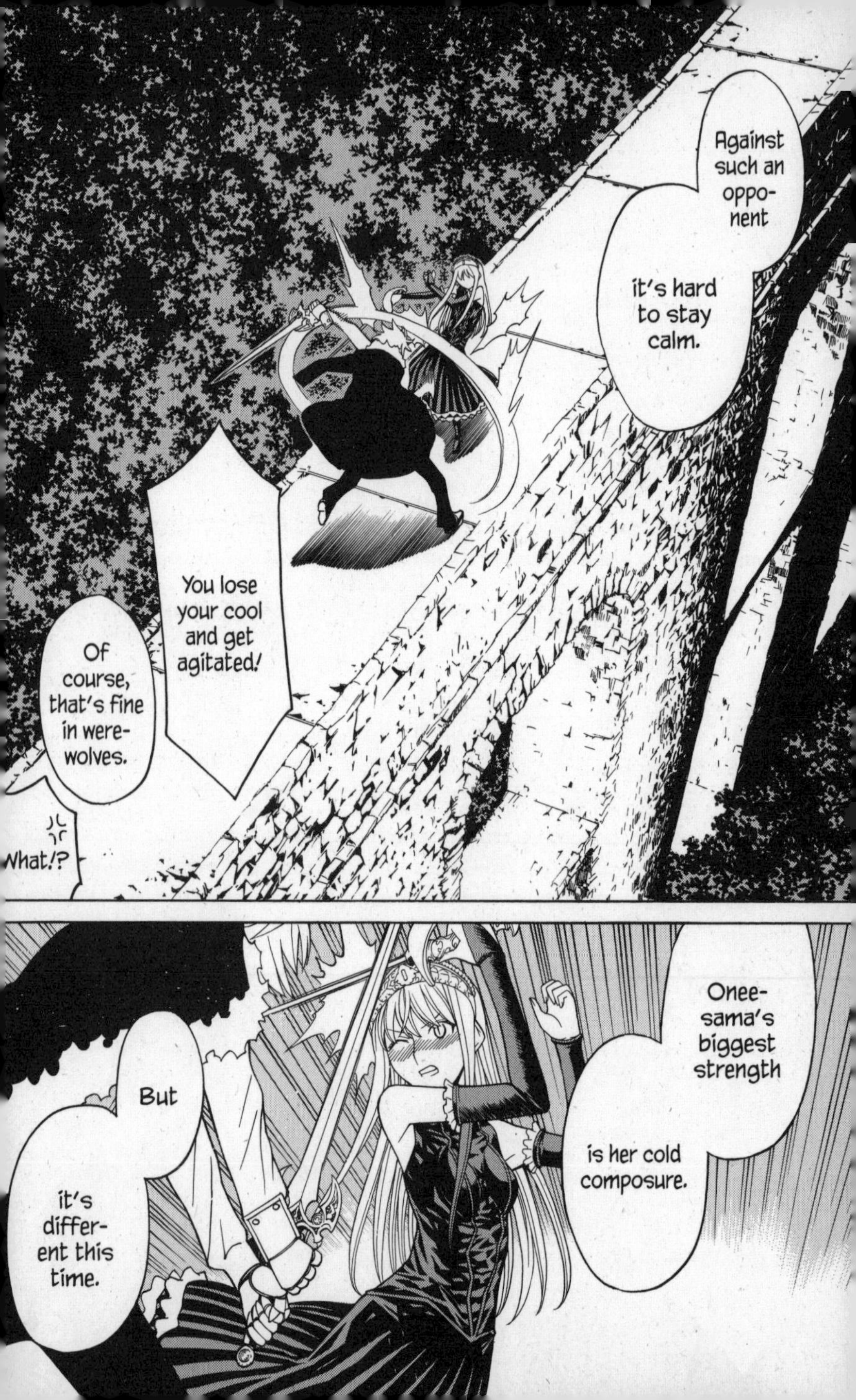
Against such an opponent
it's hard to stay calm.
You lose your cool and get agitated!
Of course, that's fine in werewolves.
What!?
Onee-sama's biggest strength
is her cold composure.
But
it's different this time.

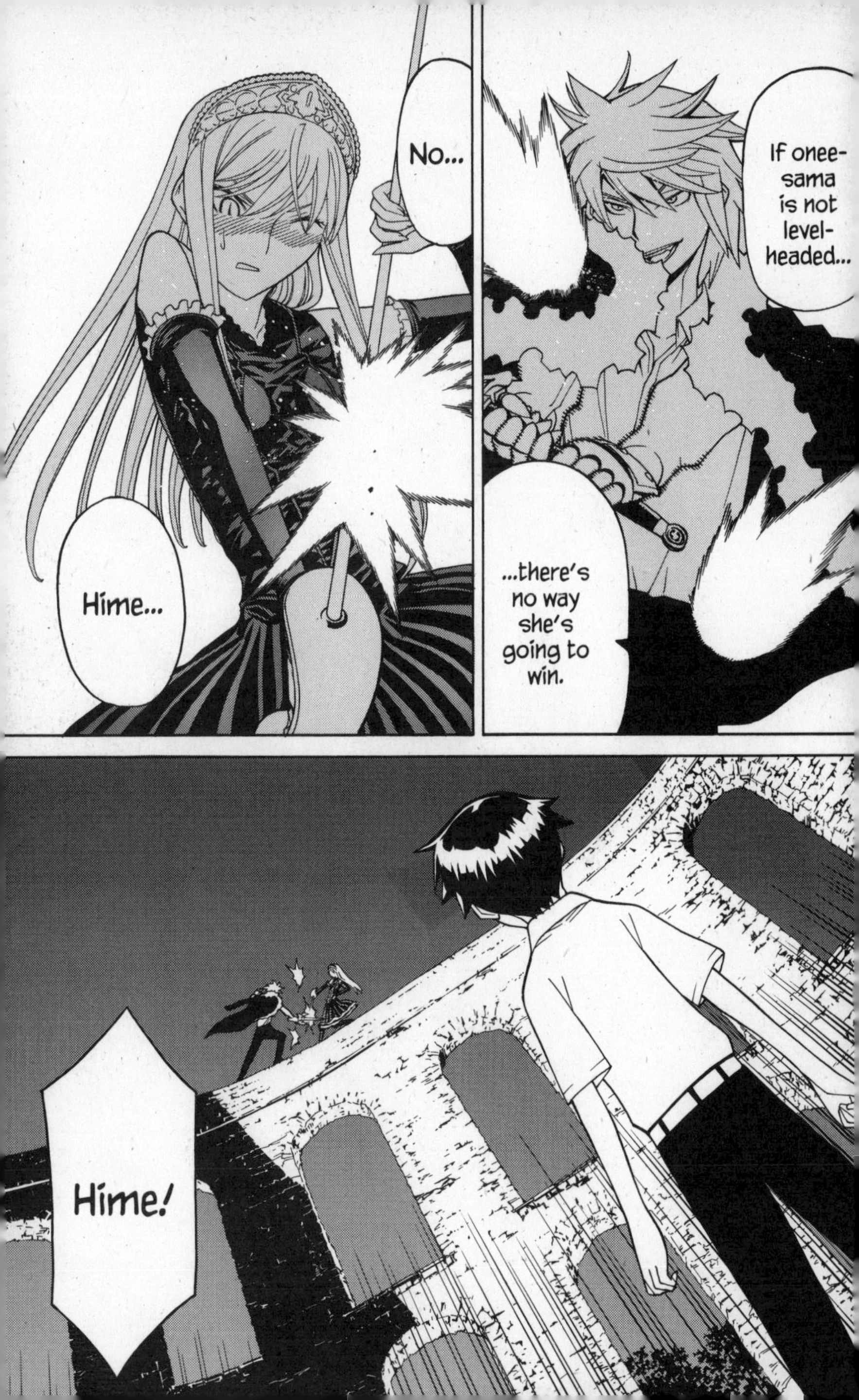
If onee-sama is not level-headed...
...there's no way she's going to win.
No...
Hime...
Hime!

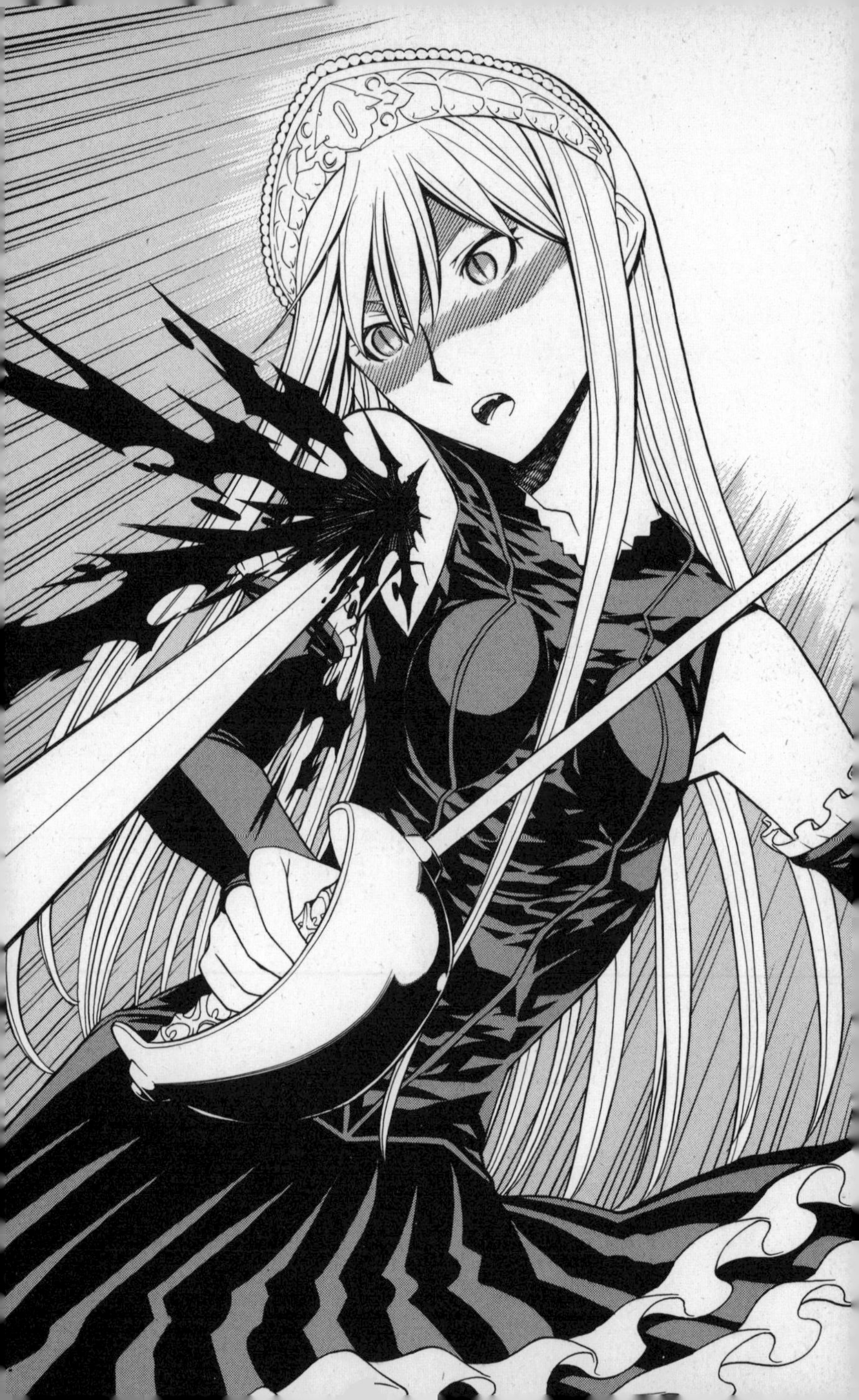

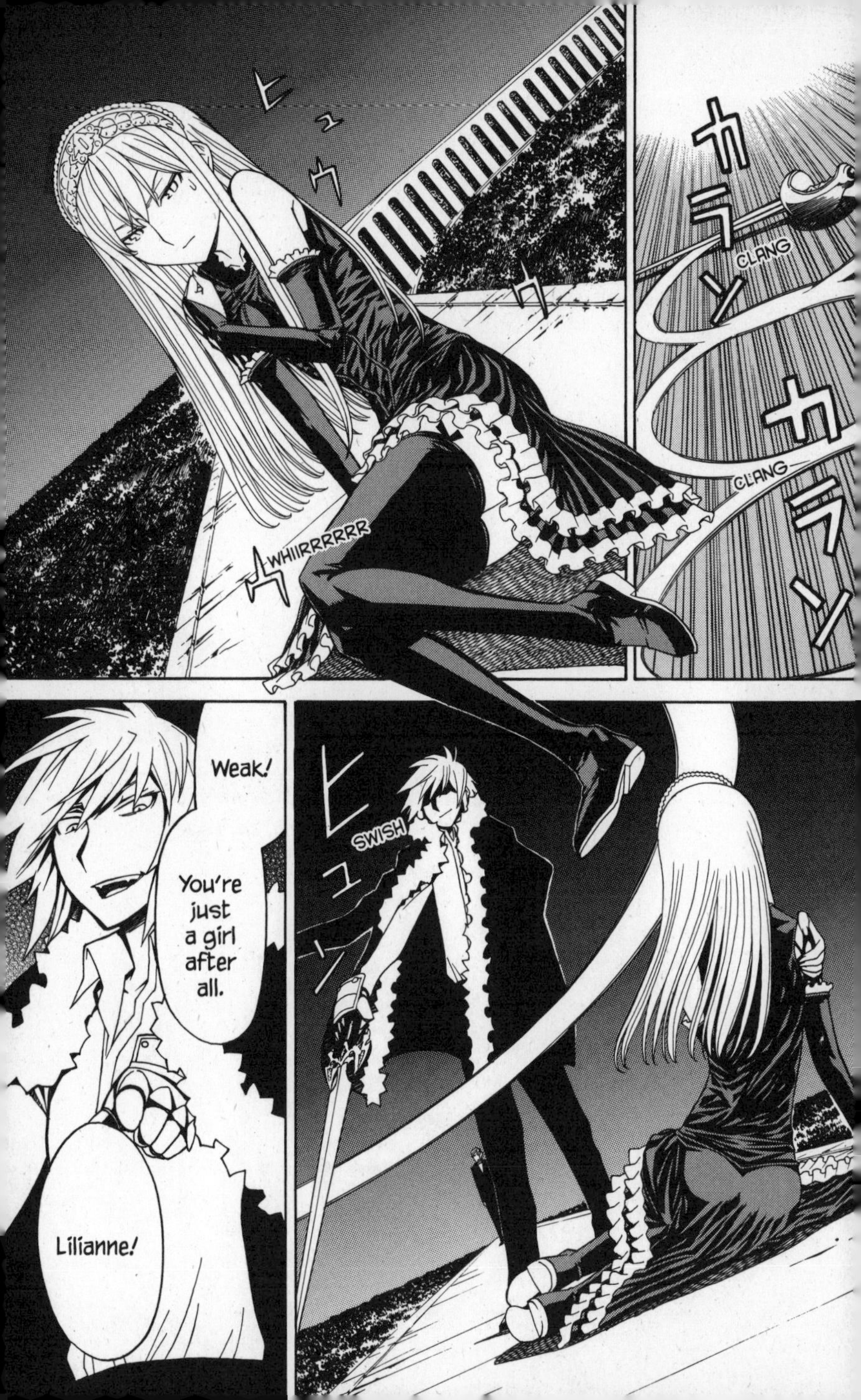
カラン
CLANG
カラン
CLANG
ヒュウ
WHIIRRRRRR
ヒュ
SWISH
Weak!
You're just a girl after all.
Lilianne!

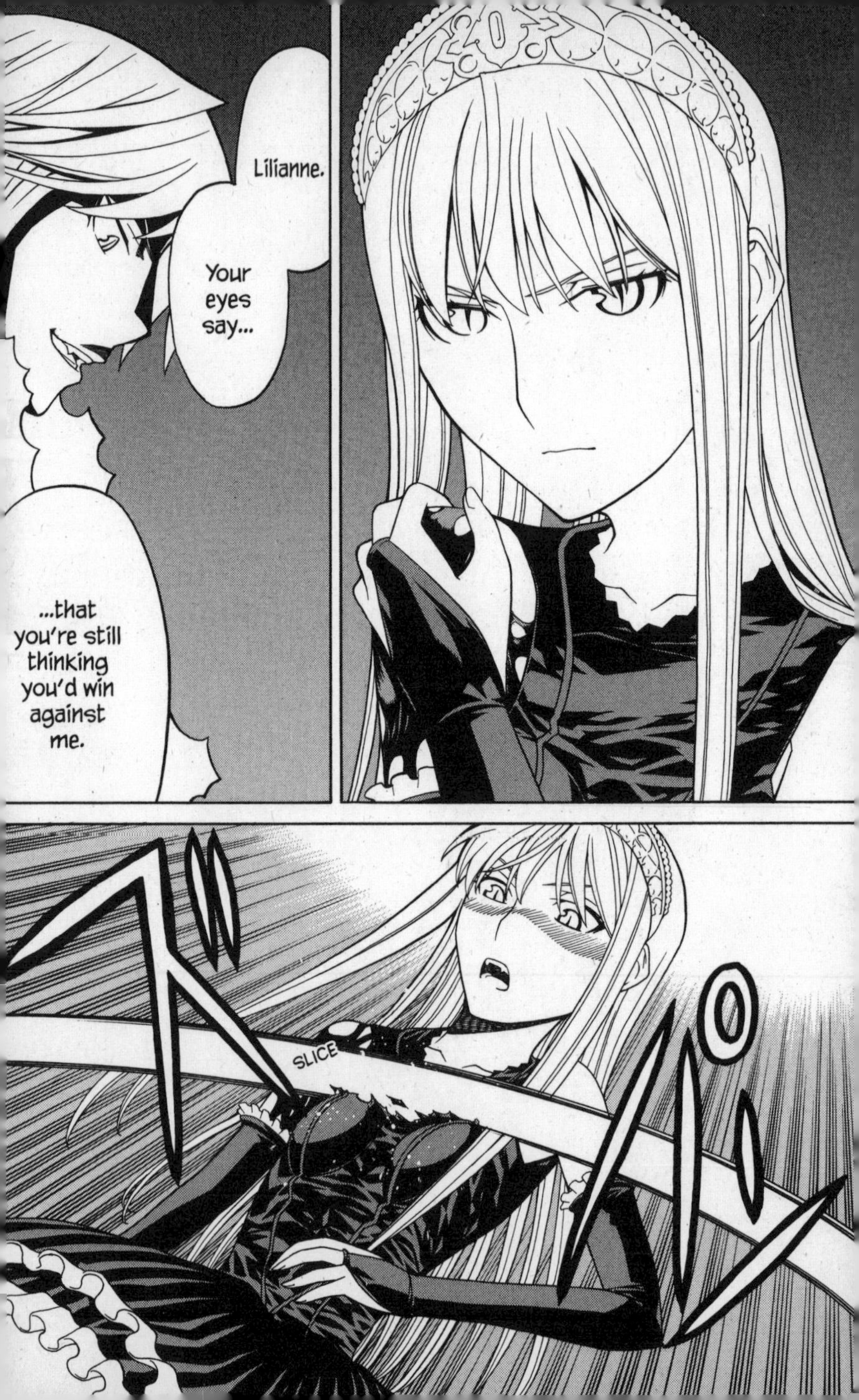
Lilianne.
Your eyes say...
...that you're still thinking you'd win against me.
SLICE

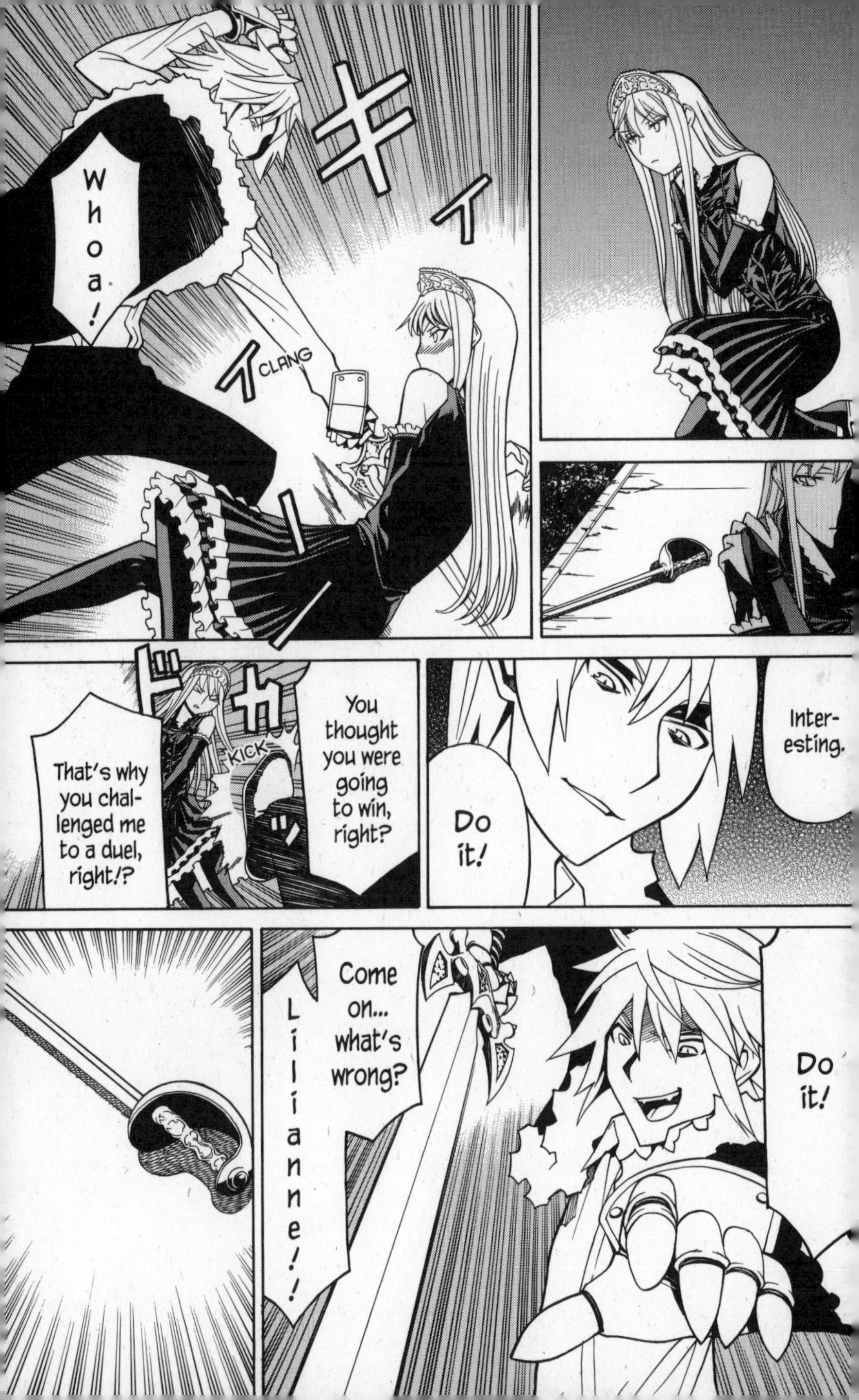
キイイー
Whoa!
CLANG
Interesting.
Do it!
You thought you were going to win, right?
ドカ
KICK
That's why you challenged me to a duel, right!?
Do it!
Come on... what's wrong?
Lilianne!!

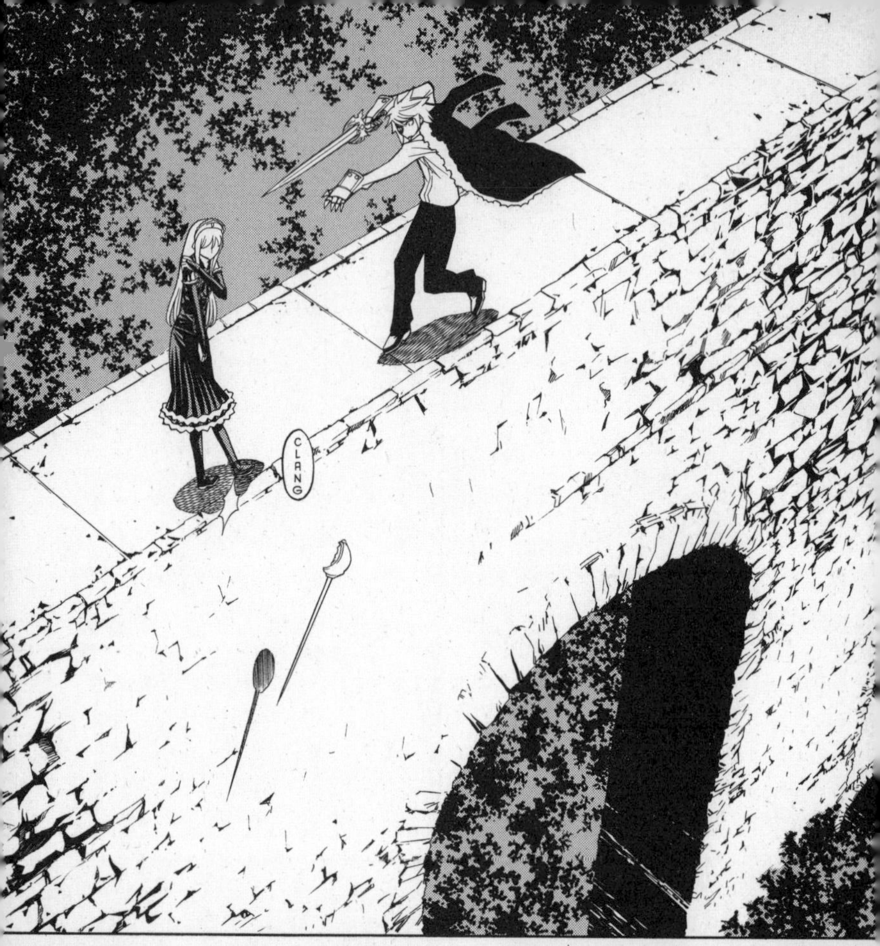
CLANG
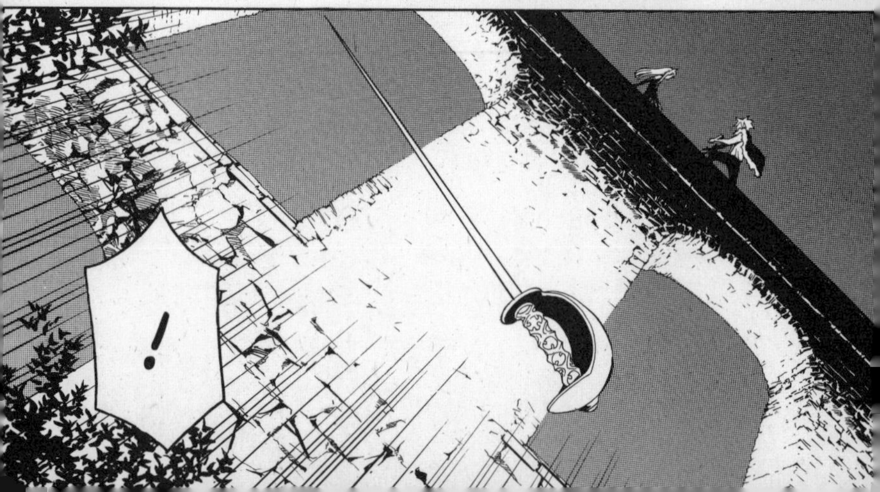
!

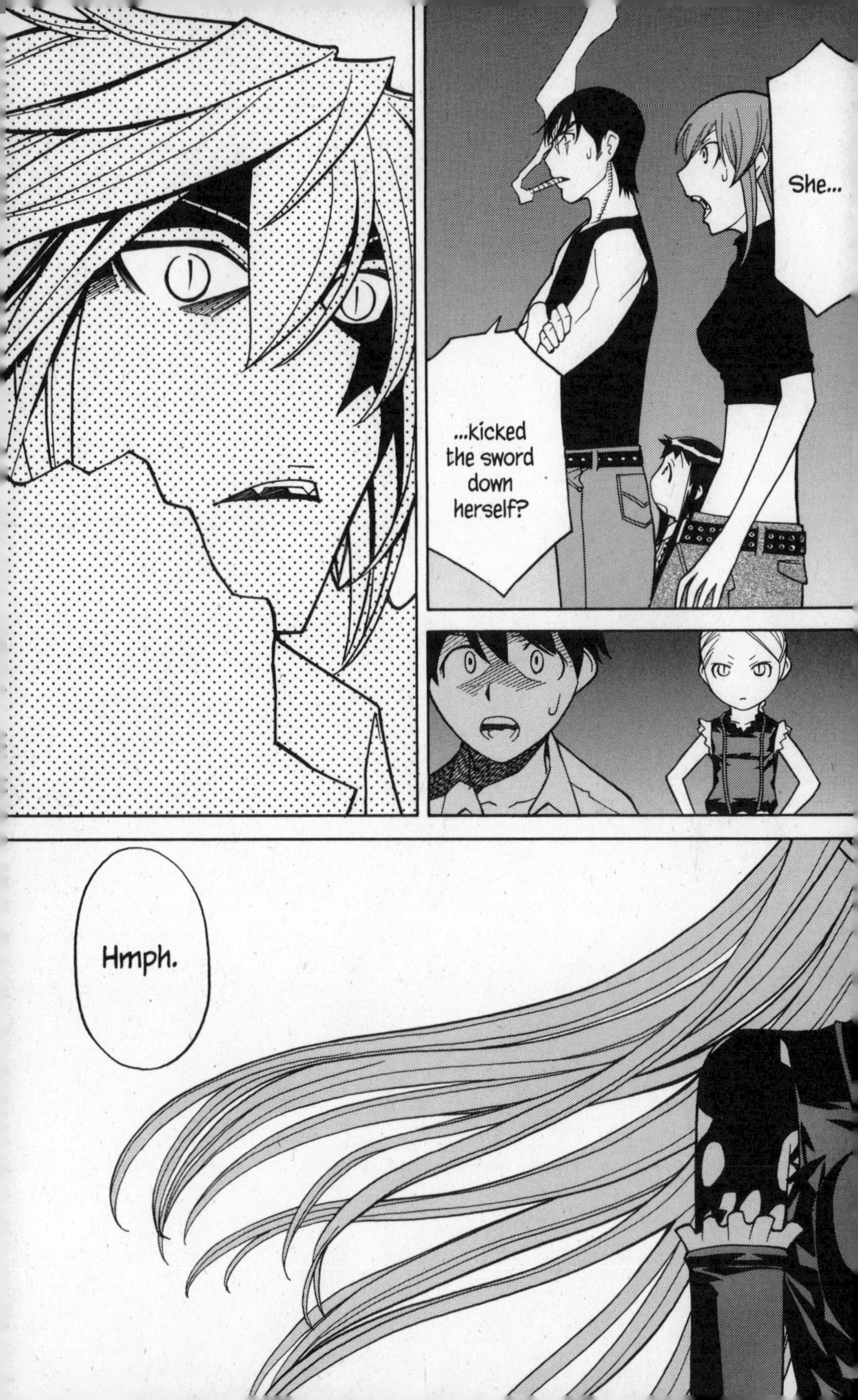
She...
...kicked the sword down herself?
Hmph.

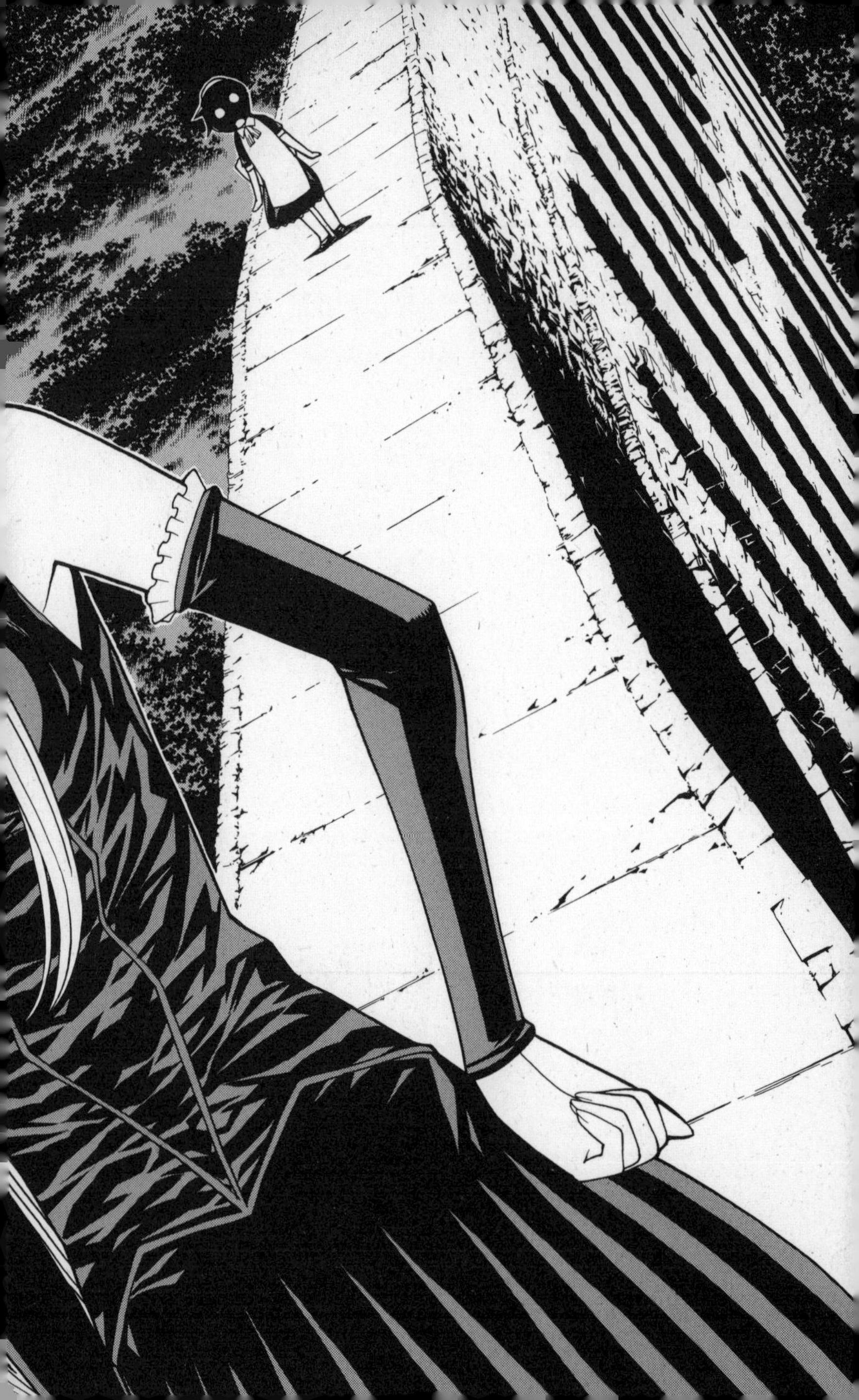

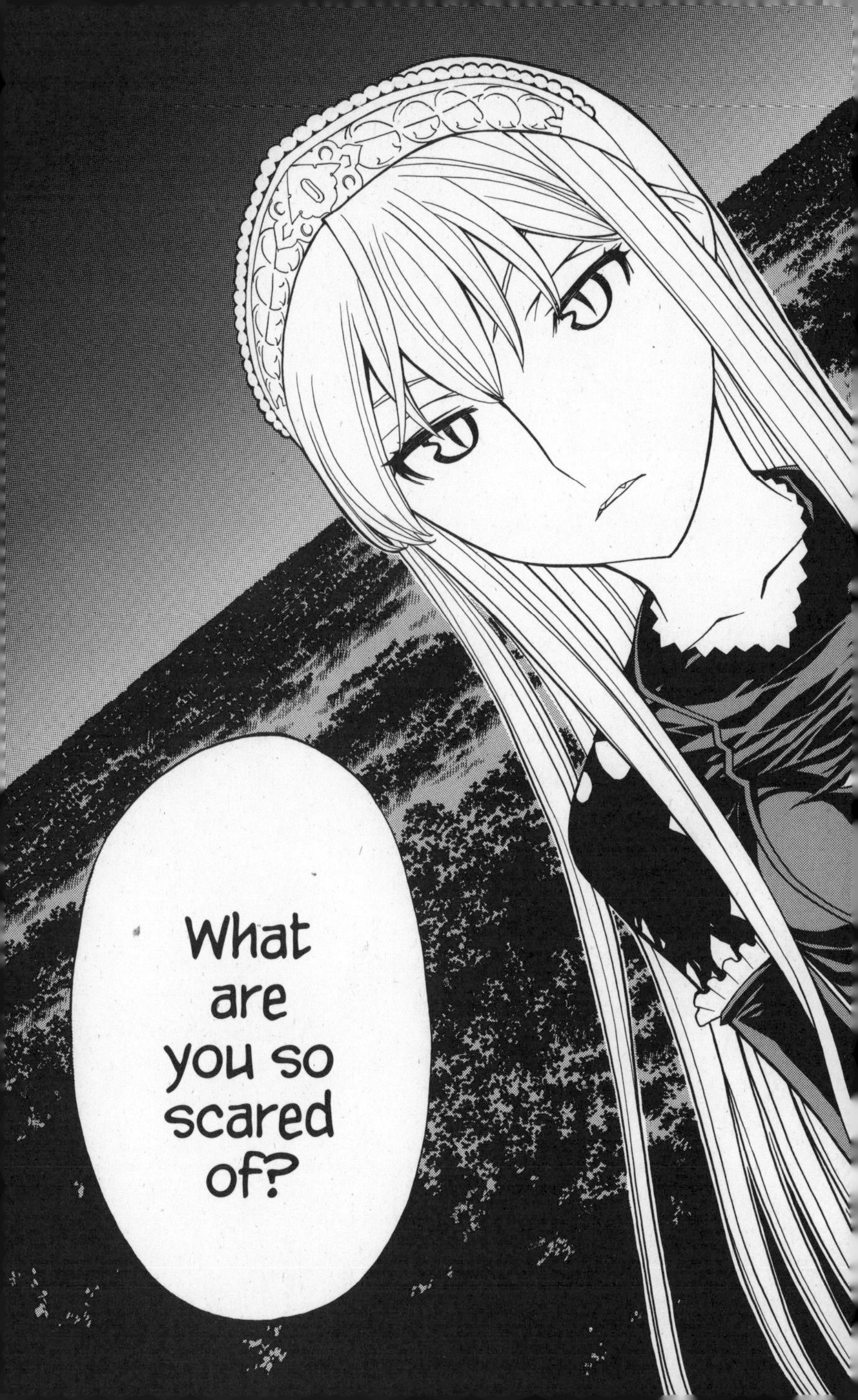
What are you so scared of?

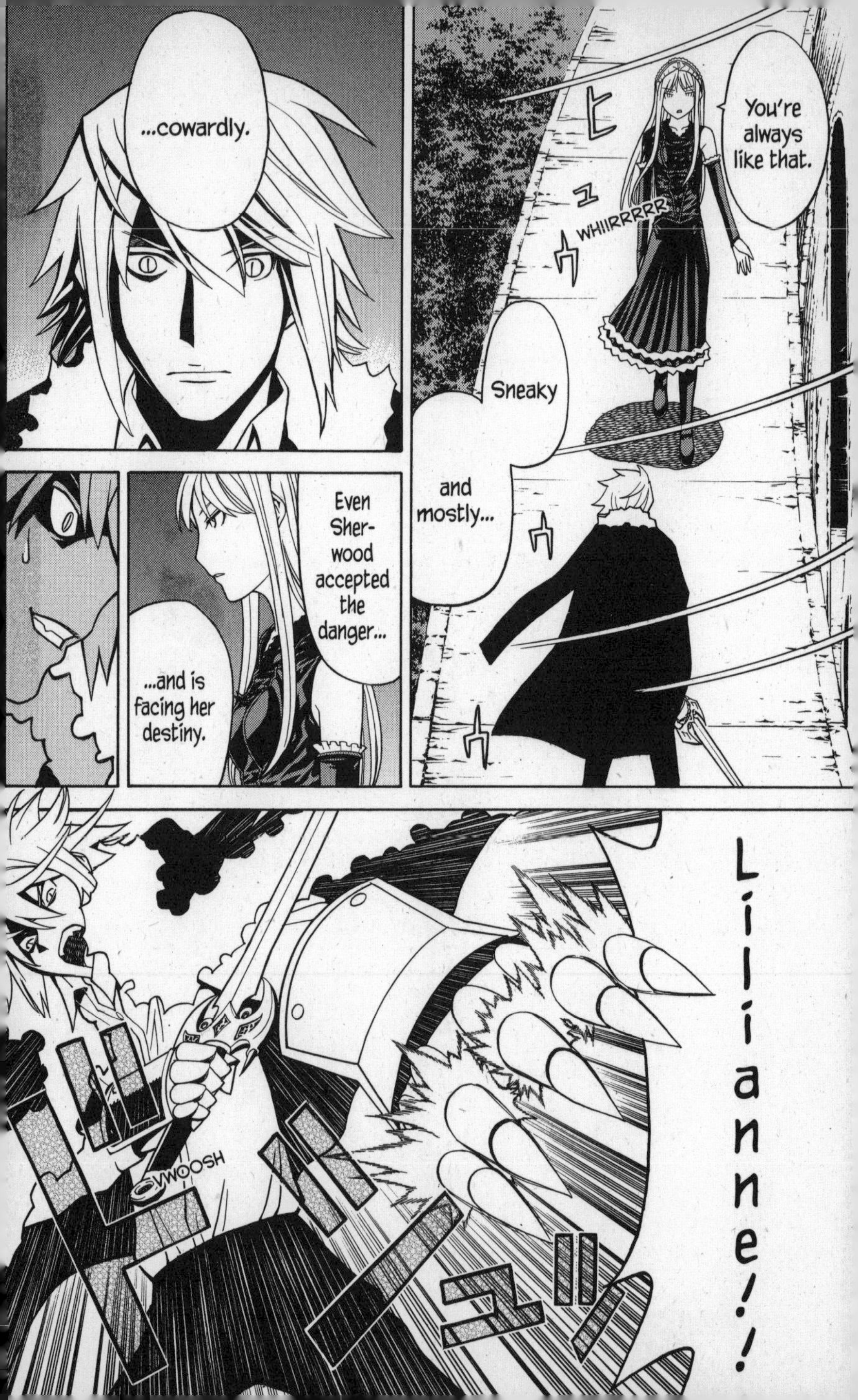
You're always like that.
WHIIRRRRR
Sneaky
and mostly...
...cowardly.
Even Sher-wood accepted the danger...
...and is facing her destiny.
WOOSH
Lilianne!!

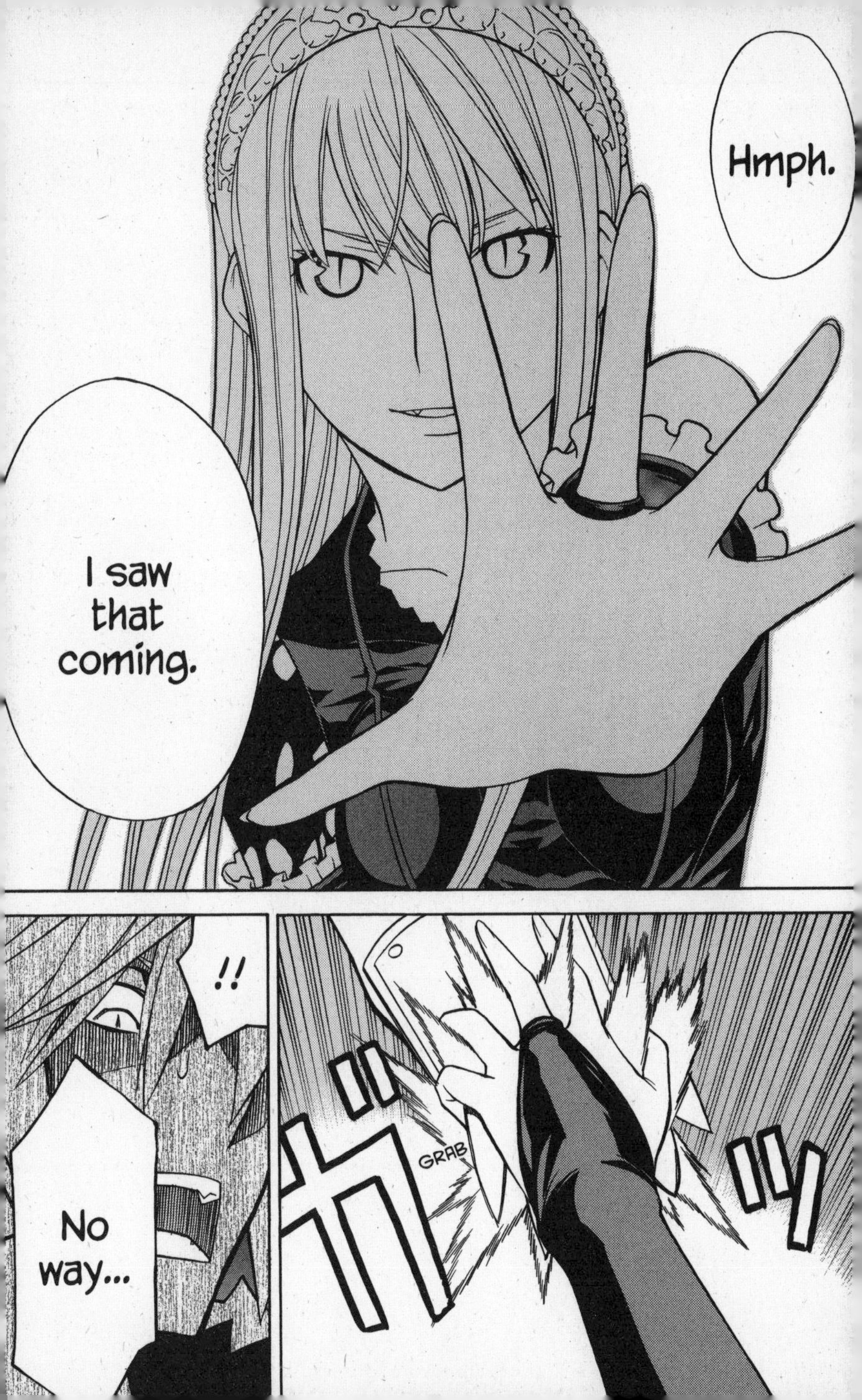
Hmph.
I saw that coming.
GRAB
!!
No way...

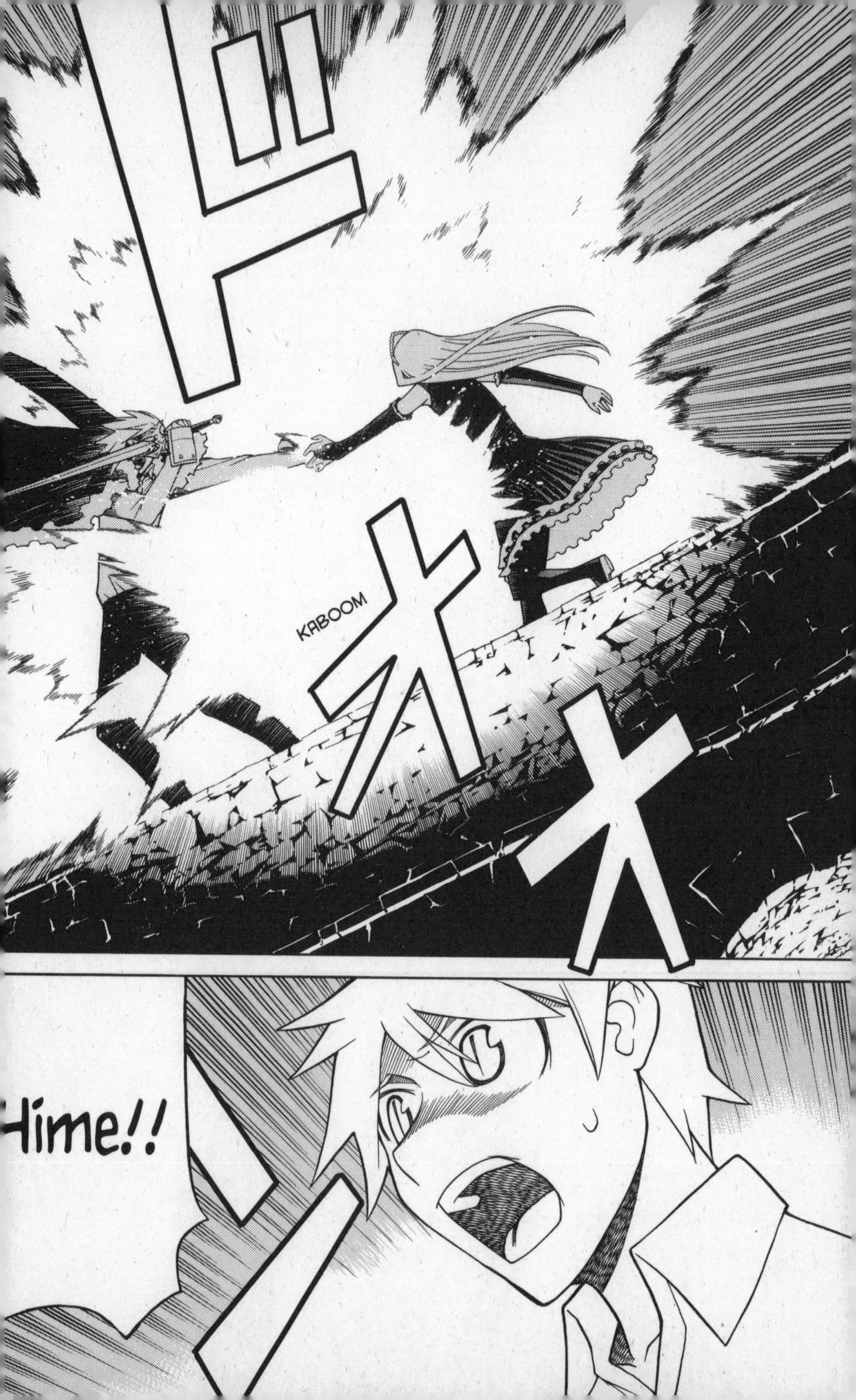
KABOOM
Hime!!

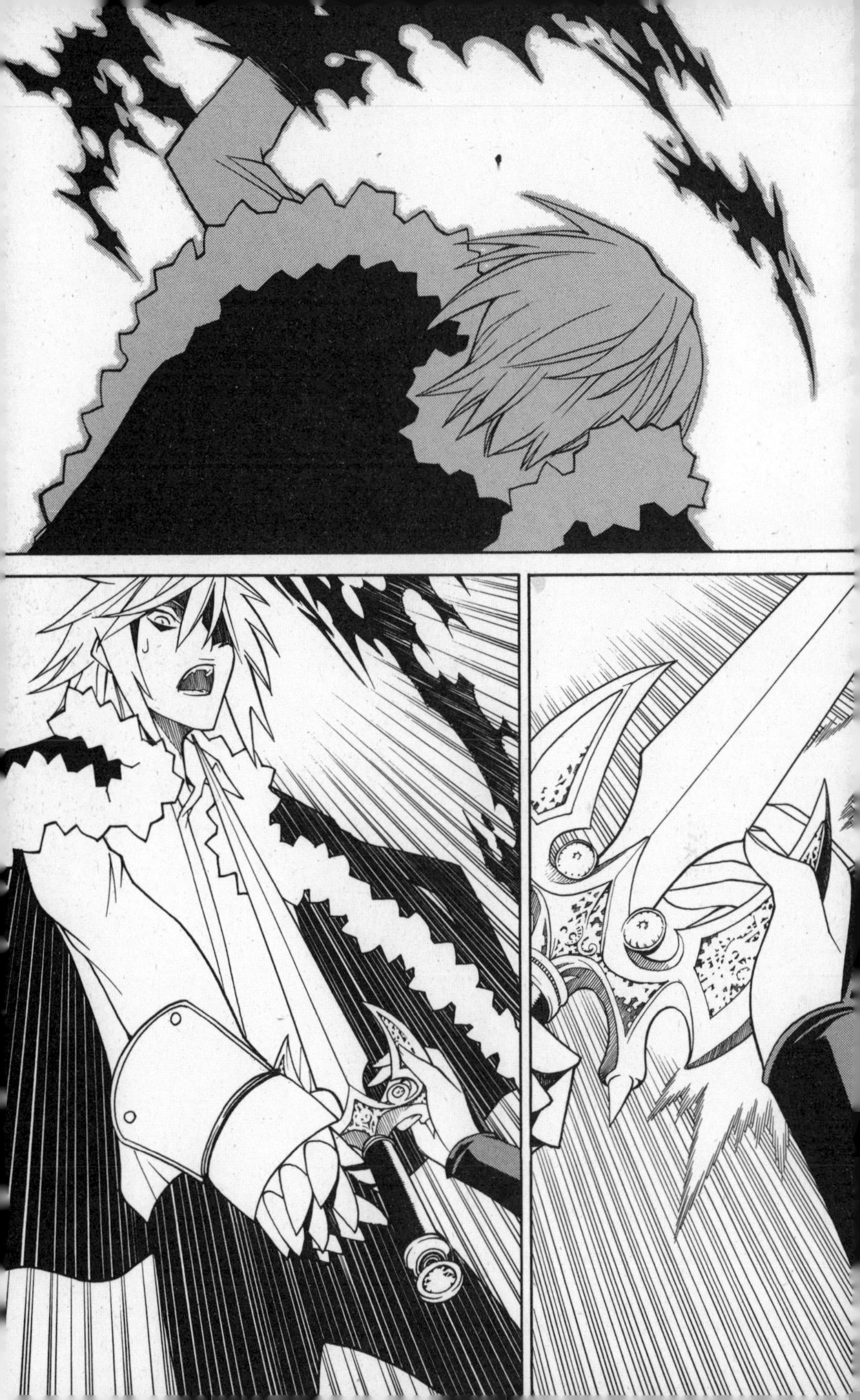

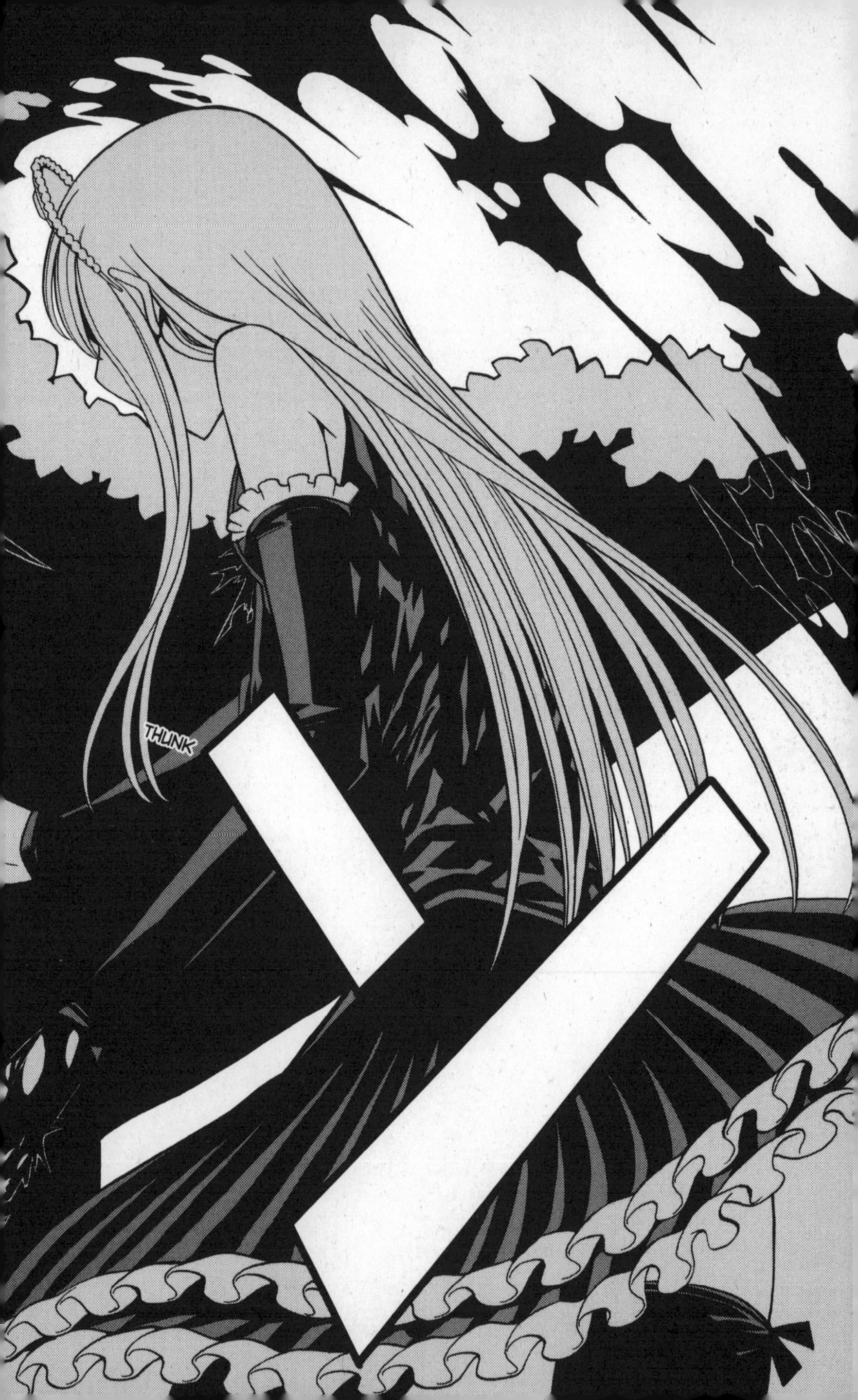
THUNK

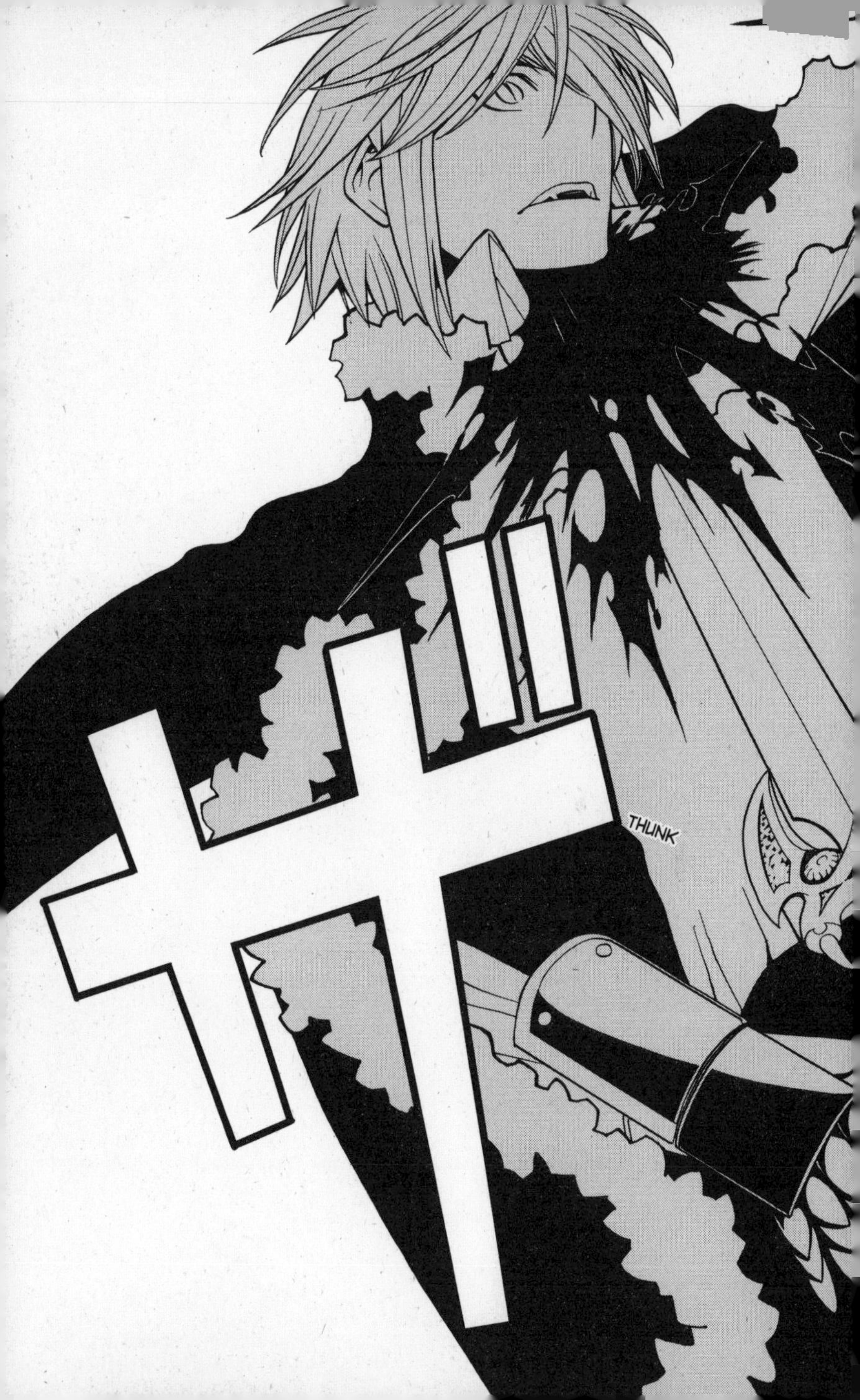
THUNK

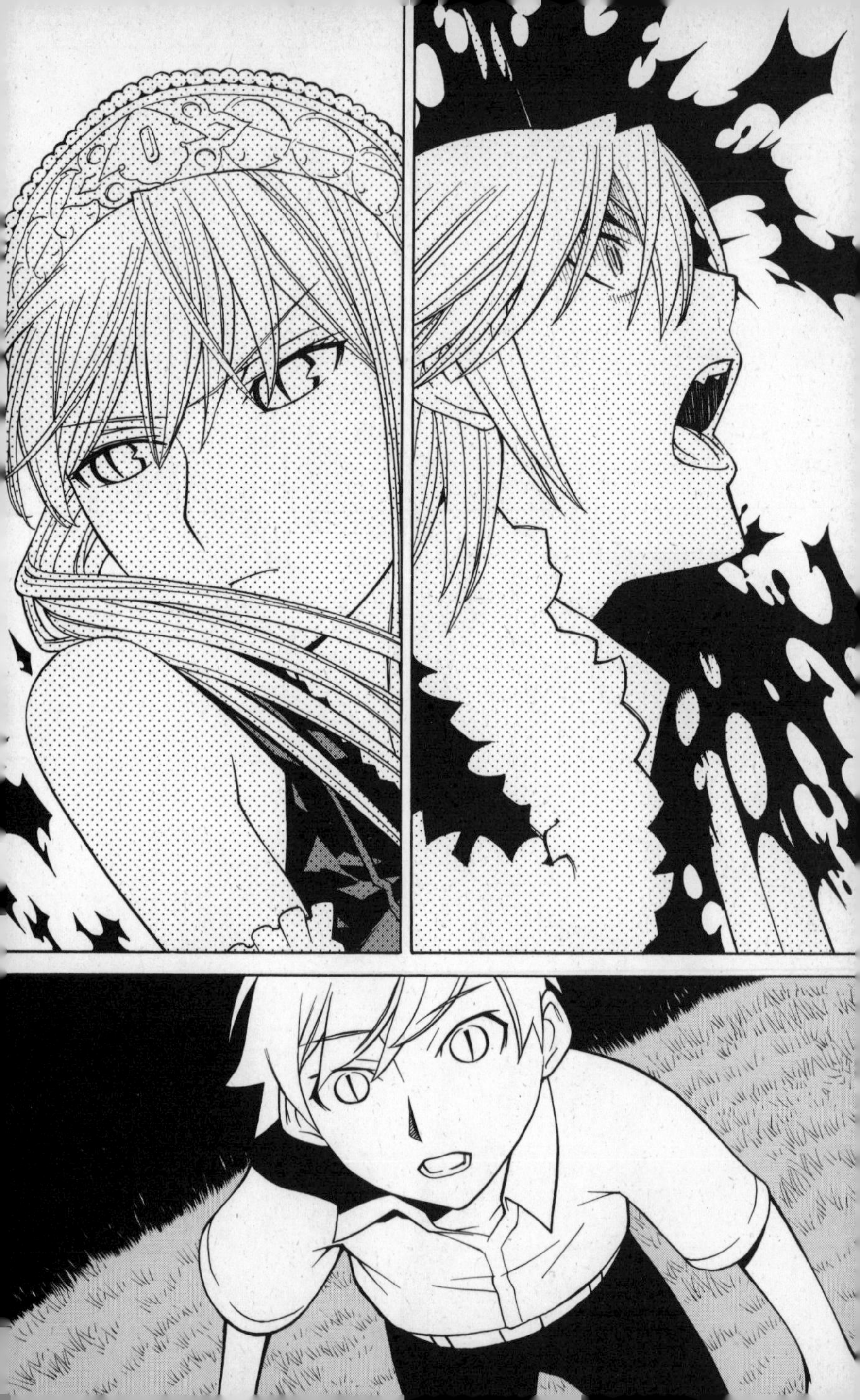

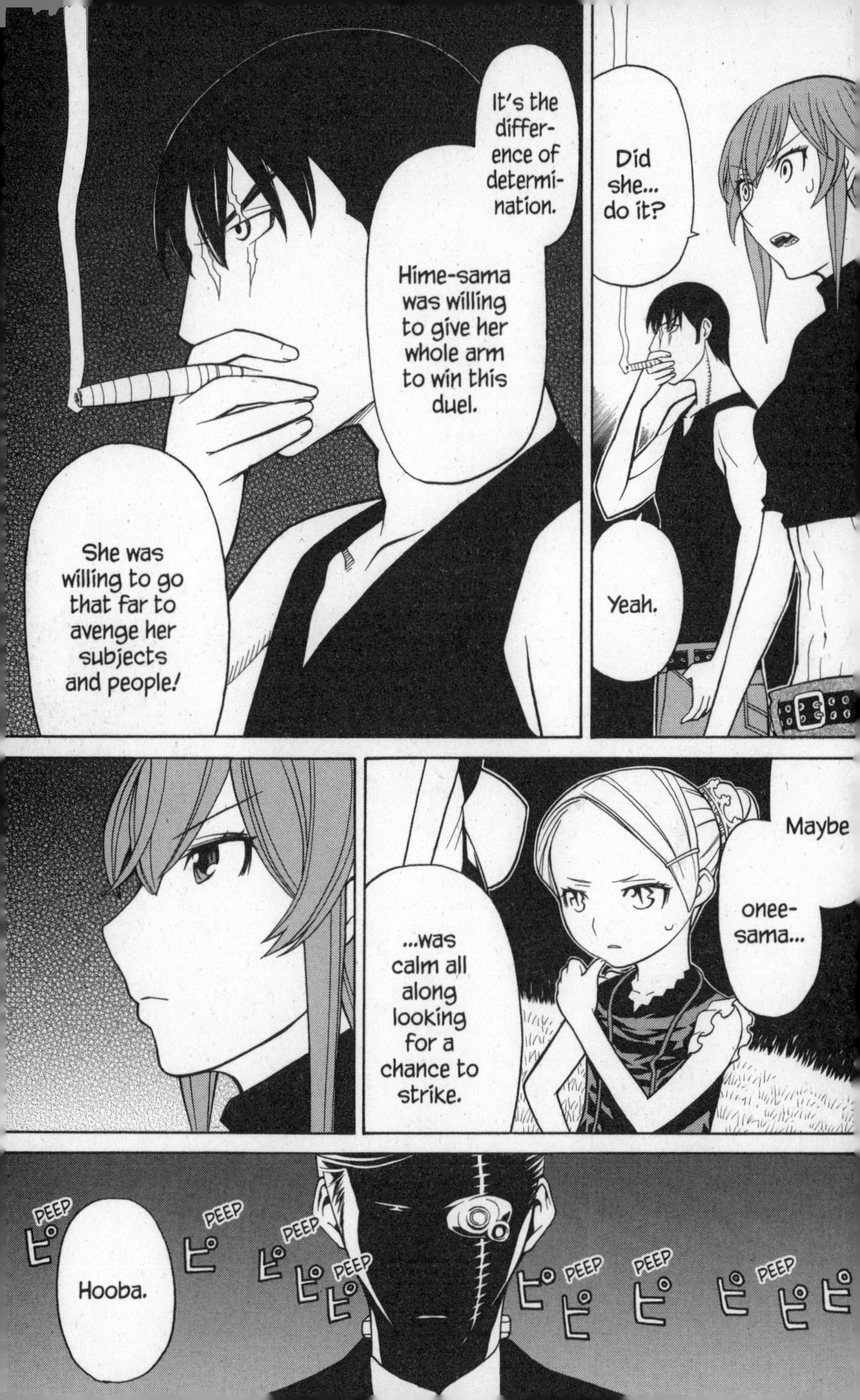
Did she... do it?
Yeah.
It's the differ-ence of determi-nation.
Hime-sama was willing to give her whole arm to win this duel.
She was willing to go that far to avenge her subjects and people!
Maybe onee-sama...
...was calm all along looking for a chance to strike.
PEEP ピ PEEP ピ PEEP ピ PEEP ピ PEEP ピ PEEP ピ PEEP ピ PEEP ピ
Hooba.

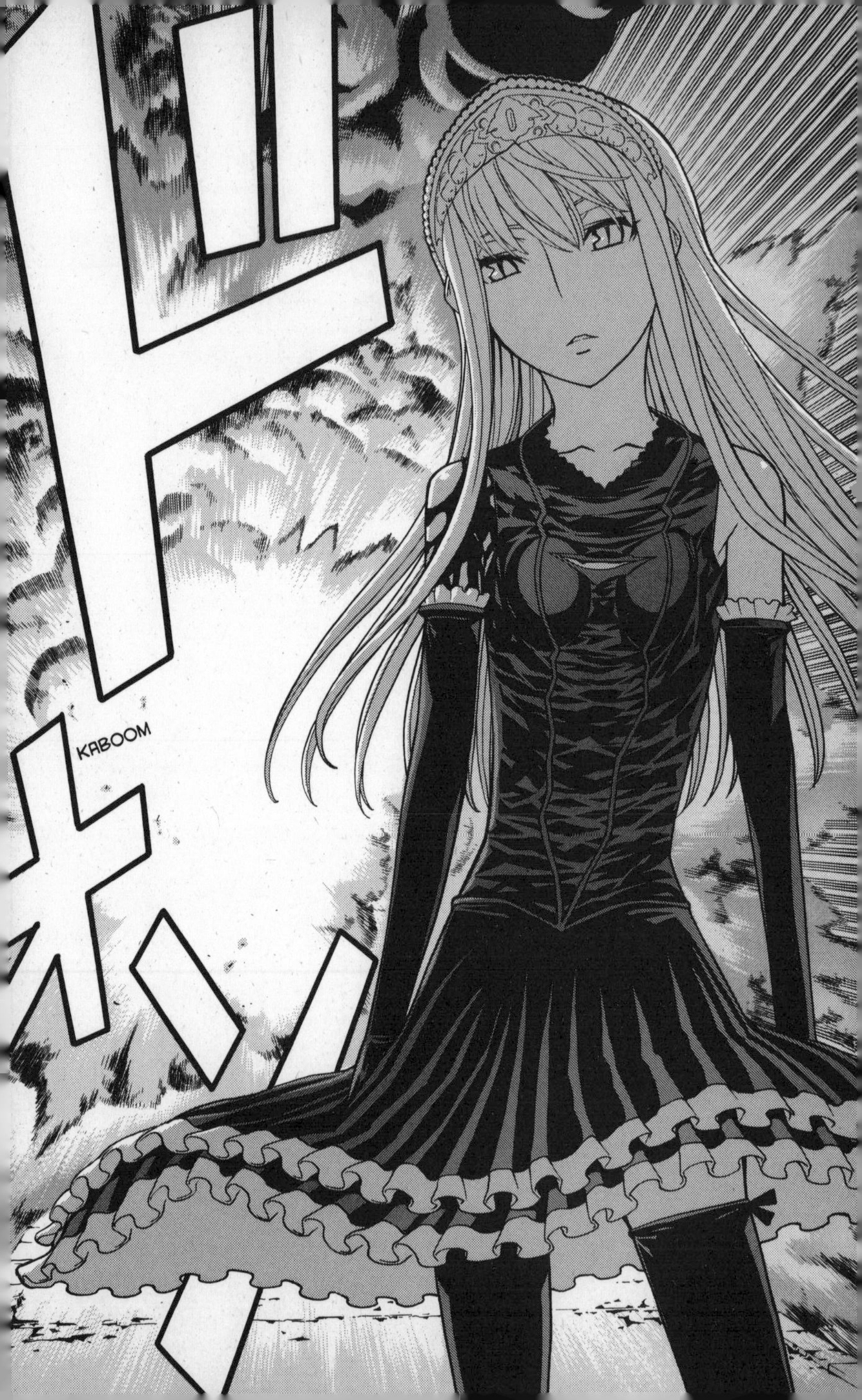
KABOOM

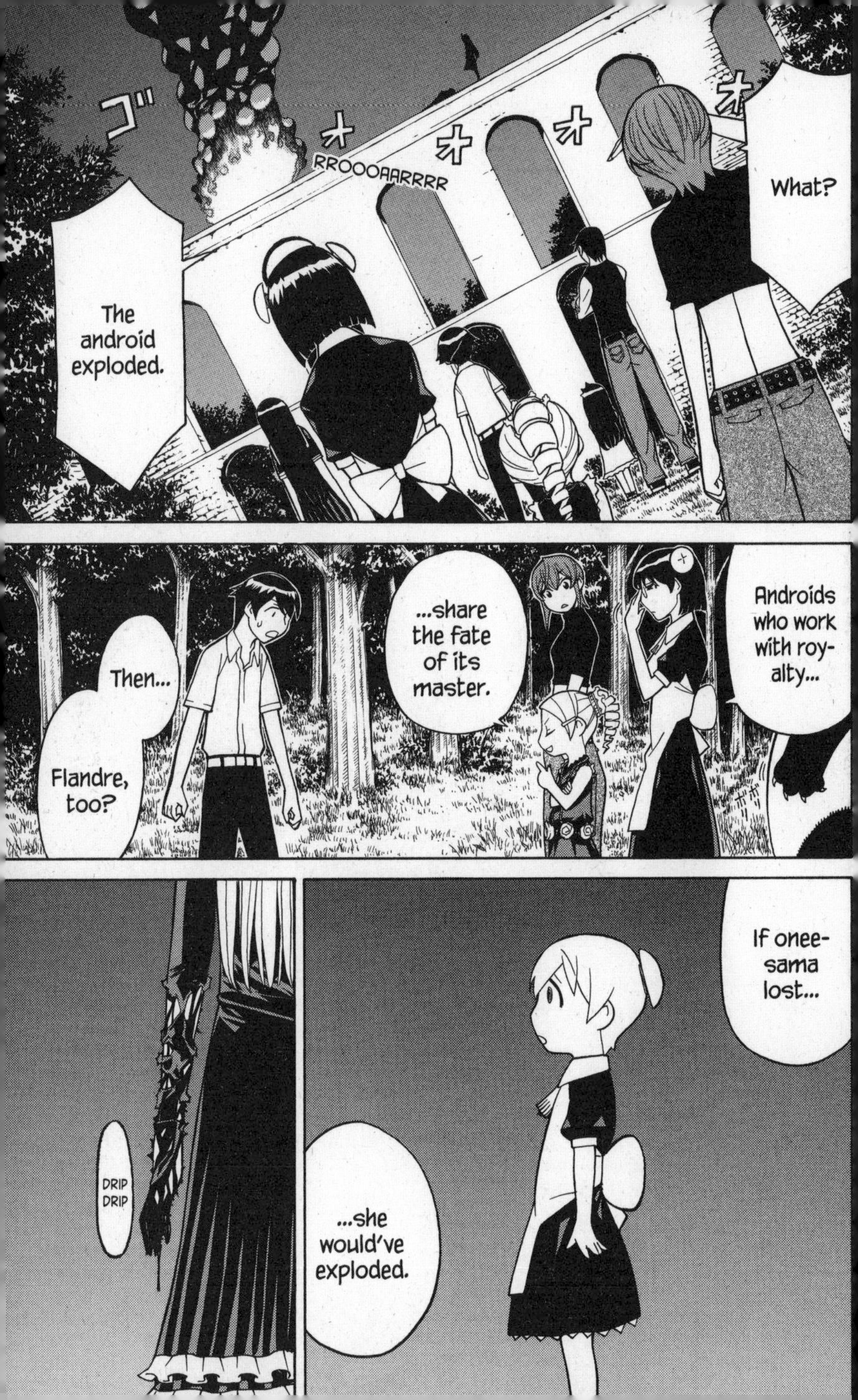
What?
ゴオオオオ
RROOOAARRRR
The android exploded.
Androids who work with royalty...
...share the fate of its master.
Then...
Flandre, too?
If onee-sama lost...
...she would've exploded.
DRIP DRIP

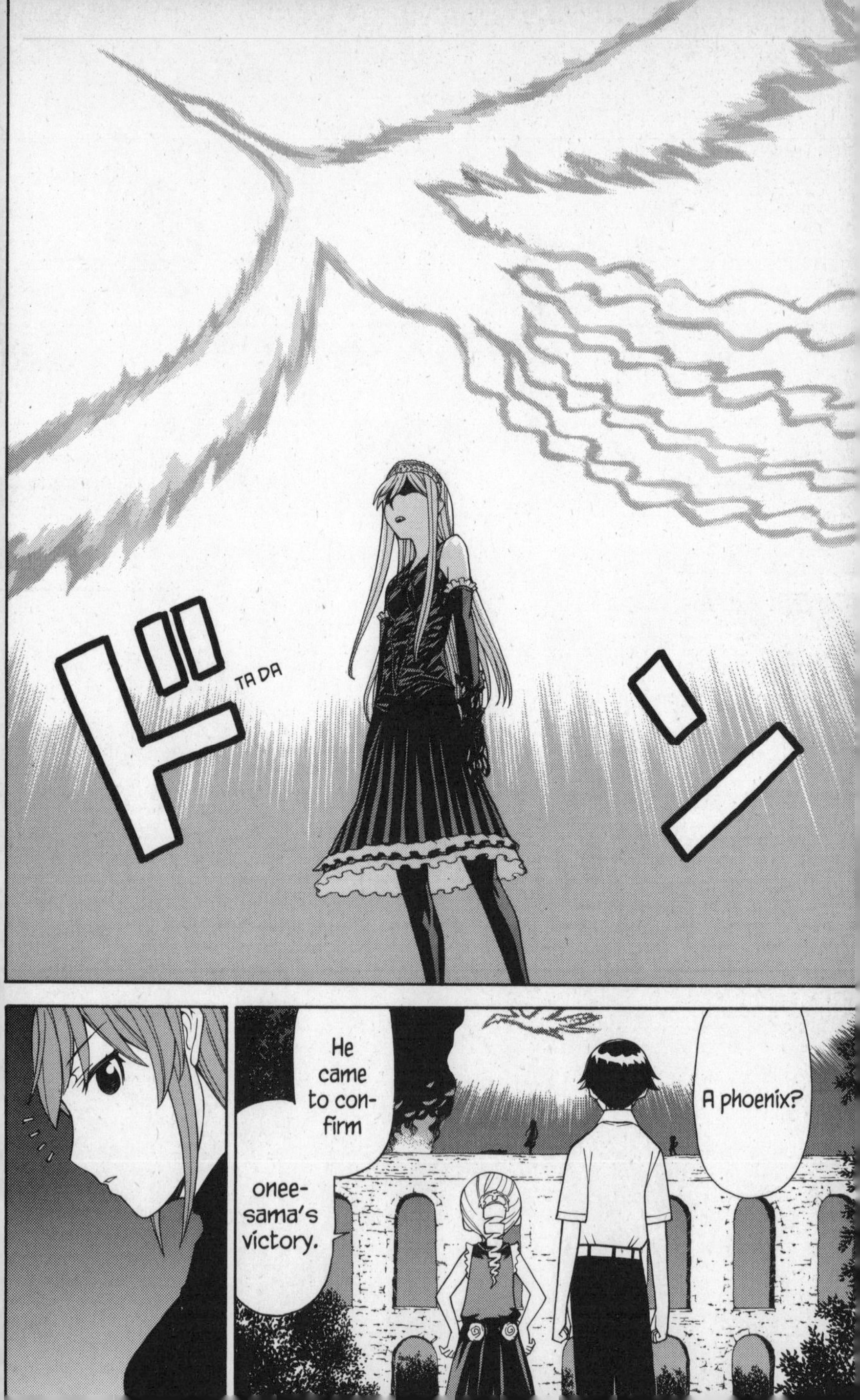
ドン
TA DA
A phoenix?
He came to confirm
onee-sama's victory.

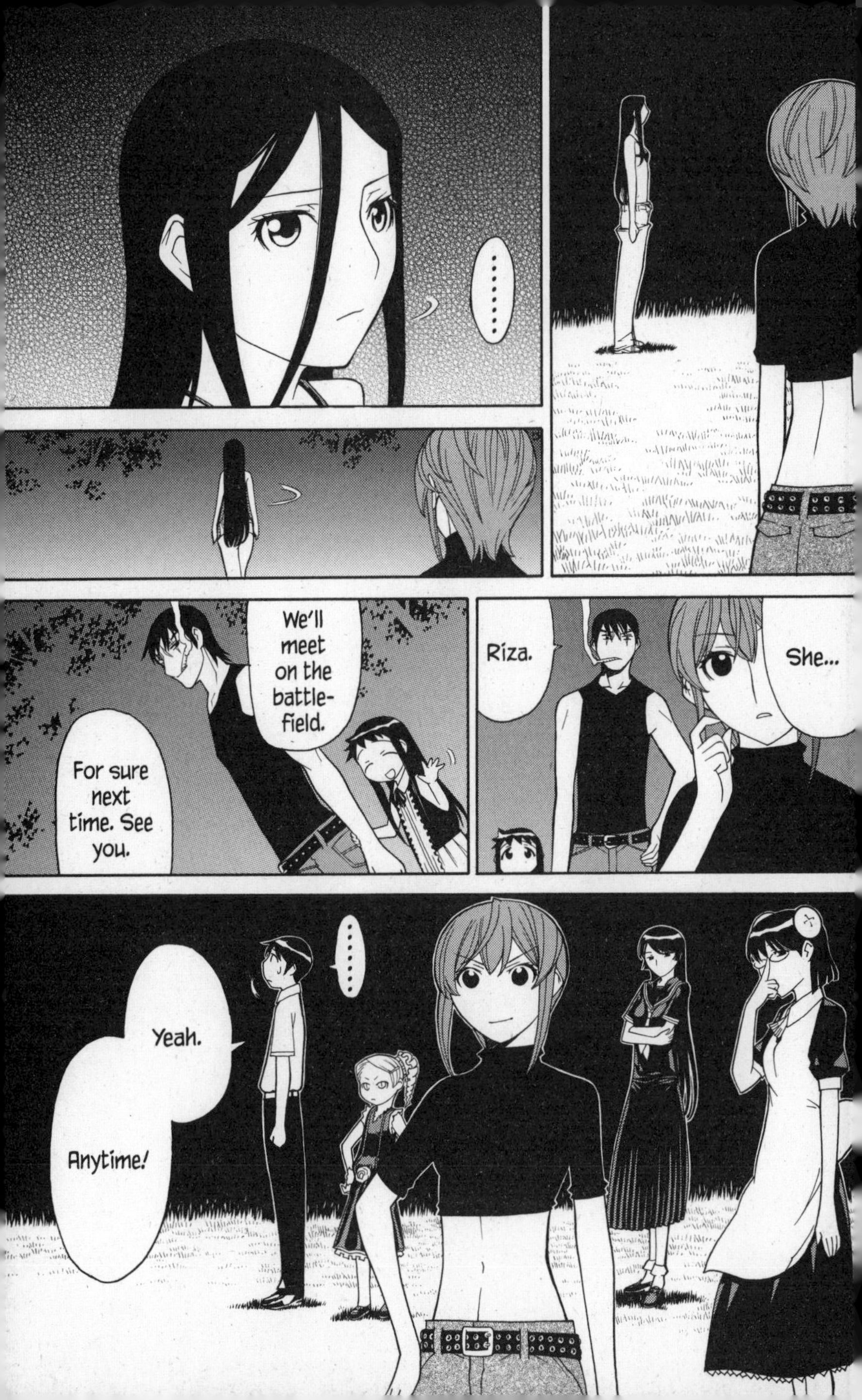
……
She...
Riza.
We'll meet on the battle-field.
For sure next time. See you.
……
Yeah.
Anytime!

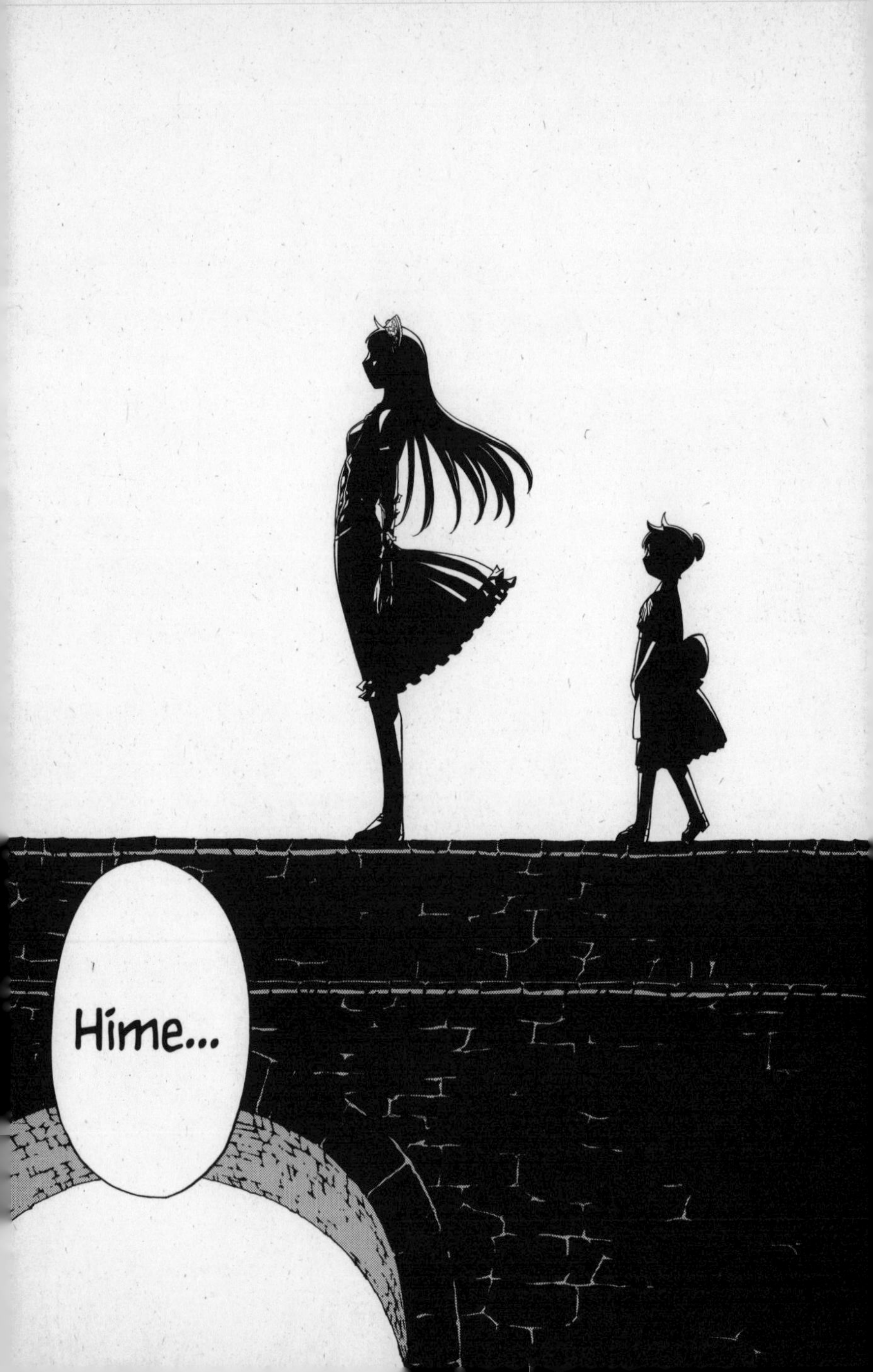
Hime...

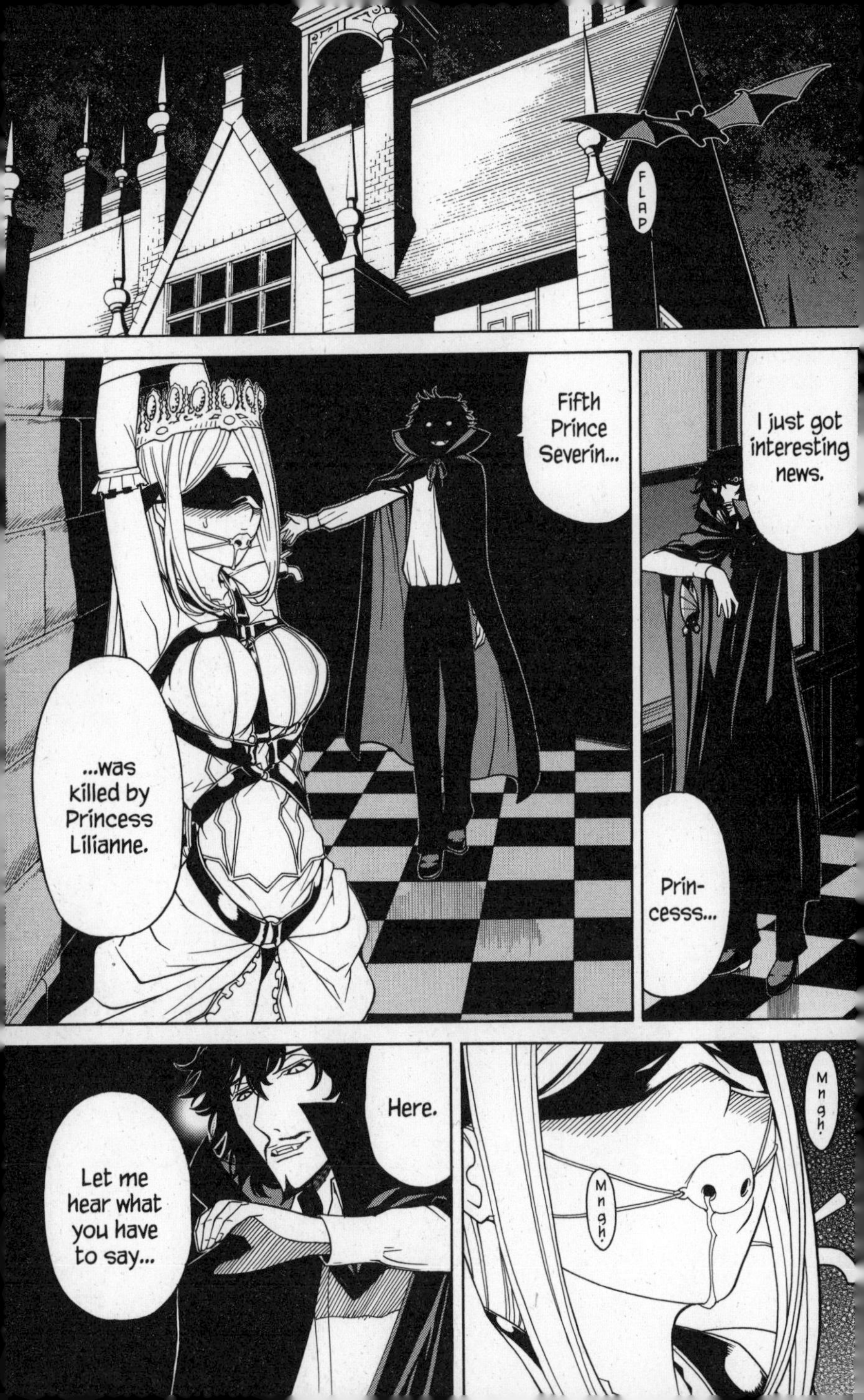
FLAP
I just got interesting news.
Prin-cesss...
Fifth Prince Severin...
...was killed by Princess Lilianne.
Mngh.
Mngh.
Here.
Let me hear what you have to say...

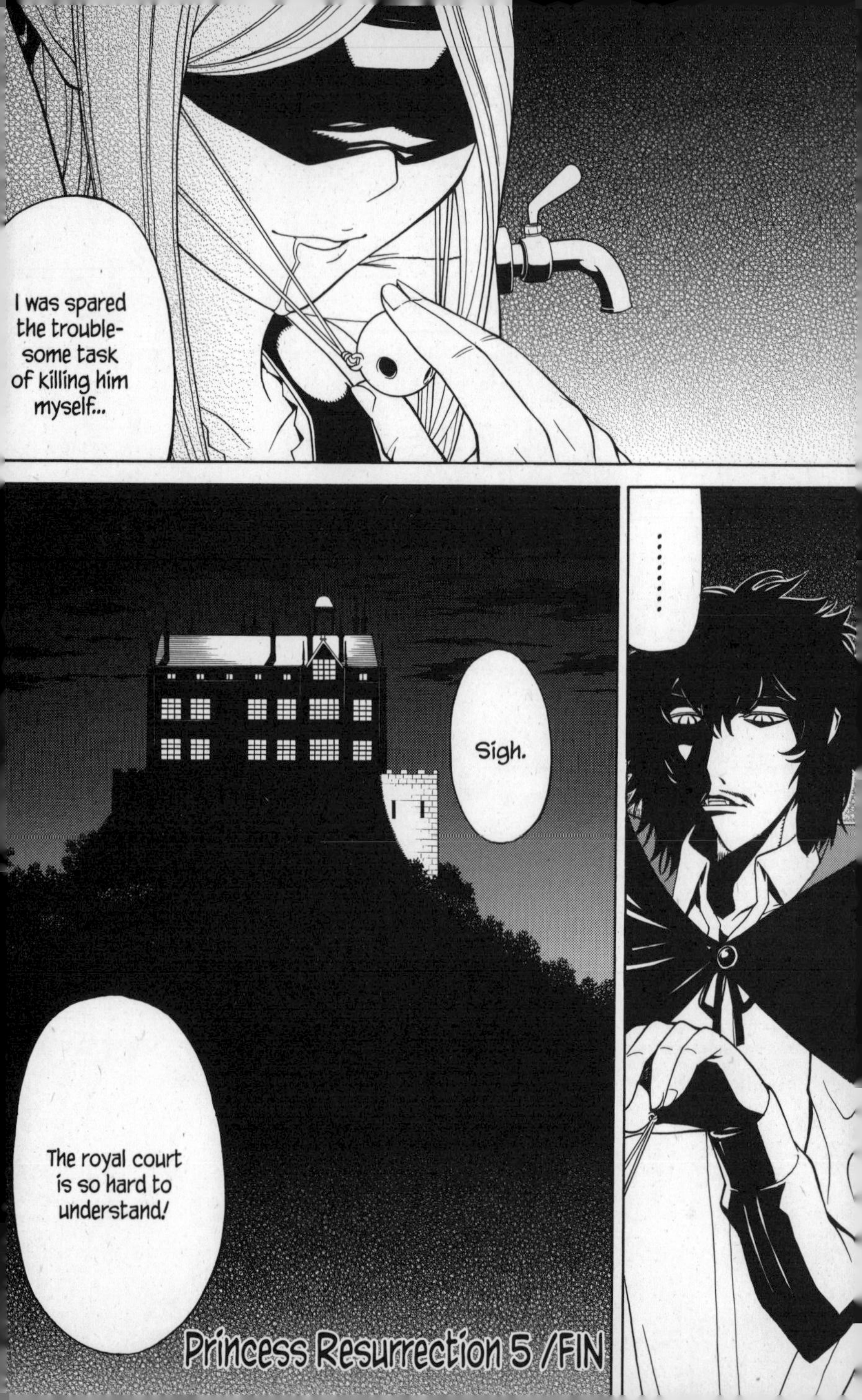
I was spared the trouble-some task of killing him myself...
......
Sigh.
The royal court is so hard to understand!
Princess Resurrection 5 /FIN

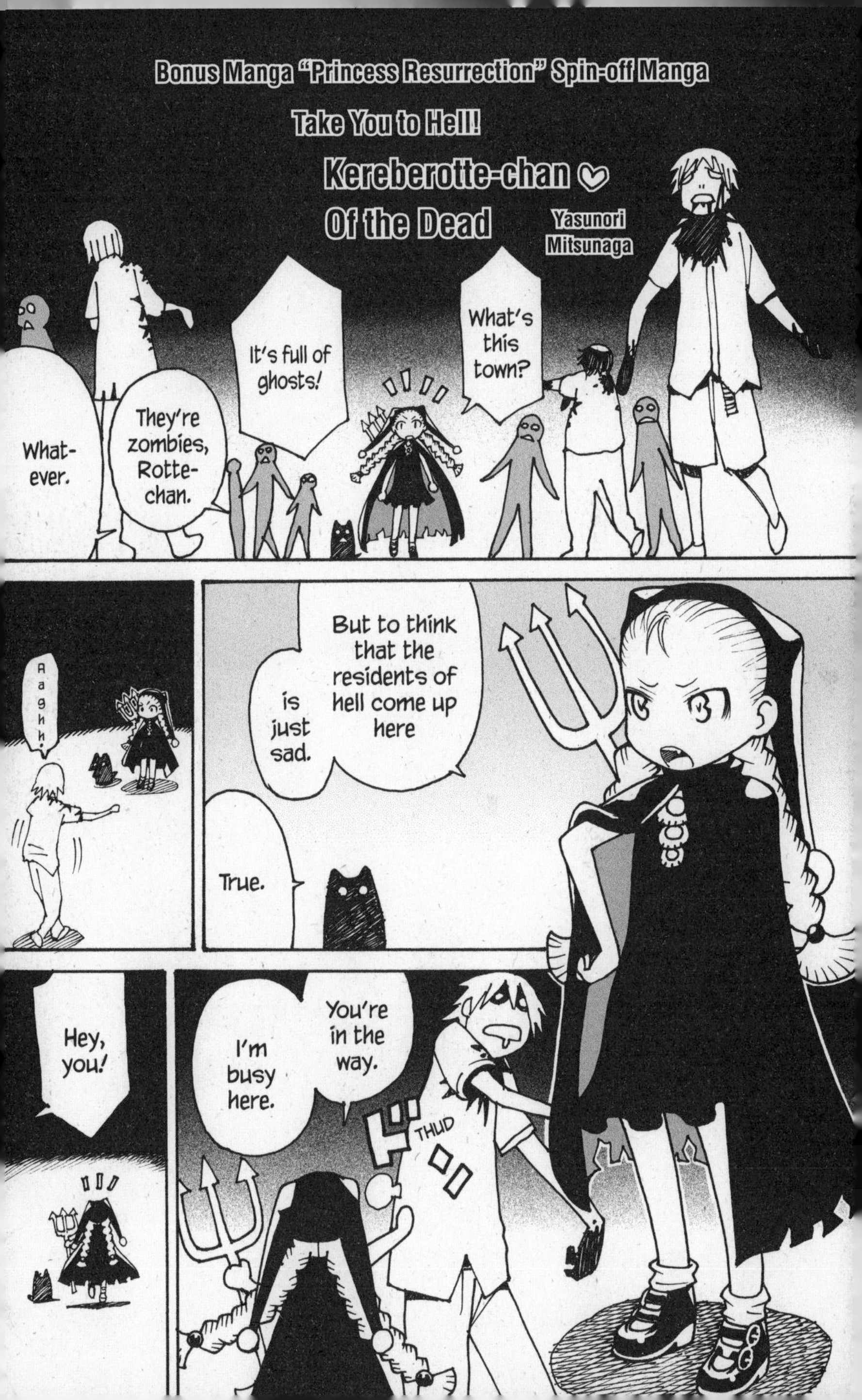
Bonus Manga "Princess Resurrection" Spin-off Manga
Take You to Hell!
Kereberotte-chan ♡ Of the Dead
Yasunori Mitsunaga
What's this town?
It's full of ghosts!
They're zombies, Rotte-chan.
Whatever.
But to think that the residents of hell come up here is just sad.
True.
Aghh!
You're in the way. I'm busy here.
THUD
Hey, you!

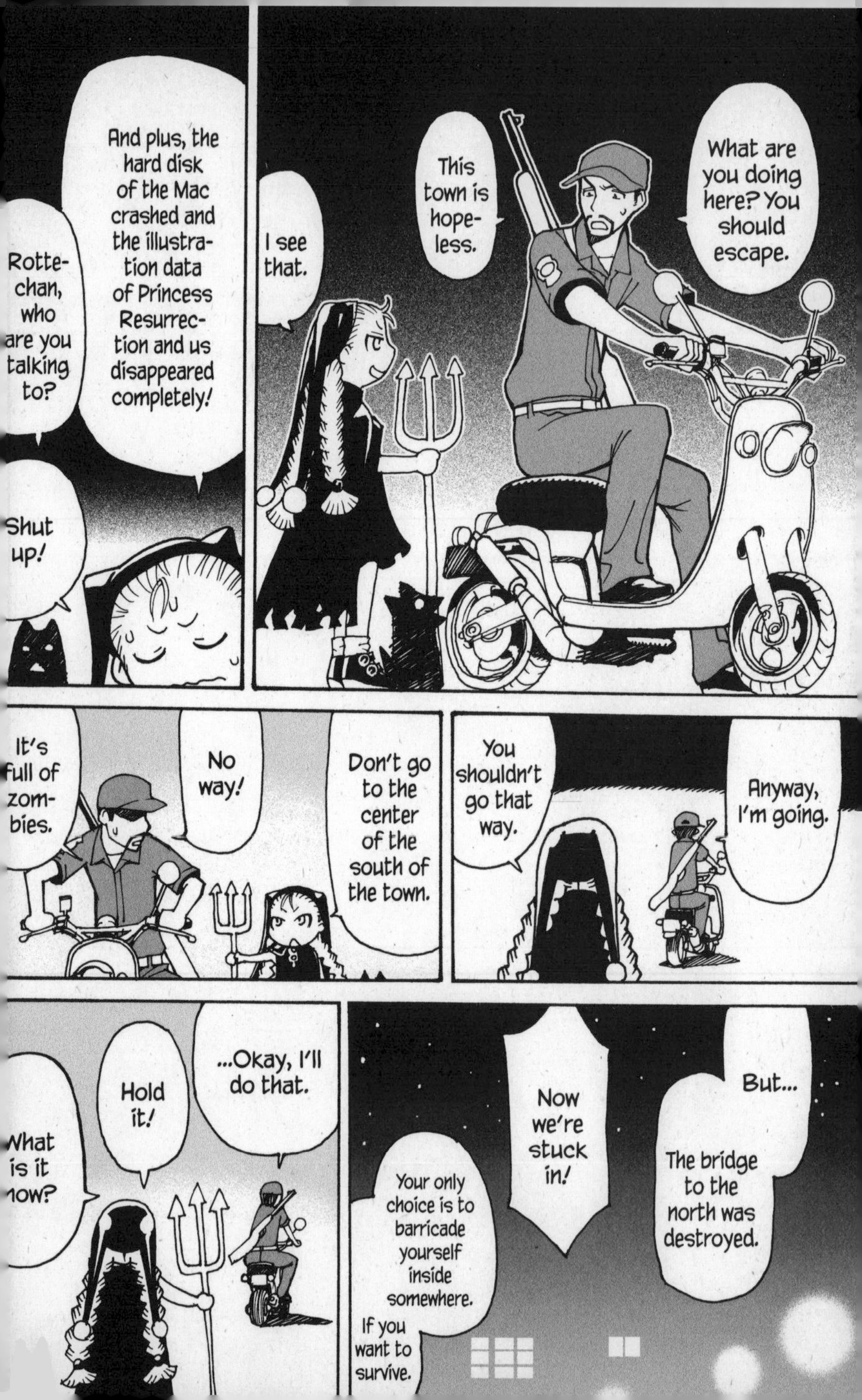
What are you doing here? You should escape.
This town is hopeless.
I see that.
And plus, the hard disk of the Mac crashed and the illustration data of Princess Resurrection and us disappeared completely!
Rotte-chan, who are you talking to?
Shut up!
Anyway, I'm going.
You shouldn't go that way.
Don't go to the center of the south of the town.
No way!
It's full of zombies.
But...
The bridge to the north was destroyed.
Now we're stuck in!
Your only choice is to barricade yourself inside somewhere.
If you want to survive.
...Okay, I'll do that.
Hold it!
What is it now?

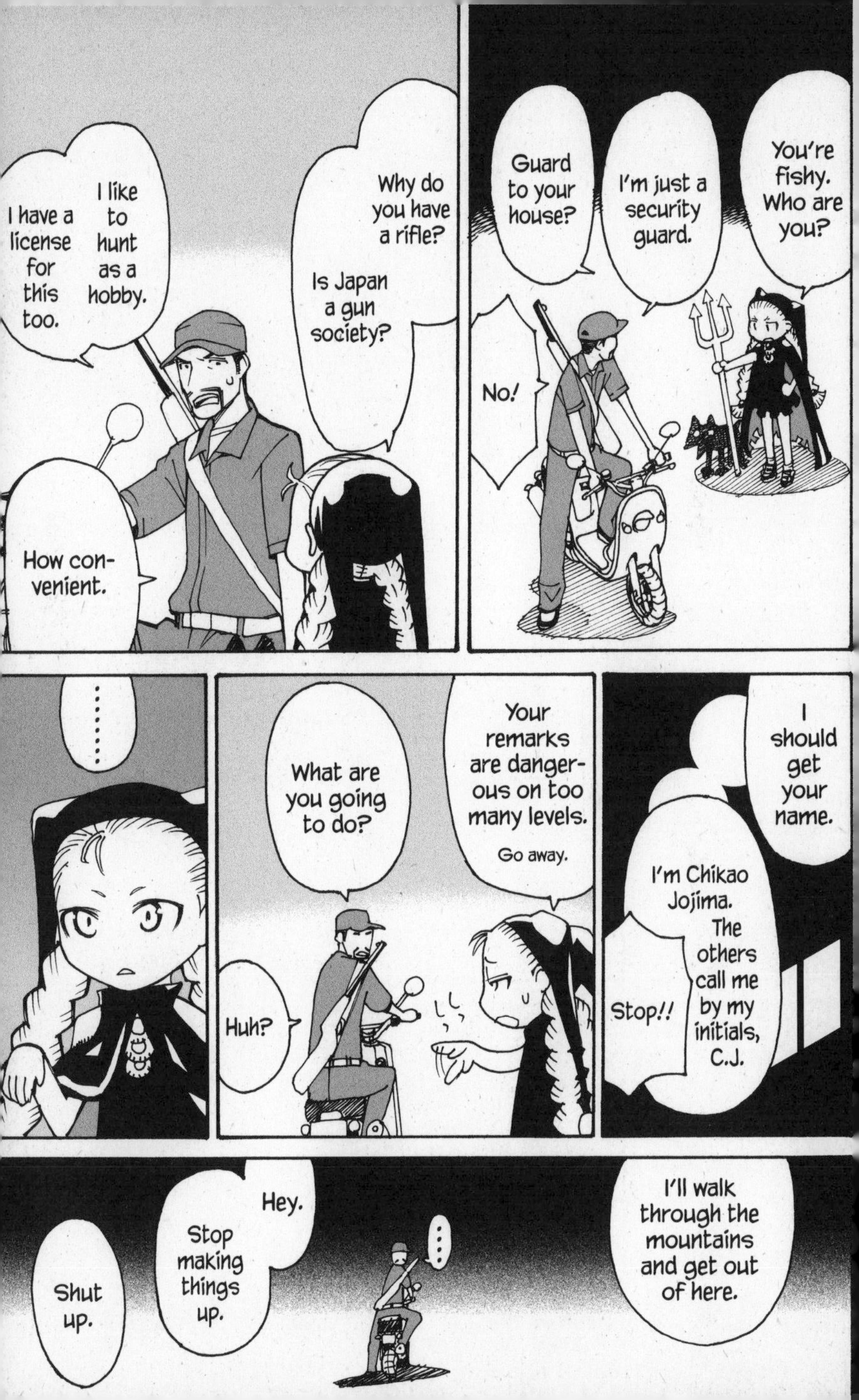
You're fishy. Who are you?
I'm just a security guard.
Guard to your house?
No!
Why do you have a rifle?
Is Japan a gun society?
I like to hunt as a hobby.
I have a license for this too.
How convenient.
I should get your name.
I'm Chikao Jojima. The others call me by my initials, C.J.
Stop!!
Your remarks are dangerous on too many levels.
Go away.
What are you going to do?
Huh?
......
I'll walk through the mountains and get out of here.
...
Hey.
Stop making things up.
Shut up.

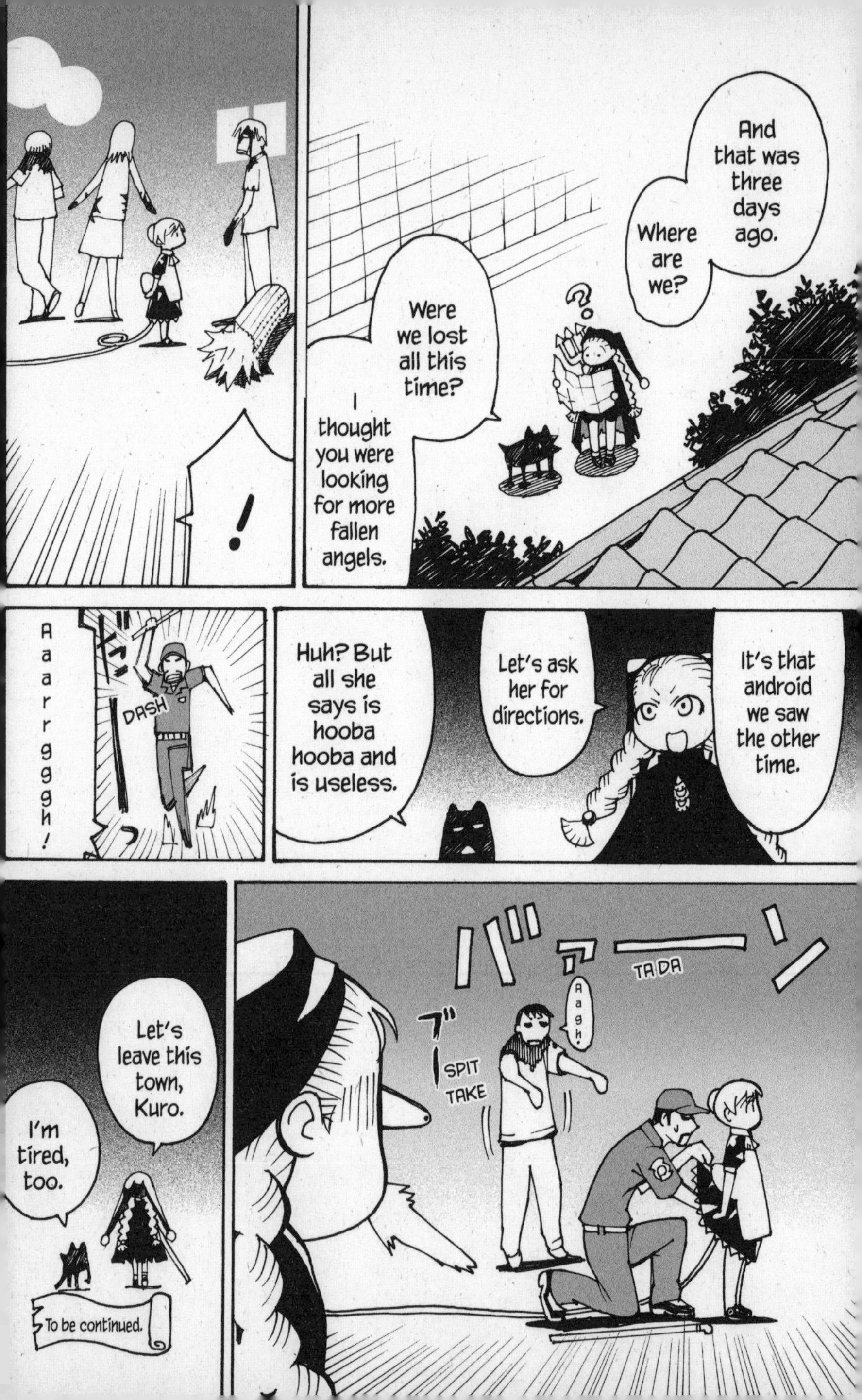
And that was three days ago.
Where are we?
Were we lost all this time?
I thought you were looking for more fallen angels.
!
It's that android we saw the other time.
Let's ask her for directions.
Huh? But all she says is hooba hooba and is useless.
DASH
Aaarrgggh!
TA DA
Aagh.
SPIT TAKE
Let's leave this town, Kuro.
I'm tired, too.
To be continued.

Translation Notes

Japanese is a tricky language for most Westerners, and translation is often more an art than a science. For your edification and reading pleasure, here are notes on some of the places where we could have gone in a different direction, or where a Japanese cultural reference is used.

Onee-sama, page 80

Onee-sama is an honorific way to say "older sister."

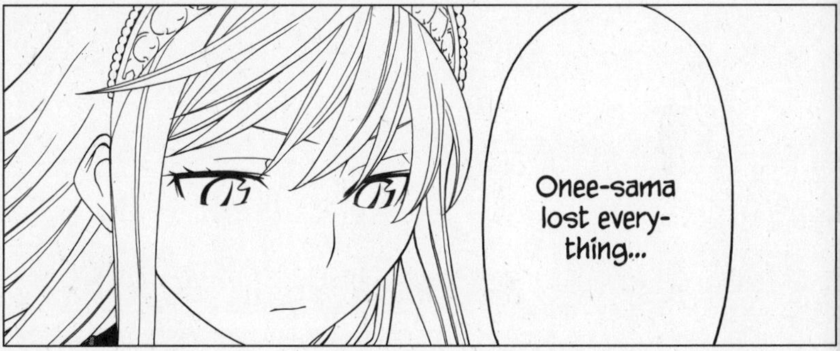
Onee-sama lost every-thing...

Nii-sama, page 159

Nii-sama is an honorific way to say "older brother." You can add "o" to the end to indicate more respect, but it is not needed.

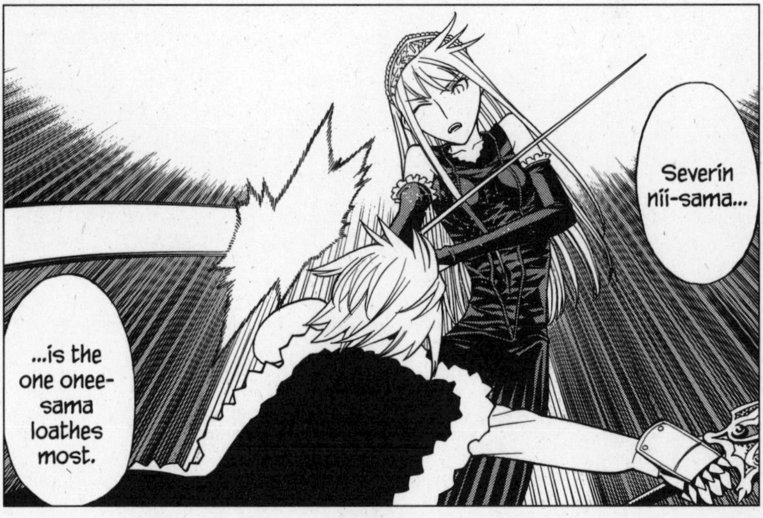
Severin nii-sama...
...is the one onee-sama loathes most.

Preview of volume 6

We're pleased to present you with a preview of volume 6. Please check our website (www.delreymanga.com) to see when this volume will be available in English. For now you'll have to make do with the Japanese!

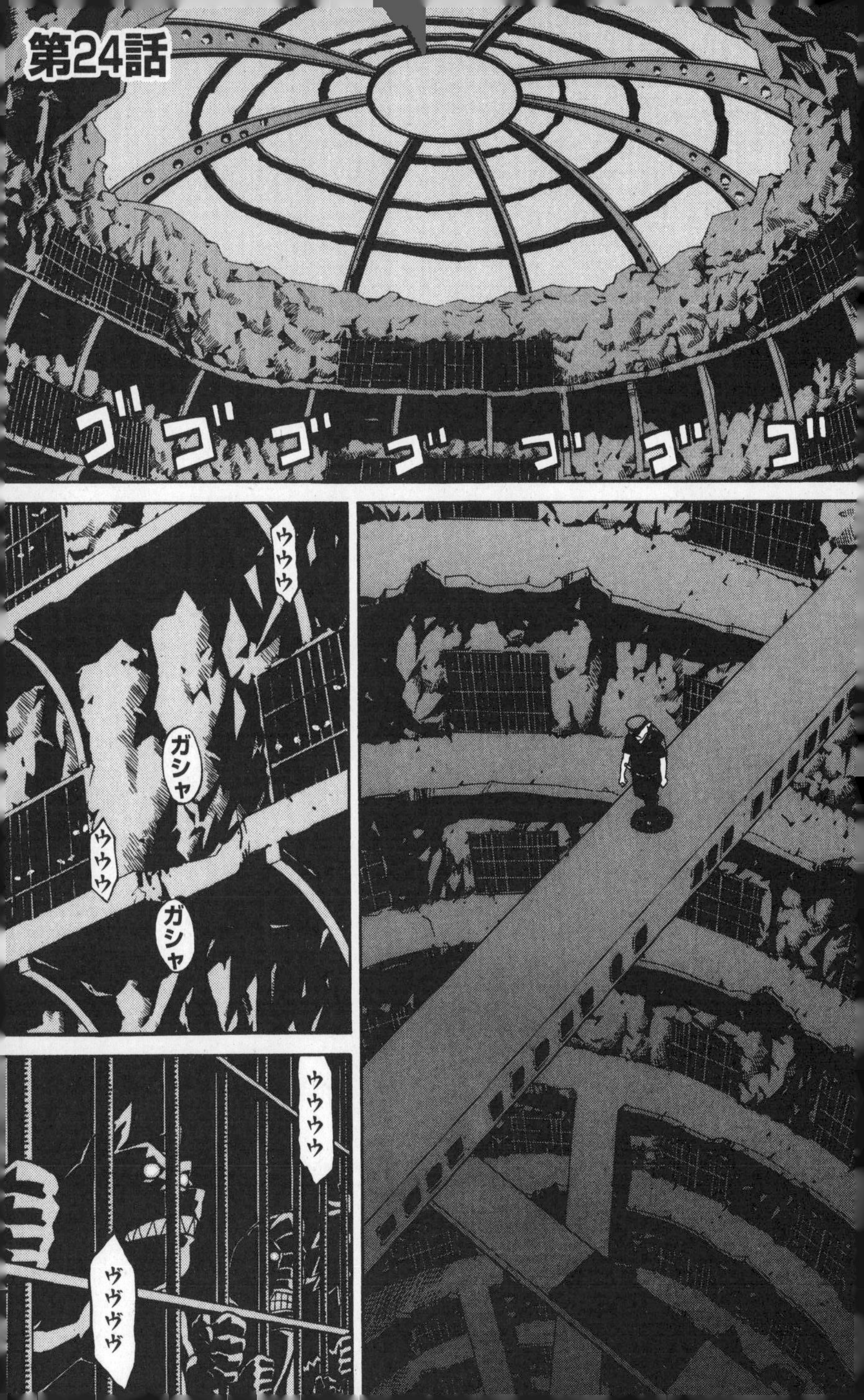
第24話
ゴゴゴゴゴゴゴ
ウウウ
ガシャ
ウウウ
ガシャ
ウウウウ
ヴヴヴヴ

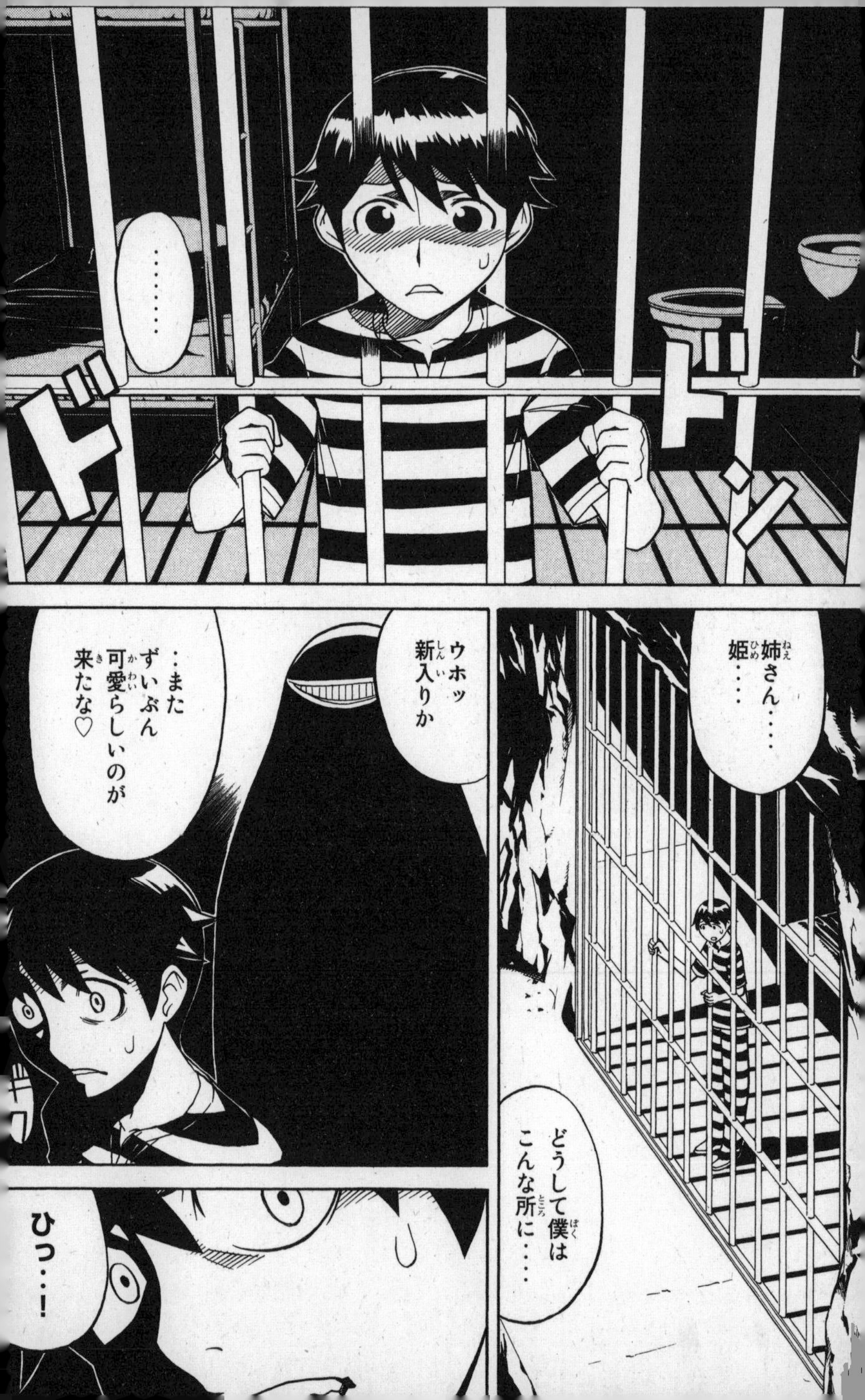
……
ドドン
姉さん……姫……
どうして僕はこんな所に……
ウホッ新入りか
…また ずいぶん可愛らしいのが来たな♡
ひっ…!

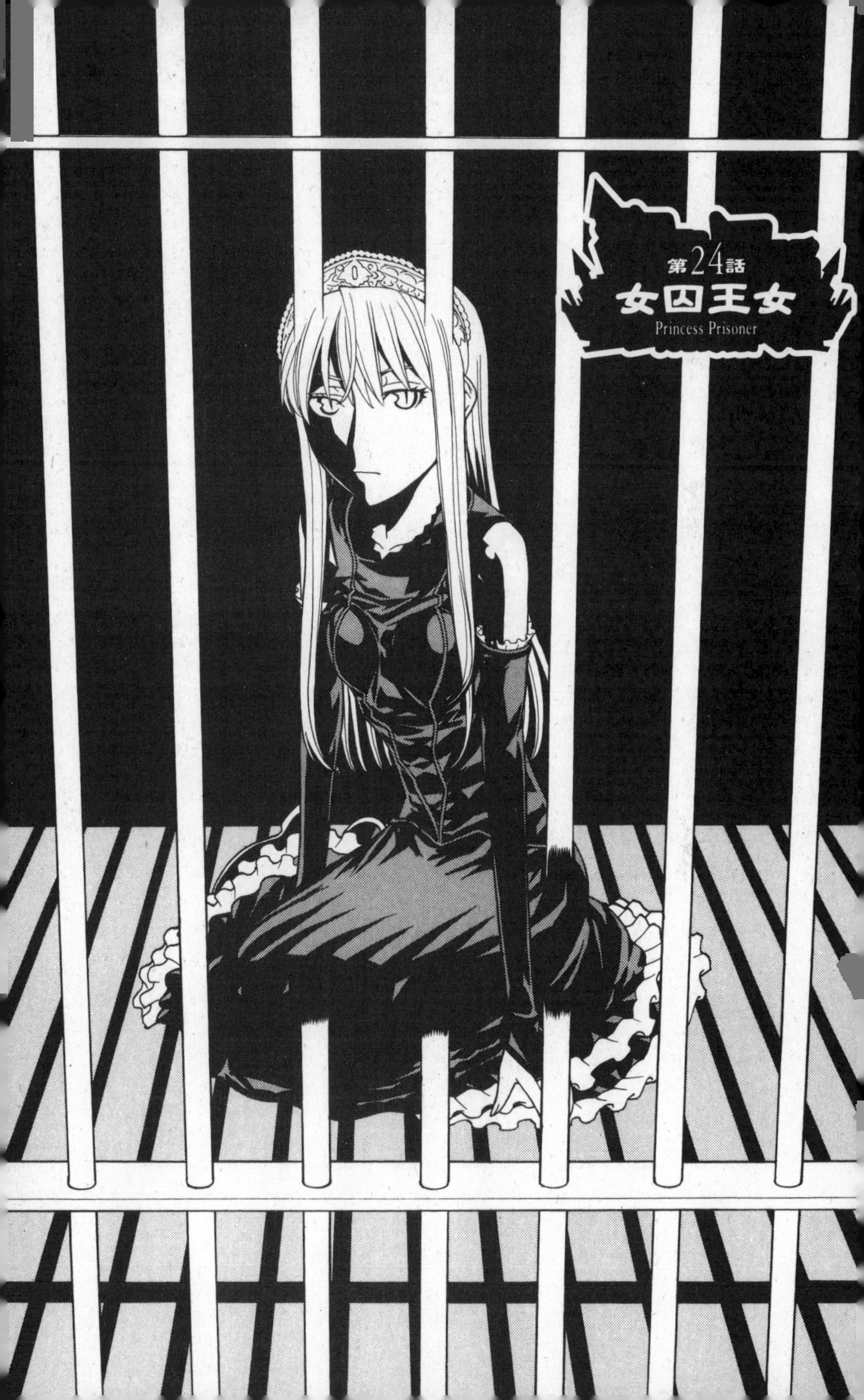
第24話
女囚王女
Princess Prisoner

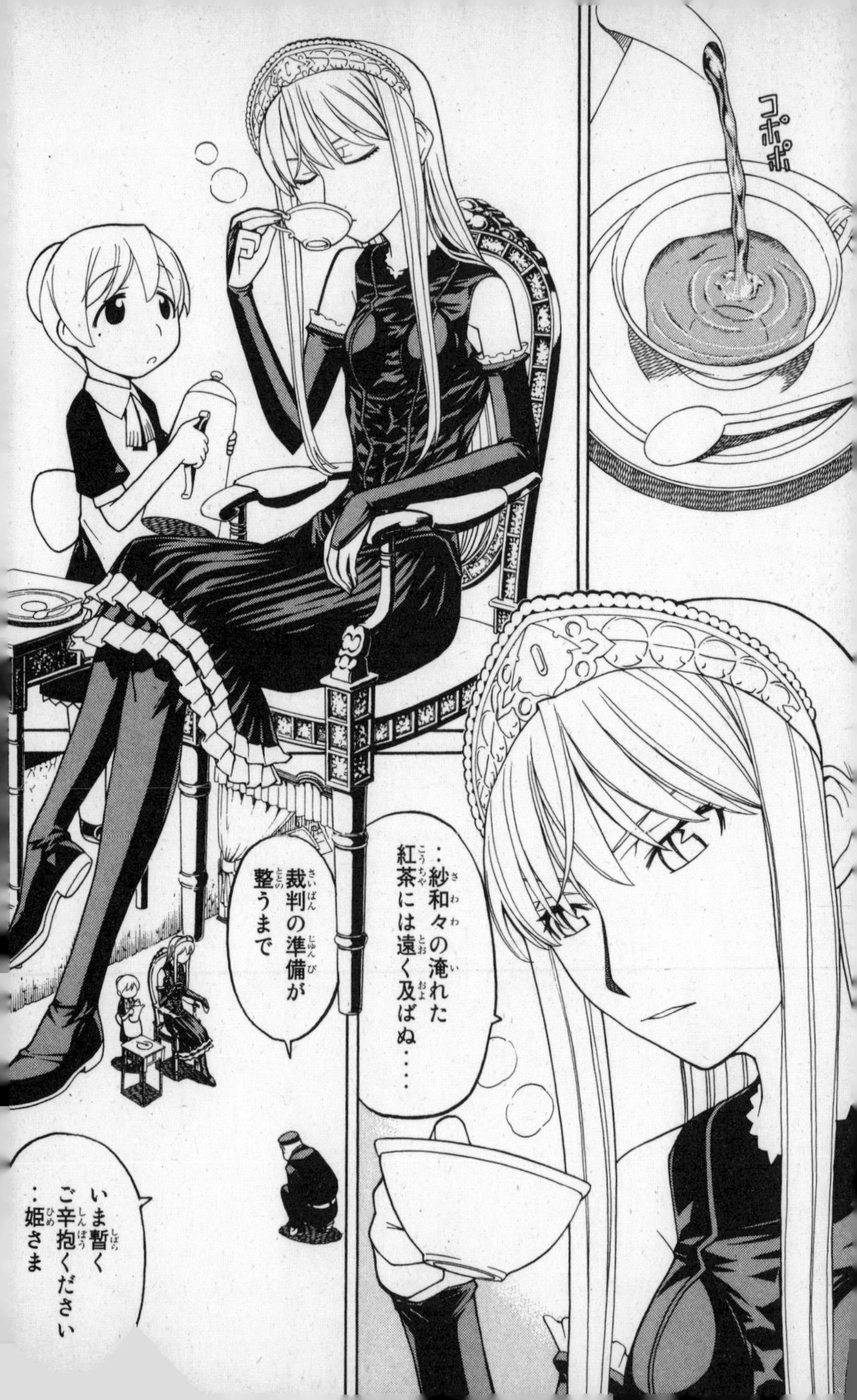
コポポ
…紗和々の淹れた紅茶には遠く及ばぬ……
裁判の準備が整うまで
いま暫くご辛抱ください…姫さま

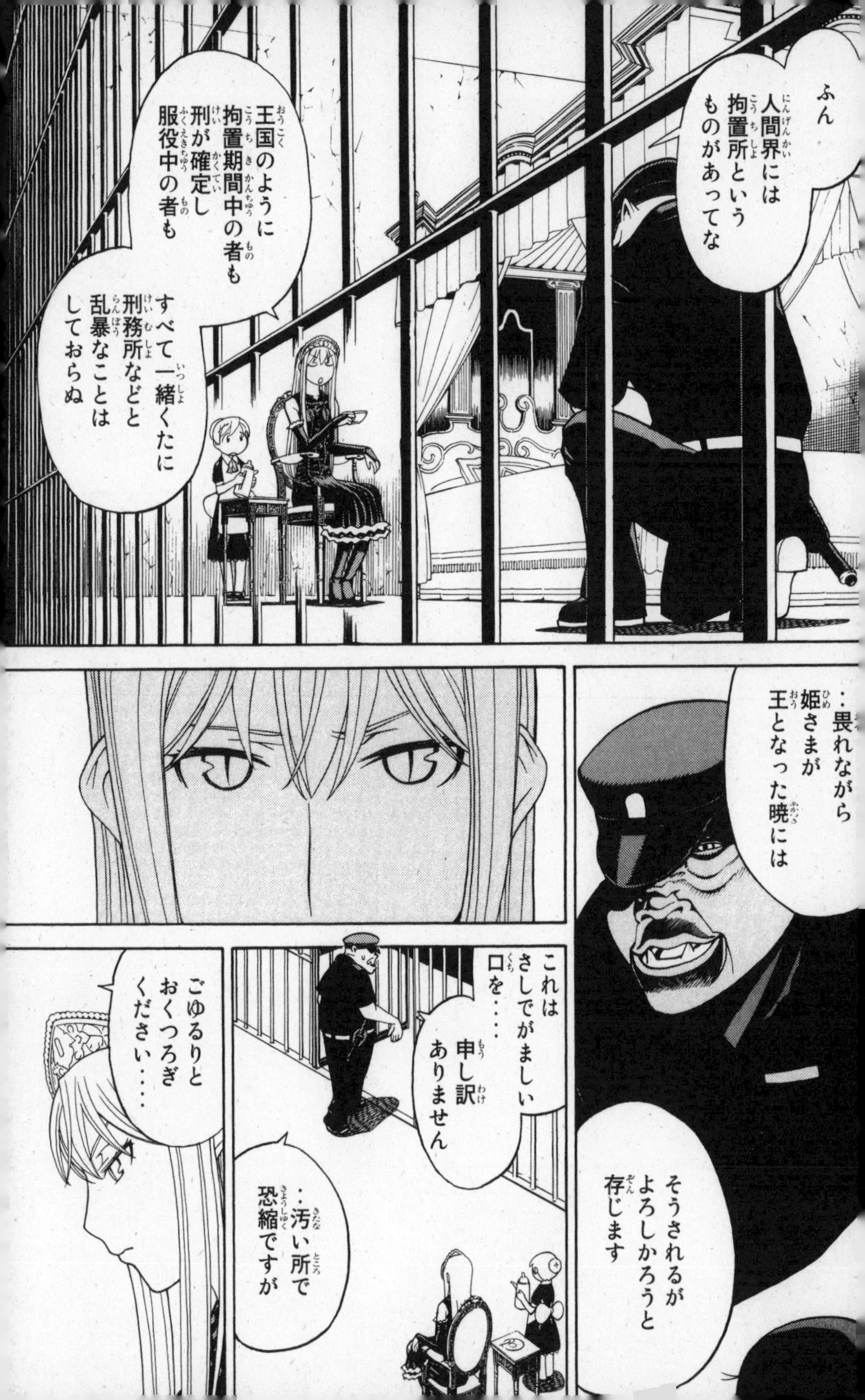
ふん
人間界には拘置所というものがあってな
王国のように拘置期間中の者も刑が確定し服役中の者も
すべて一緒くたに刑務所などと乱暴なことはしておらぬ
…畏れながら姫さまが王となった暁には
そうされるがよろしかろうと存じます
これはさしでがましい口を…・
申し訳ありません
…汚い所で恐縮ですが
ごゆるりとおくつろぎください…・

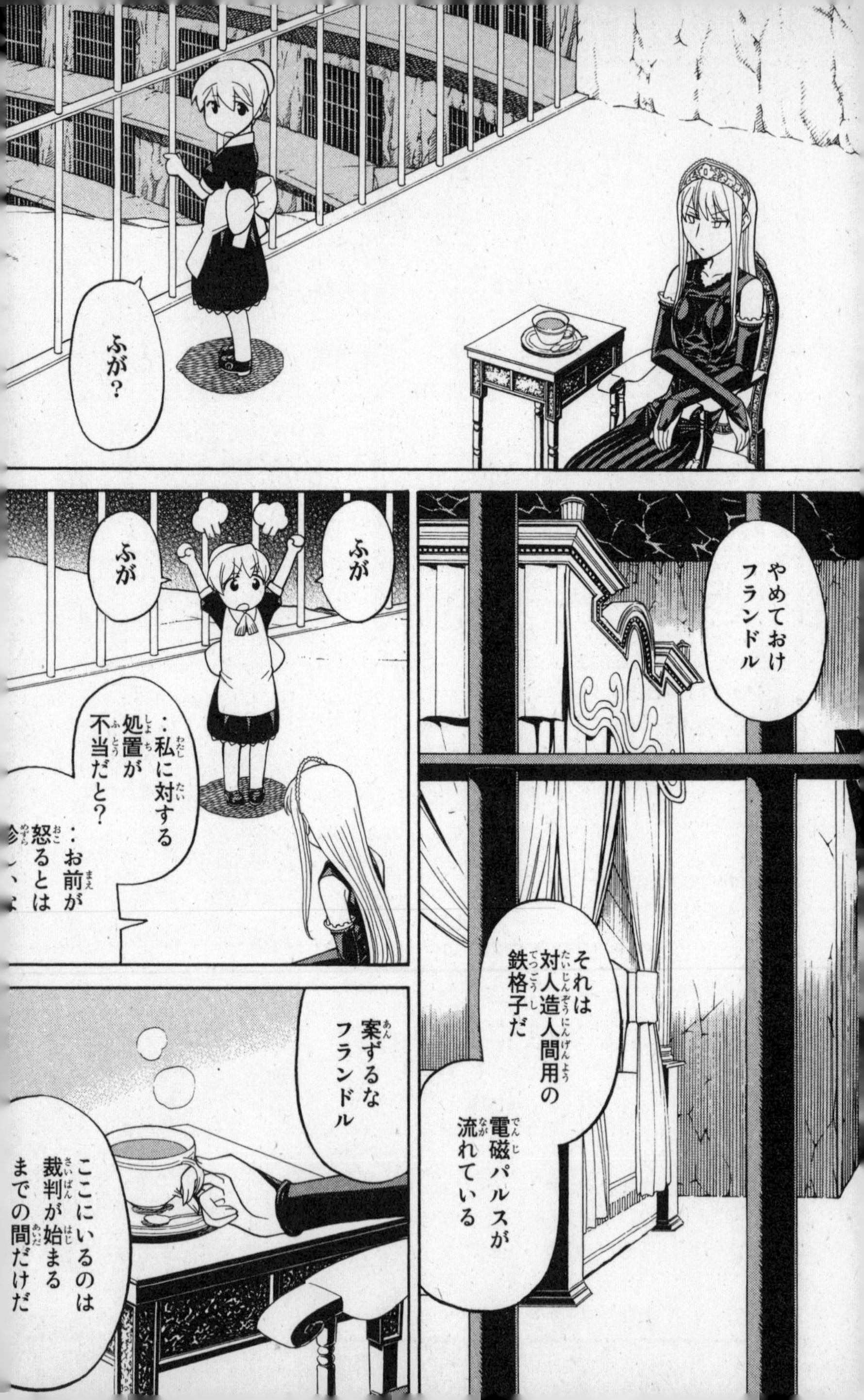
ふが?
やめておけ フランドル
ふが
ふが
…私に対する処置が不当だと?
…お前が怒るとは
それは対人造人間用の鉄格子だ
電磁パルスが流れている
案ずるな フランドル
ここにいるのは裁判が始まるまでの間だけだ

PARASYTE

BY HITOSHI IWAAKI

THEY DESCEND FROM THE SKIES.
THEY HAVE A HUNGER FOR HUMAN FLESH.

They are parasites and they are everywhere. They must take control of a human host to survive, and once they do, they can assume any deadly form they choose.

But they haven't taken over everyone! High school student Shin is resisting the invasion—battling for control of his own body against an alien parasite committed to thwart his plans to warn humanity of the horrors to come.

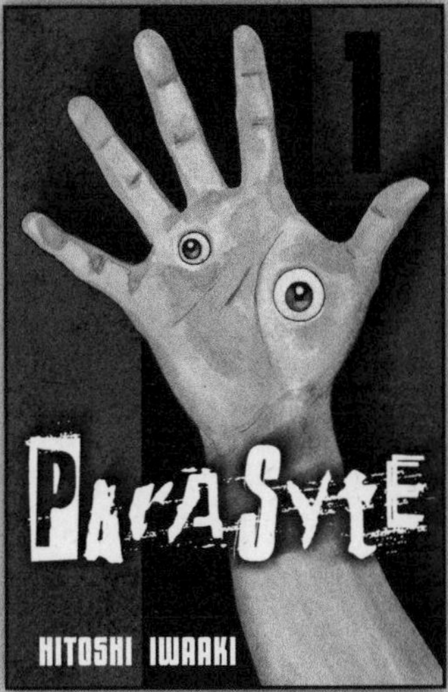

- *Now published in authentic right-to-left format!*
- *Featuring an all-new translation!*

Special extras in each volume! Read them all!

Le Chevalier d'Eon

STORY BY TOU UBUKATA
MANGA BY KIRIKO YUMEJI

DARKNESS FALLS ON PARIS

A mysterious cult is sacrificing beautiful young women to a demonic force that threatens the entire country. Only one man can save Paris from chaos and terror, the king's top secret agent: The Chevalier d'Eon.

- Available on DVD from ADV Films.

Special extras in each volume! Read them all!

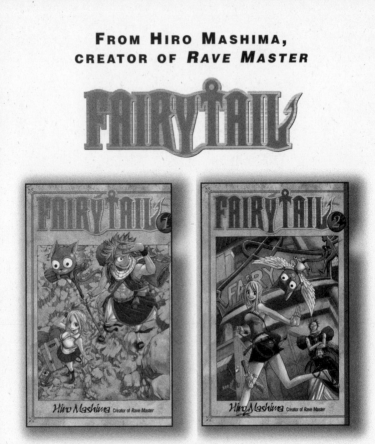

SHIN MIDORIKAWA

NEVER STOP BELIEVING

Since ancient days, the Gaius School of Witchcraft and Wizardry has trained the fiercest swordsmen and the most powerful wizards.

Now one boy could become the greatest of them all. If he studies hard. If he is true to his friends. If he believes.

And if he survives . . .

Special extras in each volume! Read them all!

TOMARE!

You're going the wrong way!

Manga is a completely different type of reading experience.

To start at the *beginning*, go to the *end*!

That's right! Authentic manga is read the traditional Japanese way—from right to left, exactly the *opposite* of how American books are read. It's easy to follow: Just go to the other end of the book, and read each page—and each panel—from right side to left side, starting at the top right. Now you're experiencing manga as it was meant to be!